A Cab at the Door
& Midnight Oil

Short Stories
The Spanish Virgin
You Make Your Own Life
It May Never Happen
Collected Stories (1956)
Sailor, Sense of Humour and Other Stories
When My Girl Comes Home
The Key to My Heart
Blind Love and Other Stories
The Camberwell Beauty and Other Stories
Selected Stories
On the Edge of the Cliff
Collected Stories (1982)
More Collected Stories
A Careless Widow and Other Stories
The Complete Short Stories

Novels
Clare Drummer
Shirley Sanz
Nothing Like Leather
Dead Man Leading
Mr Beluncle

Biography
Balzac
The Gentle Barbarian: the Life and Work of Turgenev
Chekhov: A Spirit Set Free

Literary Criticism
In My Good Books
The Living Novel and Later Appreciations
Books in General
The Working Novelist
George Meredith and English Comedy
The Myth Makers
The Tale Bearers
A Man of Letters
Lasting Impressions

Travel
Marching Spain
The Spanish Temper
London Perceived
(with photographs by Evelyn Hofer)
Foreign Faces
New York Proclaimed
(with photographs by Evelyn Hofer)
Dublin: A Portrait
(with photographs by Evelyn Hofer)
At Home and Abroad

A Cab at the Door
& Midnight Oil

V. S. PRITCHETT

The Hogarth Press
LONDON

Published in 1991 by
The Hogarth Press
An imprint of
Chatto & Windus
20 Vauxhall Bridge Road
London SW1V 2SA

A Cab at the Door first published in 1968 by Chatto & Windus
Midnight Oil first published in 1971 by Chatto & Windus
Combined volume first published in 1979 by Penguin Books

A CIP catalogue record for this book is available from the
British Library

ISBN 0 7012 0930 5

Printed in Finland by
Werner Söderström Oy

To Dorothy

A CAB AT THE DOOR

CHAPTER ONE

IN our family, as far as we are concerned, we were born and
what happened before that is myth. Go back two generations
and the names and lives of our forbears vanish into the common
grass. All we could get out of mother was that her grandfather
had once taken a horse to Dublin; and sometimes in my father's
expansive histories, *his* grandfather had owned trawlers in
Hull, but when an abashed regard for fact, uncommon in my
father, touched him in his eighties, he told us that this ancestor,
a decayed seaman, was last seen gutting herrings at a bench in
the fishmarket of that city. The only certainty is that I come
from a set of story tellers and moralists and that neither party
cared much for the precise. The story tellers were for ever
changing the tale and the moralists tampering with it in order
to put it in an edifying light. On my mother's side they were all
pagans, and she a rootless London pagan, a fog-worshipper,
brought up on the folk-lore of the North London streets; on my
father's side they were harsh, lonely, God-ridden sea or country
people who had been settled along the Yorkshire coasts or
among its moors and fells for hundreds of years. There is enough
in the differences between North and South to explain the
battles and uncertainties of a lifetime. 'How I got into you lot, I
don't know,' my mother used to say on and off all her life, looking at us with fear, as if my father and not herself had given
birth to us. She was there, she conveyed, because she had been
captured. It made her unbelieving and sly.

A good many shots must have been fired during the courtship
of my parents and many more when I was born in lodgings over
a toy shop in the middle of Ipswich at the end of 1900. Why
Ipswich? My parents had no connexion with the town. The
moment could not have been worse. Queen Victoria was dying
and my mother, young and cheerful though she was, identified
herself, as the decent London poor do, with all the females of
the Royal Family, especially with their pregnancies and funerals.
She was a natural Victorian; the past with all its sadness meant

9

more to her than the hopes of the new century. I was to be called Victoria, but now surgery had to be done on the name, and quickly too, for my father's father, a Congregationalist Minister in Repton, was pressing for me to be called Marcus Aurelius. The real trouble was more serious.

On my birth certificate my father's trade is written 'Stationer (master)'. An ambitious young man, he had given up his job as a shop assistant in Kentish Town and had opened a small news-agents and stationers in the Rushmere district of Ipswich. He did not know the city and had gone there because he thought he had a superb 'opening'. He did not know the trade but he had found 'premises' – a word that was sacramental to him all his life. He spoke of 'premises' as others speak of the New Jerusa-lem. He had no capital. He was only twenty-two; the venture was modest, almost pastoral; but he had smelled the Edwardian boom and it enlarged a flaw that had – I have been told – even then become noticeable in his character. One of nature's sales-men, he was even more one of nature's buyers. He looked at the measly little shop, stripped it and put in counters, cabinets and shelves ('You know your father, dear'). The suspicious Suffolk folk hated this modern splash and saw that he had spent so much on fittings that he had nothing left for stock. The bright little shop stood out as a warning to all in a crafty neighbour-hood. Few customers came. The new paint smelled of sin to them. At the age of twenty-two my young father was affronted and flabbergasted to find after a few months that he was bank-rupt, or if not legally bankrupt, penniless and pursued.

There is a picture of him a year or two before this time. He is thin, jaunty, with thick oily black hair, a waxed moustache, and eyes caught between a hard, brash stare and a twinkle. He would be quick to take a pencil out and snap down your order. He wears a watch and chain. Not for long: he will soon pawn them – as he had done before – and my mother's engagement ring too, escape from the premises, put her into those rooms over the toy shop. Once I am born, the young Micawber packs us off to his father's Manse in Yorkshire, while he goes indig-nantly back to London to get a 'berth'. The fact that he has gone bust means nothing to him at all. He goes to the nearest Wes-leyan Church – for he has already left the Congregationalists –

10

and sings his debts away in a few stentorian hymns. And so I, dressed in silk finery and wrapped in a white shawl, go screaming up to Yorkshire to meet my forbears.

Our journey to the Manse at Repton is miserable. Love in a nice little shop had been – and remained for life – my mother's ideal. Now, though a cheeky Cockney girl, she was wretched, frightened and ashamed. ('We never owed a penny; us girls were brought up straight.') She was a slight and tiny fair-haired young woman with a sulky seductive look. In the train a sailor pulled out a jack knife and tossed it about: she called the guard. The sailor said he was only doing it to stop the kid crying. The arrival at the Manse was awful. My grandmother was confirmed in her opinion – she had given it bluntly and within earshot, when my father had first taken my mother there, wearing her London clothes – that her favourite son had been trapped and ruined by a common shop-girl of whom she said:

'I lay she's nowt but a London harlot.'

She said she'd take the baby.

'She tried to snatch you away from me, Vic dear, and said she'd bring you up herself,' my mother often told me.

Mary Helen, my father's mother, was a great one for coveting a dress, a brooch, a ring, a bag, even a baby from any woman. As for choice of words – this bonnie little white-haired woman with a smile that glistered sweetly like the icing of one of her fancy cakes, fed her mind on love stories in the religious weeklies and the language of fornication, adultery, harlotry and concubinage taken from the Bible, sharpened by the blunt talk of the Yorkshire villages. Harlots was her general name for the women of her husband's congregations who bought new hats. The old lady assumed that my mother, like any country girl, had come to leave me and would return next day to London to take up her profession again.

In the early years of my boyhood I spent long periods at the Manse. I have little memory of Repton, beyond the large stone pantry smelling of my grandmother's bread and the pans of milk; and of the grating over the cellar where my grandfather used to growl up at me from the damp, saying in his enormous and enjoyable voice:

'I'm the grisly bear.'

My grandmother had always lived in small Yorkshire towns or villages. Her maiden name was Sawdon and she came from a place of that name near the moors inland from Whitby; it is a purely Scandinavian part of England – and she was the youngest, prettiest and most exacting of three daughters of a tailor in Kirbymoorside, in the godly Pickering valley near by. My father was born there and spoke of seeing the old man sitting cross-legged and sewing on the table in the window of his shop. Grandma was vain of her clothes and her figure. She usually wore a dark blue-and-white spotted dress. She had pale-blue eyes deeply inset, a babyish and avid look, and the drooping little mouth of a spoiled child. Her passion for her husband and her two sons was absolute; she thought of nothing else and me she pampered. With outsiders she was permanently 'right vexed' or 'disgoosted'.

Her 'Willyum', my grandfather, was let out of her sight as little as possible. The minister had the hard northern vanity also, but it differed from hers. He was a shortish, stout, hard-bellied and muscular man with a strong frightening face, iron-grey hair and looked like a sergeant major who did not drink. He was a man of authority with a deep, curt sarcastic voice used to command. When I was a child I had the impression that he was God and the Ten Commandments bound together by his dog-collar. He was proud of his life story.

Gradually I learned that he was the youngest son of a fishing family in Hull – his father was a trawler seaman – and that all his brothers had been drowned between Hull and the Dogger Bank. His mother had picked him up and taken him inland to Bradford, away from ships, and had brought him up there in great poverty. He had known what it was to 'clem'. He grew up and worked on the roads for a time; then ran off and joined the army, (this would have been in the sixties) and since only the hungry or the riff raff did this, he must have been in a poor way. He chose the artillery. This led to an event of which he boasted.

There is a strain of truculence and insubordination running through our family: at any moment, all of us, though peaceable enough, are liable to stick our chins out and take our superiors down a peg or two if our pride is touched. We utter a sarcastic jibe especially at the wrong moment and are often tempted to cut off our noses to spite our faces, in a manner very satisfying to ourselves and very puzzling to amiable people. My grandfather was kindly enough, but one noticed that, at certain moments, he would raise one fine eyebrow dangerously, the eyes would widen into a fixed stare, the pupils would go small and look as hard as marbles, and the sharp arc of white would widen above them, as a horse's eye does when it is bolting. This is the moment of cold flat contradiction; also the moment of wit. And there is a grin at the startled face of the listener.

This must have been the expression on my grandfather's face one day when his battery was stationed outside some seaside place, I believe, on the Mersey. They were at artillery target practice, firing out to sea, and the safety of passing vessels was regulated by a flag signal. It is quite in my grandfather's character that he fired his gun when the flag was up and contrary to orders and sent what he used to tell me was a 'cannon ball' through the mainsail of a passing pleasure yacht. There was a rasp of glee in his voice when he stressed the word 'pleasure'. He told me this story more than once when I was a child, sitting with him under a plum tree and eyeing the lovely Victoria plums in his garden at Sedbergh on the Fells – to which he moved after Repton. The yacht, of course, belonged to a rich man who made a fuss and my grandfather was arrested and court-martialled. He was dismissed from the Army. The moral was that you could never get a fair deal from the officer class; he could, he conveyed, have wiped the floor with any of them. The tale would end with him getting a stick for me – I was about five at the time – and putting me through military drill. We had the movements of 'Ready! Present: Fire!' and, more alarming, the 'Prepare to Receive Cavalry'. Down on one knee I went in the manner of the first lines of the British squares, with the stick waiting to bayonet the impending charge of Lancers on their horses. He had a loud, resonant voice and, being a fairish actor, could evoke the gallop of horses and spears instantly. The peaceful minister concealed a very violent man, and religion had made him live well below his physical strength and natural vitality. He then gave me a Victoria plum and moralized. He pointed out that war was wicked – on wickedness he was an expert – and that to become a soldier was the lowest thing in life, though he was proud of knowing what lowness was. And, he would add, that his wicked younger son – my father's brother – had brought sorrow on them all by running off to be a soldier in turn. The news had turned my grandmother's hair white – 'in a night', of course. And, my grandfather said, they had got their savings together and gone off to York to buy the boy out at once for £25. I did not understand, at the time, but this episode was traumatic for them. My grandfather never earned more than £150 a year in his life and, when he died, all he left was £70 in Co-op tickets which were kept in a tea-caddy on the kitchen mantelpiece. That £25 must have drawn blood.

How and why did my grandfather, uneducated and living by manual labour, become a Congregationalist Minister? In the middle of the nineteenth century, and especially in the industrial north where the wealth was made, the pessimism and anarchy of the early industrial times had passed. Even Manchester – the world's byword for poverty and revolutionary class-hatred – was becoming respectable. The idea of self-improvement was being dinned into the industrious poor; ambition was put into their heads by the dissenting churches, religion of this kind became a revolutionary force, for if it countered the political revolutionaries, it put a sense of moral cause into the hands of the ambitious. The teachings of Carlyle – the gospel of work – and later of Ruskin had their effect on hundreds of thousands of men like my grandfather. Snobbery and the Bible are dynamic in English life; respectability or – to be kinder – self-respect is the indispensable engine of British revolution or reform; and revolutions occur not in times of poverty but when certain classes are getting just a little better off. As you rose socially so – see the novels of George Eliot – you rose in virtue. There is no doubt also that among Protestants, the tendency to break up into sects comes from a nagging desire to be distinctive and superior, spiritually and socially, to one's neighbours.

After he was thrown out of the Army, my grandfather got a job as a bricklayer. It is a chancy and travelling trade and he went from town to town. He did most of his travelling on foot; thirty or forty miles a day was nothing to him. Eventually he appeared in Kirbymoorside. By this time religion must have been strong in him. It sounds as though the court martial had given him a sense of injustice: he had been in the wrong; all the more reason to reverse the verdict and assert that by the higher law of God's justice he was in the right. The more wrong, the more right, the Old Testament offering its eloquent and ferocious aid.

It was easy to become a preacher in those days; gospel halls and missions were everywhere; the greater the number of sects, the greater the opportunities for argument. Soon he was at it in the evenings, after he had put down the hod. Yet to have got religion would not have been enough. I think that what impelled and gave him a rough distinction was his commanding manner and the knowledge that he had a fine voice. He was a good singer, he loved the precise utterance of words. He loved language. All we ever knew was that a pious, spinster lady in Kirbymoorside, heard him and was impressed by his militant looks, his strength and his voice. She got him off the builder's ladder and arranged for him to be sent to a theological college in Nottingham.

But the flesh – and ambition – were as strong as the spirit in grandfather. He was courting the tailor's daughter and perhaps as a common workman he would not have got her. So at nineteen or twenty, on his prospects, he married her and went off with her to Nottingham as a student, and in a year was a father. He had only a small grant to live on. He got odd jobs. He told me he learned his Latin, Greek and Hebrew travelling on the Nottingham trams. He saved pennies, for it was part of the arrangement that he should pay back the cost of his education at so much a year in five years. My father had unhappy memories of a hungry childhood, and one of great severity. But once his training was over grandfather triumphed. At twenty-two – the family legend is – he 'filled the Free Trade Hall in Manchester' with his harsh, denouncing sermons.

Why was it, then, that after this success he was to be found in Bradford and then – getting smaller and smaller – in the little towns of the moors and the fells? It may have been that all his energy had been spent in getting out of the working class and becoming a middle-class man.

CHAPTER TWO

PERHAPS Granda – as we always called him – was tired of hearing other women decried by his wife in the Manse; he was kind to my mother and liked her good sense and common London ways. She thought him a hard man, too God-fearing for her, but decent.

'I belong to the poor old Church of England, say what you like about it,' she used to say to us.

When I was about seven, just before my youngest brother was born, I used to go up to her bedroom in the afternoons at a house we had in Ealing and worry her to let me go and work on the building site opposite our house. I had studied the builders and could tell her exactly how building was done. You dig a trench, you put the bricks in.

'Go on, Mum. Why can't I? Let me,' the perpetual song of small boys. She told me bits about my grandfather. I stood fidgeting at her dressing-table. Once I picked up a hand mirror with a crack in it. 'Put that down.' She snatched it – she was a fanatical snatcher – and said, 'I don't want another seven years bad luck. I've had my troubles. Gran had her troubles, too.'

> Needles and pins,
> Needles and pins,
> When a man marries
> His trouble begins.

'Give me that brush.'

She was brushing out her long straight hair and she looked like a funny witch with a narrow forehead. I hated, but with fascination, to see her dressing and undressing. Those bloomers! That corset!

She was always talking about her troubles. 'Things you don't know about.' Then she would laugh and sing a music-hall song.

> At Trinity Church I met me doom
> Now we live in a top back room
> Up to me eyes in debt for rent
> That's what he done for me.

'Go on, Mum.'

'That's enough. Look at my hair. I can't do anything with it. You have a go, Vic.'

So I brushed her hair.

'Your dad fell in love with my hair,' she said. 'But it's fine, thin, look at it. You can't do anything with it. My poor sister Fanny had such long hair she could sit on hers. So can Ada. Ada's is thick.'

'Mum, can't I go out to the builders?'

At this time she did her fair hair on top in a tea-cake-like shape which was full of hair pins. She had salty, greyish-green eyes – 'Green eyes jealousy' she used to say. 'That's me. I'm a wicked girl' – a longish nose, a talkative, half-sulky mouth not quite straight and quick-tempered elbows, one with a large mole on it. She was lively, sexy and sharp-spoken in the London way and very changeable, moody and, in the long run, not to be trusted.

Mother had grown up in the London jungle, in the needy streets of Kentish Town, Finsbury Park and off the Seven Sisters Road. Her father came from Bedfordshire. He had been a stable boy and gardener who went up to London to be coachman and gardener to a tea merchant who lived in Highgate. I never saw this grandfather, he died when she was a girl. From his picture he was a tall noble looking young fellow, with a beard that spread wide over his chest like a fine mist, fond of canaries, dogs, horses and chrysanthemums and tomatoes – said to be fatal to him because they gave him cancer – 'It grew all over him like a tree, from those blessed pips.' He was a touchy servant. One day, the tea-merchant's lady said to her maid: 'Put my jewellery away, the window cleaner's coming.' Grandfather Martin said to the maid: 'Take my watch, too, if there are dishonest people about.' This was meant as a reproach to his mistress. Death walked in and out of the Martin family in dramatic ways. My grandfather drove the carriage to the tea-merchant's office to pick him up one evening, and found his employer dead at his desk. He carried the body out to the carriage, propped it in a respectable attitude inside and drove him home to his wife. Soon after, grandfather died too.

The Martins were left without a penny. Gran, his widow, had

been a pert little barmaid in an Oxford public house – she had relations in the fish business in Uxbridge – and now she was left with three daughters in North London. There was Fanny, the eldest and laughing girl, the 'cure'; she was so funny as to be 'chronic'. There was Ada, funny, coquettish but more demure. These two girls were apprenticed to a well-known City shop called Spiers and Ponds when they were fourteen. My mother, the youngest and the pet, was to be kept at home to work in the house, for Gran had taken in lodgers. But Fanny sickened; she was a gay consumptive. There was a cab rank opposite their house and Fanny trained the parrot to say 'Walk up. Walk up', at which the dozing cabbies would wake up, whip up their horses, because they thought the leading cab had been hired. Fanny who read *Little Meg's Children* and *East Lynne* to her sisters, making them weep voluptuously, herself became a fading Victorian heroine. She died, saying as her last words, 'Oh! Illuminations.' She had entered heaven.

Ada worked in the china department at Spiers and Ponds and eventually married another 'cure', a young man called Frank Tilly who was in gents tailoring at a shop called Daniels in Kentish Town. He had the waxen look of the young Chatterton and waving long dark hair. 'Poor Frank' was a consumptive too; he married Ada and before the year was out he died. They had emigrated to South Africa, he collapsed in Cape Town, took the next ship back, and died at sea in the middle of 'the worst storm for forty years'. The Union Jack floated over his body at the burial, while Ada prayed in the storm saying 'Oh God, let the ship go down.' She was pregnant.

So Gran had seen three deaths and poverty too, in a few years. Her relations helped her – the fishmonger at Uxbridge, Louis, her cousin, a poor dressmaker, a skeleton figure out of a Gissing novel; Emmy, a lady's maid, brother Gil who whipped up the fish cart. Gran's grief had made her a savage little figure, terrifying to be with, for she had a prickly, bearded chin and the sour smell of stout, port, cheese and onions was on her breath. She would sit in her bonnet, with the veil that covered her face raised to her wicked red nose, swallowing her quart of stout, and the crumbs of the bread catching on to her veil. She looked like a damp and injured beetle. Her temper was violent for her knuckles were swollen with gout and rheumatism. She was embattled in pain. Worse was to happen to her in the end, years later, for Ada's gay little girl, Hilda Tilly, was to grow up and die also of consumption in her twenties. I was grateful to Gran for one thing. One day in Ipswich she pulled me off the outside W.C. when I was six or seven and was screaming with terror. I thought I was falling in. The neighbours called her.

But Gran had one fantastic stroke of luck and, in fact, it was a good deal responsible for my existence. One morning she traipsed off, grousing to herself as usual, to the butcher's. 'I've got something for you, Mrs Martin,' said the butcher pulling out a piece of blood-stained newspaper. It contained the Missing Money column. There the lawyers appealed for the relatives of a Mr Hawes. Sure enough it was Gran's brother who had died in Australia and Gran inherited a small sum of money. She was able to buy a house in Medina Road and take more lodgers. One of them was an actor, the other a young man who had lately become shopwalker in Daniels. He was to be my father.

It struck me a few years ago that I was born into a family of pets and favourites. Granda, a Pritchett, a youngest son, a pet, saved from the sea; Grandma Pritchett, the youngest pet daughter of the tailor; father a pet also, for his brother showed early signs of being a distress; and mother, the youngest pet of her sad family. It was ominous.

For at the age of seventeen, three years later than her sisters, my mother was sent as an apprentice to work in this large draper's shop. At Daniels mother was put into the millinery and there my father saw her. He saw her fair hair. She looked – he told me – like a goddess in her mutton-chop sleeves and so desirable with her tiny waist. ('Eighteen inches', she would put in). She was so quick with the customers, he said, so clever with trimmings! She could put an ugly hat on a grumbling woman, give a twist, snatch a feather or a bunch of cherries and so dazzle the customer with chatter and her smiles.

As for my father, Mother was astonished by him.

'He was so clean, dear. You never saw anything so clean.' The poorly paid shop assistant fed in the basement, slept in the attics and went out to get drunk when the shop closed.

'Eight to eight, weekdays, eleven o'clock Saturday nights,'

Mother would say. 'Old Daniels was a beast.'

They worked in the cold draughts and the poisonous, head-aching smell of gaslight.

'He was high up in Masonry and a Wesleyan' my father would say, correcting my mother's temper.

'So clean' my mother would go on, 'and so particular about his clothes – you know your father. Always the silk hat and spats. Countrified though. I could tell that. Rosy cheeks. He might have got some bad girl if he hadn't had me.'

She was in awe of him; he kept his nails perfect and there was a pleasant smell of Pears' soap and cachous about him and his teeth were white. He cleaned them – as his mother did – with soot or salt.

At this period my father – who was eventually to become very fat indeed, going up to eighteen stone in his time – was a slender young man. He looked grave, his fine brown eyes seemed to burn, and he could change from the effusive to the canny hard look of the brisk young Yorkshireman out for the 'brass'. But there was sometimes a hollow-eyed and haunted look on his face. The fact is – and this is what he told my dumbstruck mother when they talked together – he had had a wretched childhood. My grandfather, so benevolent to me, had been a harsh, indeed a savage, father.

I had seen the minister in his easy country days, idling with his small congregations of country folk, talking of Carlyle and Ruskin and English history. My father had known him as the disciplinarian not long out of the Army, living from hand to mouth in industrial towns, sending his children off to school hungry. They were forbidden to sit down at meals: it would make them soft. He made them stand rigid at the table in silence while they ate their food. His sons were in barracks. My father and his brother were not allowed out of the house after six in the evening, not even when they were grown up. What schools they went to was never made clear to me by my father. He evaded the subject, either out of shame or because he hated being definite about anything. I know he had a French lesson for he had learned by heart the phrase 'Trois hommes voyag-eaient en France'. Education was expensive and my grandfather who used to talk at large about the beauties of education seems to have been able to give little to his two sons. He lived – as my father was to do – in a dream. At fourteen my father had gone to work as a grocer's errand boy and then worked behind the counter. At sixteen or so, he seems to have had an interesting friendship with a young doctor in the village. This – in view of what I shall tell later about my father – was important. The boy was eager to become a doctor or surgeon which would have been far beyond my grandfather's means. One evening he went to the doctor's surgery and watched him dress a man's poisoned thumb. The sight of pus and blood was too much: my father fainted. This led to delay in getting home. He arrived there after dark just before eight in the evening, to find my grandfather waiting with a carriage whip in his hand. Whipping was common in the family, but now my father was nearly a man. My grandfather roared at him for disobeying orders, accused him of drinking or going after women – a scene which was to be re-enacted by Father in his turn and for similar reasons, when my brother Cyril and I were in our late teens – and when Father answered back he was struck across the face and the back by the whip, two or three hard blows. That was enough: hatred had been growing for years. Father went up to his room and in the middle of the night climbed out of his bedroom window, hid in the railway station and went off to York next morning to stay with an uncle. Then he went to London. He had a cousin, Sawdon, in the rag trade: after short jobs in the drapery, Father arrived in glory in Kentish Town.

'I could tell,' said my mother, feeling sorry for him as well as being in awe, 'he had never met a girl before. And his mother standing there, doing nothing, seeing her son horse-whipped – I could have limbed the old . . .'

Mother was an expert in leaving her sentences unfinished.

Daniels was a Wellsian establishment. It was a good 'crib' or berth and the workers were scared of losing it. From Mother's account of it, it was the leading humorous establishment in North London. 'What us girls used to get up to. The nerve we had, dodging across the street, under the horses' heads, playing tricks on your poor father, he looked so stuck up till you got to know him, putting fly papers on old Daniel's chair. . . . Oh, I was a young limb. One day I tipped a whole pile of hat boxes, the white cardboard ones dear, on top of your dad. Us girls were always giggling round corners. Frank' – this was Ada's young man – 'was a cruel mimic. Everything was in farthings in those days and poor Mr Thomas could not pronounce his "th's". Frank used to go up to him and say, large as life, "What's the price of this, Mr Thomas? Free free farvings?" and Old Thomas would go wild and say "I'll free free farvings you with a fump." '

My mother's laugh was always near hysteria. She would sit on her chair by the fire with a long skirt pulled up over her knees to the elastic of her grey bloomers and rock back and forth as she talked. And when she came to the comic point she would spread her excited fingers over her face and stare through the gaps at us and go into fits until her untidy hair started to come down.

Frank's other gift was to say people's names backwards. This kept the shop 'rocking'. Ecirtaeb Nitram was my mother's name. My father's, which was difficult, became Retlaw Tetchirp.

'Dad didn't like it, you know he's proud.'

Father was certainly easily offended. He soon told her something that alarmed her: he was not going to stay at Daniels at the end of the year. 'My name's Walker,' he said. He was going out 'on the road'. He was going to get a job with a 'good comm. and A.i. expenses'. Mother cunningly persuaded him to come and lodge at her mother's house: he noticed that she was a flirt and playing him up with one of the other assistants, so he moved so as to keep possession of her.

He had a shock when he met Gran. There had been no drink at the Manse. At Medina Road someone was always going round to the off-licence. And Gran was not very clean. She could not cook as well as his mother and he complained that London water was hard and did not get the dirt out of the pores of one's skin. He sent his shirts and underclothes back to Yorkshire to be washed and starched or ironed by his mother. What ever you liked to say about his relations in Yorkshire, he pointed out, they were not servants, they didn't kow-tow; they didn't keep pubs and they were all out to improve their position. The Martins were stagnant and, like all southerners, they were all servile smiles and lies to your face. When he was in a rage with Mother in the years to come I am sorry to say that he would shout: 'I raised you from the gutter' and, with a glance of appeal to us, would say 'You can't make a silk purse out of a sow's ear.'

These insults were no more than Yorkshire plain-speaking. All his relatives talked cheerfully like this to one another. As a Cockney Mother had a tongue, too. She would mock Father's piety with phrases like 'two-faced Wesleyans' and 'Hallelujah, keep your hands off'.

Gran Martin, of course, hated Father. She called him only by his surname for years. Father did not hide his feelings that the Martin family needed cleaning up. Morally, in particular, for he was soon taking my mother on Sundays to hear the famous preachers at the City Temple. Spurgeon and others. He loved their dramatic manner. One of these preachers told how, when he was coming into the City Temple that morning he heard two young sparks debating whether to go in or not. 'Damn it, what odds,' said one and went in. My father admired his remark. He quoted it for years. He wanted religion to smarten up and get snappy. He liked the evangelical singing and sang well for he had been trained in one of the excellent Yorkshire choirs. But he sang mainly hymns, his favourite being 'Tell me the old, old story' which came so richly from him that it brought us nearly to tears when we were very young. He knew how much preachers were paid. 'Big men' he would say. He liked 'big men'. It was the age when the Victorian Grand Old Man or Great Men were beginning to be succeeded by the Big, like Selfridge and the new race of great shopkeepers in London, Manchester and Chicago. He did not really distinguish between the big shopkeepers and the popular Nonconformist preachers, who had also broken with the theology of the Victorian age: for suddenly money was about, commerce was expanding, there was a chance for the lower middle class. They would have a slice of the money the middles had sat so obdurately on for so long. The difference between 'goods' and 'the good' was fading. My father took to smoking cigars and my mother, hunching her pretty shoulders a little before his self-confident ambition, also sparkled and admired. He always ended by saying how hungry he was. Oysters – a poor man's food in those days – were pretty

23

cheap. My father's later size was due to early hunger. He ate to make up for the craving of his childhood. He became cheerfully gluttonous. He talked for hours about food as much as he did about religion. Sixty years later when he died his last coherent words were 'That woman meant well but she did not give me enough to eat.' He was speaking of his landlady. It was untrue. The hunger of his boyhood grew and grew as he neared death.

Beatrice Martin's idea of pleasure was Hampstead Heath Fair and the music halls. My father could not stand a dirty joke; and he mildly complained that in any music hall she was the first in the audience to see the joke and give her hysterical laugh so that voices from the gallery shouted admiringly at her and egged her on.

So my father and mother courted in Finsbury Park and Parliament Hill, went boating out on the Thames, rioted with the mob on Mafeking Night, he carrying her on his shoulder round Trafalgar Square while she waved a Union Jack. He walked out, as he had promised, from Daniels and got another berth; then the minister married them and they set off for Ipswich and bankruptcy, where Gran and Mother's sister, Ada, lately widowed, appeared too. The battle between North and South was on.

CHAPTER THREE

Such was the family I was born into. There was this cock-sparrow, my father, now a commercial traveller, dressy and expansive with optimism, walking in and out of jobs with the bumptiousness of a god. And there was our sulky moody mother, either laughing or in tears, playing *The Maiden's Prayer* on the piano – she could 'cross hands' too – and also *The Mocking Bird* which was closer to her nature. She would sink into mournful tales of illnesses and funerals, brood on railway accidents and ships lost at sea. She loved a short cry, easily went pink on her check-bones with jealousy or flew out into a fish wife's tempers. She was a hard-working woman. We were in a small villa of damp red brick in Woodford. I had a brother now, Cyril, eighteen months younger than myself. My parents' bedroom contained a large lithograph called *Wedded*. A Roman-looking couple are walking languorously along a city wall. The man had strong hairy legs and, I believe, wore a tiger skin. I confused him with my hairy father. In the twenties I met an Italian who had sat for the legs of this figure, one more blow to my sense of the uniqueness of our family. There was another lithograph called *The Soul's Awakening*, a girl with her night-gown falling off in the wind as she was swept up to heaven. On the washstand there was yellow chinaware which had a pattern of Dutch girls and boys. Hidden behind the chamber-pot in the cupboard was a small copy of Aristotle's 'masterpiece' on gynaecology with startling pictures of the moronic foetus in the womb. In another cupboard were my father's leather top-hat boxes; already he was buying clothes for himself in notable quantities. There were 'words' if mother had not washed and ironed his underclothes or starched his cuffs and collars as well as his mother had done.

In the small dining-room there was red and blue linoleum of floral pattern. There was a small palm in a pot. There were ornaments with mottoes on them. 'Dinna trouble trouble till trouble troubles you' and 'Don't Worry It May Never Happen'.

Also a picture which gave me my first lesson in the 'who' and 'whom' difficulty. Two old men in red robes with their backs to each other, but looking with medieval grumpiness over their shoulders, held an antique parchment in their hands on which the following words were printed:

In Men Whom Men Condemn as Ill
I find so much goodness still,
In Men whom Men pronounce divine
I find so much of sin and blot
I hesitate to draw the line
Between the two where God has not.

This poem was often bandied about and pointed at when Granda Pritchett came down to London and denounced my father's latest religion, for Father was continually going one better in the matter of faith. The other picture showed simply an envelope on which was written:

Messrs Sell and Repent,
Prosperous Place,
The Earth.

This was the spirit of the early 1900's. Things, as Father said, were beginning to hum.

My parents rarely stayed in one house for as long as a year. After Woodford there is a dash to Derby where Father hoped to do well with a Canadian Insurance Company, and where, in north-country fashion, we had a pump beside the sink; in a month or so we are back. We had various London addresses: Woodford again, Palmers Green, Balham, Uxbridge, Acton, Ealing, Hammersmith, Camberwell are some of them; then back to Ipswich again, on to Dulwich and Bromley. By the time I was twelve, Mother was saying we had moved fourteen times and Father went fat in the face with offence and said she exaggerated. At this, she counted up on her fingers and said she now made it eighteen.

We moved mainly to small red-brick villas, the rents running from 9s. and even to 12s. a week, once or twice to poor flats. It seemed to us that Father had genius. By the time there were four children – three boys and a girl – Father seemed as sumptuous as a millionaire and my mother was worn down. It was like a marriage of the rich and the poor. She cooked, cleaned, made our clothes and her own, rarely had the money to pay for a girl to help her and went about a lot of the day with a coarse apron on, her blouse undone and her hair down her back. Patently genius was lacking in her. For it was he who came home in the evenings or at week-ends from places like Glasgow, Bournemouth or Torquay, having stayed in hotels with names like Queens, Royal or Majestic, palaces of luxury. We learned to wait at the door and to open it for him when he came home, because he was affronted if he had to let himself in with his own key. We would often wait for an hour. When he got in he walked into the front room where we ate, sat down in an arm-chair and, without a word, put out his foot. Mother's duty was to kneel and unbutton his boots until laced boots came in, when she unlaced them; eventually we squabbled for this honour. 'Ease the sock' Father would say with regal self-pity. And he would tell her about the orders he had taken that week. His little order books were full of neat figures and smelled warmly of scent.

And then – the magic of the man! – without warning we would, as I say, get up one morning to find my mother in her fawn rain-coat (her only coat), and hat, ourselves being pulled into coats too. A cabby and his horse would be coughing together outside the house and the next thing we knew we were driving to an underground station and to a new house in a new part of London, to the smell of new paint, new mice dirts, new cupboards, and to race out into a new garden to see if there were any trees and start, in our fashion to wreck the garden and make it the byword of the neighbourhood. The aggravating thing was that my mother was always crying in the cabs we took; and then my father would begin to sing in his moving bass voice:

> Oh dry those tears
> Oh calm those fears
> Life will be brighter tomorrow.

Or, if he was exasperated with her, it would be

> Tell me the old, old story
> For I forget so soon.

27

I look back on these early years and chiefly remember how crowded and dark these houses were and that, after Uxbridge, there is always a nasty smell, generally of sour breadcrumbs at the edges of the seats of chairs, the disgusting smell of young children, after my sister and youngest brother were born. And there was the continual talk of rudeness. It was rooted in our very name for we soon learned that Pritchett was the same as Breeches for other children; one polite little boy called my mother Mrs Trousers because he had gathered that 'breeches' was rude. Mother – and especially her mother, Gran – were the sources of a mysterious prurience. Gran liked chamber-pot humour and was almost reverent about po's, mentioning that Aunt Short said that the best thing for the complexion was to wash one's face in 'it' – and good for rheumatism too. The bottom was the most rude thing we had, and, in consequence, the Double U. Rudeness became almost mystical if we caught Gran on the Double U when she left the door unlocked. Girls were rude because of their drawers; women, because of their long skirts, and more rude than men because they had so much more to cover. To crawl under a table and lift the hem of a skirt was convulsingly rude. At certain times Mother and Father were rude – not when she was in bed and her astonishing titty-bottles slipped out of her nightdress, like a pair of follies; but when she and Father went for a walk together and we walked behind them. We felt that it was rude to see a marriage walking about in front of the neighbours. Granda and Grandma Pritchett were never rude; but Mother was rude in herself – she wore 'bloomers' and often 'showed' them – but Father, on his own, never. I was ashamed for years of a photograph of us children. The corner of my sister's silk dress had lodged on my knee as I sat next to her. *I* was rude.

One thing became noticeable in our removals. Very often my father and mother went to different destinations – she to the new house while my father and I would find ourselves at Euston station in the middle of the night. I was off by the midnight train to my grandfather's in Repton and later to Sedbergh, to be away in the north for weeks or even months. My brother, it seemed, was off to Ipswich to stay with my mother's sister, Ada. My sister and baby brother were at home. At one time I found

28

myself sitting on the carrier of my father's bicycle travelling from Nottingham to Derby. Another time I remember travelling in a hansom to Paddington and yet again standing one winter's morning beside the driver of a horse tram down Tooley Street on a roundabout journey via Tower Bridge to King's Cross. So began my love of change, journeys and new places. As many London children do, I skilfully lost myself in the streets and was twice picked up by the police. Most of these journeys which my father thoughtfully provided were, as I say, to the north. Repton I scarcely remember; but to Sedbergh, Kirby-moorside and Appleton-le-Moors I went again and again. We would get out of the night train, my father and I, at a junction near Kendal, at the gateway through the mountains to the Scotish border, cross the lines and take the little train to Sedbergh, that neat town of grey stone lying under the bald mountain I thought was called the Berg. The horse brake would take us up the main street, following a herd of cows. By the Manse and chapel, Granda was waiting. In the distance, on her whitened doorstep and close to a monkey-puzzle tree, stood Grandma in her starched white apron, her little pale iced-cake face and her glasses glittering. I remember an arrival when I was six. My Grandmother would not let me into her clean house until she looked me over.

'Eeh Walter, for shame, t'lad's buttons are off his jersey, his breeches have a hole in them. I'm raight vexed with your Beatie, letting a son of hers come up with his stockings in holes and his shoes worn through. Eeh, he looks nowt but a poor little gutter boy. For shame, Walter. For shame, Victor. I lay you've been playing in the London muck. I dassn't show you to the neighbours. Nay, look at his breeches, Willyum.'

'Mother made them.' I stuck up for Mother, not for her sake but because of the astonishing material she used – mostly curtains from our house. Nothing covering a window, a table or a sofa was safe from my mother's scissors when the sewing fit was on her. 'I'll get those old curtains down.' She was an impatient woman.

My grandmother took me inside, undressed me in the hall and held the breeches up and looked at them.

'Eeh Willyum, come here. They're not stitched. They're just tacked. T'lad'll be naked in 't street.'

It was true. Mother's slapdash tacking often let us down.

On these visits, the minister would be having a sarcastic argument with his son about the particular God of the moment, for Father had left the Congregationalists, the Baptists, the Wesleyans, the Methodists in turn, being less and less of a Jehovah man and pushing his way – it turned out – towards the Infinite. He was emerging from that pessimism which ate at his Victorian elders. The afternoon bus came and he went. Up the back step of the station brake he skipped, to pick up a couple of hampers of traveller's samples in Manchester. I was glad to be rid of the family and scarcely thought of my mother or my brother and sister for weeks. Here was what I was made for: new clothes, new shirts, new places, the new life, jam tarts, Eccles cakes, seed-cakes, apple puffs and Yorkshire pudding. My grandparents looked at each other and then at me with concern for my character. I did not know that almost every time we moved house Father had lost his job or was swinging dangerously between an old disaster and a new enterprise, that he was being pursued by people to whom he owed money, that furniture had 'gone back' or new unpaid-for furniture had 'come in'. I did not know that my mother wept because of this, even as she slyly concealed, clenched in her fingers a half sovereign that some kind neighbour had given her. And I remember now how many times, when my father left in the morning for his work, she barred his way at the door or screamed at him from the gate, 'Walt, Walt, where's my money?' But I did see that here in Sedbergh there was domestic peace.

It is a small old town smelling of sheep and cows, with a pretty trout beck running through it under wooded banks. The fells, cropped close by sheep, smelling of thyme and on sunny days played on by the shadows of the clouds, rise steeply behind the town and from the top of them one sees the austere system of these lonely mountains running westward to the Pikes of the Lake District and north to the border. One is almost in Westmorland and, not far off, one sees the sheepwalks of Scott's *The Two Drovers*, the shepherd's road to Scotland. The climate is wet and cold in winter; the town is not much sheltered and day after day there will be a light, fine drizzle blowing over from Westmorland and the Irish Sea. When it begins people say 'Ay, it's dampening on.' These people are dour but kindly.

Yorkshire is the most loved of all the many places of my childhood. I was sent to my first school, the village school at the top of the town, up the lane from the Manse garden – it is just as it was when I was a child sixty years ago. The school sat in two classes and, I suppose, each class had about forty or fifty boys and girls, the girls in pinafores and long black or tan stockings. Douthwaite, Louthwaite, Thistlethwaite, Braithwaite, Branthwaite were the common surnames. The children spoke a dialect that was hard to understand. They came from farms and cottages, both sexes brisk and strenuous. We sat in three tiers in the class-room, the upper one for bigger children. While I was doing pothooks and capital D's from a script, the others were taught sums. Being a London child with a strange accent I began to swank, particularly to the girls. One who sat with me in the front offered to show me her belly if I lowered my own breeches. I did so, being anxious to show her my speciality – a blind navel, for the cord had been so cut that my navel was closed. In her opinion – and that of others – this was 'wrong' and foretold an early death because no air could get inside me. This distinction made me swank more. She did not keep her part of the bargain, neither did any of the other girls in Sedbergh. She put up her hand and told teacher. This was the first of many painful lessons, for I instantly loved girls.

This incident was reported to the Manse. Also a scuffle or two in the school yard, being caught pee-ing over a wall to see how far we could go, with a lot of village lads, and a small burglary I got into with a village boy who persuaded me to slip into an old woman's cottage and steal some Halma pieces from her desk. We lied about this. My grandfather, waiting to catch me naked in the bath tub, gave me a spanking that stung for hours. I screamed at him and said that I hoped he would be run over by the London express at the level-crossing the next time he crossed the line at the Junction. More spanking. I was removed from the school because the neighbours were talking. I was surprised for I was a pious little boy, packed with the Ten Commandments and spotless on Sundays: the farmers' boys, the

31

blacksmiths' sons and all the old wheelwrights, tree fellers, shepherds thought I was a townee and a softie. I would never be able to herd sheep, shoe or ride a horse, use a pickaxe or even work in a woollen mill. My secret was that I was going to be a preacher like my grandfather; he had begun teaching me Latin, pointing out the Latin words on a penny – *fidei defensor*. I was to be defender (with spears and guns if necessary) of the faith, 'prepared to receive cavalry'. For years I thought this and Calvary were the same thing.

The Manse at Sedbergh smelled of fruit and was as silent as church and had even churchy furniture in yellow oak, most of it made by country craftsmen, who in a fit of fancy, might carve, say acorns or leaves all round the edge of a table. There was no sound but the tick tock of the grandfather clock. Everything was polished, still and clean. One slept in a soft feather bed and woke to see the mist low down on the waist of the Berg. On the old brick wall of the garden my grandfather grew his plums and pears, and in the flower-beds his carnations, his stock, his roses and his sweet-williams; and under the wall flowed a little stream from the mountains.

It was a kind, grave house. My grandparents were in their early fifties. For my grandmother cleanliness was the first passion. Whenever I stayed in my first years with her she bathed me in a zinc tub before the kitchen fire and was always scrubbing me. Once she tried to remove a mole from my nose, thinking it was a speck of tar. For two days, on and off, she worked at it with soap, soda, pumice and grit and hard brushes, exclaiming all the time like Lady Macbeth; while my grandfather growled 'Let it bide, you're spreading his nose all over his face.' He had a genial sadistic touch, for he loved to point to a scar on the tip of my nose which seemed to shine like a lamp and make me ridiculous; and also to say that my nose was the nearest thing to an elephant's foot he had ever seen. He enjoyed making me angry. It was Yorkshire training.

Grandma always kept her white hair in curlers until a late hour in the afternoon, when she changed into one of her spotted blue dresses. The only day on which she looked less than neat was Monday. On this terrible day she pinned a man's cloth cap to her hair, kirtled a rough skirt above her knees, put on a pair of wooden clogs and went out to the scullery to start the great weekly wash of sheets, pillow-cases, towels, table-cloths and clothes. They were first boiled in a copper, then she moved out to a wash-tub by the pump in the cobbled yard and she turned the linen round and round with the three-legged wooden 'dolly' – as tall as myself – every so often remarking for her neighbours to hear that her linen was of better quality, better washed, whiter and cleaner than the linen of any other woman in the town; that the sight of her washing hanging on the line – where my grandfather had to peg and prop it – would shame the rest of the world and the final ironing be a blow to all rivals. The house smelled of suds and ironing. Her clogs clattered in the yard. But, sharp at five o'clock she changed as usual and sat down to read the *British Weekly*.

On Tuesday, she made her first baking of the week. This consisted of different kinds of bread and I watched it rise in its pans to its full beauty before the fire; on Thursday, she made her second baking, concentrating less on bread than on pies, her Madeira cake, her seed-cake, her Eccles cakes, her puffs, her lemon-curd or jam tarts and tarts of egg 'custard', operations that lasted from seven in the morning until five in the afternoon once more. The 'bake' included, of course, the scouring of pans and saucepans which a rough village girl would help her with. At the end, the little creature showed no sign of being tired, but would 'lay' there was no better cook in the town than herself and pitied the cooking of her sisters.

On Wednesdays she turned out the house. This cleaning was ferocious. The carpets were all taken up and hung on a line, my grandfather got out a heavy stick to beat them while she stood beside him saying things like 'Eeh Willyum, I can't abide dirt.' There was some nasty talk among the Congregationalists in Sedbergh about my grandfather's carpet-beating; they got their own back for the boasting of my grandma and some said out loud that he was obviously not the class of man to be teaching the word of God in that town. (Forty years later when I went back to the town after his death, one or two old people still spoke in a shocked way of their working-class minister who was under the thumb of his 'stuck-up' wife. That came of a man's marrying above himself.)

After the carpets, the linoleum was taken up and Grandma was down on her knees scrubbing the floor boards. Then came hours of dusting and polishing.

'Woman,' Granda often said on Wednesdays, standing very still and thundery and glaring at her, 'lay not up your treasure on earth where moth and dust doth corrupt.'

'Eeh Willyum,' she would reply, 'wipe your boots outside. Ah can't abide a dirty doormat. Mrs So-and-so hasn't whitened her step since Monday.'

And once more she would settle down as pretty as a picture to an evening, making another rag rug or perhaps crocheting more and more lace for her dresses, her table-centres and her doilies. By the time she was eighty years old she had stored away several thousand of these doilies, chests full of them; and of course they were superior to the work of any other woman in the country. In old age, she sent boxes of them to her younger son who had emigrated to Canada, thinking he might be 'in want'.

I remember a tea for Sunday-school teachers at the Manse. They came, excited young men and bouncing young women who went out in the fields and trees along the beck to see who could collect and name the largest number of different species of wild flower in an hour. An older woman won with fifty-seven different kinds. We got back to my grandmother's parlour where the sun shone through the little square lights of her windows, to see one of my grandmother's masterpieces, a state tea laid on the table. The scones, the tea-cakes, Eccles cakes, jam tarts, iced tarts, her three or four different kinds of cake, sultana, Madeira, seed and jammed sponge, her puffs and her turnovers were set out in all their yellows, browns, pinks and, as usual, in her triumph, my grandmother was making a pettish little mouth, 'laying' that 'nowt like it' would be seen on any table in the town. The company stood reverently by their chairs and then, to my disgust, they broke out into a sung grace, conducted by the eldest of the teachers, each taking parts, bass and tenor, soprano and contralto, repeating their variations for what seemed to me a good twenty minutes before setting to. To my wonder – for I had been nicely brought up by my grandmother – the eldest teacher who was a very old man with the big hands of a labourer, tipped his tea into his saucer, blew on it and drank.

'Look at the man,' I shouted. 'He's being rude.'

There was a silence. The old man was angry. Grandma was vexed. There was a dispute about whether I should be told to leave the room. One of the girls saved me. But the old man kept coming back to it and it was the whole subject of the tea-party, and for days the minister and his wife had the matter over with me. If that was 'London manners', the old man growled when he left, he didn't want owt of them. Such slights are never forgotten in the north; they go all round the town and add to its obdurate wars. The story was reported to my father in London and was brought up indignantly year after year. To think that a boy, a relation of the minister's, too, and already known to have exposed himself in school, should say a thing like that. One experience I feared to tell them. That day of the flower hunt, I had found a beautiful white flower like a star growing near the river. I had never seen a white flower so silky and star-like, in its petals, and so exquisite. I picked it, smelled it and dropped it at once. It stank. The smell was not only rank, it suggested rottenness and a deep evil. It was sin itself. And I hurried away, frightened, from the river, not daring to mention it and I never walked through that field again. For many years I thought of this deceit. I did not know this flower was the wild garlic, the most evocative of our aphrodisiacs, the male to the female musk.

The general portrait of the country people of Haworth which is given by Mrs Gaskell in her life of Charlotte Brontë, very closely fitted the character of my Yorkshire relations if one allows for the taming effects of lower middle-class gentility. Haworth-like tales were common among the Sawdons. They were proud, violent, egotistical. They had – according to your view – either a strong belief in the plain virtues or a rock-like moral conceit. Everything was black or white to them. They were blunt to your face, practical and unimaginative, kind yet iron-minded, homely and very hospitable; but they suspected good manners, they flayed you with their hard and ironical eyes. They were also frugal, close and calculating about money – they were always talking about 'brass' – and they looked on

35

outsiders with scorn. They were monosyllabic talkers but their silences concealed strong passions that (as Mrs Gaskell said) lasted for life, whether that passion was of love or hatred. Their friendship or their enmity was for ever. To listen to their talk was like listening to a fire crackling. They had no heroes. They were cautious and their irony was laconic. I was in the city of York soon after it was bombed in the last war and I said to a railway worker,

'Well they didn't destroy the Minster.'

'Ay, they say as how Hitler says he's going to be married there next May. But ah doan't know . . .'

With that last phrase dryly uttered he gave me a look as hard as steel.

Year after year I went to Sedbergh to sit on the stool by my grandmother's fire, staring at the pots that hung simmering on their shining chains over the coals, smelling the green country bacon and the rising bread. One day a boy from the famous Public School at Sedbergh was called in to tell me how many years it would be before I reached the verb 'sum' in Latin and could enter the school and go for their terrible fifteen mile 'runs' across the fells, the toughest schoolboy run in England. I often saw the boys slogging along near the ravine. This was one of the many schools I never went to.

My grandfather's home life was laborious and thrifty. Coals were bargained for in the summer and sacked down, carefully counted piece by piece, in a heap near the stone shed. He would then grade the pieces in sizes and (reverting to his brick-laying days), he would build them into a wall inside the shed. Each day he would collect, one by one, the various sizes of coal needed for an economical fire. They were small, slow burning fires, often damped down in order to save, but in the winters of valley fog or snow, we were thickly clad in Yorkshire wool and I remembered no cold. After his work in the house he had work to do in his garden also. He had to dig all of it. There were his vegetables and his raspberries which, in the ripe season, he sold at twopence a cup to the town. Notices saying, Thou Shalt Not Steal were placed on sticks on the wall by the school lane. He had little time or peace for his ministry; or opportunity for his secret vice: cigar smoking. The Congregationalists would not

36

have tolerated tobacco smoking in their minister, any more than they would have stood for drinking, but I've known him drink a glass of strong home-brewed ale at an isolated farm and, as for the cigar, his habit was to sneak off to the petty or earth closet at the end of the garden, latch himself in with Bible and writing-paper, light up, take his ease and write his sermon. My grandmother was always frantic when he was out of her sight for a minute – she did her best to stop him going on his parish visits, for she would 'lay' the men would be out at work and he would have to see the women, which raised her instant jealousy – and on his cigar days her delicate nose would sometimes catch the smell coming out of the top of the petty door. She would run down the garden and beat on the door with a yard-broom, shouting.

'Willyum, Willyum, come out of that, you dirty man.'

Sunday was his day. On this day my grandmother respected him and herself withdrew into a silent self-complacency as her Willyum prepared for the Christian rites. He had an early and a late service in the mornings, another in the afternoon and one in the evening. He prepared for the day in soldierly way, as for battle. He shaved so closely that there was generally a spot of blood on his chin and his cheeks were pale. His surplice was a disappointing, cotton affair, like a barber's sheet – poor quality I came to think, shop-shoddy – as he set off across the gravel path to the chapel which made one side of his garden cold and damp. I was put into my Sunday best – sailor collar, vest that choked me, linen breeches that sawed at the crotch and cut me above the knees when I sat, legs dangling, swelling and aching in the pew; and my grandmother had on her best bonnet and costume. We smelled of new cloth, but she relieved this by soaking her handkerchief in Lily of the Valley and gave me a sniff of it. She also took smelling salts. Then comes the agony of sitting in those oaken pews and keeping my eyes fixed on Grandfather. What he says I never understand but he goes on and on for a long time. So do the hymns. There is the cheerful break when the plate goes round, the happiness of putting in a penny; and then there is the moment which makes me giggle – and at times (when my brother was with me), the joke was too much. My grandfather would give out notices and announce the sum of last Sunday's collection, a sum like eight shillings and three pence halfpenny. (His living, by the way.) His voice is harsh, but what convulses me is his way of pronouncing the word half penny; he calls it, in curt northern fashion ha'penny with the broad 'a' – 'hah-pny'. I often tell my father of this later in London who points out I have no call to complain when, in pure Cockney I talk of a boy who lives 'dahn ahr wy'.

Back we go to cold beef for it is wicked to cook anything on Sundays – except Yorkshire pudding. This is sacred. Light as an omelette yet crisp in the outer foliations of what it would be indelicate to call crust, it has no resemblance to any of that heavy soggy fatty stuff known all over England and America by the name. Into it is poured a little gravy made of meat and not from some packaged concoction. One might be eating butterflies, so lightly does it float down; it is my grandmother's form of poetry. Grandfather asks if I would like 'a small bortion more' for Non-conformists often affected small changes of consonant, 'p' becoming 'b' and an 's' becoming a 'z', and then asks his wife what she thought of the sermon. The faithful always called themselves 'uz', the 'z' separating them from sinners. Her reply is to ask if he noticed Mrs Somebody's terrible new hat and to add that she didn't think owt to the material of the new coat Mrs Somebody Else had dressed herself up in.

The afternoon is more serious. I had no toys or games at my grandfather's – nor did my father when he was a boy – and I did not miss them. There was enough in garden, country or the simple sight of things to keep me occupied and, for years, in my parents' house the smell of toys seemed unpleasant and their disasters too distressing. One always thought of the money they cost. On Sundays at Sedbergh I was allowed into my grandfather's study. It was a small room with a few hundred books in it, almost all sermons, and he would read to me some pious tale about, perhaps, a homeless orphan, driven to sleep on straw, in some shed in Manchester, surrounded by evil-doers. The boy resists starvation, and after a long illness, is rescued by benevolent middle-class people.

When I tried to read these tales I found the words were too long and so I gazed at the green Berg, watched the cloud shadows make grey or blue faces on the grass, and the sheep nibbling there. The quiet and loneliness were exquisite to me; and it was pleasant to smell the print of my grandfather's paper and hear him turn over the pages in such a silence. When I grew up the Christian God ceased to mean anything to me; I was sick of Him by the twenties; but if I think of a possible God some image of the Berg comes at once to my mind now, or of certain stones I remember in the ravine. To such things the heathen in his wisdom always bowed.

I did not understand my grandfather's sermons. My mother who had sat through many told me his manner was hard and monotonous and that he was one to whom hatred and the love of truth were very much the same thing, his belief being that truth is afflicting and unpleasant. He argued people into hell, not in the florid manner of the melodramatic hell-fire preachers who set the flames dancing so that in the end they became like theatre flames to the self-indulgent. My grandfather's method was to send people to hell rationally, contemptuously and in-tellectually. He made hell curtly unattractive; he even made it boring. This was an error; later on, his congregations dwindled, for he offered no beanos of remorse, salvation or luxuriant ruin. He could not see that sin is attractive and that therefore its condemnation must be more voluptuous.

Frankly the congregations expected an artist and they discovered instead a critic. They were puzzled. That enormous success in the Free Trade Hall at Manchester was not repeated. Grandfather was essentially an intellectual and some said – my parents among them – that his marriage to a vain, houseproud and jealous girl who never read anything in her life except the love serial in the *British Weekly* and who upset the ladies of his many chapels by her envies and boastings, was a disaster for an intellectual man. The Congregationalists invite their ministers and the news of her character got round. But how can one judge the marriages of others? There are families that are claustro-phobic, that live intensely for themselves and are indifferent to the existence of other people and are even painfully astonished by it. His truculence in the Army was a symptom of solitary independence.

The pious story of the Manchester orphan had one impor-tance: for the first time I heard of the industrial revolution. This was real to the north-country people. We knew nothing about it in the commercial south. There were little mills in the valleys where my grandfather took me to see the mill girls at their machines. There were the tall chimneys of Leeds and York. One spoke of people, not by who they were, but by what they did. Their work defined them. Men who met at street corners in Sedbergh knew of strikes and labour wars; and my grandfather told me of masters and men with war-like relish. These stories were not told in terms of rights and wrongs very much, though my grandfather was radical enough; Carlyle's *Past and Present* fitted his view. The stories were told with a pride in conflict itself. Hard masters were as much admired as recalcitrant workmen; the quarrel, the fight, was the thing. The fight was good because it was a fight. Granda's youth was speaking when he told of this.

The Ten Commandments, of course, came into my grandfather's stories, particularly the commands to honour one's parents – though of mine he clearly had a poor opinion – because that led to obedience; then stealing the old lady's Halma pieces, the allure of apples, raspberries and Victoria plums. Finally murder. About murder he was vehement. It attracted him; he seemed to be close to it. I felt I must be close to it too. I had a younger brother whose goodness (I jealously knew) was palpable. How easily I could become Cain. To the question 'Cain, where is thy brother Abel?' how glad I was that I could honestly reply 'Uxbridge, near the canal', though I had once tried to push him into it. Granda kept on year after year about murder. When I was nine or ten and the famous Crippen cut up his wife and buried her in his cellar, Granda made me study the case thoroughly. He drew a plan of the house and the bloody cellar, for me to reflect on. He had a dramatic mind.

In the summer my grandparents took a holiday, paying for it out of a few preaching engagements. We took the train across Yorkshire to the North Riding. For the first week we would stay with my Great Uncle Arthur and his wife Sarah, who was my grandmother's sister. After the placid small town life of Sedbergh, York was a shock. We were in an aristocratic yet industrial city. The relations were working-class people. The daughters of the tailor in Kirbymoorside were expectant heiresses in a small way, but both had married beneath them. Very contentedly too: the difference cannot have been very great and was bridged by the relative classlessness of the north – relative, I mean, to life in the south.

We arrived at one of an ugly row of workers' houses, with their doors on the street, close to the gas works, and the industrial traffic grinding by. A child could see that the minister and his wife thought themselves many cuts above their York relations. Great Uncle Arthur was a cabinet-maker in a furniture factory. The minister glittered blandly at him and Uncle Arthur looked as though he was going to give a spit on the floor near the minister with a manual worker's scorn.

Great Uncle Arthur was a stunted and bandy man, with a dark, sallow and strong boned face. He looked very yellow. He had a heavy head of wiry hair as black as coals, ragged eyebrows and a horrible long black beard like a crinkled mat of pubic hair. A reek of tobacco, varnish and wood-shavings come off him; he had large fingers with split unclean nails. The first thing he did when he got home from work was to put on a white apron, strap a pair of carpet knee-pads to his trousers, pick up a hammer or screw-driver and start on odd jobs round the house. He was always hammering something and was often up a ladder. His great yellow teeth gave me the idea he had a machine of some kind in his mouth, and that they were fit to bite nails; in fact, he often pulled a nail or two out of his mouth. He seemed to chew them.

Uncle Arthur's wife was Grandma's eldest sister and in every way unlike her. She was tall, big boned, very white faced and hollow-eyed and had large, loose, laughing teeth like a horse's or a skeleton's which have ever since seemed to me the signs of hilarious good nature in a woman. Though she looked ill – breathing those fumes of the gas works which filled the house cannot have been very good for her – she was jolly, hard-working and affectionate. She and Uncle Arthur were notorious (in the family) for the incredible folly of adoring each other. She doted on her dark, scowling, argumentative, hammering little gnome: it seemed that two extraordinary sets of teeth had fallen in love with each other.

For myself, Uncle Arthur's parlour, Aunt Sarah's kitchen and the small back yard were the attractions. The back yard was only a few feet square but he grew calceolarias there. It gave on to an alley, one wall of which was part of the encircling wall of the city. Its 'Bars' or city gates, its Minster are the grandest in England and to Uncle Arthur who knew every stone in the place I owe my knowledge and love of it. One could go up the steps, only a few feet and walk along the battlements and shoot imaginary arrows from the very spot where the Yorkists had shot them in the Wars of the Roses; and one could look down on the white roses of York in the gardens near the Minster and look up to those towers where the deep bells talked out their phenomenal words over the roofs of the city. They moved me then; they move me still.

Uncle Arthur's house had a stuffy smell – the smell of the gas works and the railway beyond it was mixed with the odour of camphor and camphor wax. The rooms were poorly lit by gas jets burning under grubby white globes; air did not move easily, for there were heavy curtains in the narrow passage-way to the stairs. But the pinched little place contained Uncle's genius and the smell of camphor indicated it. The cabinet-maker was a naturalist – he used to speak of Nature as some loud fancy woman he went about with and whom his wife had got used to. On the walls of his kitchen hung pretty cases of butterflies and also of insects with hard little bubble bodies of vermilion and green – creatures he had caught, killed and mounted himself. In the lower half of the kitchen window he had fixed a large glass case of ferns in which he kept a pet toad. You put a worm on the toad's table – one of Uncle's collection of fossils – and the spotted creature came out and snapped it up.

The smell of camphor was strongest in the small front parlour. A lot of space in the window corner was taken up by another large glass case containing a stuffed swan. This enormous white bird, its neck a little crooked and sooty, was sitting on a nest of sticks and seemed to be alive, for every time a lorry or a train passed, it shook and – by it's stony eye – with indignation. In two other corners there were cabinets containing Uncle's collection of birds' eggs; and on the mantelpiece was a photograph of Uncle being let down by a rope from the cliffs of Whitby where he was collecting eggs under a cloud of screaming gulls.

Granda was the sedentary and believing man; Uncle was the sceptic and man of knowledge. He had been born very poor and had had next to no schooling. He told me he could not read or write until he was a grown man. A passion for education took him. He took to learning for its own sake and not in order to rise in the world. He belonged – I now see – to the dying race of craftsmen. So he looked for a book that was suited to his energetic, yet melancholy and quasi-scientific temperament. At last, he found it: he taught himself to read by using Burton's *Anatomy of Melancholy*. This rambling and eccentric compendium of the illnesses of the brain and heart was exactly suited to his curious mind. He revelled in it.

'Look it up in Burton, lad,' he'd say when I was older. 'What's old Burton say?'

He would quote it all round the house. Burton came into every argument. And he would add, from his own experience, a favourite sentence:

'Circumstances alters cases.'

Burton was Uncle Arthur's emancipation: it set him free of the tyranny of the Bible in chapel-going circles. There were all his relations – especially the minister – shooting texts at one another while Uncle Arthur sat back, pulled a nail or two out of his mouth and put his relatives off target with bits of the *Anatomy*. He had had to pick up odds and ends of Latin and Greek because of the innumerable notes in those languages, and a look of devilry came into his eyes under their shaggy black brows. On top of this he was an antiquarian, a geologist, a bicyclist and an atheist. He claimed to have eaten sandwiches on the site of every ruined castle and abbey in Yorkshire. He worshipped the Minster and was a pest to curators of museums and to librarians.

In short, Uncle Arthur was a crank. When the minister and he sat down in the parlour they looked each other over warily. The swan shook irritably in its glass case as they argued and there they were: the man of God and the humanist, the believer and the sceptic; the workman who had left his class and the workman who scorned to leave it. The minister said Uncle

43

Arthur was naïve and a joke; Uncle Arthur regarded the minister as a snob, a manual worker who had gone soft and who was
hardly more than his wife's domestic servant. The minister was
prone to petty gossip as the clergy are apt to be. Uncle Arthur
said 'Let's stop the tittle tattle.' He wanted a serious row. He
puffed out his chest and grinned sarcastically at his brother-in-
law; the minister responded with a bland clerical snort. They
were united in one thing: they had both subscribed to the saying,
often heard in Yorkshire: 'Don't tha' marry money, go where
money is.' They had married heiresses.

I fancy Uncle Arthur's atheism was weakening in these days,
and that he may have been moving already towards spiritualism, theosophy and the wisdom of the East – the philosopher's
melancholy. There was a ruinous drift to religion in these
northerners. I did not know that, in this room, there was to
occur before very long, an event that would have a calamitous
influence on my family but one that would play a part in starting my career as a writer. Uncle Arthur had two sons and a
daughter. She was a brisk, jolly Yorkshire girl who was having
a struggle with her parents. She was about to be married and,
after coming home from work her idea was to go round to the
house she and her fiancé had found a few streets away. He
would be painting and papering it and she would have more
things like fire-irons, or a coal-bucket, to take there. Uncle
Arthur and Aunt Sarah thought this might lead to familiarities
before marriage and would not allow her to go unless she had
one of her brothers with her, but they were rarely at home.

The clever girl saw that I was the answer and petted me so
that I was delighted to go with her. I was the seven-year-old
chaperon and I fell in love with her. It piqued me that when
we got to the house, her young man would spring out at her
from the front door and start kissing and cuddling her. 'Oh, give
over,' she cried out and said 'I'm going to marry him,' pointing
to me. I did not leave them alone for a minute. A bed had come
to the house and the excited young man soon had us all bouncing up and down on it, rumpling my hair with one hand while
he tickled her with the other, till she was red as a berry. At last
the wedding day came and I was sad. I longed to be with them
and wanted to be their child and was sad that I was left out of

it. Aunt Sarah teased me afterwards and said that since I was in the photograph of the wedding group, I was married too. This cured me of my passion. For at home in London we had a book, bought by my father, called *Marriage on Two Hundred a Year* which, like my mother's song 'At Trinity Church I met me doom' caused words between my father and mother. I was beginning to form a glum opinion about married life. Why did these tall, adult animals go in for what – it seemed – was nothing but worry?

Uncle Arthur's eldest son was a tall, sad young man, with puffy cheeks. Whenever I was in York and he was at home he took me out rowing on the Ouse. He was a hero to me for he was a post office sorter who worked on the night mail train to London. He had the superb job of putting out the mail-bags into the pick-up nets beside the line, as the train screamed through at sixty miles an hour.

It was the other son, a lithographer whom I saw only once, who made the strongest and most disturbing impression on me. There are certain pictures that remain with one all one's life and feed disquieting thoughts. I was taken to a poorish house in the winter one evening and there he sat, a pallid and ailing man, with blue circles under his eyes, with medicine bottles beside him. Several young children were playing on the floor: the mother was giving the bottle to a new baby. There was – to me – the sickly smell of young children which I hated, for being the eldest of my family, I had often to look after my brothers and sisters when they were tiny. This second cousin of mine was very ill, he had lost his job as a lithographer because of his illness, and looked as if he were dying. In fact, he was no more than a nervous sickly dyspeptic, one of the victims of the Yorkshire diet of pastry, cakes and strong tea; and my grandfather said with disapproval that he was an artist. One was shown a lot of people in Yorkshire who were 'warnings': after the picture of Crippen the murderer in the papers, there was the town drunk of Sedbergh, the town fighter, the town gambler. This cousin of mine was the warning against the miseries of art, unwise marriage and failure. (When I was eighteen I wanted to be a painter and the sick smell, above all the sensation of defeat and apathy in that room worried me.) Years passed. I must have been about eleven when father brought home the news that the dying Cousin Dick had been suddenly and miraculously cured by Christian Science.

It was on one of these stays in York that my grandfather took me along the walls to the Minster and showed me the Lincoln green glass. I had already had many pernickety tours with Uncle Arthur, who pointed out bits of joinery and stone masonry, and explained every historical detail. He was a connoisseur of carving and especially of tombs. His was a craftsman's attitude. It was a sight to see him standing, bandy, threatening and bearded in the aisle, with bicycle clips on his trousers – for he rarely took them off – and looking up to the vault of the aisles with an appraising eye. He often had a ruler sticking out of his jacket pocket and on my first visit I really thought he was going to pull it out and start measuring up. He didn't go so far as to say he could have built the place himself, but once we got to the choir stalls and started on the hinges and dove-tailing, he looked dangerously near getting to work on them. The choir stalls appealed to him because there are often pot-bellied and impish bits of lewd carving under a seat or on the curl of an arm, and he always gave me a pagan wink or nudge when he found one. Once he said 'That'd vex t'minister.' Uncle Arthur behaved as if he owned the place and would get into arguments with vergers and even bewilder a clergyman by a technical question.

My grandfather's attitude was different. The grandeur, height and spaciousness of the place moved him. He was enraptured by it. But, pointing down at the choir, he said that it was sad to know that this lovely place was in the possession of the rich and ungodly and a witness not to the Truth but to a corrupt and irrelevant theology.

The Minster was scarcely the house of God any more but the house of a class.

'And you cannot,' he said severely, 'worship God freely here. You have to pay for your pews.' The clergy, he said, were like the Pharisees in the Bible.

We left the cathedral and went up to the steps to the walls once more at the point where the railway runs under an arch into the old York station where Stephenson's Rocket stands;

46

and we sat in one of the niches of the battlements and looked down on the shunting trains, the express to Edinburgh coming in, the Flying Scotsman moving out to London, under their boiling white smoke. And there he told me about the wrongs of England and of a great man like Carlyle and of another, John Ruskin, who had hated the railways.

'Great men,' he said. 'God-fearing men.'

The granite walls, the overpowering weight of English history seemed to weigh on us. To choose to be a great man was necessary; but to be one one must take on an enormous burden of labour and goodness. He seemed to convey that I would be a poor thing if I didn't set to work at once, and although the idea appealed to me, the labour of becoming one was too much. I wasn't born for it. How could I get out of it? In the south fortunately we were feebler and did not have to take on these tasks. I loved the North but I was nervous of its frown; and even of the kindly laughter I heard there.

After York we used to take the train to see the remaining sister of my grandmother, the third heiress. She lived upon the edge of the moors above Kirbymoorside where my grandmother came from, in a hamlet called Appleton. This was wild and lonely country. You drove up five or six miles in the carrier's gig; if it was raining, the passengers all sat under one enormous umbrella. There was a long climb to the common, with the horse snorting and puffing, and then you were in the wide single street of the hamlet, with wide grass verges on either side and you were escorted in by platoons of the fine Appleton geese. You passed the half-dozen pumps where girls were getting water for the cottages and arrived at a low flint cottage where my Great Aunt Lax lived.

The frown went off Grandfather's face when he left his York relations. His preaching was over. He was free. He was back in his wife's country. Aunt Lax had a farm and land that she now let off. The industrial revolution, the grim days of Hull and Nottingham and Bradford were forgotten, we were in true country and had gone back a century and Granda forgot his respectability and took off his clerical collar.

At first sight Aunt Lax looked hard. She was a tallish and skinny woman with iron-grey hair which she kept in curlers all the week except Sundays. She had a long thin nose, a startling pair of black eyebrows like charcoal marks, wore steel spectacles and was moustached and bearded like a man. Not only that, like a man, she was always heaving things about – great pails of milk in her dairy – churning butter, clattering about on clogs, shouting across the street; and her skirts were half the time kirtled to her knees. Her arms were long and strong and bony. On a second look you saw that her lizard-like face had been beautiful; it was of a dark Scandinavian beauty. But the amusing thing about this spinsterish creature – and perhaps it was what made her so gay and tolerant – was that she had been married three times. The rumour was that there had been a fourth. These marriages were a shock to the family, but Lax in name, Lax in nature, this indefatigable Wesleyan did well out of her weddings and funerals and had a long stocking.

When I was six I met the last Mr Lax. He was a dumb giant who sat on a chair outside the cottage in the sun. He was very old and had a frightening glass eye. Since there were many ploughs, carts and traps and gigs in her farmyard, I came to think he was a moorland farmer, but this was not so. A few years ago, sitting in a pub at Lastingham near by, I found an old shepherd who had known him well.

'Nay, he was nobbut t'old watchman up at t'lead mine,' he told me. If Aunt Lax had done well out of her two previous husbands, the third was obviously a folly. And a strange one. The chimney of the lead mine – now abandoned – stands up like a gaunt warning finger in the middle of the heather that rolls away from Lastingham, and when she was a girl she was locked in the house, as all the village girls were, when the miners came down on Saturday nights to the village pub. North-country love is very sudden. There it was: a miner got her in the end.

Year after year I went to Appleton, sometimes alone, sometimes with Cyril, the brother who was a year or so younger than I. Aunt Lax had no children of her own so that there was nothing possessive or spoiling in her affections. We hauled water for her at the pump and, for the rest, she let us run wild with the jolly daughters of the blacksmith and anyone we came across. We scarcely ever went to chapel. The smell of bacon woke us in the morning and we went down from our pretty room which contained a chest of drawers made by Uncle Arthur, to the large kitchen where the pots hung on the chains over the fire and where she sometimes cooked on a spit. Her baking days were less fanatical than my Grandma's and her washing days were pleasanter. Even the suds smelt better and there were always the big girls to chase round with us when the washing was brought in from the line or the hedges when the day was over.

When her third husband died, it was thought that amorous or calculating Great Aunt Lax would take a fourth. She had picked her second and third at the funeral feasts at which dozens of local farmers could form a sound opinion of her as a caterer and housekeeper. They had a good look round at her stables when they came, knew her acres and her fame as the leading Wesleyan for miles around. Instead, she took in a female friend, a Miss Smith. She, too, died and on the very day my brother and I arrived at the cottage. We arrived in a storm and were taken at once to one of the outer sculleries where a village girl came in, stripped us, scrubbed off the London dirt and swore to us she'd let us see the body upstairs. We longed to see it, but the girl took us off to the blacksmith's where we had to stay. More promises were made but we never saw the body. But we were allowed to play in a barn and watch the country people coming to the funeral feast. We avenged ourselves by opening six or seven bales of rag strips which Aunt Lax used for her winter occupation: making rag hearth-rugs. We threw them all over her orchard.

She was not very vexed. There was a lot of questioning of us afterwards in York and in London about who had come to the funeral, for Aunt Lax was supposed to have added to her wealth by Miss Smith's death, and everyone was trying to guess if there would be a fourth or whether other relations were on the prowl. She grew to be rather witch-like.

The moorland life was eventless. Every so often Aunt Lax would dress up in a heavy grey tweed costume, put on her hat and go off to Kirbymoorside Market, sitting by the carrier. It was a state visit. She would go there to buy cloth, or stones of flour and other things for her bins, and to see her lawyer. Once a week a pedlar would come round or a man selling herrings from Whitby and she gossiped with them. She understood boys. She told us of all the local crimes and knew the sites of one or two murders. She sent us down to the mill because a man had murdered his wife there years before. One year when I was nine I came up from London terrified with street tales about Jack the Ripper and I tried to get her to tell me he did not exist or had at any rate died long ago.

'Nay,' she said. 'He's still alive. He's been up here. I saw him myself at 'Utton-le-'Ole last market day.' (None of our Sawdons had 'an aitch to their names'.)

This cured me of my terror of the Ripper: the fears of childhood are solitary and are lasting in the solitariness of cities. But in villages everyone knows everything that goes on, all the horrors real or imaginary; people come back from prison and settle down comfortably again; known rapists drink their beer in the public house in the evenings; everyone knows the thieves. The knowledge melts peacefully into the general novel of village life.

But one alarming thing occurred when I was five or six, in Appleton. It had the Haworth touch and it showed the dour, dangerous testing humour of the moorland people. We all set out one afternoon in a gig, my grandparents, Aunt Lax and myself, to a farm, a lonely stone place with geese, ducks and chickens fluttering in the yard. A few dark-leafed trees bent by the gales were standing close to it. We had tea in the low ceilinged kitchen and the farmer noticed that I was gazing at a gun which hung over the mantelpiece.

'T'lad is looking at yon gun of yours, Feyther,' said his wife.

'Ay,' said the farmer. 'Dost know what this is lad?'

'A gun. It shoots.'

'Ay. And what does it shoot?

'I don't know.'

'Would 'ee like to see it?'

'Eeh. He'd be fair capped to touch it,' said my grandmother. The farmer got the gun down and let me touch it, then (helping me, for it was heavy), he let me hold it.

'Dost know how it works?'

I murmured.

The farmer broke the gun, showed me where the cartridges

went, closed it, clicked the safety catch and the trigger. He gave it to me again and allowed me to do this. I was amazed.

'Would 'ee like to see the cartridges?'

'Yes.'

'Yes please,' said my grandmother.

'Please,' I said.

He got a couple of cartridges from a drawer and loaded the gun.

'There you are. It can shoot now. Hold it.'

'Ready! Present! Fire!' said my grandfather. 'You can shoot a rabbit now.'

The farmer steadied the gun which swayed in my small hands.

'Ay,' said the farmer. 'Take offt' safety catch. Now if you pull t' trigger now it'll fire.'

I trembled.

'Would it kill rabbits?' I asked.

'Ay,' laughed the farmer. 'And people. Come, Mother, come Grandma and Mrs Lax, stand over against the wall, t'lad wants to shoot you.'

'No,' I said.

'Ay he does,' said the excited farmer, waving them to the dresser and there they stood laughing and the gun swung in my aching hand.

'Eeh t'little lad wouldn't shoot his grandma as makes him those custard pies,' Grandma said.

'Safety catch off. Now if you pull t' trigger – has 'e got his finger on it? – they'll all be dead.'

'No,' I said with tears in my eyes and nearly dropped the gun. The farmer caught it.

'Eeh well, it's a lesson,' said the farmer hanging the gun back on the wall.

'Old Tom likes a joke,' they said, going home, but Aunt Lax said the kitchen was small and that was the way Mr Robinson shot his wife down 't Mill, no accident that was. But all the way my grandma moaned:

'Eeh, who would have thought our Victor would want to shoot his grandma. Eeh. Eeh, well.'

I sulked with misery and, after a couple of miles, she said to me: 'He's got a monkey on his back,' a sentence that always roused my temper for I felt at my back for the monkey and screamed 'I haven't. I haven't.'

That was the night I told my grandfather again I hoped he'd be knocked down by a train at the Junction when he crossed the line and I got my second spanking.

I came home from these Yorkshire visits sadly to whatever London house we were living in and would see in my mind's eye the white road going across the moors, like a path across a swollen sea, grey in most seasons but purple in the summer, rising and disappearing, a road that I longed to walk on, mile after mile. I was never to see one that moved me so strangely until, in my twenties, I saw another such in Castile. It brought back my childhood and this was the cause of my walking across Spain. So, when one falls in love with a face, the reason may be that one saw such a face, perhaps of an old woman, that excited one in childhood. I always give a second look at any woman with Aunt Lax's eyebrows and her lizard-like face.

CHAPTER FOUR

WHEN I look back upon our history I see my grandfather as much an immigrant in a new country – for that is what his middle-class life was – just as, say, an Italian is when he comes to settle in England or America. The process is exhausting; Grandfather retained the violence of his forbears. His son – my father – is the first emancipated generation who, brought up in the early struggle and marked by it, is excited and able to take advantage of the new world and rapidly dramatizes and exaggerates his role in it. All the Yorkshire relations were as rooted, settled and certain of themselves, as any of their ancestors had been since the time of the Danes: my father quickly rid himself of these traits; if emotionally he was still an obstinate boy from a small town in Yorkshire, his mind and speech soon became a Londoner's. Yet London was not a deeply known reality to him as it is to a real Londoner, to a real inhabitant of the big city; to him it was a fantasy and encouraged fantasy in himself. At no time did he seem to belong to the city, as my mother did, but rather to float and flutter about over it, even to regard it piratically as loot. Fantasy he had, but little imagination – my mother, as he continually complained, was the imaginative one – for imagination grows from indigenous deep roots; his energetic power of exclamatory self-renewal, was really a weakness, a sign of superficiality.

Postcards came from hotels, north and south and west:

'Big orders. Back Friday. Love to self and chicks. Walt.'

On Friday Mother calms her fears of the railway system by having her weekly bath and puts on a white silk blouse with a net front and a high lace collar. She won't let us come near her. She has a racy smell and is restless and disturbing. She now belongs to him and not to us. He arrives hours late; he is always late. We hear the cab horse blowing at the gate. Father has brought her a present – a Dover sole or a joint in a skewered basket. She says how worried she has been; he chases her round the house, almost falls over the sofa and she screams with pleasure. 'Don't, Walt, you'll kill me.' The thin young man is now fat and bounces about like a ball.

There is a canal at Uxbridge, but for him it is not a canal. For him it is the Thames, the Ouse, the Severn, the Scottish salmon rivers. He buys himself a yachting cap, a blazer and cream trousers suitable for the Royal Yacht Squadron and Cowes and walks grandly among the old men fishing with worms off the towpath. Uxbridge is impressed by this young yacht owner especially as he puts up a monocle, for a lark, from time to time. This get-up is one of his incarnations. The fishermen put an idea into his head: he buys waders, a rod for perch and a rod for salmon and even a gaff and sets off to fill the family larder. The malicious anglers on the canal watch him hook himself to trees and even to passers-by.

At home he gets out his little notebooks in which he writes his orders. He reads the long list of items aloud. They are his poetry. So many gross of table-runners, cushions, or tea-cosies and so on, sold to the big drapers. Occasionally he does a sketch of the article he is selling for he is good at sketching. He can draw better than most people. He has heard of *art nouveau*. This puts an idea into his head. He decides that my mother ought to be an artist and out he goes to buy an expensive box of oil paints, brushes, an easel, canvases. He sees her as a glamorous woman painter. She had been so clever in the millinery at Daniels. She might turn out a good line in the manner of *Wedded*. There are two chocolate-coloured prints of dreamy-bosomed ladies, their transparent gowns slipping off their shoulders, pale, large-eyed languorous Guineveres, with their long waving hair falling over their shoulders: these are his notions of what my mother is like or ought to be like. They are excessively Woman, to my mind; embarrassing. Art has been put into his mind by a side line of his; the new Art Pot fashion. There are a number of samples on the mantelpiece; he has gone in for this line on his own and over-bought, so there they are. Very expensive, he says. One enormous flower bowl has blue Chinese dragons on it and I spend hours of my childish years working out which dragon is chasing which.

Ideas, he says, are everything. What did Emerson say? Father's got it written down in his notebook. Something about

54

the world carving a path through the woods to the door of the man who has an idea? The world is a wonderful place, he repeats, and buys stout shoes for shooting, pumps, high boots, low boots; button boots are going out. This leads him on to suits, overcoats, hats and shirts and pants. His under-clothes are sacred. Everything underneath must be clean – and at this his jolly face goes pale and a look of disgust comes over him. He has a double chin now. Very often he goes off to wash his hands, runs his fingers along the edges of tables to see if there is dust.

'He's just like his mother,' Mother says. 'She'd scrub a goose inside and out with a scrubbing brush.'

Their best friend at Uxbridge has a chemist shop and is about to start up in a new building estate at Gerrards Cross. We all drive out there in a horse charabanc to look at the new shop. We play with rolls of wallpaper and later get ourselves filthy among old tins in a rubbish dump among the gorse, while our parents are at the public house. We see a tramp asleep on the common and run away frightened: it is his sleep that has frightened us; perhaps he is dead. In the evening, we come home with the fast-trotting brake loaded with grown-ups who are singing 'Daisy, Daisy', cuddling and occasionally throwing out a beer bottle. At home, my father toys with the economics of the pharmaceutical trade, but the idea drifts away, for obviously something better has turned up. Father points out that the chemist is a small-minded man, without ambition, and he has better things to do.

At Uxbridge, when we are naked after a bath in front of the fire, I snatch my glass slate from my brother and sit on it so that he cannot see what I have drawn. The slate smashes and cuts two large slices in my bottom. Mother rushes screaming with me to the surgery, is saved from wheeling me into the canal in the pitch dark by a policeman. At the surgery I am given a sniff of chloroform and, coming to, see the doctor walking upside down on the ceiling. 'Another inch,' says the doctor, 'and he would have had them off.' What? I get a fort, soldiers, a fire in my bedroom for this. It is worth it.

Suddenly we leave Uxbridge for the suburb of Ealing, to another small but newly built villa, our first new one, with a small white balcony a foot wide and three feet long. 'I'll have my breakfast on it,' father says, fancying himself on the Riviera. We can watch the trains go by from our bedroom window and have a maid called Edna who steals. We are prosperous. Father goes about humming airs from Wagner or a few hymns, subscribes to a business magazine called *System* which contains pictures of the loading yards of factories, grain elevators, the offices of large corporations and portraits of their owners. 'A big man,' he says, gazing at the glum, cropped-haired businessman with admiration. 'Poor Father,' he says (reflecting on the minister). 'He did not realize his opportunities.' Any moment now, our meaty magician announces, he is going off to the United States, first-class on the *Mauretania*, all ex's paid – New York, Chicago, the city of the future. And this is no fancy: a cabin trunk, suits, shirts, pants, vests, socks, clothes of all kinds come into the house in larger quantities. Preparing for America he has himself fitted out with horn-rimmed spectacles and false teeth – impresses the customers – looks more serious. We are awed by the flash of the new white teeth. He walks to mirrors trying on grave expressions. He comes home one day and announces he has seen *Peter Pan*. He took a customer. We are told the plot.

'Do you believe in fairies?' the actor says and a wonderful thing happens: all the children in the audience say 'Yes' to stop a fairy called Tinker Bell from dying. This has moved Father so much that he has to wipe a tear from his eyes.

We, my mother, brother and I, are not envious or jealous. We have no desire to see things like the pantomime or *Peter Pan*: other children see such shows, but we prefer to send father there on our behalf; it will be one more chapter of his fantastic life. For example, it is he who is asked to carve the joint in the commercial room of hotels; it is he who commands cab drivers to carry his hampers of samples, tipping them a shilling. He knows managers. Some of them are hostile and won't touch his stuff; but they soon find their mistake. They come crawling 'on their hands and knees' – we see men in frock-coats crawling down the street after him begging now for what they foolishly refused. There are rival travellers, sinister spying creatures, but they usually drink and lose their jobs or their trade and Father snaps it up. He threatens, in a crisis, to 'knock them down'. We see a number of men get a straight punch from our hero and lying flat on the floor. There are also a number of men at the top who think they are sitting pretty, but in fact, any moment, they will be down in the mud.

While we were away in Yorkshire my sister was born. My brother Cyril and I were silenced by this incomprehensible piece of news. Were our parents not satisfied with us? No sooner are we in Ealing than there is another baby, my youngest brother. Another betrayal. Why clutter up the place? It happens on my birthday, too. It cannot be a good thing because Mother is always ill and talks about funerals and the illnesses of all her relations, and some woman comes in and cooks mutton stew which we refuse to eat. My little brother is called Gordon – after the General, and my sister, after one of Father's trips to Dublin, is called Kathleen, after Mavourneen, and my mother now remembers her grandfather once took that horse to Dublin. Father sings 'Kathleen Mavourneen' now. The horn of the hunter sounds in the amorous house.

With all our moving, school has been a nuisance. Father has no time to see about it. Education is very important, he says, we must not rush into it. Mother is opposed to education. All you want, she says, is schooling. Like she had. St Anne's Church of England; every morning the school bell sang out, she says, 'To St Anne's School. To St Anne's School.' At last there is an emotional outbreak at home and we are rushed off – by Father – in the middle of term and arrive about eleven o'clock when the children are painting irises. The paint runs. We have had a few weeks at a penny a week school – we take the penny on Monday; we've been to rough schools, kept by Wesleyans. I am getting stuck in the chorus recital of the multiplication tables, also the capes and rivers of England. At history I am trapped by Stephen and Matilda for several years. One day I throw my brother's cap on to a high hedge and we are just going into the garden to get it when we see an old lady looking out of her window at us. We are terrified and run for our lives; we never came back from school by that street again and have to tell a few lies about the cap.

Then, very suddenly, that haunting cab is at the door. No trip to Yorkshire this time. We are heading for Hammersmith

Broadway, mother crying as usual, father singing. We arrive at a shop close to the tube station in that rowdy, traffic-jammed neighbourhood. Thousands of people ooze out of the tube station, the streets are criss-crossed by thousands of legs, the buses (motor buses now) stink and grind; radiators boil over. Dray horses fall down. Our bedroom looks out on to a London gin palace; our back yard is a few square feet behind a wall that looks down on the tube station. Half the night the trains whine, the porters shout out 'Mahnd the dow-ers.'

Something has gone wrong. The *Mauretania* has sailed without Father. The dozens of shirts are piled up on the bed unworn and my mother walks at a distance round the bed with a hostile look as if looking at snakes. Father has opened up instead in the second-hand clothes business – society women's clothes resold. He also sells off his shirts. Mother serves in the shop. Left alone, my brother and I get out her oil paints, which she never used, after squeezing out paint on to the curtains to see the effect, go to the yard, take our clothes off and paint each other all over.

One Sunday we all go off to a shop in Edgware Road to meet a woman called Mrs Murdo who is an important figure in the old-clothes trade. We go through the suffocating smell of scores of coats and dresses and see a tall, stout woman, robed in red velvet. She has glossy black hair, a plummy, booming way of talking and great breasts that look as though they are going to tumble upon us. We wonder why she has not been fined for having breasts so large. She has a loving mouth and little eyes. She loves us and is going to be our greatest friend and we can't help noticing that Mother, wearing a brown felt hat with a feather in it and her old raincoat, makes a poor figure compared with this voluptuous woman. Later on Mrs Murdo is not quite our best friend: some question of an invoice. Just as well, the noise and dirt and smoke of the Edgware Road gave us headaches. Mother has them often now.

Usually there is no girl to help in the flat we live in above the shop, but one comes in sometimes and takes us to the Salvation Army. I begin to note that everyone drops his aitches here, like Mother, and has a sweaty smell. Going home through noisy streets, the girl tells us to hurry or the Fenians or Anarchists will get us. They will throw bombs.

There is danger at Hammersmith. We can sniff it in the gassy, coal-gritty London air. Few customers come into the shop and Father amuses himself by ringing up the till; but sneak thieves, beggars and drunks have a go at our lives. One morning a beautiful woman comes in, asks a fulsome question and falls full length smiling on the floor where she looks wide at the top and flat in the middle of the body, tapering like a parsnip. Mother drives us upstairs and we spy distantly a police barrow carrying the lady away, leaving a smell of whisky behind her.

Another curious incident occurs at Hammersmith. I suddenly, without knowing it, become a writer and cause the first of a long line of serious questionings. Someone at the Wesleyan school has set us the task of writing a sentence containing the word 'berth'. Nothing easier in our family: Father and all his friends are always leaving one 'guv'nor' for another and getting new 'berths' or 'cribs'; Father had even had a 'berth' in the *Mauretania*. I reject this family obsession and write a confusing sentence. An evening or two later, after a report from the school-teacher, I am questioned closely by my father and mother who are in a hateful state. Mother is pink in the cheeks – a bad sign with her – she has her sulky look of offended decency. This is absurd in a woman who goes about half-dressed, showing her breasts and leaving bloody things in the po. She sends angry signals to my father asking him to defend her from me. I have written on the paper:

'Last night I went to see the berth of a child.'

Now what (says my father, egged on by my angry mother), did I mean by 'last night'? Did I go out? Wasn't I at home? And then who was the child and what did I see? Well, I saw a berth. Like a berth on a ship or a child being born? How do you spell it? says my father. 'What does he mean he saw "the berth" of a child,' says my mother with a small scream. 'That's a funny thing for the boy to say.' I see that something has gone wrong, but what? I begin to invent, or rather I describe how I have invented something. I was a doctor, I said, and I went along to see a child born. He brings a baby, I saw him bring it. 'Now, keep quiet, Beat,' says my father to my mother. 'I want to say something to you, Victor. You are not a doctor. You made this up. You're not telling the truth.'

59

'It's all the kid's imagination,' said my mother indignantly.

'He gets it from you, old dear,' grins my father.

'Not in front of his mother, I won't have it,' says my mother. 'Do something, Walt.'

'Who gave you this idea?' says my father kindly.

'You said berth. . . .' I say, beginning to cry. 'I heard you.'

'You'd better look after your spelling,' says my father. I perceive that my father and mother are in a nervously excited state.

'What I can't understand is where he gets his ideas from,' says my mother looking at me mistrustfully. 'At eight I was helping Gran in the house.'

'You ought to help your mother, you're the eldest,' says my father. I stopped sniffling. The thing that worried me was the news that I had 'ideas'. This sounded like a curse or an illness. Had this some connexion with my closed navel? Perhaps I was going to die young like my mother's poor sister Fanny? The thought was voluptuously interesting.

Thank heaven, the cab was again at the door soon afterwards. Having attacked provincial towns, having tested the defences of the London suburbs, Father now decided to strike boldly at the heart of this dirty city that became smokier as you got to the centre of it. We arrived at Camberwell Green, in a street off Coldharbour Lane in which the smell of vinegar from a pickle factory hung low, a street of little houses, like Great Uncle Arthur's in York, and little shops that sent out such a reek of paraffin and packages that one's nostrils itched, we settled into one of our most original residences. It was, to our excitement, a flat. People lived above us. We could hear them trampling on the floor. Children raced up and down till the ceiling shook. We all got measles. A strange smell that had puzzled my parents soon showed its cause. Dry Rot. We woke up one morning to find our bed was at a steep slope. The foot of the bed had gone through the floor. Father was equal to this, of course. He 'got hold of the landlord' and said 'Confound you. For two pins I'd knock you down.' In a day we moved to an upper flat next door. We were then able to see the beauty of our situation. A yard or two from our bedroom window at the back was one of the largest machine bakeries in London, and next to it the Camberwell Roller Skating Rink. I was enchanted by the lurid quality of industrial London. It all looked like something in a newspaper. The sound of these machines, their humming clatter, was in our ears all day long. It became warm and assuring at night when the factory lights were on and we could see men in white coats and hats at the ovens, and hear their shouts, and wake up after midnight and still see the show. In the small hours the delivery carts and vans woke us up. Competing with the noise of the bakery was the high, rattling, swirling rumble of roller skates at the Rink and from this came the screams of girls and the thump of a band. Life had speeded up. Gentility — we appreciated — had gone. Something rank and urgently sordid was in the air. It scared me but I liked it. Responsibility came to me. I had to look after my brother Cyril and my sister and wheel the baby out. It was I who had to shout 'Mum, Mum, quick. He's done his business in his trousers.' Mother might send me out to get a basin of pease pudding and a few slices of pickled pork, or a pennyworth of pickles, or fish and chips in a newspaper; I bought firewood and paraffin, too.

The south of London has always been unfashionable and its people have stuck to a village life of their own; they were often poorish, but poverty, or rather not having much money yet managing on it, has its divisions and sub-divisions of status. Respectability, the dominant trait of the English and certainly of the two-faced London mind, prevailed. Camberwell had gone downhill since the days when the Ruskins kept a carriage there or the Brownings thrived, and we were in one of the reach-me-down parts of it, a place of street markets and within call of the costers of the Walworth Road, known for selling rabbits at fourpence. We soon learned to say we'd give each other 'a fourpenny one in the clock.' We were close also to Loughborough Junction noted for a dirty limerick; to go 'up the Junction' was one of our street trips. There was the yelling and selling of the Brixton Arcades on Saturday nights. Within a few weeks my brother and I were pissing happily off the so-called roof garden of our flat into the yard below and swinging on ropes hung round the lamp-posts outside. Soon we would 'bung a brick' through the lamps.

Instantly I knew I was, and always had been, a London child

61

and understood with pride my grandmother's word about the gutter; not that we had lived in it, but to feel we were close to it, cheered us. The school I was sent to – here my mother, nearer in spirit to her own home ground, must have made her sole gesture on behalf of my education – was a rough Church of England school called St Matthew's. (The church it was attached to, the school, and a lot of the neighbourhood, including our flats, were destroyed by bombs between 1940 and 1944.) A couple of hundred boys from seven to fourteen were in this sooty, churchy building and sat in one great varnished hall. The teachers stood in a row with their canes before us unruly cattle; the headmaster, a little man with a long white beard, stood in the middle of the school on a dais. At a rap of his cane, we began with prayers and the school hymn.

Loudly old Mathusians rally
At the sound of the reveille.

In shrill Cockney voices we yelled it, kicking and giving punches to our neighbours as we finished off the scuffles of the school yard. Then a glass partition was drawn across the hall, the school was divided into two and a couple of teachers got to work. In the middle of sums you would be distracted by the geography and history going on a yard or two away. My mind was a mixture of everything that was going on and brought to a standstill when, every now and then, a boy would be called out to be caned across the hand or, in bad cases, to be sent to the headmaster whose cane was thicker. I was used to elementary schools and had been deadened by the turgid sing-song of the Wesleyans teaching by incantation; St Matthew's was Dickensian. But there was one strange lesson – given, I suppose, because male shorthand writers were in demand at that time – Pitman's shorthand. Being bad at handwriting and spelling, I enjoyed the secrecy and elegance of those little signs and when I got home used to practise them. It was the beginning, for me, of the desire for other languages. For the rest, small and alarmed by the violence of the bigger boys, I joined in the daily riot: the rabid games of marbles in the yard, with a fight every time a glass alley was hit. I learned to save mine to play with quieter boys along the gutter of Coldharbour Lane. There was often a

62

shout of 'Hump the Knacker, one, two, three.' In this game you leapfrogged over a row of lads, the leader having bent against the wall. Heavy boots, soled with hobnails, crushed one's shoulders. To complete the Victorian picture, the bearded headmaster suddenly died and we had a great funeral orgy. We had to walk round his coffin in the church next door. According to the sermon, the headmaster had been a second Dr Arnold.

At St Matthew's the Health Inspector came round once a month to take the lice out of the heads of some of the larger girls and boys. They came out in front of the class and as the inspector cracked the lice and dropped them into a basin of water beside him, the lads would wink or grin proudly at us and we would laugh back. There was a tall boy who worked in the market, whom we called Uncle because of his good nature.

'Cor, look at Uncle!' we said admiring his distinction. One half wanted to find a louse oneself, but Mother was good at combing out the nits.

There was a Hippodrome at Camberwell and on Saturday nights many of the bigger boys, the rowdy ones, used to get into the Gallery. We soon found ourselves 'in the fashion'. For ragtime had just come in and we picked up 'Alexander's Ragtime Band', 'Hitchy koo' and 'Waiting for the Robert E. Lee' from the lads as they sang it going home in the streets. These we added to our mother's music-hall collection. More often now she sang:

> At Trinity Church I met me doom
> Now we live in a top back room

but would alleviate this by 'A Bicycle Made for Two', 'My Old Dutch' and 'Only a Little Jappy Soldier'. I loved this last sad song. This year I nearly won the 200 yards, and would have done if my shorts hadn't fallen to my ankles only a few yards from the tape, while the crowd cheered. King Edward came to Camberwell and we waved our Union Jacks at that smiling man with the short legs and sloping stomach, his elegant Queen and his two solemn sickly-looking children.

This was the peak; after that a decline. Everything went wrong. To start with, I set off to school and stopped to stare, unbelieving at the posters all edged in deep black. King Dead, they said. Death of the King. I ran back to tell my mother who began to shake and say 'Oh poor Queen Alexandra'. There was a picture of his bedroom in the papers and of his faithful white dog looking up at the empty bed. Mother cried and began on her long litany of royal troubles and funerals which had a wide European range: moving from these to her dead Dad, her poor sister Fanny, poor Frank buried under the Union Jack in the Atlantic, and then on to her dog Rover and a lovely little canary the cat got, which broke her heart. Somehow, one felt, they had all died for England and the Empire and I felt this year that my life was wrapped in patriotic flags and that my very body was stained red, white and blue every time I sang 'Hurrah' for it. My mother was adept at these tribal purgations.

Then a terror began to be whispered about our school. It was the terror about which I was to consult Aunt Lax at Appleton within the next twelve months. We would be standing, a row of us, in the stinking school jakes, happily seeing who could pee the highest, when the whisper would start: Jack the Ripper was about in Camberwell. What did he do? He took girls' knickers down and slit them up the belly: better informed boys said, 'up the cunt'. We left school in terror, and for me, with an agonized responsibility. I had the duty of collecting my sister from a girls' school in the next street and Jack the Ripper was known to wait there. For weeks the boys talked of nothing else. I believed it, yet did not believe it. But one afternoon something sinister happened. It was in the winter and already a little dusk. I fetched my little sister and I walked, holding her hand, up Coldharbour Lane. Presently a shabby man with a feeble, knowing face came up beside us and said something like 'Hullo, going home from school? Is that your little sister? Going down this way? I'll buy you a toy.' And with this he took my hand. I was chilled with terror. The shop was just along the street, the way we were going, he said. I choked out 'No' and sulkily said 'I don't want a toy.' He kept on about the toy shop he knew, gripping my hand and stepping out with determination. ' 'Ere y'are, in 'alf a mo',' he kept saying. Very soon we were outside the shop window that was lit up and full of toys: talk of Satan taking Jesus up a high mountain and offering him the world. The story came naturally to my mind after staying in Yorkshire. ' 'Ave this one. I'll give you sixpence.' The philanthropist and child-lover looked ill, pale and seedy. 'No,' I said. 'Come on, I'll give you a shilling – say what you want. 'Ere y'are, a shilling.' 'No.' 'I'll hold your sister's hand, you run in and get it.'

Now there was no doubt: he was the Ripper.

By a stroke of what looks like genius to me now and, in my agony, I said, 'That one,' pointing to the biggest toy fort in the window. I could see it was the most expensive in the shop. 'I'll look after your sister,' he said excitedly. 'You go and get it,' I said. 'No,' he said and, like a fool, he let go of my hand to put a shilling in it. It was my chance. I dropped the shilling and ran off with my sister as fast as I could. I was nearly screaming. We ran all the way home, past the shops, the long line of hoardings by the wasteland, the skating rink and the bread factory and hammered on the door of the flat. I made my sister swear she would say nothing, as we went up the stairs. And she didn't; she had noticed nothing strange and even now does not remember the incident. I had been too frightened to call for help in the crowded street and was too frightened to tell my parents. When I was in my twenties I told them at last and they said I was making it all up.

'You have your mother's imagination,' my father said.

London was dangerous. We had a girl to help my mother for a few weeks and her mind, like the mind of the one at Ealing, was brimming with crime. She took me to the Camberwell Bioscope to see a film of murder and explosions called *The Anarchist's Son*, in which men with rifles in their hands crawled up a hill and shot at each other. When the shed in which one of them was living blew up, the film turned silent, soft blood red and the lady pianist in front of the screen struck up a dramatic chord. In the Bioscope men walked about squirting the audience with a delicious scent like hair lotion that prickled our heads.

On the way to school we had to pass the hoardings, a hundred yards of them. There were cryptic ones. There was the huge portrait of an unshaven tramp under which were the words advertising Pears' soap: 'Ten years ago I used your soap, since when I've used no other.' There were the Election posters. Lloyd George was trying to get rid of the House of Lords and there were comic pictures of dukes and earls with coronets toppling off their heads. He was also introducing Health Insurance and the words 'Ninepence for Fourpence' were printed in bold letters, a worry to me. But there were two far less jolly. One showed the British working man in moleskin trousers tied by string below the knee, the general uniform of the labourer, sitting down to sausage and mashed in his cosy kitchen with his wife and children. But the kitchen door is open and a snarling wolf called Socialism is coming in to rob the family of their dinner. Considering the state of the London poor at this time – a dock labourer's wages were about 11s. a week and the mass of English people had reached the lowest level of nutrition since 1760 – as we know now from the researches of the Drummonds – this picture was a political crime, on the part of the Tory party.

I did not understand these pictures, but they showed that London had the melodramatic spirit. There was another which I did in a way understand and which agitated my fancies. I must return first to the private life of our family to explain why.

As we ran about the streets during the day, as we swung on our rope from the lamp-post, with the Catchpole brothers after school – they lived next door, their father was a gas meter inspector who came in to collect the sixpences from our slot machine – as we hung on to the tail boards of carts or lorries while the other kids shouted to the driver, 'Put your whip behind, guv'nor,' the street cry of the period, we were aggressively happy. To show our mood – our Aunt Ada's daughter, Hilda, aged seventeen came down from Ipswich to stay with us, the one who went to 'a boarding-school for the daughters of gentlemen'. This, as they say, killed us. She caught my brother and me at our occasional sport of peeing off the roof and was angry with us. I cheeked her back. She persisted, so I said,

'I'll kick you up the arsehole. I'll bung up your lug.'

She said I was a nasty, common little boy, so I kicked her on the shins. She looked at me scornfully and went away.

We uneasily knew that we had become sordid and that the lives of our parents had, in some way, changed. My mother looked bedraggled. Her hair was always coming down, the coarse apron was round her waist. She plonked saucepans on the table, full of rice or sago, boiled in water, and made stews full of fat which we could not easily eat. It turned out she was a bad cook. She had whitlows on her fingers and we had them too.

At night, the soothing sound of the machines at the bakery were driven out by shouts and shrieks from the room next door to us. My mother was shouting at my father, my father rumbled and then roared back. We had never heard them quarrel before, but these shouts went on for hours. We listened acutely for key words. The only one we could catch was . . . 'That woman . . .' This was disturbing for it had somehow got into my head that the word 'woman' meant something wrong; my granda often addressed my grandma as 'Woman' when he was rebuking her.

'Let's call for water,' my brother said.

So we started up. 'I wanta drinka water.'

There was no answer. At last we got out of bed in our night-gowns. Our mother looked at us slyly and with derision. She got us the water and pushed us back to bed quickly and then continued with her tirade. Night after night this went on.

A few days after this, my father – looking very much the dandy – caught us swinging on the lamp-post. He looked sick with anger and drove us inside. Mother turned on my brother and said he was round-shouldered, stupid and the image of my father's brother Edward, the casualty of that family; to me, she said that I thought I was clever but I wasn't. She now sat by the fire-guard muttering to herself. She pulled us about and punched us, and her appearance, the hair falling over her face, was witch-like. One evening, waiting for my father's return, she said she had toothache and called for brown paper and vinegar and made me warm it by the fire. Her face was swollen, she said, and when it was heated she held the paper to her face. Father got home, grave and dignified. Mother went to the oven, banged down a plate of chops on the table and said:

'There it is. Eat it.'

'What is the matter with your face, old dear?'

'You know what's the matter.'

'She's got toothache,' we said.

'Toothache?' said Father. 'What is that? Now, Beat, you know what I've been telling you. There is no such thing as toothache. You only think you've got it.'

This interested us for Father said this in the kindest and most rational of voices and, in fact, Mother had said nothing about toothache earlier in the day. We were anxious for the discussion to be continued but we were sent to bed and then the nightly rumpus began again. It was still about 'that woman'. Who she was we could not find out and indeed did not find out for many years, but from this moment there was a shadow in our lives, often forgotten, but always there. The houses we went to live in, particularly the dining-rooms and kitchens, seemed darker. I tried to wheedle the secret out of my mother, but she would give a steady dishonest look, mocking, flirtatious and obstinate and sometimes say, very comfortably, 'I'm a wicked girl.'

Now on the hoardings in Coldharbour Lane, there was for two or three weeks a poster that offered a confused solution to the mystery. There was something evil about all these gaudy posters, because through cracks in them you could see a piece of waste ground littered with tins and rubbish and rank weeds, and among them old men could often be seen loafing about, looking for things, men of the Jack the Ripper type. My key poster was the most sinister of all. It was a theatre poster. It showed a bedroom. At the dressing-table a woman, in rather naked evening dress, sits doing her hair – just as my mother did – and she is just about to give a stroke of the brush when she sees in the mirror that the bedroom door is opening. In the doorway stands a tall, dark man with a pointed black beard, startling eyes and wearing a cloak over his evening dress. There is an expression of horror on the girl's face. Above the picture is the title of the play – it is at the Hippodrome – the title is *The Bad Girl of the Family*.

Day after day I gazed at this picture when I passed. For some time, I related the scene in the picture to another notice, stuck at the bottom of it: Commit No Nuisance. People 'committed suicide', 'committed murder', were 'committed for trial' and so on. 'Committed' was an evil word. The man in the picture was clearly about to 'commit a nuisance' whatever that was; but the phrase was repeated on other posters, so that Lloyd George, Pears' soap, the House of Lords were engaged in the same monotonous crime. I gave up this theory and tried again. I began to suspect that the woman at the dressing-table might be Mother – as I say, I was often with her when she did her hair; and although I knew she did not mean it, she often said she was a bad or wicked girl. Who was the man? I could think of no man for the part. Uncle Edward was wicked too, but I had seen him once and he was shuffling, lazy and fair-haired, not handsome like the man at the door. The only handsome man was my father and he certainly was not a villain. Yet (for my emotions were stirred) I had my first jealous sense that my father *just* could be the intruder in that room. And there was this curious underlying feeling that woman had some side to her nature that it would be unlucky to know. It would be like falling into the canal and drowning. Even so, I knew – but in a child's way, without consciously knowing it – that the scene came out of a play about a girl being seduced by a villain. My mother's story-telling was always reckless and suggestive, because when she got to the sexy bit, she would stop short and not finish the sentence, but give a knowing nod. (This became a habit all her life so that, by not finishing a simple sentence, she could make any innocent thing sound lewd.)

'So I said to the shopkeeper, I want a pair of . . . and ran home and took off . . . and he said, Mrs P, just hang them on the . . .'
or
'So I sat down in the . . . and closed the . . .'

So, to return to the picture; it was a mixture of our life and a fiction. The bad girl was in a poetic way, my mother, the man was my father; but who 'that woman' of these new, violent rows was, was beyond me. There was no other woman but my mother, though you saw imitations in the street. My mother was Woman herself.

About these quarrels we were as indignant as little lords. By what right did these two grown-up animals have these consuming battles, put on these tremendous plays and not only keep us out of them, but in doing so, ignore us. It was intolerable. There was a growing feeling in my brother and myself, that we ought to tell them so; and that they were selfish. This feeling was getting very strong in me.

Left out of the battle, I sulkily threw myself into the rough and tumble outside. I swapped my father's fishhooks for a skate and lost it in a fight on Denmark Hill – had he been alive Ruskin might have seen an incident which has no parallel in *Et Praeterita* – I fell in love with a girl who lived with the theatricals two doors down. I pinched, at last, a pound packet of haricot beans and threw them at the school-teacher and tore up my writing book. I got a couple on the hands for this and was made to stand on the bench in school after everyone had left. You could usually see three or four solemn figures doing this after school. Once a girl wetted her drawers and they swelled out like a white balloon. We had to wait for the teacher to release us. One by one the others were released, but my teacher did not appear. It was winter. The school darkened. I decided to escape. I got down and crept to the door and there I ran into the teacher. Now, I thought, I'm in trouble, but to my surprise, he said:

'Good heavens, I forgot about you. Come home to tea. Then I'll take you home. I live near you.'

There followed the most memorable tea of my life. The master and his wife gave me strawberry jam and cakes. Their room was full of books and had three armchairs. I sat in an armchair. We had only one in *our* flat. The teacher and his wife spoke to me as if I was their age and, being a talker, I told them all about my father and grandfather. Then the teacher took me home.

'I will speak to your father,' he said. 'I think you ought to go to a better school. You're good at shorthand.'

What passed between my father and the master I do not know, but my father – and, surprisingly, my mother – were impressed by the shorthand. I was even congratulated and my father, instead of being simply good-natured, was almost respectful to me. I did not go to a better school, but the very next day, my brother and I were sent off on the late train to Sedbergh. We had our classic arrival: torn jerseys, holes in breeches and stockings. It was our last visit for many years and after a month we were sent off from York, not to London, but to my birthplace, Ipswich. A new upheaval had occurred in my father's life – my grandfather had hinted as much and he too suggested there was a wicked woman concerned in it; for the moment my grandparents supported my mother and said that, except for cooking, housekeeping, sewing, etc., she was sensible. It appeared also that fortunately 'certain people' did not know we had been living in Camberwell: we were there, it seems, in hiding. Father had gone bankrupt at Hammersmith and had started up again, somewhere else, in Mother's name.

CHAPTER FIVE

In these sudden crises in our lives when I went off with my father to Yorkshire, my mother sometimes took my brother Cyril to her sister's at Ipswich and left him there. When the two of us met again we would be astonished to see how long our legs had got and scarcely recognized each other's voices. Mine had the hard Yorkshire strain, he had the softer, politer voice of the south. Unlike myself he was an affectionate boy and he observed more of the true situation in our home than I did. He was an easy victim and he early became a very bad stammerer. This vanished at our Aunt's house where he was the little gentleman, used to the drawing-room, to servants and Edwardian niceties. When he came back to our rough and tumble, the sight of a table not properly laid and of rooms ill-furnished and knocked about by our life, made him nervous and upset. He talked in a careful and elderly way at that time.

But now we were both leaving York for Ipswich on our own. The train ran through the empty landscape of the Fens lying under the wide skies that had moved the Norwich painters. We saw powerful Ely cathedral on its hill in that flat land and were in sweetly rolling East Anglia, the country of large village churches, monastic buildings and pretty white, pargeted and timbered houses, some of the loveliest things in England. This region had once been rich when England's great wealth was in wool and before the water power and steam engine of the north had captured the trade a century before. Strange names like Eye and March excited me. I had read *Hereward the Wake* and knew of fanes and that 'silly Suffolk' meant holy Suffolk.

I saw the reason for my brother's distinction when we got out at Ipswich station. We were met by a tall man of fifty who had a domed head like a very large pink egg, fluffy white hair and a short white beard. He looked like a pious ram. Perhaps those mild blue eyes and red wet lips were roguish – as my mother often blurted out in her cheery way – but he had a slow, considerate manner and the voice had the straying educated bleat.

71

He was, I had heard, notorious for knowing everything and he had the most enlightened views. My plump cousin, Hilda, the girl whose lug I had threatened to bung up, shook hands in a condescending way. She was his stepdaughter. Instead of hiring a cab at the station, as bounders and commercial travellers did, we crossed Ipswich economically by tram, sitting on top under the sparks of the trolley. Our uncle – for so he was by marriage – pointed out the shipping on the River Orwell, mentioned the chief trades of the city, noted the birth-place of Cardinal Wolsey (a man, he said, ruined by ambition), and the ancient streets of the town, in a serious, prosing East Anglican sing-song. Now and then my cousin pointed to a couple of houses belonging to her relations, houses that seemed like mansions to me and lying in luxurious grounds, protected by laurels, the most moneyed of English shrubs. She handed out lady-like social chit-chat. We were wearing cloth caps and she asked, snobbishly I thought, where our school caps were. We hadn't got any, I said. She was put out. Obviously we who had come out of the depths were about to soar to the heights; but we had yet to know about family strategy. The tram set us down in a district of humble little villas on the outskirts of the city and there we found our house. Only Mother was there, waiting for us with the other children. Father had gone. He had left us. He lived seventy miles away in a flat in London and was to come very rarely during the next year for a day's visit. Our new uncle baa-ed some charitable words to my mother, as indeed he had done to the tram conductor and a couple of people on the tram who had deferred very markedly to him; and then went off. He was our aunt's second husband.

Our aunt had brought off a *coup*. She was a cleverer, more independent and collected woman than my mother and though she had my mother's chattering gaiety, was far more discreet in tongue and manner. Laughter with her had become a refined giggle. After she had buried poor Frank at sea and had given birth to her daughter, she had settled in Ipswich (after Father's abrupt departure in 1900) where houses were cheap and she lived with Gran who kept lodgers. Gran Martin looked after Hilda while Ada, her mother, went to work in a Post Office. For years, sitting behind the grill she had sold stamps to this well-off and philanthropical gentleman who, hearing her story, proposed to her. He was much older than she was. They were married. It was a joke in both families.

Her Fred was the eldest and most solemn of thirteen children. His grandfather, I believe, had begun life as a cobbler in Norwich; in the next generation a small fortune was made out of leather; our new uncle retired young on his means, became the director of several waterworks and managed his property. He was a strong Presbyterian and active in Liberal politics and was, among other things, one of the trustees of the local Mechanics' Institute – one of those hundreds of libraries established privately over England for the education of industrial workers. The high point of the family's social distinction was reached when Uncle let the house he had been brought up in to the German Kaiser on one of his visits to England. Among his brothers, sent to great Public Schools, was a barrister on the Eastern Circuit, famous at murder trials, an architect, an artist and one enormously successful businessman in the wholesale provision business, supposed to be worth half a million and a partner of the famous Lipton. He had taken the house of a peer of the realm and – my mother said – drank champagne for breakfast. The only girl was one of the first women to go to Girton and looking after her mother half her life, married another well-off man, who was in the trade. So it was respectfully reported to us, but they belonged to the sober generation of new wealth and were shocked by any sons or daughters who went in for high social pretentions. They were Presbyterians, public-spirited, bought pictures at the Academy, and were very respectable.

There was only one flaw in this family. This part of England had been settled in the early centuries by the Teutons and by the de Burghs, the family name indeed of the Dukes of Norfolk, and, although he made no absurd claims in the matter, my uncle was careful to recall that this was the origin of his name. But the English have always mumbled foreign languages: my good uncle's name became Bugg. This he proudly stuck to, but many of his brothers couldn't stand it. They changed theirs to avoid low jokes. The news that dear Ada had married a Mr Bugg sent my mother into fits; and Gran, who thought second

marriages were wicked, grimly called her son-in-law plain Bugg
for the rest of her life, and after a drink or two, would mutter
about 'the old bugger'. It took the kind, patient man about
twenty years to win her round.

The Buggs lived in the fashionable end of Ipswich and
ourselves had been carefully placed at the other: there was no
desire to make acquaintance. Even the two dear sisters scarcely
communicated. We were that humiliating plague – poor relations. Far from ascending we were sent off to a rough school
in Cauldwell Hall Road. Not that that mattered to us: we were
free, spending our spare time in the Suffolk countryside where
at harvest time we were to see the rows of men cutting the corn
with sickles in the fields. We brawled on the 'Pansy', the name
of a meadow near the school, and back, as far as education went,
I went to reciting the capes and rivers of England and learning
the dates of Stephen and Matilda.

It was odd, considering my uncle's principles, that he was
reluctant to see us; eventually because he was a man of strong
moral sense he told us one of the reasons and gossip between
the sisters soon revealed the rest. One day, Mother said, putting
on a mocking voice, 'You are going to the Highlands. High up –
high in name, high in nature.' It was the name of the house. We
dressed in our best clothes and walked up the long hill to the
house. The house seemed to us immense but it was really an
ample but unpretentious Victorian villa. There were far larger
ones about it of the kind which are either pulled down or
turned into flats nowadays. It was approached by a small drive,
its two lawns were sheltered by pines, sycamores and a cedar.
The dining-room had its heavy furniture and heavy curtains.
Two bronze gladiators gallivanted on the black marble mantelpiece with a marble clock like a temple between them. On
the walls were oil paintings bought from the Academy which
looked like dark gravy mixed with cabbage. They were cribs
from Morland and Constable. In the morning room two thousand books were in their walnut cases – the works of Gibbon,
Mill, Macaulay, Prescott, Motley, the life of Garibaldi – indispensable to our uncle's generation – political, historical or philosophical volumes, and his classics as well. No fiction was
allowed. After breakfast the three maids were called in for

prayers. Our uncle who was working his way chronologically through the bible had got once more to Kings and intoned a chapter in a voice of deep, rebuking melancholy; then all knelt down and listened to a long prayer. After breakfast we walked round the garden as far as the conservatory where our aunt talked in a fanciful way to the gardener and then sat under a sycamore tree and my cousin Hilda brought out one or two improving books, for I was known to be a reader. I had read every line of several volumes of the *Home Magazine* – especially a grotesque serial called 'The Wallypug of Why', an enjoyable fantasy about the plots of a cathedral gargoyle: also bits from the *Children's Encyclopaedia*, *Hereward the Wake*, comics and *Marriage on Two Hundred a Year*, one of the popular handbooks of the period. My cousin asked me what I thought of Montesquieu who, it turned out, was French. That bowled me out so she set about correcting my English. In the afternoon we walked with my aunt in the Arboretum where she paused at each unusual tree. She had gone in for carrying a lorgnette, as a lady-like thing, and raised it when she read out the botanical name. We returned then to her drawing-room, done in the prettiest Edwardian fashion, and she got her lorgnette out once more as she took us on a tour of her collection of water-colours by a local artist called Barlow Woods. My aunt had a flirtatious manner: I decided, on the spot, to become a painter.

By now Uncle Bugg thought the time for seriousness had come. We were taken to a spare bedroom. There he unlocked a wardrobe door and from a shelf he took down five or six books bound in black cloth which had a cross and crown in gold monogram on them.

'I keep these books here, locked up, and for a special reason,' he said. 'In order,' he said with a sly but forcible smile, 'that no one shall ever read them. They belonged to one of my sisters whose life was ruined by them and, when she died, my first step was to go to her house and take them away. They are the works of a fraudulent American woman: Mary Baker Eddy. I am sorry to say that your father – who perhaps hasn't had the opportunities for education – has become a follower of that woman. I have told him that she is one of the false prophets the

New Testament warns us against. It has already distressed your grandfather, and, I am glad to say, your mother has understood the evil of this woman who has misled your father. His judgement in many things is weak. He has good qualities but he is easily carried away. I have explained to him that this is trash.'

My uncle smiled gravely. He had a general vanity in knowing more about everything than anyone else and his talk – as we got to know him – was a catalogue of moral and intellectual victories over everyone, from the Liberal Party down to his servants.

This news meant only one thing to me. A mystery was solved. 'That woman', who had rocked our nights at Camberwell, was an American prophetess. That was why my father was not with us. Instantly, but silently, we rallied to Father. It had gradually become clear to us that he was a natural follower. He followed all kinds of people. It struck us as rather fine. Just as he went to the theatre, stayed at big hotels, went to smart restaurants, for our sake, as if we had sent him there in order to save ourselves the trouble of it, so we felt about his friendship with Mrs Eddy. She would get a good deal out of it. We felt proud of him. He was far above us. It was not surprising that he had sailed into this high position and had left us.

Yet, once Uncle Bugg had locked the wardrobe door, I became uneasy. On our way home Mother told us Father was coming to see us on Sunday. My brother, who adored him, was pleased; but I was not. I did not miss him. I did not think about him. He would spoil our Sunday. We would have to give up going to the camp in the pea-field we had made with our gang of children in the street. We would not be able to sit up in the chestnut tree and smoke cigarettes for which some stored window blinds served as tobacco. We would not be able to go off down the Orwell to watch the steamers. And – it now occurred to me – Uncle Bugg's story put a new meaning on that poster showing the scene from *The Bad Girl of the Family*. The handsome man in the opera cloak who looked in at the bedroom door and frightened the bad girl, would frighten me no more. He was my father for certain now and the Bad Girl was Mrs Eddy. He had moved on to a prophetess.

I told Mother what Uncle Bugg had said, in order to find out more from her. But the moment I spoke, I could see her devious watchful look coming on. I knew she would lead me on to find out what I knew and would then turn on me and laugh in my face. And then she would stop looking shrewdly and keenly at me and would look away up at the ceiling or out of the window and go into thoughts of her own. Out of these she would speak and mysterious sentences would come.

'I dunno what to make of it,' she said. 'I told him not to do it.'

'Who, Mum?'

'What are you talking about?'

'You said you didn't know what to make of it, told him not to do it.'

'Did I? Well don't you do it either.'

'I haven't done anything.'

'Haven't you? Littering up Mrs Bowser's hall with all those notes you wrote to that girl – her mother came round and said for you to stop it.' Now, this was true. One of my twenty hour passions had blown up for the pretty little daughter of Mrs Bowser down the street, and I had been delivering notes there at the rate of two or three an hour. But I knew my mother. I knew she was escaping by turning the tables on me.

Presently, having won her victory, she changed her mind.

'It all started with your Uncle Arthur up at York. I don't know how I got in with such a lot but when you're young you're thoughtless. It was his cousin Dick.'

And now one of her stories came out. That cousin of my father's, the ill and miserable lithographer who couldn't keep his food down and was out of work, had been cured by this American woman, Baker something. The whole family had been converted – except Uncle Arthur. He had stuck to Burton and 'circumstances alters cases' and fought back angrily against them.

'Your father believes it,' she said.

'Like Uncle Bugg said,' I said.

She looked wary again.

'And there's been all this trouble,' she said.

But at this she broke off and would not say what it was.

I could see there was a battle going on inside Mother's mind, one which she was losing, but because of her tenacity, never losing for good and what it was about would come out only in hints, or in shouts in the next ten or fifteen years. It tore my loyalties and my heart in two.

The 'trouble' (gradually my mother and I put it together) was this. Father's proposed journey to America had been a device of his employer. The villain wanted to get Father out of the country, while he fiddled the books. A telegram from the woman bookkeeper of the firm – she had come to see us at Ealing – brought my father back from Liverpool when he was embarking. He came back to London and hearing that the man had also been making advances to the unwilling girl, he had had a stand-up fight with him in his office in Aldersgate Street. It was a curious fight, for the man had locked himself in his office. My father, though short, was heavy and strong and, under his bland manner, had stores of violence: he charged at the door and broke it in, and of course 'knocked the man down'. The sequel is vague. Undefeated, Father suddenly decided to go into the high-class second-hand clothes business in Hammersmith and, having once been bankrupt in Ipswich, he opened up in Mother's name. That shop had failed too. He had fled to Camberwell and then, not to be crushed and having good connexions in his trade, he started up again in the art needlework trade in Newgate Street, opposite the Old Bailey. This new being, exalted by a new religion, heard of his sister-in-law's rich marriage and advanced hopefully upon Ipswich to get Uncle Bugg to put money up for his new firm. Father had placed us there as an outpost. Uncle Bugg considered my father's career and decided that he was too volatile an investment and also chaffy in his religious life. It was because of this and not entirely because we were poor relations that we were put at the other end of the town. Aunt Ada was not going to have her lucky marriage wrecked from the beginning by a begging brother-in-law.

We knew nothing of this for years. Nor did we really know anything of my father's religion or even what it was called. George V was crowned that year and in Ipswich the affair was celebrated in the park by a mock attack on an Afghan Hill Fort which went up in smoke. Soldiers in red coats and pill-box hats walked about the streets. It was a fine summer. My cousin was kinder. Down to the Art Gallery we went and saw a huge picture of Lucrezia Borgia offering poison to a page while the wicked Pope looked treacherously on. Hilda said she liked the Borgias. They were not Presbyterians nor were they followers of a mealy-mouthed American prophetess.

Hilda hated her stepfather and especially his religion. She was High Church and took me to see the ritual and smell the incense of that fashionable religion. I was bored.

There was trouble with my accent. I had given up Yorkshire speech and had quickly picked up the Suffolk sing-song. At school we called each other 'boa' – from the Teutonic *bauer* – and lilted to one another phrases like 'Where y'now goin' boa?' And when we parted we always used the pretty Suffolk habit of saying 'Farewell, boa', instead of 'Good-bye'. My brother and I spent hours in our chestnut tree smoking. We had moved to elderberry pipes now, but we went on with the window blinds. There were a dozen of these blinds to get through. They were made of stiff dressed blue calico and were stored in the roof. Though scorching to the tongue the blinds tasted better and burned better than chrysanthemum leaves. We finished all except two pairs that year. On April Fool's Day we got a lot of gents off their bikes by shouting out 'Your tyre's flat' and bawling 'April Fool' at them. My mother sent us to the Congregational Sunday School, but it was a riot of thrown hymn-books. She tried us with the Church of England, but not having heard of its theology or prayers, we were at a loss and were offended by the classy accents of the clergyman and congregation. It is odd, considering my father's religiosity: I was never baptized. Like the closed navel, it was a distinction I stuck to.

Then came the Saturday night when my father arrived and stayed until tea-time on Sunday. Well-dressed and graver than I remembered him, he stood like an intruder among us. He surprised us by bringing us to order; he stopped us running out to the chestnut tree. He was in a temper about the blinds, the first temper I had ever seen him in. And he and my mother quarrelled, my mother shouting about 'that woman' again, and

79

asking him what he thought we lived on and of course the Bugg family was dragged in. These rows made me jealous and I stopped the quarrel by calling out:

'Dad, Dad. Thou shalt not divorce thy wife. It says it in the Bible.'

'There you are,' said my mother. 'Your own children know.'

My father said sternly, 'Little boys are to be seen and not heard.'

'There you are,' cried my mother passionately to me and changing sides in a flash as she always did, 'You dare talk to your father like that.'

And then she started crying and said her dear sister Ada would take her in and Father said her 'dear sister Ada' had scarcely spoken to her though she lived scarcely two miles away.

'And you know why,' cried my mother.

At tea-time a cab came for my father and we were glad to see him go; or at least I was. But Mother repented. She was a bad girl, she said, with a wicked tongue and Gran had a wicked tongue too. 'Your father is doing everything for the best. He has got faith, remember that. He always had. When we were at Daniels,' she went on, and she would soothe us and herself with the story of her life, looking nervously at the door when she did. For we noticed now that for a year or more – it had begun in Camberwell – she was frightened of doors, especially the front one. 'Go and peep, don't let them see you. See who it is.' Once we heard her talking at the door to a man.

'No one of the name of Pritchett here,' she said. 'Never heard of them. I'm the maid.'

We stared at her. She gave us a threatening look, her greenish grey and fretful eyes quick and full of lies. We felt we were either floating in the air or sinking through the earth.

CHAPTER SIX

WE were off again, of course. The year's soft and lazy affair with my birthplace had passed. We had scarcely heard the word God at all for a twelvemonth in this pagan holiday. We had made two or three more visits to our Aunt Ada's. I see her, on one of them, duck-breasted, wearing a fanciful dress and under a large Edwardian hat, raising her lorgnette to the one or two nudes in a local picture exhibition and te-he-he-ing in her bird-like way to me, telling me to come over and admire. Mother would have gone pink and pushed me out of the gallery. Uncle, a believer in practical education, sent my brother and me up the vertical ladder of one of the towers of his water-works on Rushmere Common and instructed us in the digging of artesian wells and the economics of diesel power. There was an election that year and a crowd of us went into town singing:

> Vote, vote, vote for Mr Churchman
> Kick old Goddard in the eye.

At Felixstowe we saw the sea for the first time. It seemed like a wide-eyed face pressing against our faces and tingling in our hair. Mother talked of ships going down on the Goodwin sands and shouted from the shingle 'Don't go in deeper.' An hotel caught fire.

In Yorkshire and in Suffolk there had been peace. No one spoke about money or the struggle for existence; there was none of our family talk about 'getting on'; there was no anxiety. My brother and I had the freedom of country life; we need not 'get on' at all. These influences slowly made me feel that although I was not as clever as many boys at school, I was clever enough and egotistical enough to be able to do what I liked with my life, and that my mind was already deciding what this should be. Money would have nothing to do with it. Just as I could feel myself grow and urge myself to grow more, so I felt that the important thing was to be alone – alone in the

81

street, in the fells or on the Suffolk commons. And always walking and moving away.

My aunt's pictures gave me a hint of how this would be possible: not her gravy-coloured Academy landscapes, but the water-colours of Barlow Woods. This gentleman was alive. He was also young. He was witty, my aunt said. He sat down alone in a field by the Orwell and painted the trees by the water, the tide ebbing from the silvered mud banks. I liked painting and I wondered, when I walked to the lane where Gainsborough had painted his elms, whether some of that influence would fall upon me. The thought of being a writer had not occurred to me. I did feel that I could choose some studious kind of life but the barriers to knowledge seemed to me far too great. I would not have to read or know, to be a painter. A picture took one instantly through a door into another world, one like our own, but silent. There were no raised voices. There were no rows. And there, alive, was Barlow Woods creating these scenes. I never saw him. Whether he was a good painter or a poor one, I do not know. But, unlike ours at home, his pictures were done in real paint. In Ipswich, in that peaceful interregnum of my boyhood, the idea of being a painter began to dawdle in my mind.

But we left.

There is a short tunnel on the south side of Ipswich station and we all came out of it in a cloud of smoke and steam, with the solemn knowledge that we were now heading for London's aching skies. We had one glimpse of the blue spear of sea in the Stour estuary and of the sailing boats of Manningtree – except for those days at Felixstowe we were sea-starved children and often went into moans of self-pity because of this. We had said our last Suffolk 'Farewell, boa' to the lazy and forgotten country of slow-talking Suffolk people who had been stunned by the east wind. We got two shillings and some cultural advice each from Uncle: not bad.

We arrived on a dull May day, in London, at the pleasant suburb of Dulwich. The centre of Dulwich is still a Georgian village of fine houses and stately trees. There was the College and the old College chapel; and near it the small and famous Art Gallery. Everywhere one saw notice-boards reading Alleyn's College of God's Gift. College boys in their blue striped caps were in the streets. Ruskin, always dogging me, had often visited the Gallery; Browning had walked in the woods that overhung the village; and the Crystal Palace, built for the exhibition of 1851 and moved to Sydenham Hill, dominated all with its strange glass towers and its lolloping glass dome, like a sad and empty conservatory. From the Parade, at the top, one could see the dome of St Paul's only a few miles away, and a distant slit of the Thames.

We noticed that the family fortunes had gone up a little when we got to Dulwich. Our destination was not the sedate part of the district but on the outskirts at the Norwood end. We found ourselves in a rather taller villa than usual in a street where dozens of houses were to let, for this was the period of the Edwardian housing slump. Father was indignant at the rent: 16s. a week. He was often in arrears with it. But the house had one distinctive feature – he proudly pointed out – dark-blue fireproof paper in its front room.

But the London air was mottled with worry. We had come back to a father who had changed his character. The merry, bouncing fellow with the waxed moustaches and the cigar, the genial carver of the commercial rooms, the singer of bits of Kathleen Mavourneen had shaved off his moustache, and had been replaced by a man whose naked face was stern. In the past year he also had experienced freedom – freedom from us. He had been living in a comfortable furnished flat and had had leisure to re-make his own life. He had found another self. We had come back and this new self was trapped in a situation he could not get out of. He stared at us and the corners of his mouth drooped: he saw the ineluctable. When I was eighteen he once said bitterly 'I'm warning you. Don't make my mistake. I married too young, before I knew my own mind.' I hated him then and even more for saying this. At Dulwich it was plain that he had passed through some crisis and not a simple one. The idea of righteousness was very powerful in him, despite his unreliability; it was this idea, I believe, that began to corrupt him. An emotional struggle – I would guess – and then righteousness killed his heart. His gaiety vanished. Self-punished, he slowly drifted into punishing us. How else to account for his black moods?

83

But his losses had their gains – perhaps after all the will meant more than the heart to him. One short-term gain for him was his new religion which, since Mother rejected it, he kept to himself. We knew nothing about it, but we knew it existed. He was determined to keep *that*, a romantic compensation and counsellor which corrupted him very quickly. Or, perhaps he corrupted it. He once told me more about his conversion. Mother was wrong in saying that Cousin Dick's peculiar recovery from chronic dyspepsia was the main cause. The decisive thing – and the decisive would always be personal for him – was the death of a friend of Cousin Dick's. This man was dying of tuberculosis but believed that he could be cured by Christian Science treatment. The worse he got, the more he believed; and just before he died he declared that he knew it was 'the Truth' and made my father swear to stick to it. It was this tragic failure, arriving at a moment when I think Father himself felt he was in a desperate situation, that converted my father.

The second gain was remarkable. He had refused to give in to bad luck in his business and now he had at last succeeded. In that year while he was alone in Dulwich and with the help of the clever woman who had got him back from Liverpool in the nick of time, he at last realized his dream. And this time it was no deception. He had got out of the despised retail trade; he had left the jaunty and vulgar world of the commercial traveller and out of that came one remarkable change, one that separated us from him, as if there had been a real divorce. His name had changed. Until now, he had been Walter S. Pritchett; now the Walter was dropped. His second name appeared. He was Sawdon Pritchett, a name so sonorous, so official, so like a public meeting that we went off into corners and sniggered at it. He would, all the same, lower his eyes with his touching modesty when he said it. He pulled out a card to establish his new name with us. There it was:

> Sawdon Pritchett Ltd.,
> Art Needlework Manufacturers,
> Offices and Showrooms Newgate Street.

'Opposite the Old Bailey,' he pointed out.

> When will you pay me
> Said the Bells of Old Bailey,

> When I grow rich
> Said the bells of Shoreditch

Mother sang. Ominously too.

He took us to his office. Pigeons laid their eggs on the dirty balcony of his floor of the building. The crowds queued outside the Courts for the murder trials and down below, on the wood blocked streets, scavenger boys in white coats dashed in and out of the traffic with brushes and wide pans to sweep up the horse manure. My brother and I envied their dangerous and busy life and their wide brimmed hats.

Father's elevation and dignity had a silencing effect on our home. The words, Managing Director, put him in a trance. He told us that we now had many privileges; first we were the children of a Managing Director, living in a refined neighbourhood among neighbours who would study our manners. We had also the privilege of living within a couple of hundred yards of a remarkable family and an even more remarkable woman, the secretary to the Company whose brother, high in financial circles, played tennis at a most exclusive club. My father doubted if this family would feel able to know us immediately, but if by some generous condescension they did, we would remember to have our hands and shoes clean, brush our hair, raise our caps and never sit down until told to do so. Father's face had lost its roundness. It had become square, naked and authoritative. It also looked pained; as if he were feeling a strange, imposed constraint.

Mother supported him vigorously; in fact, as we soon saw, with unnatural vigour. It was irony on her part. Our debt to this family and to this lady was total, she said. The lady appeared almost before Father finished speaking, which took my father and mother aback, my mother's hair (as usual) being not quite in a state for receiving another woman. And we were taken aback too. We had expected perhaps another operatic Mrs Murdo in red velvet; instead a tall, beautiful young woman with burning brown eyes, and black hair, came in. Her eyelashes fluttered. She had alluring lips and, on the upper lip, a few black hairs at the corners which, before the fashion changed, made women sensually disturbing. Her voice was a shade mannish, low and practical, she was slender and wore a business-like coat and skirt with a white blouse. She struck us as elegant, even fashionable. To our delight she teasingly addressed our father as 'Father' which made him blush. She even called him 'Sawdon'; it was as if she had called him Lord. She put us so much at our ease that we loved her at once and got boisterous; my father deferred to her and so did my mother who also blushed.

One of her first questions to me was: when was I going to sit for a scholarship to the College? This was startling to me and I looked for help to my father.

'When he is ready,' said my father. 'I do not want him to imagine that just because his father has his own business he has only to sit about waiting for everything to fall into his lap.'

'Which school are you going to send him to?' she turned to my mother.

'I really don't know,' said my mother.

'We are considering the matter,' said my father in his board-room manner. 'It may be this or that. It may be the College, though we shouldn't limit ourselves to that. There may be other, better schools, than the College.'

My father's evasions stopped. Certainty appeared and a look of polite but firm rebuke came to his face. He liked the gaiety of the lady but he was not going to allow her to lead the way in his family or anywhere else. The matter was raised to a graver, higher and crushing tribune.

'He will go where the Divine Mind wishes him to go, for he is a reflection of the Divine Mind, as Mrs Eddy says.'

This puzzling remark lifted me into a region I had never heard of before; my head seemed to stretch painfully. I thought someone had put on me a hat that came down over my ears.

My mother looked appealingly and mistrustfully at the lady. 'Are you in this too?' she seemed to signal anxiously, but what she said was: 'I never had much education myself.'

'We were brought up very poor but my parents were careful. We had to earn our living early, my brother and I. We worked hard and went to evening classes. Father made us get our diplomas,' said the refined lady in her precise way. 'My brother qualified as an accountant.'

My spirits fell. After the gaieties of Ipswich we were once more caught by the doctrine of hard work and bleak merit. Mother's neck wobbled in a pained way as if she had been shot, but was too lady-like to mention it.

'If I may offer a thought there,' said my father, for he had not quite lost touch with the charms of an easy life. 'What these boys need, what we all need, is the Truth.'

'Stick to the point,' said my mother, desperately blinking at him.

'I'm sure you've been too busy to think about it yet,' said the lady tactfully, but mother did not take it as tact, and gave her one of her looks.

'Why don't you do something about it, making a fool of me in front of that woman?' my mother shouted at my father when the lady went. 'And why don't you get those boys to a school?'

Father pointed out that now my mother had a friend and we all had a friend and that soon our general tone would be raised by this fortunate contact. This did not happen. In the years to come my mother kept herself apart from this family.

'Who was her father? Only a man on the railway and the mother takes lodgers. Why are we beholden to her?' Mother said. For many years the lady was known to us only as 'Miss H'.

There was my father sitting in that office with 'that woman' all the week; Mother said: why didn't he stay with her if she was so wonderful. We know she put up the money. How did she get it? Cheese paring. My mother was not going to cheapen herself by visiting them. She might not be educated but she knew the difference between sixpence and a shilling and had been brought up straight. We were shocked. Mother was jealous. There were two women; Mrs Eddy and this lady, Miss H.

And why had we got to be so polite to her? The Business, that's what it was, Mother said. The Business. Our father had ceased to be our father. He now became 'the Business'. It was a shadow in our fire-proof room.

And then this woman, Miss H, was a woman and women are woman-like, Mother said. Not that she had any doubts about Father, for she knew he was true, but if women don't get one thing, they go for another. They don't let go.

87

As for Father being true, this is as certain as anything can be. He really hated women. He despised them. They existed to be his servants, for his mother – as my mother said – had waited on him hand and foot. Of course he charmed women; they liked talking to him, he appealed to their masochism. If they fought back or showed any signs of taking charge of him, his face went cold. His favourite gesture was to hold up his hand, palm upwards and wag it insultingly up and down, silently telling them to shut up. Their role was to listen to him and he had a lot to say. But once let them discuss, differ or suggest another idea, and the hand went up, playfully at first but, if they persisted, he was blunt with them. He described these incidents to us often. His phrase was 'I put her in her place'. It was unlucky that he had not met Mrs Eddy. She was dead. It was unlucky also that in his trade most of the workers were women. It must be said that several of these, who admired his vitality, loved him all their lives. Perhaps Miss H the bookkeeper did; Mother scornfully thought so.

At Dulwich the question of schools became grandiose for my brother and me. We were the sons of a Managing Director: our value rose. Prospectuses came in from half the great Public Schools of England. Eton and Harrow were dismissed easily; it was astonishing how many boys from such schools uttered false cheques in the course of a decade and got into the papers. We saw ourselves at Dulwich College, swaggering arm in arm like the College prefects in their tasselled hats. We walked behind them listening with awe to their astonishing man-of-the-world talk about girls. We caught drawling hints of musical plays and lavish disputes about whether the Indian Civil Service or the Army were to be preferred. One day we heard a youth pity another whose father was in a Line regiment. These snobberies had – I now see – the effect of gin upon our unaccustomed fancies. We began to live double lives. I read the prospectuses eagerly. At these schools one was away from home, and that I longed for. But I saw the fatal difficulty: I knew no Latin. For twopence cadged off my mother I bought a second-hand Latin Primer. I decided to teach myself and enter paradise.

I was defeated on the very first page. There was a sentence that ran 'Inflection is a change in the form of a word'. There was no dictionary in the house. Mother had never heard of the word 'inflection' nor had Father. But I had heard of 'form'. But how could a word have form? It wasn't a thing like a table, or a vase. I drew a pencil line carefully following the shapes of the letters round a word or two; that led nowhere. I skipped to 'mensa' but what on earth did 'by with or from a table' mean? I'd never heard anyone say it. Mother hadn't either. As for the verb 'sum' mentioned idolatrously by my grandfather when I was five or six, I couldn't find it in the book.

One morning there was a click at the letter-box and Mother said, in a panic: 'What was that?'

'Someone at the door,' we said, but all stood still, knowing that this was a dangerous moment.

'Stay here,' said my mother. 'Vic, open the kitchen door and peep up the hall.' I peeped. No person stood beyond the coloured glass of the front door, which threw a sad and bloody light on the passage, but a letter was on the linoleum.

'A letter,' I said.

'Wait,' she said, drying her hands on her apron; then all advanced towards the letter. My mother stopped about a yard away looking cautiously at it. Then she made a dart at it and picked it up. It was only a circular.

'It give me a turn,' said Mother whose English had deteriorated in the last year.

It was a circular begging on behalf of Treloar's Home for Crippled Children and contained pictures of the school rooms, and workshops, the dormitories, the playgrounds by the sea in the south of England where these children lived. I envied them. How lucky to be a cripple. If only, in some game of football in the Park, I could get my leg broken, go on crutches and, helped on to a train, go to this place. The thought was luxurious. For an hour or two I tried limping.

Then, with the suddenness with which everything happened to us, Father having gone off at seven to be at his workroom before the 'hands' got there to see they did not cheat him of his time, Mother put the two youngest children with the next-door neighbour and marched my brother and me for a mile and a half, muttering to herself, to Rosendale Road School, near Herne Hill.

'I've brought these two boys,' she said, giving us a push, to a dapper little man in a tail-coat and who looked like a frosted pen-nib. His name was Timms.

What Mr Timms said I don't know, but I was aware of what I looked like. Mother had a hard time making both ends meet and, on a day like this, wanted us to be dressed in something respectable. The day before she put the sewing-machine on the dining-room table, took out a paper pattern and set about making me some trousers. She made many of her own dresses and a lot of our clothes; indeed, if she was making a dress for herself or my sister, I was often the model. I had to stand up while she pinned patterns all over me. She was often puzzled by the strips of pattern that were left over. If only she had her cousin Emmy or better still Cousin Louie, the dressmaker, she would say; for it was a fate with her often to cut out, say, two left sleeves, or to be short of a quarter of a yard on the length. She knitted our stockings and never learned how to turn a heel, so that a double heel often hung over the backs of our boots: jerseys for us she never finished; but for herself – for she did not want to make victims of *us* – she would knit recklessly on while I read the instructions to her, and turn out narrow tubes of wool that she would stretch, laughing till she cried, to her knees. She had to pay for the material for her dressmaking out of the house-keeping money and she would raid any free material in sight. I have described her attacks on our curtains. Her own bloomers were a byword: for in gay moments she would haul up her long skirts above her knees and show my father – who was always shocked – what could be done with a chair cover or something robust of that kind. 'You want me in the business instead of "that woman",' she'd say.

For she had a vengeful streak in her, and looking at our father, the impressive Managing Director, and counting his suits and knowing how she couldn't get a penny out of him for our clothes, she attacked his wardrobe. She found a pair of striped trousers of the kind worn with morning dress. Just the thing for me. Out came the scissors. Slicing the enormous trousers roughly at the knees she saw that my brother and I could get into them both at once. She was upset by our laughter. She now slashed at the trousers again and narrowed them to my size. The insoluble difficulty was the fly buttons; these she pulled round to the side of one leg; cutting and then tacking her way up the middle while they were on me at the final try-on, she sewed me up totally in front.

'I won't be able to *go*, Mum,' I said.

She was flabbergasted, but in her careless way, she snipped a couple of stitches in her tacking.

These were the trousers I was wearing as I stood before Mr Timms, very pleased by Father's fashionable stripes and willing to show any boy who was interested the original touch of having Savile Row fly buttons down the side of one leg. What I feared was happening: the hole was lengthening in front. I could feel an alarming draught. I dared not look down. I hoped Mr Timms would not look down, as my mother chatted on and on about our family. Nothing happened. I went to my classroom; at playtime I dared not run, for fear the tacking would go. When I pulled the thread to tighten it I was left with a length of thread hanging down from the vulnerable part. When I went home after school the thread went altogether and I had to cover myself with my hand.

So my first day at Rosendale Road School began. Wearing my father's classy cut-downs I knew the distinction of our family and its awkward difference from the families of all the other children. No one else had a Managing Director's trousers on. No one else had (I was sure) our dark adventures. We were a race apart; abnormal but proud of our stripes, longing for the normality we saw around us.

I was eleven. Between the age of ten and fourteen a boy reaches a first maturity and wholeness as a person; it is broken up by adolescence and not remade until many years later. That eager period between ten and fourteen is the one in which one can learn anything. Even in the times when most children had no schooling at all, they could be experts in a trade: the children who went up chimneys, worked in cotton mills, pushed coster barrows may have been sick, exhausted and ill-fed, but they were at a temporary height of their intelligence and powers. This is the delightful phase of boyhood, all curiosity, energy and spirit.

I was ready for a decisive experience, if it came. It did come.

At Rosendale Road School I decided to become a writer. The decision did not drop out of the sky and was not the result of intellectual effort. It began in the class-room and was settled in the school lavatory. It came, of course, because of a personal influence: the influence of a schoolmaster called Bartlett. There were and are good and bad elementary schools in London. They are nearly as much created by their districts and their children as by their teachers. The children at Rosendale Road, which was a large school, were a mixture of working class and lower middles with a few foreigners and colonials – Germans, Portuguese, Australians, French and one or two Indians. It was a mixed school. We sat next to girls in class and the class was fifty or sixty strong. We had overgrown louts from Peabody's Buildings and little titches, the sons of coalmen, teachers, railwaymen, factory workers, sailors, soldiers, draughtsmen, printers, policemen, shop assistants and clerks and salesmen. The Germans were the children of people in the pharmaceutical trades; they had been better educated than we were and had more pocket money. One dark satanically handsome boy owned a 'phonograph' and claimed to be a direct descendant of Sir Francis Drake and did romantic pictures of galleons. At fourteen the girls would leave school, work in offices, in factories like my father's or become waitresses or domestic servants.

In most schools such a crowd was kept in order by the cane. Girls got it as much as the boys and snivelled afterwards. To talk in class was a crime, to leave one's desk inconceivable. Discipline was meant to encourage subservience, and to squash rebellion – very undesirable in children who would grow up to obey orders from their betters. No child here would enter the ruling classes unless he was very gifted and won scholarship after scholarship. A great many boys from these schools did so and did rise to high places; but they had to slave and crush part of their lives, to machine themselves so that they became brain alone. They ground away at their lessons, and, for all their boyhood and youth and perhaps all their lives, they were in the ingenious torture chamber of the examination halls. They were brilliant, of course, and some when they grew up tended to be obsequious to the ruling class and ruthless to the rest, if they were not tired out. Among them were many who were emotionally infantile.

A reaction against this fierce system of education had set in at the turn of the century. Socialism and the scientific revolution – which Wells has described – had moved many people. New private schools for the well-off were beginning to break with the traditions of the nineteenth century and a little of the happy influence seeped down to ourselves. Mr Bartlett represented it. The Education Officer had instructed Mr Timms to give Mr Bartlett a free hand for a year or so and to introduce something like the Dalton or tutorial system into our class. The other teachers hated him and it; we either made so much noise that the rest of the school could hardly get on with their work, or were so silent that teachers would look over the frosted glass of the door to see if we had gone off for a holiday.

Mr Bartlett was a stumpy, heavy-shouldered young man with a broad swarthy face, large brown eyes and a lock of black hair wagging romantically over his forehead. He looked like a boxer, lazy in his movements and his right arm hung back as he walked to the blackboard as though he was going to swing a blow at it. He wore a loose tweed jacket with baggy pockets in which he stuck books, chalks and pencils and, by some magnetism he could silence a class almost without a word. He never used the cane. Since we could make as much noise as we liked, he got silence easily when he wanted it. Manners scarcely existed among us except as a scraping and snivelling; he introduced us to refinements we had never heard of and his one punishment took the form of an additional and excruciating lesson in this subject. He would make us write a formal letter of apology. We would make a dozen attempts before he was satisfied. And, when, at last, we thought it was done he would point out that it was still incomplete. It must be put in an envelope, properly addressed: not to Mr Bartlett, not to Mr W. W. Bartlett, not as I did, to Mr W. W. Bartlett Esquire, but to the esquire without the mister. It often took us a whole day and giving up all the pleasant lessons the rest were doing, to work out the phrasing of these letters of shame.

At Rosendale Road I said good-bye to Stephen and Matilda and the capes and rivers of England, the dreary sing-song. We were no longer foredoomed servants but found our freedom. Mr Bartlett's methods were spacious. A history lesson might go on for days; if it was about early Britain and old downland encampments he would bring us wild flowers from the Wiltshire tumuli. He set up his easel and his Whatman boards and painted pictures to illustrate his lesson. Sometimes he changed to pastels. And we could go out and watch him and talk about what he was doing. He made us illustrate our work and we were soon turning out 'Bartletts' by the dozen. He set us tasks in threes or fours; we were allowed to talk to each other, to wander about for consultations: we acted short scenes from books at a sudden order.

For myself the lessons on literature and especially poetry were the revelation. No text books. Our first lessons were from Ford Madox Ford's *English Review* which was publishing some of the best young writers of the time. We discussed Bridges and Masefield. Children who seemed stupid were suddenly able to detect a fine image or line and disentangle it from the ordinary. A sea poem of Davidson's, a forgotten Georgian, remains in my mind to this day: the evocation of the sea rolling on the shingle on the coast between Romney and Hythe:

> The beach with all its organ stops
> Pealing again prolongs the roar

Bartlett dug out one of James Russell Lowell's poems, *The Vision of Sir Launfal*, though why he chose that dim poem I do not know; we went on to Tennyson, never learning by heart. Bartlett must have been formed in the late days of pre-Raphaelitism, for he introduced us to a form of writing then called half-print. He scrapped the school pens, made us use broad nibs and turn out stories written as near to the medieval script as possible. (This and German script, four years later, ruined my handwriting for ever.) We had a magazine and a newspaper.

Many of Bartlett's methods are now commonplace in English schools; in 1911 they were revolutionary. For myself, the sugar-bag blue cover of the *English Review* was decisive. One had thought literature was in books written by dead people who had been oppressively over-educated. Here was writing by people who were alive and probably writing at this moment.

94

They were as alive as Barlow Woods. The author was not remote; he was almost with us. He lived as we did; he was often poor. And there was another aspect; in Ipswich I had been drawn to painting and now in poems and stories I saw pictures growing out of the print. Bartlett's picture of the *Hispaniola* lying beached in the Caribbean, on the clean-swept sand, its poop, round house, mainsails and fore-tops easily identified, had grown out of the flat print words of *Treasure Island*. Bartlett was a good painter in water-colour. When we read *Kidnapped* he made us paint the Scottish moors. We laughed over *Tom Sawyer* and *Huckleberry Finn*. The art of writing became a manual craft as attractive – to a boy – as the making of elderberry pipes or carpentering. My imagination woke up. I now saw my grandfather's talk of Great Men in a new light. They were not a lot of dead Jehovahs far away; they were not even 'Great'; they were men. I went up to dirty second-hand bookshops in Norwood where I had found the Latin grammar; now, as often as I could cadge a penny off my mother, I went up there and out of the dusty boxes I bought paper-backs called *The Penny Poets*. One could have a complete edition of *Paradise Regained* (but not, for some reason, *Paradise Lost*) or Wordsworth's *Prelude*, the *Thanatopsis* (but what on earth was that?) of William Cullen Bryant, the poems of Cowper and Coleridge. To encourage my mother to open her purse or to reward her with a present, I bought penny sheets of second-hand music for her. I was piqued by her laughter.

'This old stuff,' she said, sitting down at the piano. 'The Seventh Royal Fusiliers'.

'The gallant Fusiliers, they march their way to glory,' I sang out.

'You're flat,' she said. 'Where did you get it?'

I had found a collection of the worst patriotic songs of the Crimean War, full of soldierly pathos. The music sheets were very dirty and they smelled of hair oil, tea and stale rooms.

That I understood very little of what I read did not really matter to me (Washington Irving's *Life of Columbus* was as awful as the dictionary because of the long words.) I was caught by the passion for print as an alcoholic is caught by the bottle. There was a small case of books at home, usually kept in the backroom which was called my father's study. Why he had to have a study we could not see. There was an armchair, a gatelegged table, a small rug, piles of business magazines usually left in their wrappers; the floor boards were still bare as indeed were our stairs; Father had temporarily suppressed his weakness for buying on credit. I had not dared often to look much at his books. It is true I had read *Marriage on Two Hundred a Year*, because after all the quarrels in our house, marriage was a subject on which I had special knowledge. From the age of seven I often offered my parents bits of advice on how to live. I knew what the rent was and what housekeeping cost. I had also read *Paper Bag Cookery* – one of Father's fads – because I wanted to try it. Now I saw *The Meditations of Marcus Aurelius* in leather: it defeated me. Wordsworth and Milton at least wrote in short lines with wide margins. I moved on to a book by Hall Caine called *The Bondman*. It appeared to be about a marriage and I noticed that the men and women talked in the dangerous adult language which I associated with *The Bad Girl of the Family*. *The Bondman* also suggested a doom – the sort of doom my mother sang about which was connected with Trinity Church and owing the rent.

Hall Caine was too thundery for me. I moved to Marie Corelli and there I found a book of newspaper articles called *Free Opinions*. The type was large. The words were easy, rather contemptibly so. I read and then stopped in anger. Marie Corelli had insulted me. She was against popular education, against schools, against Public Libraries and said that common people like us made the books dirty because we never washed, and that we infected them with disease. I had never been inside a Public Library but I now decided to go to one. Mr Bartlett had advised us to get notebooks to write down any thoughts we had about what we read. I got out mine and I wrote my first lines of English prose: hard thoughts about Marie Corelli.

This exhausted me and the rest of the notebook was slowly filled with copied extracts from my authors. I had a look at *In Tune with the Infinite*. I moved on to my father's single volume, India paper edition of *Shakespeare's Complete Works* and started at the beginning with the *Rape of Lucrece* and the sonnets and continued slowly through the plays during the coming year. For relief I took up Marie Corelli's *Master Christian* which I found more moving than Shakespeare and more intelligible than *Thanatopsis*.

On the lowest shelf of my father's bookcase were several new ornate and large volumes of a series called the International Library of Famous Literature. They were bound in red and had gold lettering. They had never been opened and we were forbidden to touch them. I think Father must have had the job of selling the series, on commission, at one time: I started to look at them. There were photographs of busts of Sophocles and Shakespeare. There were photographs of Dickens, Thomas Hardy, of Sir James Barrie and Sir Edmund Gosse in deep, starched wing collars, of Kipling rooting like a dog at his desk and of G.K. Chesterton with his walking-stick. There was Tolstoy behind his beard. The volumes contained long extracts from the works of these writers. I found at once a chapter from Hardy's *Under the Greenwood Tree*; and discovered a lasting taste for the wry and ironical. I moved on to *Longinus on the Sublime* and could not understand it. I was gripped by Tolstoy and a chapter from *Don Quixote*. In the next two or three years I read the whole of The International Library on the quiet. These volumes converted me to prose. I had never really enjoyed poetry for it was concerned with inner experience and I was very much an extrovert and I fancy I have remained so; the moodiness and melancholy which fell on me in Dulwich and have been with me ever since, must have come from the disappointments of an active and romantic nature; the forms of Protestantism among which I was brought up taught one to think of life rigidly in terms of right and wrong and that is not likely to fertilize the sensibilities or the poetic imagination. The poet, above all, abandons the will; people like ourselves who were nearly all will, burned up the inner life, had no sense of its daring serenity and were either rapt by our active dramas or tormented by them; but in prose I found the common experience and the solid worlds where judgements were made and which one could firmly tread.

An extract from *Oliver Twist* made me ask for a copy for Christmas. I put it in our one green armchair and knelt there reading it in a state of hot horror. It seized me because it was

97

about London and the fears of the London streets. There were big boys at school who could grow up to be the Artful Dodger; many of us could have been Oliver; but the decisive thing must have been that Dickens had the excited mind, the terrors, the comic sense of a boy and one who can never have grown emotionally older than a boy is at the age of ten. One saw people going about the streets of London who could have been any of his characters; and right and wrong were meat to him. In all of Dickens, as I went on from book to book, I saw myself and my life in London. In Thackeray I found the gentler life of better-off people and the irony I now loved. To have been the young man in *The Virginians*, to have travelled as he did and to find oneself among affectionate genial and cultivated families who enjoyed their fortunes, instead of struggling for them, must be heaven. And I had seen enough in our family to be on the way to acquiring a taste for disillusion.

My mother's tales about her childhood made the world seem like a novel to me and with her I looked back and rather feared or despised the present. The present was a chaos and a dissipation and it was humiliating to see that the boys who lived for the minute and for the latest craze or adventure, were the most intelligent and clear-headed. Their families were not claustrophobic, the sons were not prigs, as I was. There was a boy with a Japanese look to him – he had eyes like apple pips – who had introduced me to Wells's *Time Machine*. He went a step further and offered me his greatest treasures: dozens of tattered numbers of those famous stories of school life, the *Gem* and the *Magnet*. The crude illustrations, the dirty conditions of the papers, indicated that they were pulp and sin. One page and I was entranced. I gobbled these stories as if I were eating pie or stuffing. To hell with poor self-pitying fellows like Oliver Twist; here were the cheerful rich. I craved for Greyfriars, that absurd Public School, as I craved for pudding. There the boys wore top-hats and tail-coats – Arthur Augustus D'Arcy, the toff, wore a monocle – they had feasts in their 'studies'; they sent a pie containing a boot to the bounder of the Remove; they rioted; they never did a stroke of work. They 'strolled' round 'the Quad' and rich uncles tipped them a 'fivah' which they spent on more food. Sometimes a shady foreign-language master was seen to be in touch with a German spy. Very rarely did a girl appear in these tales.

The Japanese-looking boy was called Nott. He had a friend called Howard, the son of a compositor. The *Gem* and the *Magnet* united us. We called ourselves by Greyfriars' names and jumped about shouting words like 'Garoo'. We punned on our names. When anything went wrong we said, in chorus: 'How-'ard! Is it Nott?' And doubled with laughter dozens of times a day and as we 'strolled' arm in arm on the way home from school.

I knew this reading was sin and I counteracted it by reading a short life of the poet Wordsworth. There was a rustic summer-house at the end of our back garden. It had stained-glass windows. Driving my brothers and sisters out, I claimed it as my retreat and cell. When they kicked up too much noise I sat up on the thatched roof of the house where, when life at Grasmere bored me, I had a good view of what other boys were doing in their gardens. I forgot about prose and said I was going to be a poet and 'Dirty Poet' became the family name for me. Sedbergh is not far from the Lake Country: destiny pointed to my connexion with Wordsworth. We had a common experience of Lakes and Fells. His lyrical poems seemed too simple and girlish to me: I saw myself writing a new *Prelude* or *Excursion*. Also the line 'Getting and spending we lay waste our powers' struck home at our family. I read that Wordsworth had been Poet Laureate: this was the ideal. To my usual nightly prayers that the house should not catch fire and that no burglar should break in, I added a line urging God to make me Poet Laureate 'before I am twenty-one'. This prayer lasted until I was sixteen.

One day Mr Bartlett made this possibility seem nearer. He got us to put together a literary magazine. Nott and Howard efficiently produced a pair of thrillers, one set among the opium dens of Hong Kong. I got to work on a long poem. Finding – to my surprise – that Wordsworth was not a stirring model, I moved to Coleridge's *Cristabel*. My first line thrilled me. It ran: 'Diana, goddess of the spectre moon'. I turned in fifty or sixty lines of coagulated romantic images in this manner and waited for the startled applause, especially from Mr Bartlett. There was silence. There was embarrassment. Nott and Howard were stunned by the poem. Ginger Reed, a little red-haired Cockney flea, skinny, ill and lively, who skipped around cheeking me in the streets and clattering the hobnails of his brother's boots that were too heavy for his thin legs – Ginger Reed tore the poem to bits line by line: why call a 'bird' Diana? Why 'spectre' – was the 'bird' dead? Metaphor and simile, I said. Stale, he said. I was very small, but he was smaller and people in Herne Hill might have been surprised to know that one urchin pestering another at a street corner were on the point of fighting about a poem, while a pale child with owlish glasses called Donald stood there as a kind of doleful referee. The thing to do was to wait for Bartlett, but he would not speak. At last I was driven to ask his opinion as he walked in the school yard.

'Too many long words,' he said. And no more.

I was wretched. A gulf opened between myself and Coleridge.

To me, my Diana was a burst of genius. I have never had the sensation since.

I went home and sitting in our attic on a tin trunk, which I called my desk, I gave up poetry for prose once again and started on my first novel. My father had sensibly given us the *Children's Encyclopaedia* and in that I had found some more Washington Irving, simplified and abridged from his book about the legends of the Alhambra. The thought of that ethereal Moorish girl rising from the fountain entranced me. Here was a subject: the story of that girl who rises and is caught in the wars of the Moors and the Spaniards. There was more than a boyish interest in war in this choice of subject. Nasty wars had been boiling up in Edwardian Europe. We had had an illustrated history of the Boer War at home; and in the illustrated papers there had been dramatic pictures of contemporary wars in Greece and the Balkans, pictures of destroyed muddy towns and fleeing people. The Balkan wars seeped into my novel. When I was short of invention – I could never make the Moorish girl do anything except wave her langourous arms – I put in a battle scene, usually a tragic defeat, ending with my stock device: a lament by the Moorish women looking on the battlefield for their dead. Laments had an intimate appeal; my mother lamented often in these days. Day after day I wrote, until my novel reached about 130 pages, and I showed some of it to my friends.

'How-'ard is it Nott?' they said, tactfully advising me to cut out the laments. I kept the MS. from Ginger Reed. He was spiteful in these months. He always came top in arithmetic and was leaving school to become a van boy: stunted, he was older than the rest of us, we discovered. He was over fourteen and he jeered bitterly at us. We were rich, he said. We had opportunities, he jeered, as he ate his bread and dripping (his breakfast), as he danced about us in the school yard.

Then two bad things happened and their effect was to poison my life and was lasting. It took me many years to recover from them. Father discovered I was reading the *Gem* and the *Magnet*. To think that a son of a Managing Director of a Limited Company which had just paid off its debentures, a son who was always putting on the airs of a Professor, and always full of Mr Bartlett This and Mr Bartlett That: who had been brought up in the shadow of his grandfather's utterances about John Ruskin and possibly even deceived himself that he was John Ruskin, should bring such muck into the house.

We were sitting at tea. It was Sunday. The family looked at the criminal and not without pleasure. I had tried to force books on them. I had cornered them and made them listen to my poem and my novel. I had read *Thanatopsis* at them. I had made them play schools which they hated. I had hit out at the word Dirty Poet and had allowed no one near the tin trunk and, in fact, had put an onion in a jar of water on it, as a piece of Nature Study, to mark the intellectual claims on the spot. Naturally they couldn't help being a little pleased. My mother, always capricious, liable to treachery and perhaps glad not to be the centre of a quarrel herself for once, betrayed me also.

'He reads them all day. Dozens of them. Dirty things.'

'Where are they? Bring them down,' said my father. I went upstairs and came back with about twenty or thirty grubby *Gems* and *Magnets*.

'Good godfathers,' said my father, not touching the pile, for he hated dust and dirt. 'I give you your Saturday penny and this is what you're doing with it. Wasting the money I earn. I suppose you think you're so superior because you have a father who has his own business and you spend right and left on muck like this.'

'I borrowed them. A boy lent them to me.'

'A man is known by the company he keeps,' said my father. And getting up, his face greenish with disgust, he threw the lot in the fireplace and set fire to them.

'Walt, Walt, you'll have the soot down,' screamed my mother. 'You know we haven't had the sweep.'

But father liked a blaze. What could I say to Howard and Nott?

'Why do you read that muck when you could be reading John Ruskin?'

'We haven't got any of Ruskin's books.'

'He writes poetry. He wants to be a poet,' said my brother Cyril.

'He's writing a book, all over the table instead of his home-work,' said my mother.

'No, upstairs.'

'Don't contradict your mother. What's this? So you are writing a book? I hope it will improve us. What is it? Where is it?'

'Upstairs,' the traitors chimed. 'Shall we go and get it?'

'No,' I shouted.

'Go and get it.'

'Oh, if he doesn't want us to see it . . .' my mother began.

'I suppose a boy would want his own father to see it,' said my father. Anger put me on the point of tears. Very easily I cried when father reprimanded me.

I brought the manuscript and gave it to my father.

'The Alhambra – remember we used to go to the Alhambra, Beat?' he said.

'It's the Alhambra in Spain,' I said scornfully.

'Oh, superior!' said my father. 'Let's have a look at it.'

And, to my misery, he began reading aloud. He had scarcely read ten lines before he came across the following line:

'She adjusted her robe with ostentatious care. She omited to wear a cloak.'

'Ostentatious,' exclaimed my father. 'That's a big word – what does it mean?'

'I don't know,' I sulked.

'You wrote a word and you don't know what it means?'

'It means sort of proud, showing off. . . .' I could not go on. The tears broke out and I sobbed helplessly. I had got the word from Marie Corelli.

'Ostentatious,' said my father. 'I never heard of it. And what's this? "Omited". I thought they taught you to spell.'

'Omitted,' I sobbed.

'Don't bully the boy,' said my mother. I tried to rescue myself in the Howard-Nott manner.

'O mite I have done better,' I blubbered.

'O-mite, omit – it's a pun,' I said and sent up a howl.

It ended, as trouble usually did in our house, with a monologue from Father saying that he had always dreamed – for a father always dreams – that having founded a business, he might have a son who – if he were worthy of it – might conceivably be invited to come into it, a privilege hundreds of young men less fortunately placed would give their eyes for. Only this week he had had an applicant. A young man who thought just because he was his father's son (his father being something big in the trade and making two or three thousand a year), he could just walk into anything. A matter on which Father instantly put him right, for he might have been to Eton and Harrow, but that meant nothing. For my father's business was God's business. Unlike other businesses, it was directed by the Divine Mind. 'And by the way,' Father said, 'I always look at a man's boots when he applies for a job.' My father's voice became warmer and more benign as he expanded on the subject of the Divine Mind, who was his manager, and we drifted into other fields. My mother's mind, less divine, wandered.

I took my novel back. I put it inside the tin trunk. Blackened by hatred, I did not touch it again. I hated my father. And one morning in the winter the hatred became intense or rather I decided I could never talk to him again about what went on in my mind.

It was an early morning of London fog. The room was dark and we had lit the gas. I was reading Shakespeare in bed. I had by now reached *Measure for Measure* when my father came in.

'Get out of bed you lazy hounds,' he said. 'What are you reading?' He took the book and started reading himself and was perhaps startled by Claudio's proposal.

'Poetry,' he said. Then very seriously and quietly said: 'Do you really want to be a poet?'

'Yes I do.'

He went red with temper.

'If that's what you want,' he shouted, 'I have nothing more to say to you. I won't allow it. Get that idea out of your head at once.'

Why my father raged against my literary tastes I never really knew. He had been very poor, of course, and really feared I would 'starve in a garret'. He wanted – in fancy only – to found a dynasty in business; and he heard no word of money in writing poetry. At this time he had many anxieties and the family, from my mother down, exasperated and tormented him. He was a perfectionist. He was also an egotist who had identified himself – as indeed I was doing – with an ideal state of things. And then there comes a time when a man of strong vitality finds it hard to bear the physical sight of his growing sons. He found it harder and harder; and he was to be even more severe with my brothers and my sister, especially Cyril who adored him. We were at the beginning of a very long war; these were the first rumblings. One by one, we fell into secrecy. In self-preservation we told him lies.

He was behaving exactly to us as his own father had behaved to him; there was a strain of gritty, north-country contempt and sarcasm in all of us.

CHAPTER SEVEN

ONE thing is now clear that was not clear then. When I was twelve my mother came to collect us from school one day. She scarcely ever did this. She walked along in her raincoat and felt hat muttering to herself and worried. 'The Business' – that shadow – was on her mind. She had come out to calm herself. For my father, in his hot-headed way, had brought a legal action against his landlord in the city; had won it, but had lost it on appeal. It had cost him £800, an enormous sum for him.

'You can never win against Property in the City,' he said.

'He's a fighter,' she said with pride, but also in terror.

There were often noisy scenes in our house. Money was one trouble; Mother could not get it out of him. The Business made him neglect her. He went off at seven or half past in the morning and returned at eight in the evening; on Saturdays he came home at seven. They had no pleasures; my mother did all the household work herself. He did not buy clothes for her. He hated her talking to the neighbours and perhaps feared her careless tongue; was she telling them about his bankruptcies?

'Other men take their wives out.'

'I am not other men, as you are pleased to phrase it.'

'Mr Carter does, so does Mr O'Dwyer.' (They were our neighbours.)

'Civil servants!' said my father. 'They're living off me. And let me give you a thought there. I don't want neighbours. God is my only neighbour.'

'The boys ought to have friends.'

'Their father is their friend. They will realize it one day.' The dispute would soon get out of hand; the two began shouting. There were knocks on the wall from the Carters next door. Father, in a temper, knocked back with the poker. 'Perhaps that will shut them up.'

The Carters and the O'Dwyers were so unlike us, their lives – to our minds, so normal – that we felt we must be foreigners. Mr Carter, aged forty-five, was a doggish, grey-haired clerk married to a much younger wife. They sang for the local choral society and were Fabian socialists. Mr Carter had a complete set of classics and I tried to read Thucydides in his house: there they were, another thirty volumes, exposing the fact that I had a mountain before me. Would I 'catch up' – my mania?

Mr and Mrs Carter wished to civilize us. I had made a toy theatre, a rocky construction in cardboard which kept falling to pieces for I was not a very practical child: the Carters saw it and at once put it to rights and made me give a performance of *Aladdin* to some guests in their sitting-room. These guests paid 6d. The performance was in aid of Jim Larkins's dock strikers in Dublin. I had mixed feelings about my theatre being taken over by people cleverer than myself; I had simply wanted to muddle away with it in my own way – a feeling I still have about writing. I still feel this jealous fear when I hear that someone has read what I have written – No (I think) this is a private thing. I do not want it to be seen. Or not yet.

One evening Mr and Mrs Carter knocked at the door while one of our rows was building up. They were civilizing again.

'We *heard* you were at home,' they said darkly, in refined voices, 'and came to apologize if our singing practice disturbs you. The walls are very thin.'

They indeed drove my father to anger by their scales.

'Ah ah ah ah ah; ah, ah, ah, ah ah,' went Mrs Carter's soprano; then, at the breaking point, intolerably down the scale, Mr Carter would join her. Mother was excited by these allies. She often spoke over the garden wall to them. She spied on them. She was flushed with merriment when she found out they lay down on their bed together on Saturday afternoons.

'We often have a word, don't we?' she said flirtatiously to Mr Carter.

'This very morning in fact, Mrs P,' said Mr Carter waggishly.

'Oh,' said my mother, beginning to blush and laugh and covering her face with her hands. 'I was hanging out my . . .'

'Something long, I was too polite to mention it,' said Mr Carter. 'Made of wool. Tubular.'

'Combs. Two pairs,' said my mother, giving a scream.

'I didn't like to mention them, but since *you* have, Mrs P, I noticed the articles in question,' agreed the lewd Mr Carter.

'And *his* long pants too,' screamed my mother.

Father looked very shocked.

'You work too hard, Mrs Pritchett. Why don't you get out? You never go out, do you?' said Mrs Carter.

'Only once to Brixton a year ago. Meat is cheaper there,' said Mother, disloyal and defiant. 'Because of "the Business".'

My father intervened here, the tone of conversation rose. Mr Carter was in favour of Cooperatives. He asked ironically if London Bridge 'paid'. My father was opposed to this. Cooperatives were the enemy of the small man. He'd seen enough of that in Yorkshire. An argument about capitalism began, the cash nexus and the profit basis – all news to me – but Father ended in astonishing Mr Carter by telling him that he, Father, did not run his business, but God did. Ah, ha, we thought, admiring our father – Mr Carter had never thought of that. Hence Father was not going to have a lot of socialists running it.

Afterwards Father said:

'I put that old fool in his place.'

We agreed.

But the Carter children went to the grammar school. The youngest, aged eight, said that he knew how babies were got and born. I did not believe him. His sister, a romping, red-headed girl with freckles, joined in and snubbed me.

'Our parents told us,' she said gravely. 'It's true. You can ask them. Haven't your parents told you? I expect not. They're religious, aren't they? We are rationalists.'

'I don't believe you,' I said.

'You go into your outside lav, I'll undress and I'll show you,' she said. 'Go on now. I'll be there in a minute.'

I went to our lavatory and waited but she did not come back.

'Oh, I changed my mind,' she said next day and laughed at me and said, 'Let's go up the garden and talk about torture and cruel things.' We sat by her fence and talked about torture. Mr Carter who was pruning his roses on the other side of the fence put his head over and said:

'I've heard everything you said. I have never heard such disgusting children. Talk about something interesting.'

The Carters held high-class Badminton parties on Saturdays. The voices of schoolmasters and dons came over the fence.

'Look at Mrs Carter,' cried my mother, excitedly peeping from behind our curtains. 'You can see right up her ...'

If the Carters were clever advanced people, the O'Dwyers were negligent and cheerful. Mrs O'Dwyer was French.

'Oh, Mrs Preech,' she called over the wall. She would be standing on a beer crate and put her fat, wild face over the wall and looked like an untidy sorceress. 'Vere is that clever son? I want to have a conversation with him about Racine.'

'Racing?' said my mother.

I went into a dirty sitting-room, where the ashes of a week's fires were all over the grate, reviews and books were thrown about on tables and chairs among beer bottles and glasses. Mrs O'Dwyer was only half-dressed, greasy-looking and bearded. She looked at me with merry, gloating eyes and kissed and tickled me; then talked to me about France.

'Vat are you reading? Wordsworth. I don't like him. I'll read Racine to you. I will teach you French if you want. You want? I'll give you another kiss.'

Mrs O'Dwyer's enormous breasts nearly knocked me over. She declaimed some Racine to me. Oh God! The Carters with the classics, now the O'Dwyers with Racine: the road lengthened every day. She had been a singer, she said in Paris – not like those snobbish little Carters who tra-la-la'd in the ridiculous local choral society and spent their summer holidays in Ventnor. 'La belle France' for her!

Mrs O'Dwyer had two sons of about fifteen and seventeen with whom she boxed in the garden. She put up a rope ring and trained them to fight till her blouse was half off and her hair down. Often a light blow knocked her over, for her fat body wobbled on her heels and she went down on her bottom, calling out 'Bring me a glass of beer'. Then she drove them indoors to their studies. She stood over her sons while they worked, brought them beer and made cold compresses to put on the clever one's head as he read for his university exams. The sons often chased her round her house with a broom. One day she peeped out of her bathroom window and saw one of the boys climbing the drainpipe towards her. She got a pail of water and emptied it on him. These youths adored this fat and merry mother. She helped the one who was a naturalist to skin his guinea-pig and mount the skeleton. Beer crates clattered in the yard and she would sometimes shout over the fence.

'Mrs Preech, vy don't you educate yourself. Give up the vashing. I'm reading a book, vat are you doing? Read. Improve your mind.'

Our dog Jim and the O'Dwyer's dog got on well. They used to rush up and down, each on its side of the fence, barking at each other and tearing at the palings. Jim had caught our family hysteria. He frothed at the mouth and licked and slobbered over palings in his frenzy. When a paling fell down loud laughter came from Mrs O'Dwyer's kitchen. Like ourselves the O'Dwyers were garden wreckers. On summer evenings Mr O'Dwyer, austerely silent, sat in the wreckage of his garden smoking his pipe and drinking a glass of whisky.

Mother had her own amusement. Mrs O'Dwyer might box, Mrs Carter might play Badminton, Mother's sport was moving furniture. She would be sitting in the dining-room when, without warning, she would say:

'I can't stand that old piano over there. Help me move it, you boys.'

But the room was so crowded that you could not move one thing without moving the rest. We would all lift the table first.

'From me to you. From you to me. Lower a bit. Tip it,' my brother would say, mocking the many removal men we had seen at work. This brought all those removals to mother's mind and she would drop her end of the table or piano, whatever it was, and start on the tale. Soon the room was in confusion.

'Don't be a cure, Cyril,' Mother screamed.

In an hour everything was in a new place and we stopped for breath.

'No,' she would say. 'I don't like it. Get it all back as it was.'

'Back with it!' we shouted.

We started shoving and lifting. The piano chimed.

'Bang goes the Maiden's Prayer,' said Cyril.

We always said these words. She would sit down and say:

'I get sick of these things stuck in the same place. You've only got one life.'

Down at Rosendale Road we talked of football, 'Jocks' and sex. 'Jocks' were members of a small secret society who talked in a peculiar baby language they had invented or picked up from one of the Comics. I longed to be a Jock but was shut out. The anti-Bartlett campaign succeeded: the progressive movement was defeated and we were moved *en bloc* to a more conventional class, even more crowded. Mr Williams, the geography master taught the geography of India and told me I was Welsh: my name derived from Ap-Richard. I denied that I was Welsh. Boys who had lovingly called me Pritch, Prick or even Shit, now called me Taffy. There was an effusive Cockney music master, all roar and spit, who taught us to sing a song of Pope's. He sang out the words:

> Where e'er you walk
> Cool Giles shall fan the glide

in a fine voice. I at once took to reading Pope's *Essay on Man* during algebra.

The worst thing was that our new teacher was a woman. All the boys in the class hated her. Her figure was ridiculously beautiful, going in and out from bosom to waist and hips like a bottle: to walk behind her and see her lovely bottom sway made us giggle. One of the masters, a gingery hairy curly fellow like a barber, was courting her. We decided that she was 'hot' and that he 'had it up' with her. I felt the desire to kick her. This woman had a high-class voice and finished herself for me by telling us that Bartlett was an out of date Impressionist in painting. I did a picture of Tower Bridge and she told me it was a mess. I told her I was not trying to put in every brick but that I was trying to get the 'effect' of the bridge, not a copy. What, she asked, exactly did I mean by 'effect'? 'Well "effect",' I said. 'You have been badly taught,' she said.

'Volume' and 'shading' were what we had to aim for. Imagine: a whole hour drawing a pudding basin in pencil and then shading it. But Dexter, the draughtsman's son who sat next to me in this class told me his father said she was right and that Bartlett was a slapdash old fool. A painting I had done of a

Yorkshire moor in a storm was removed from the place of honour on the wall.

Holidays were getting near. The teacher said they were an opportunity to see unusual things. She would give a prize to the value of 5s. to the child who brought back a drawing of the most unusual thing they had seen. Five shillings! But how, since we never went away for holidays, would we see anything unusual. Five shillings – the books one could buy for that! I was nearly mad with determination to get it. I had a brilliant idea which I am afraid exposes the dirty cunning, the 'deediness' as mother called it – and flightiness of my priggish character. I decided that museums were a store of unusual things. I dragged my younger brother and sister for a couple of miles across Dulwich Park – because I had to look after the children – stopped them from playing on the way, with bribes of ginger beer, and got to Horniman's Museum. Oh sacred and blessed spot, oh temple of knowledge, oh secret Bore, I dragged the kids round the cases. Mr Bartlett had been keen on stone arrow heads and flints, Uncle Arthur had gone in for fossils and quartz – I had bought a book on geology and had tried to memorize the names of rocks: the craze lasted a week or two – but what was unusual about them? And, in any case, how difficult for an 'effect' artist like myself to draw things like these. I searched for something foreign, exotic and simple. I found it. There was a collection of amulets from India. Quickly I drew the childishly simple shapes and noted the colours. I took the other children back home, got out my paints and did a full page of amulets, inventing some extra ones as I went along. Some I called Indian; at a venture, I lied and called some African. The whole swindle in yellows and purples looked pretty and saleable. I longed for the holidays to be over. I had turned my mother's talent with curtains and her husband's trousers into something approaching an aesthetic.

My culture-snobbery and faking were successful. Most of the boys and girls in the class had forgotten to go in for the prize. Howard had spent his time selling newspapers; Nott had been to Somerset and had seen stalactites in caves but could not draw. Those self-indulgent rivals had been caught napping. They were not obsessional boys. I won the prize, the only one of my school life.

III

'And what would you like for your five shillings,' the teacher said.

'A book.'

'That's good. Which book would you like? Henty? Conan Doyle?'

'No, Ruskin.'

'What?' said the teacher. 'He wrote a great many books'.

I did not know the titles of any of Ruskin's books.

'Any one. Some.'

'You realize he was a social reformer and art critic?'

'On art,' I said blindly, sucking up to her love of volume and shading, and remembering Aunt Ada and Barlow Woods.

The woman with the ludicrously beautiful figure whom we mocked and whom I had wanted to kick, presented me a few weeks later with eight volumes of Ruskin – *Modern Painters*, *The Seven Lamps of Architecture*, *The Stones of Venice* and – most enlightening of all – an Index. I had blotted out the *Gem* and *Magnet* fiasco.

I went home and opened the first volume of *Modern Painters*. The title startled me. This surely could not have been the writer Grandfather admired. It contained nothing about social justice. I was faced by an utterly strange subject: art and the criticism of art. Those pictures I had admired for their silence and their peace, even their self-satisfaction as images, were not – it seemed – at peace at all. I struggled to understand the unusual words and nearly gave up; but I was kept going by Ruskin's bad temper, his rage against Claude and Poussin – whoever they might be – and his exaltation of Turner. Ruskin was in a passion. Until now I had never been inside Dulwich Gallery, but now I went. And there I stood in those empty polished rooms, that sometimes smelled of the paint of a copyist who had left his picture on its easel, in Ruskin's world. Here were the Dutch, the Italians. Here was Rubens. Here was Mrs Siddons as the Tragic Muse. I was happier than I had been in my life, but I was also oppressed. It was the old story: I was self-burdened. There was too much to know. I discovered that Ruskin was not so very many years older than I was when he wrote that book.

It took me a year to get through the first volume of *Modern*

Painters. The second I skipped. The third bored me until I got to the chapter on the Pathetic Fallacy. This I read easily: in the conflict between painting and literature, literature always conquered. I was shocked to see Pope attacked. I was shamed to see that I was on the side of the Pathetic Fallacy. I had not realized that there was unrest in literature, too, and that one was allowed to attack 'the great'. Seeing that Homer was praised I bought Chapman's Homer from the second-hand box. How could Keats have been bowled over by it? Why no 'wild surmise' for me? All the great poets had praised the *Iliad*. I was bored by it. Slowly Coleridge and Wordsworth drifted away into regions that were, evidently, unattainable.

There was presently talk at home of my sitting for a scholarship for a place at the Strand School, a secondary school at Streatham. (Many a time I had walked over to Streatham Common in the belief that it was an approach to the Sussex Downs where Mr Bartlett had found coltsfoot. There were only dandelions on Streatham Common.) Miss H had been nagging my father about scholarships; and because of the Ruskin 'prize' he was impressed and I was in a state of euphoric self-confidence.

Soon, Father and I were on a bus going to Streatham. I was going to sit for the examination. I was impressed by being at a school where there was a dining hall and where boys could buy buns, chocolate and drink cocoa in the break. They also wore long trousers. There was a touch of Greyfriars in this. I was sick with fright and had had diarrhoea, of course, but I felt I could rely on my genius. But when I sat down to the examination papers I found that my genius was not being called upon. The effect of Mr Bartlett's system was that I was totally unprepared and ignorant – even in English. I could answer scarcely any of the questions and I could only hope to get by in Scripture. There was a question about Noah and the Ark; something about the numbers of people aboard, size and location of the ark, the duration of the flood, and how many times the dove flew in and out and with what in its beak? I had inherited my father's dislike of a fact. I ignored the question and wrote at full speed a dramatic eye-witness account of the Flood, ending with that favourite device – a Lament. I made the drowning millions lament. A month later I heard the inevitable news: the genius, the inhabitant of a higher plane, had failed to win a scholarship.

I did not know how to bear the shame of this. It was made worse by hearing that I was older than all the other boys who were sitting. I could never sit again. I found it hard to face my brother. He who hated school, and except in carpentry always did badly – Cyril welcomed me to the brotherhood of failures. He had had a worse humiliation. A school inspector had come to the school and Mr Timms, to show off his efficiency had sounded the Fire Alarm for Fire Drill. Everyone appeared except my brother who didn't hear the alarm. He was hauled up to the platform in the school hall, where Mr Timms made a speech saying that all had obeyed the call of duty, that call irresistible to the heart of every true Englishman, except this miserable specimen beside him – my brother. He had disgraced the whole school and, what was more, before a representative of the London County Council.

Failure to win a scholarship was a blow to vanity and to hope. For me it would be decisive. In those puzzled hours at the desk my future was settled. How often my grandfather and my father had urged me on with the joke 'Victor – always victorious'. I wasn't and I began to be cowed by my morally pretentious Christian name and to hate it. I was never good at examinations and was never near the top of the class in spite of all my efforts. In English I was always near the bottom of the list. My memory was poor. Mr Bartlett had scorned to teach English Grammar and I knew nothing of it until I learned French and German. I was bad at spelling and had – I have still – bad handwriting. The most serious result of this failure was that it was now certain – although I did not realize this – that I would never go to the University. If I had passed I would have stayed at school until I was eighteen and would surely have got another scholarship to London University; probably I would have become a teacher or an academic. I had had a narrow escape. But I would have had friends whom I would have met again and again in life and, in university days, they would have helped as much as my tutors to put some order and direction into a drifting and chaotic mind.

So farewell to Greyfriars, for the moment; back to Rosendale

Road. A gang of us used to go to Brockwell Park, put down our coats for goal posts and play football on Saturday afternoons in the autumn and winter, tagging on to the brother of Fatty Page who had a job and who treated us to American gums and ice-cream sodas made of R. White's ginger beer. My brother and I were well-equipped for football; we wore football boots to school every day, blackened over, for we had no others. Ford cars were coming in and we went home shouting down the street:

> Old iron never rust
> Solid tyres never bust.

The school was beaten by Effra Road Higher Grade – boys stayed until fifteen there and were heavier than we were – on a frosty morning, near the railway arches, one to nil. It was a desperate game. The assistant teacher came with us and sang the school song on the touchline, in his weak, Cockney voice. Roses was pronounced 'Rowsis'.

> Roses on the ball, Roses on the ball,
> Never mind the half back line
> The Roses beat them every time.
> Give the ball a swing
> Right over to the wing,
> Roses, Roses, Roses on the ba-a-ll.

His eldest son who had left school a couple of years before came to visit us. A few of us gathered in the school lavatory with this hero who knew the outside world, to hear about life and his experiences. We asked him what his work was. He said – to our amazement – that he hadn't decided anything yet. But he was not going to settle into some dull nine to six office job. He was determined to travel, take some job that would get him out of the country, be a reporter, on 'some rotten paper', edit a 'cheap magazine'. I pricked up my ears. If he thought it was possible to write and to begin on a rotten paper, it must be; one could postpone being Poet Laurence for a year or two until one found one's feet.

He was an expert on sex, too. He told us what went on in the bushes on the allotments opposite the school. All of us talked about sex at school but few knew the facts of life; he told us. As far as I was concerned, a god suddenly fell. I did not believe a word of what he told us. I had not believed the Carter child either.

'Not the King and Queen, too,' I said scornfully.

'Of course, he screws her,' he swanked.

'Liar,' I said.

And walked home indignantly and troubled, presently remembering Aristotle's masterpiece behind the chamberpot in my parent's bedroom.

We looked at the girls and the girls pouted and put out their tongues and giggled and their warm eyes winked at us. Their dresses, pinafores, jerseys; their tapes and buttons and ribbons fascinated me. A rough-tongued girl called Kate sat next to me in class, pushing, snubbing and wheedling. The descendant of Sir Francis Drake wrote romantic notes in medieval handwriting to one of the beauties. Asked by Kate which girl I liked best in the class, I dreaded that she expected me to choose her; but was wise enough to conceal from her the name of the child I admired, the little oval-faced Portuguese who sat behind me, who scarcely spoke and had neat handwriting. I dissembled and chose a tall blonde creature called Gladys who wore glasses and who gave herself queenly airs. Her gold glasses attracted me. They magnified her blue eyes. I told this choice to Kate in secrecy and she let it out at once: a lesson there. Gladys walked giggling near me for a yard or two, looking me up and down as if I were a meal. We dropped each other at once. Our sizes were incompatible.

There was a large sallow sulking Jewish girl with big breasts called Sadie who – we all knew – had started her 'monthlies'. This led one of our biggest louts to snatch a Bunsen burner off the master's desk and make it protrude erect from his fly buttons and walk up and down to the laughter of the class when the master was out of the room. But the German boys and girls were the licentious ones. They lived up our way. The youngest, a child of seven, had found her father's contraceptives and, blowing one out, chased her sisters and brother round their garden with it.

The year before the 1914 war and especially in the spring and summer before it started, my brother and I were great friends with the German boys and girls. A straggling gang of us used to go to the beautiful park in Dulwich and we learned to say, *'Liebst du mich? Ich liebe dich'* over and over again, when we had nothing else to say. We played cricket, or rounders. If we had enough money we rowed on the lake, which in honour of Wordsworth I tried to think was Ullswater and in honour of Scott, Loch Lomond. I saw Alan Breck land on its concrete banks under the bushes.

But we talked all the time of who had 'had it up' with whom. These innocent erotic fantasies were exquisite to us. There were three sisters: a clinging romantic Lolita of about eight, a freckled tomboy of twelve, and a very pretty older and petulant one of fifteen called Greta, a girl with black curls, long eye-lashes and blue speckled eyes like a blackbird's egg who was already coquetting with the youths of the neighbourhood. We all used sometimes to go into a vacant patch of building ground, a place of long grass and trees, hidden by the railway bank, and there we would light a fire and kiss and bicker. To show off to her I climbed the embankment and put a halfpenny on the railway line and waited for two trains to pass over it – for it was a busy suburban line. Two trains could flatten a halfpenny and spread it to the size of a penny. Then you slipped along to West Dulwich Station and got chocolate out of the slot-machine with it.

I could not take my eyes off the inciting Greta. One day I jumped on her and wrestled with her. I was instantly in love. This was different from my other childish loves because her beauty made me afraid. I expected a slap but I was astonished to see she was pleased; now her glances confirmed me. I could not believe that a girl as sought after as Greta should look at me. What about my jersey with the holes in it and my made-up trousers? Compared with us the Germans were what we called rich. They lived in a bigger house than we did. I felt that I was in flames when she asked me to tea with her. We sat at a table in her garden and ate strawberries. She had her exercise book with her. This was the first shock. Her handwriting was childish and her mind was feeble. I told her about Coleridge and others. She gaped at me and said, offensively, that I was 'funny' and 'what's clever in that?' I went home, still alight, and rejecting the help of the Lake Poets I copied out a love-poem from the *Windsor Magazine*, a poem which ran:

> Stars of the heavens I love her
> Spread the glad news afar.

I put it in her letter-box that evening, lay awake all night and at seven in the morning slipped out to walk up and down outside her house, wondering which her room was. Back and forth I went to her house, maddened by the hours. At last she and the freckled tomboy came out. They stared and then giggled together; she laughed a laugh I shall not forget, a high chilling laugh of mockery and put her tongue out. They both put their tongues out and walked away. After a yard or two she turned round and screamed:

'I hate you.'

I stood there choking with sudden tears. At home I was sick and could not eat. Only the words from *Sartor Resartus* are turgid enough to describe my state: 'Thick curtains of night rushed over his soul.' And I had lowered myself to sending a poem from the *Windsor Magazine*. Grief changed to anger. The wound to pride was real. It was many years before I could speak to a girl and even longer before I could – as I was prone to – fall in love. And I avoided the pretty ones. But I kept up with the dreamy Lolita, the youngest of the German sisters. An errand boy followed us down the street one morning and kept shouting, 'Fancy a kid like you having a little tart.'

My mother used to say of us: it's all life and death and hammer and tongs with you. It worries me. You don't seem balanced, not in your right minds half the time.

I liked the German boys. They had a freer life than we had. They talked about Germany and they boasted about the greatness of their country in military science and in music. We used to think that it was for them the German band would come trumpeting with its brass instruments up at the corner of their street. For ourselves, we had to put up with the lavender sellers, the last of the London criers, singing, 'Will you buy my own sweet lavender? I will give you – sixteen branches for one pe-e-enny': the singing beggars who walked always in the middle of the road on Sunday afternoons, bawling with their right hand held to their jaw and over their ear. Once a year the man selling almanacs, sang out: 'Penny Old Moore, date of the War', and Mother, eager for prophecy, made us run for a copy of the paper. The muffin man rang his bell on Sundays. The 'window bang' seller came on windy days, calling out: 'Bangs for your windows, buy a window bang'. Newsboys went by calling, 'Stop Press' late at night. Tramps came for a slice of bread and butter, an incident which always made us recite a joke from one of our comics. A young man is cuddling a girl while another tramp pops his head over a hedge and dangles a pair of his dirty socks in their faces.

'Your golden locks!' says the young man.

'My stripey socks!' says the spoil-sport tramp.

They were our favourite lines of English dialogue and often brought back peace to family life.

These were ballooning days. Suddenly, low over the house-tops and looking at first like the bald heads of spying old men, would rise a group of enormous balloons sent up from the Crystal Palace and we would see the aeronaut empty out sand, and the wind creasing the skin of the great ball.

We had a struggle to keep our dog, Jim, from the fighting terrier of the street, a blood-stained murderer with torn ears and a drunken walk. I bowled my young brother's hoop under the legs of a butcher's horse and Jim got his foot run over and ran yelping mad and we had a job catching him. And there were the London thunderstorms, worse in the south, my mother said, than in Finsbury Park; she was frightened of them and ran crying to hide herself in her bedroom cupboard and sometimes put her head under the sofa cushions downstairs, clinging hysterically to my hand and moaning: 'Is it getting any lighter?'

'Artful Art' one of the boys we played with had his house flooded two feet deep in one of these storms; we envied him. On Saturdays we went up to the Norwood cinema, sat in the front row, cheered the Westerns, saw Bunny, the fat man, and Charlie Chaplin and came back wagging our shoulders in the swanking walk of the cowboys; but we did not tell our father.

The spell of the German boys still held, but their tempers were touchy. One fierce Saxon with wheat-white cropped hair, a budding young Fritz of the caricatures, carried a pair of scissors to defend himself against the Fräulein who looked after him. He had got a razor hidden under his mattresses, ready for her, he said. Another set about trying to hang himself in the bushes of Dulwich Park, after being given 'out' at one of our cricket matches. One day I saw an older girl cousin of the Germans with a quarrelling party in a boat on the lake. Her name was Else and the Germans were always talking about her. If anyone had for certain 'had it up', it was Else. She had been expelled from school because of her love affairs with two teachers. I gazed at this wicked girl with consternation. She was a tall creature with reddish hair and fine grey eyes and a wide warm mouth. Soon, as I was watching the boat-load from the path, she stood up and shouting an insult at her party calmly stepped into the water waist deep in the middle of the lake and waded across to me. I gave her a pull in and she stood grinning and dripping beside me.

'I've heard all about you,' she said in a friendly way. 'I've got a brother who wants to be a writer. Are you going to be a poet?'

I was overwhelmed that such a wicked girl should talk to me.

'Look at me. Help me get my skirt off and wring it out. Will you show me your poems? They're stupid people here.'

I stared at her sunburned legs and she was pleased.

'Could you write something about me and show it to me? I'm sure you could.'

And then she gave a loud, jolly German laugh and went off home. But before she went, she shook hands. I felt her wide eyes and woman's body drawing me to her in friendship with an amused helpless intelligence of their own. I felt I had grown a year older. I never saw her again. For the 1914 war started a month or two later and she and the other Germans were interned.

A bad thing occurred at Dulwich Park lake in the November of that year. One morning at breakfast, just as we were putting the milk on our porridge, my father and mother had a terrible quarrel. We were used to these rows, but there had never been one in the morning before. We were scared. My mother pulled me by the arm, just as I was dipping my spoon in my plate and shouted:

'I'm taking my son and leaving you. Come on.'

We usually grinned at these rows, but now she pulled off her apron, got her hat and coat, made me put mine on and pulled me with her to the front door.

My father was very pale and looked silently at her and mockingly at me. I looked appealingly at him to try and convince him that all this was against my will. I was frightened.

'I shall kill myself. I shall drown myself in the lake,' she cried out.

Her grip on my wrist was hard. She raced down the street with me and nothing I said could stop her. So we went on in the morning fog and got to the Park – I was surprised she knew the way – and made for the lake. I was old enough to know my mother's tantrums would not last. The only thing I could do was to take her the long way round the railings to the boat-house gate which I guessed would be closed at this hour. So round and round the lake we walked until she calmed down. Gradually I edged her towards home. Tactfully my father had left the front door open. She went up to her room, locked herself in and came down later with her bag packed.

'I'm going to my sister,' she said calmly.

And she did go there.

We felt she had betrayed us all and now turned to our father. He became unexpectedly kind. He explained to me how I must get the lunch for everyone and that he would be back soon in the afternoon for he had to go to his office. He kept his word and appeared with a large quantity of plaice. He put on his apron, cracked eggs, got breadcrumbs and soon fried one of his wonderful fish suppers. The house filled with blue smoke, the delicious fish was golden on the plate.

'Your mother isn't getting fish like this at the Buggs tonight,' he said. 'A bit of cold mutton it'll be, I expect.'

What a fool she was; how genial he was, we thought. A big fry of fish was always the solution to his emotional problems.

What the quarrel was about we did not know. In two days Mother came back. Mr and Mrs Bugg bored her with all their 'Yes, dear,' and 'No, dear,' she said. 'Silly old infatuated fool. Ada's spoiled.'

CHAPTER EIGHT

EUROPEAN War! Another case of 'prepare to receive cavalry'. This was good news for us, I thought, because it looked as though the worry of our household had spread beyond our garden fence and that our neighbours and the world in general had been infected by our example. Wasn't Mother always saying life was a fight? Until then we had seemed to be the only fighters. We were now the norm. We heard of Uhlans, German batteries on the Crystal Palace Parade: our personal boredom vanished. Father had customers in Frankfurt and said you could never trust Germans. One had 'gone down on his knees' – as people often did with Father – and had cried, in order to persuade him to knock a few shillings off his prices. We felt proud. Father was fighting for the Business. And as for myself, the *douceur de vivre* and the high *bourgeois* culture was at an end. Of course I had no idea that either of these amenities existed. In many ways, for us, this most shocking of wars, a cattle slaughter, was a liberation. A hungry generation pressed forward over the graves of the dead; great states and great families decayed and their certainties with them.

We knew nothing about the forces controlling us and Father was too concerned with his trade to think about them or talk about them. Mother, in her simple, practical, backward-looking way, was more aware of what was happening. Her first thought was for the Royal Family. What would happen to poor Princess this and poor Queen So-and-so? Fancy, too – all that boasting of the Bugg family that they had once let one of their houses to the Kaiser; a smack in the eye for the Ipswich lot. I went out to find one of the German boys down the street. I found him outside an ironmongers where he had just bought a wash-leather and, shouting 'Dirty German', I hit him, without more warning. He was a tall, handsome and scornful boy, Greta's brother, and would not deign to fight first of all; but I wouldn't let him alone. I wanted to knock the Rhineland or Hamburg out of him. Soon we were on the ground and I was getting the worst of it. Unlike father's customer he did not go down on his knees and cry. An old gentleman separated us with his walking-stick as if we were dogs, and said he would report us to the College. We slunk off together, sneering back at the old gentleman. I put my fingers to my nose: 'We don't go to the College.' The old gentleman caught me and cuffed me. He was scarlet with anger.

Mrs O'Dwyer put her head over the fence and told Mother about the superiority of French culture. Mother nodded; she always nodded when people spoke to her. She had learned that in the millinery and the wily doorways of Kentish Town.

'When your dad and I went over their house, Vic, (my father and mother were supposed to keep an eye on it while the O'Dwyers were away, and had the key) 'we looked under the beds and the po's had not been emptied.'

Mr Carter was upset by the lack of unity among European socialists and took up rifle shooting.

Mother groaned and said Father would be ruined and was, for once, sorry for him – and so he was, but not in the way she expected. Father considered the prospect of disaster but brushed it aside. He took a chance and, characteristically, moved his business. He took larger premises. Mother cringed at this reck-lessness and prayed for him to get a safe job like everyone else – Mr Carter or Mr O'Dwyer. Going into the butcher's shop she always opened her purse, put the money she had decided to spend on the counter, and told the butcher to cut accordingly. The new factory was a three- or four-storey building in Middle Street off Cloth Fair, close to the meat market which Father loved; indeed he was a 'follower' of old London institutions. In a glow of civic pride he even became a sidesman at St Bar-tholomew's near by, though he disliked the Anglican re-ligion.

In the evenings he showed us the plans of his factory and talked about them for hours. Every now and then Mother pointed one of her fingers in a random way at the plans and said:

'Walt, what's this here?'

'Showroom.'

'No, these.'

'Fittings.'

'Oh,' she groaned. She was thinking of those disastrous fittings in the stationer's shop when I was born.

He invited her to come and see the building. She refused. She wanted to have nothing to do with the new venture. All she said was:

'As long as it's straight. Credit, debit, I don't understand it.'

But we were excited and mocked her.

One morning my brother and I were taken to see Father's new place. We saw the dirty Thames crawling under the girders of the bridge near St Paul's and got out, with thousands of office workers, at Holborn and felt once more the dulling blow of the central London headache. Father whisked like a fly through the traffic.

Father's showroom was a large, white-walled place, newly furnished with counters and cabinets with sliding doors. Miss H, tall, accomplished and gay, came rubbing her hands together; I knew it was disloyal, but I admired her. She wore her white blouse, grey skirt, black stockings and serviceable shoes. She had a touch of scent. On the counters of the showroom were displayed pretty tea-cosies, in all colours and designs, cretonne-coloured boxes, delicate, voluptuous cushions of the best down, silk handbags, scented sachets, embroidery-worked tea-cloths. The large room smelled of heliotrope and lavender and lily of the valley. The air was pure and luxurious, the place spotless and my father himself was fastidious as he walked quietly among his goods, in a white starched dust coat and a bowler hat. He had the air of a priest. The machines hummed on the floor above as he told us that his goods were the most expensive and the most luxurious in the trade; only customers willing to pay high prices were tolerated. He preferred a few customers only. Once or twice a year he would go to Glasgow, Edinburgh, Perth or Exeter and Torquay and get large orders; outside of this he condescended to sell only to Harrods or Liberty's, but Toronto was 'on its hands and knees'. His customers were the wealthy and overfed Edwardians who were just about to be impoverished by the war – their very houses looked overfed with hangings, bric-a-brac and cushions – who lived cholerically and almost untaxed, on their means. They were above all a race who draped themselves.

I was puzzled when I saw the Sunday processions of unemployed marching with their banners and when I thought of my father's struggles in his trade; and now when I read books of nostalgia about Edwardian times, I find I remember nothing but the English meanness.

Miss H, whose accent was more precise and grammatical than Mother's North London Cockney, told us we should be proud of our father and understand that his eye for colour and original design and his gifts as a salesman were the foundation of his success.

Mother said of this:

'He gets it from his mother – thoroughness. The old b— always said she must have the best. He's got taste. He always had.'

Father might frown at home but here we saw a new being, the artist-priest, a pleasant mixture of the active, the fussing, addicted craftsman and perfectionist. A tiny defect in workmanship would send him up the stone stairs to his workroom, to start a row with the girls and we soon realized that, at home, he treated us as 'hands' also. His manner to them was censorious and sarcastic. The girls chattered and sang as their machines hummed but when the door opened and he stood there, silently, in his starched white coat, they stopped at once. His presence silenced them as he silenced us.

Until now we had had no idea that our father was an artist. We had often grinned at the number of times he washed his hands and had feared him when he passed his fingers over the edge of a table. We had been told often that many things, such as carpets, the upholstery on our chairs and the sofa – which had a violent design of peonies and parrots – were not actually ours, but belonged to the Business and might have to go back. This was true enough of the things he had bought on 'appro' or had not paid for; but the deeper explanation of his habit was that he hated things to be used or touched by anyone but himself, just as a painter will be distressed if anyone touches his painting. He saw in every room a personal dream. And when he was an old man he told me he kept his hands soft and clean because by keeping his skin in a sensitive condition, he was able to distinguish the qualities of silks and cloths; and his underlip would pout with pleasure. This possessiveness of things was also feminine. I gradually grew into a hatred of his love of Things and my mother had a recurring nightmare about it. She would dream of going into three rooms: the first, full of valuable and beautiful china and furniture; the second even more beautiful; the third, full of stench and decay.

He himself was awed by his creation and lowered his voice when he spoke in the showroom. But when we went there, he was always irritated and Miss H had to placate him and quietly take our side. It was obvious at once to us that his factory and office were another home and perhaps his real one. His office was more like a pleasant studio than an office. It had his secret collection of clocks, many articles of silver and china, far superior to those we had in our house. He and Miss H were on terms of pleasant, teasing friendship. At eleven in the morning when the machines stopped in the workroom above, a girl would bring in coffee and he would put a record on his gramophone. He would play 'Where My Caravan Has Rested' and also a song by his favourite singer, Clara Butt. A powerful, ox-like rumble came from this woman as she sang:

> If all the ships I had at sea
> Should come a-sailing home to me.

(It was feared, in the last verse, that one of these might fail to return which, in Father's case, was prophetic. It sank overloaded.)

His eyes moistened with emotion as he listened to the booming curdling voice of this man-woman: Mrs Eddy, Miss H, Clara Butt – three women in his life! He was very happy. But at ten minutes past eleven he looked at one of his watches – he had two – checked them with each other, then with the clocks and said sharply: 'The machines aren't on yet. The second time this week.'

'Sit down, Father,' said Miss H. 'I don't want you making trouble with the girls.'

Father sat down: imagine that, Father doing what a woman told him. We were amazed. The machines started up. Miss H was a miracle worker: their life was, in these days, a business illyll.

126

Better things followed. We had been brought up to London in order to get a new suit each at Swan and Edgar's, in Nash's Quadrant. Miss H came with us and easily calmed Father down, for his temper was dangerous in shops. Then he took us all to Eustace Miles's New Food Restaurant, where we ate energized bread and hygienic omelettes, for Father was now a follower of the fashionable food reformer and had a large photograph of this fat man in his office. The playing of a lady violinist and a pianist helped to waltz the reformed food down our throats. Afterwards Miss H told us, in a very serious way, that we were going to be sent to a grammar school at a great sacrifice on our father's part. Not until twenty years later did we discover that in fact Miss H paid for our education, indeed I believe for the education of the younger children too: Mother told us. I think Miss H was in love with Father and he had skilfully turned this into a love for his family.

My brother and I went back home by bus.

'What was Miss H wearing? Did she say anything?' said Mother, searching our faces suspiciously.

All we could remember was what Father had said. We decided to say no more.

Father was severe about our new school. We would have to reform our characters, he said, stop being round-shouldered to begin with. Boots cleaned, care with clothes, not playing with every Tom, Dick and Harry, and so on. A total change – or he would alter his plans. Greyfriars at last! We went home and told the Carters and O'Dwyers who were relieved, welcoming us to civilization. But we had to earn it, Father said. Jim had to be chained up so as to stop him tearing down the garden fence. So he went mad and bit his kennel. He was very like us. We had to clear up the worn-out grass, hoe the path, dig the flower-beds, weed. In the next few weeks Father himself joined in and conducted his favourite war. He hated trees. He cut them down, chopped a branch off the laburnum, killed the lilac, destroyed a pergola and soon reduced the garden to a place without vegetation. He drew a plan of a new garden. This preparation for secondary schooling was fierce and it left me with a lifelong hatred of gardening.

Our first day at Alleyn's School in Dulwich began with the

sort of shame we were used to. Our new clothes were stiff, Father was late and in a temper. It was a two-mile walk, past the old College and Art Gallery, through Dulwich Village and up the hill beyond it, to the group of high red brick buildings. He was a brisk walker in spite of his weight; he had his father's soldierly carriage and the print of insult on his face. He had the art of turning any occasion like this into something like the sacrifice of Isaac. When we sighted the school we exclaimed at the fine trees and large playing fields. He blew up and said he wasn't sending us to this school to waste our time and his money playing games. We feared he would insult someone at the school. For, as usual, we were not being taken on the first day of term: it had begun two or three weeks before, Father pointing out that his time was more valuable than any school-master's.

We got through the main gate of the school without trouble. There was an awkward quarter of an hour in a corridor while the headmaster kept us waiting; Father was beginning to pace. We peeped into the high school hall and saw a row of large portraits of Charles I and Henrietta Maria staring at us; we were to be Cavaliers here, not puritanic Cromwellians, as at Rosen-dale Road – a rise in the world. And then came the alarming encounter. Alarming, because we knew from talks with the Carters and O'Dwyers who went to the same school that in spite of Swan and Edgar's we were incorrectly dressed. It had been laid down firmly that we must wear black jackets, striped long trousers and black shoes. Father had said he was not going to allow any tu'penny ha'penny schoolmaster to dictate to him! We were pushed before him into the headmaster's study, my brother wearing a very loud yellow tweed knickerbocker suit and myself a slightly less savage brown one. We wore painfully banana-coloured shoes as well. The headmaster of Alleyn's School was a tall and leathery retired Colonel, an Anglo-Indian whose large nose stood out with a naked look. It had faced tigers. He was a terse man who looked stonily at Father. The Colonel was used to giving abrupt orders and sinking into long silences.

'You'll have to do something about those,' he nodded dryly at our suits.

Father was bland. He wasn't a salesman for nothing. He quietly pointed out, with a commercial charm, that our suits were made of the best West of England tweed from one of the finest mills in the country, its products sold all over the world – foreigners on their hands and knees for them – hard-wearing and, in fact, our colours were the new season's line as he knew well from his own tailor in Savile Row. Father said he was sure the Colonel must be aware of these facts. The Colonel said that nevertheless the school regulations were what they were and then went dumb. Father supposed that the First World War might have changed people's ideas and that as the Managing Director of a high-class business, he knew that *his* ideas had, at any rate. What was more, he said, he couldn't afford it. And whenever he said he couldn't afford anything a spacious, even wealthy look came on his face and his tone was grand. More-over, since we were three weeks late, he imagined that a wealthy foundation like Alleyn's would make a discount. The Colonel sympathized but said decidedly 'No reduction' and would Father be so kind as to see to the clothes promptly? Any-way the war, once the Russian steam-roller got to work, would be over by Christmas. My father said his time was money and he had a train to catch.

My brother and I made a striking pair at our Greyfriars that term: Father did not buy us new suits. I wore mine the whole two and a half years that remained of my school life. I was led into the Fourth Form just as Dr Ludwig Hirsch of Bonn – never interned – enormous in his black gown, his mortar-board tilted over his pale, offended face, was starting German hour.

Der Knabe: the boy

Die Knaben: the boys

and with a carnivorous and rich German laugh:

'*Mit den Knaben*, de latest news from the front, de Dative plural always ends in "n".'

Alleyn's School (of God's Gift) is one of the many good London grammar schools. There were 700 boys. Locally we were known as 'God's Gifts'. It was well-endowed by the Alleyn Estate which had founded Alleyn's College in the seventeenth century out of the fortune of Shakespeare's actor manager. But our school was really founded as a result of the Education Act of the seventies which aimed at educating the lower middle-classes and was separated from the College. The school fees were very small: a large number of the boys came up on scholarships from the elementary schools and we were intended to become the trusted clerks of lawyers, insurance companies, and bankers, cashiers to the future executives who, at this moment, were going to the Public Schools. The school claimed to be a Public School and was run very much on those lines; but we were all day-boys and in the social hierarchy we were a cut below the College boys; still our masters, we were proud to see, were almost all from Oxford and Cambridge. We had everything the College had, except the architecture – and no swimming bath – and we were taught only two languages instead of three, until we got to the Sixth, then Greek or Spanish was added. The College, when it condescended to play cricket or football with us, usually sent us their second team and beat our first; the College could pay for better coaches. The College produced many famous men – Shackleton, P. G. Wodehouse, for example, but, except for one freak Colonial Governor and some top boys in the Civil Service, Alleyn's School had not achieved much beyond that in my time; the English social system, being what it was then, made this unlikely. In my youngest brother's time the school standards were higher.

We were snobbish, of course; snobbery is one of the romantic aggressions of schoolboys. If the College snubbed us, we snubbed the rest. We had two advantages over the boarders at the College – freedom of the streets and a wider mixture of classes. We were not homesick or lonely. It was very possibly a loss, but I never heard of homosexual crushes, nor indeed of homosexuality till I was well into my twenties when a Frenchman assured me that all Englishmen were homosexual. I must have been innocent. One thing separates us Grammar School boys from those who have gone to Public Schools – we are not traumatically fixed on our schoolboy life and friendships. I have only once met a boy from Alleyn's School since I left it fifty years ago.

Father decided that since he intended me for a business career, I should go on the modern side and take French and German instead of French and Latin: French would be useful

130

in the silk business, German in the handbag trade. I hated this decision. Wordsworth and Coleridge both knew Latin and Greek – so did Grandfather. Then, I was backward; a large number of the boys had already done a year or two's Latin and French at Prep. schools; and at rising fourteen I was a year older than the rest of my form.

There was no saluting of the Union Jack as at Rosendale Road. Here we began with prayers, the Collect for the day and prayers for the soul of Edward Alleyn, our founder and benefactor. This was the first time I learned of Anglican practices. They seemed chilly. The Colonel barked out the Lord's Prayer and two or three times a week would forget the line after 'As we forgive them that trespass against us'. The pause would be long and a very audible drawling reminder came from the assistant headmaster who had a High Church accent. At lunchtime we assembled for a large meal of roast beef or mutton, very good stuff, in the dining hall, while the masters drank their beer at the high table at the end. We were fed as well as we were fed on Sundays at home. Grace was said by the school captain. In the afternoons we played games three or four days a week, or sat about in the very good library.

In the next few months I gave up literature, in fact I now concealed my desire to be a writer by saying that I wanted to be a schoolmaster. Father said I'd soon get over that and was relieved. I had never succeeded in English, but it turned out that I was good at languages. We were taught French and German every day; I learned fast and was usually far ahead of my form. Also, I secretly re-learned shorthand and could soon write sixty words a minute. Little Froggie Reydams and the Herr Doktor from Bonn were jokes to most of the boys, but not to me. Someone set fire to the Herr Doktor's gown that first winter, someone else tied a rope to the leg of Froggie's chair and pulled it off the platform just as he was going to sit on it. Froggie, a little man with a thick accent, enjoyed being ragged; but the large Herr Doktor would make sounds like a boiler bursting, then he quietened down and shook his head sadly and said we'd never beat the 'Chermans' if we didn't study like the 'Cherman' boys did. This caused loud jeers about the Germans never getting to Paris. They had just been driven from the Marne. In the end, the Herr

Doktor had to call on the form captain, a New Zealander, to bring us to order.

Dr Hirsch resembled Emil Jannings in *The Blue Angel*, his big flaccid head lolled sadly and he looked like a condemned capon. He smiled slowly at our larks and was sometimes charmingly interested in them. He was fascinated when he found that several of us had put lighted candles in our desks and were boiling our ink.

'Vat are you doing?'

'I am boiling my ink, sir.'

'In English boys, scientific curiosity, a new thing' he mocked us turning his eyes to the ceiling.

The hullabaloo did not prevent the Herr Doktor from being a good crammer. He ground German grammar into me so that I can never forget it. The discovery of foreign languages had an intoxicating effect on me.

I was not happy at home. Suburban life bored me. When I looked at the streets and houses around us, the unending stretches of London villas, the great buildings, the Town Halls, my spirits fell. I had been born into a family that was isolated – it seemed to me – from all the amenities that I had read of in English literature. There was no bridge between us and the rest of English life. Boys went to the sea for their holidays; a few had been abroad; country boys had horses, town boys went to pantomimes and theatres; they owned bicycles, went to parties, had sporting fathers, went swimming, played tennis; we did none of these things partly because our parents were locked in their own drama, partly because theatres, bicycles and holidays were too expensive and also partly because – despite appearances – my parents belonged to a timid generation. My father's grand air was a little man's fantasy. My mother, who had a terror of water, would not allow us to swim, saying she could not afford to buy us swimming suits out of the housekeeping money, and I did not learn until I was in my middle twenties: I became as frightened of water as she was. My father, very moved and almost in tears, would often exclaim when we were restive: 'I don't want you boys to grow up. I want you to keep your innocence.' We were a mixture of intense emotionalism and pusillanimity.

After a few months at Alleyn's School and although I worked
with a Puritan's fervour, I understood that I was backward and
would never pass crucial examinations. One by one masters
gave up teaching me mathematics and geometry; history was a
muddle, in chemistry and physics I was at the bottom. My
memory – being of an associative kind – was bad. Continuous
failures at English were humiliating. So words had to rescue me:
not English words, but French and German words. I now
dreamed of leaving the tedious city life of England. I could become a Frenchman – even a German when the war was over. I
had liked the German boys and girls. As I walked home from
school, I walked along the Rhine, through France, crossed the
Alps with Shelley and Byron; or, because I had read Thackeray's *The Virginians*, I could see myself on the Potomac. I saw
myself as an explorer. All the signs of commercial life – I suppose because of my early years in the Yorkshire fells and moors
– depressed me; and I was sad, uncomprehending and scornful
when I heard my school friends talk eagerly of getting into
banks and insurance offices. At Rosendale Road we had had our
Bartlett phase; at Alleyn's School there was no one to talk to
about art and writing. This was natural, for we were being introduced to that accomplished Philistinism which was the tone
set by our betters. It was a relief to have a better accent and to
be almost a little gentleman, but I was also disillusioned. I had
felt deprived of education, but – outside of French and German
– look at it! Nor was I a 'healthy-minded boy'. I liked games but
only in an undisciplined way – unable to keep my place in the
field. I hated the popular adventure books. The Librarian caught
me reading *Bacon is Shakespeare* which instantly converted me.
I was told not to be a prig and to read John Buchan. I found his
thrillers unreadable. The characters were not like human
beings. The Library did provide one real drama: two prefects
had a very ungentlemanly and savage fight, attacking each
other with chairs. It was about a girl. The school in general was
mad about 'birds' who had now become known as 'flappers'.

This was stimulated by a new gay French master, a wounded
Air Force pilot, who kept us delighted by pictures of his mistresses and of French brothels. As the war went on masters left
for the Army and tired out old masters took their place. There

was one tragic figure when we got into the Fifth. He was a Shakespeare scholar of sorts, a man with slipping glasses, and a weary, breathless, cultivated manner and almost blind. He had a distraught and noble face. He was the victim of crescendos of boot-shuffling, dart-throwing, desk-lid banging:

> We are the boys who make no noise
> Um Ha! Um ha ha!

His chair was chalked. The desks were barricaded so that he could not get at them. He would gaze at us helplessly like some contemptuous saint.

'Wretched little boors,' he used to say to us.

'And cads!' one day he said, drawn by a boy's tears. They came from an elderly-looking, pimpled orphan of loving and trusting nature, down whose neck we used to stuff decaying sausage, because the little swine came to school in a celluloid collar.

'He stinks,' several of us protested.

He loved us too much. His spotted face, his doleful large eyes, craved our goodwill; and he was kind enough to smile pacifically as he let us stuff more food down his neck.

The view was that a boy who dared to come from an orphanage in what were obviously orphanage clothes and who already shaved and had bleeding pimples, was a swine. When these attacks were over, he pulled the mess out of his collar and all he said was:

'Oh flick!'

A vulgar expression! One day he gave a roar and fell shouting on the floor: he was an epileptic.

The war became serious. Having moved his workrooms, Father celebrated the worsening times by moving house again, this time a few miles farther out to Bromley which was half country town and half suburb. There were no cabs, hymns and tears this time; in this removal we left Dulwich almost in triumph for the country.

We found ourselves in a small semi-detached late Victorian villa with a large garden facing open fields. The air was purer, Father said. It was a pity, he later said, the water wasn't soft. All his life he longed for the soft water of his Yorkshire childhood. Already having got his desire, he was dissatisfied.

'Listen to the thrush singing,' he said. Every evening, in the spring and summer, a thrush sang in our fir tree, but as it sang in the quiet summer evenings we sometimes heard a monotonously repeated bumping from the south. It was the sound of the guns in the Battle of the Somme.

Battle! Father cut down fifty yards of hedge on the road front and replaced it by expensive laurels. He also bought 500 rose bushes and made me catalogue them and plant them. Food became scarce; we went in for rabbit breeding, but there were scenes about killing the pets, so he turned to chickens. First he moved the furniture out of the back room and put in three incubators but something went wrong: none of the eggs hatched, they were fried, and left a rotten smell. We imported day-old chicks, moved them about in batteries; and then transferred them to a scientific chicken house, known as the Paradise House, which had arrived in sections. At first Father bolted the wrong walls together, then in a rage rushed off to church and left the task to my practical brother. Mother screamed when pieces fell; cats brought dying pullets, with their entrails hanging out, into the kitchen.

Father was thirty-eight or thirty-nine and he was called up to join the Army. He decided on the Navy. His fancy had been taken by the sausage-like balloons that swung over the Crystal Palace, and he applied to be a naval balloon observer and bought binoculars. He was annoyed when he was rejected because of his enormous weight.

Mother said: 'Two balloons in the air.'

But some months later as the demand for more soldiers came in, he faced a crisis. He was ordered to leave the Business and go to work in an aircraft factory. The order appalled him.

'I've had a blow, Beat,' he said to Mother.

Mother said to us: 'It seems a fate. He tries and tries and something always hits him. But your dad never gives in, I'll say that for him.'

He bought a bulldog, a sloppy bitch, to guard us while he was away but Mother was angry: one more female to contend with:

Mrs Eddy, Miss H, Clara Butt, and now this animal. When it was on heat, she screamed:

'Not in front of me, with those boys here. Walt, how dare you!'

But Father went off to Hertfordshire to the aircraft factory and left Miss H to run his business. She was a shrewd and economical woman.

In the next few months my desire to be a writer returned. It arose out of an air raid on the town. The difficulty I was in is the general one: one may love the arts but how does one know whether one has any talent? The doubt tortures and depresses; one can only try. But how? To find a subject is bad enough. It was baffling to me that Howard and Nott could dash off a thriller easily – but they were out of my life now – and that I could not come to their facility.

But now the autumn had come, the moon grew large and the Zeppelins could see their way to London. They would come, as all raiders of England have done since the days of the Danes, up the Thames Estuary and owing to the winding of the river, south-east London was vulnerable. A lost Zeppelin would often drop a bomb or two in Bromley Recreation Ground and smash a few windows thereabouts. The air-raid warning was given by a maroon which made a sharp cracking noise like a rocket. One of these went off at eight o'clock one night after Father left us, and very soon the gunfire started. My poor mother was frightened and became hysterical. She sent my brother and me to get the young children down from their bedroom, but we stayed up there to get a good view of the raid. Someone seemed to be driving nails into the sky with a hammer and knocking sparks off it; and now and then a lorry with a gun on it started rapid fire, just over the fence by our silver birch trees. Mother screamed. So we all came downstairs and she grabbed us in her fierce arms while she moaned, dragging us round and round in a circle with her, while we twisted our necks and struggled to get away in order to see the gun flashes and to hear the shrapnel coming down (we hoped) on our garden path. What we were really waiting and longing for was to hear the great naval gun go off at Pickhurst Green, across the fields, for the flash of this superb gun lit up the country for miles and the majestic detonation shook the whole town. Now, it fired and fired again, as we rocked together in my mother's grip, so that we were like some moaning animal with five heads and ten legs struggling with itself.

Next door to us lived a shaggy freckled music teacher and church organist, a young man in poor health, not long married: Mother giggled at the way this couple cuddled and kissed in the garden; Father said the man looked like a weak fellow – fancy playing the organ, ridiculous. And he needed a hair cut! When an air-raid alarm went, this young neighbour knocked on the wall with a poker, and then struck up loudly on his piano which we could easily hear through the thin walls of the dining-room. He played Sibelius to begin with and made enough noise in the louder parts of *Finlandia* to drown the sound of the artillery. He did this to comfort my mother; and in other raids went on to Brahms and Rachmaninoff's Prelude in C sharp minor. So, for the first time I heard classical music. One night during a raid, we all went to his house and Mother did not like this because she noticed that his wife had been cooking tripe and onions on the sitting-room fire and that the saucepan had burned.

'You could see she's not been married long,' Mother complained.

For other raids, we kept to our own house.

We had no telephone, so after a few raids Father came to see us. He chased a chicken to kill it for supper and made a mess of it; he wrung its neck clean off by mistake and was sick. Mother stewed some rhubarb leaves, having read in the paper that it was as good as spinach. It did us no harm but we soon learned from the papers that it was poisonous.

'Well, you see,' Father said when he recovered from beheading the chicken, 'Father comes home and everything's quiet.'

He was in a good mood. He arrived with a case full of letter files which belonged to a new filing system that was installed in the aircraft factory and explained it all to us. He worked, for £2 a week, in the Central Registry of the large organization and he was enchanted by the dreams of office organization. You could file tens of thousands of letters and papers a day with it, he said. He was going to introduce it into his business.

'But you only get a dozen letters a day,' Mother said. 'And no one writes to me, except Ada.'

'We don't want to bring Ada into this,' Father said. And went on all evening.

We went to bed. About two or three in the morning, my brother woke me up and said:

'Man, man, listen.'

A light flashed in the room. We heard guns. There was a raid.

'Shall we tell them?'

'Wait.'

We went to the window. There was no sound from our parents. We watched the beams of the searchlights cutting up the sky like scissors and then suddenly the beams stood still, four or five of them converged and tented their light. At the apex was a silver Zeppelin, but silver for only a few seconds; suddenly it became vermilion and the whole of London's sky was lit by this red light. Our own faces were reddened by it. The Zeppelin was on fire; it became a red cigar and then it buckled, broke in two and fell in two torches beyond the roofs. And then came the sound of cheering, taken up from street to street, across the city: the airship came down thirty miles away. We did not wake our parents. We wanted this show for ourselves.

At Alleyn's School next day everyone was excited. Two or three masters said we were savage little beasts. Had we no thought for the wretches burning alive in the sky? Another master, a cynical-seeming man who smelled horribly of stale cigarette tobacco, told us to 'get it out of our systems' and write an account of an air raid. What a chance! But what a problem! I knew what Howard and Nott would have done. 'Bang! Boom!' I began and could go no further. I was said never to stop talking and was as bad as my mother for my exaggerations and mimicries; I knew I was muddle-headed and given to showing off. But rocking with my mother, my brothers and sister, in that room, had moved me; and being 'the man' of the house at that time, I was sorry for her. I was suddenly released by recovering an emotion; I hit by this accident on the first duty of the novelist – to become someone else. I pretended to be my mother and, in her person, told what she felt as she called her children down and hysterically thought of her husband. And the old theme from my absurd Alhambra novel was a help: the lament of the women. The story was a lament. I think most of my stories have been laments.

The daring of this idea scared me. Obviously the story was a lie; obviously to write from the point of weakness and in the voice of a woman, would make the toughies of Fifth Form double up with laughter. I handed the story in. The next thing I knew was that the story was a success. It was read aloud in the Masters' Common Room and to the upper forms of the school. I was treated as a young marvel.

Fame is like fire. Baker, the photographer's son and Hillyard the 'knut' who oiled his hair and brushed it straight back, said Pritch had genius: he borrowed the thing and showed it to his sister, a typist, who confirmed it. '*Ma soeur* says its clever.' Jackson, who sat next to me and who had persecuted me because I would not join the masturbation gang who met in the lavatories, left me alone at last, with a final sneer. Fatty Foley, whose father had a small newsagent's business, stopped his punch ups and made flattering jokes. 'Look at old Prick! Look at old Prick!' he kept saying in wonder. Wizam, the Indian, paid me an obscure compliment. He said that I had pretended to be a woman because I never left the girls alone and had tried to seduce his sister, a child of seven, who lived near us. He shouted this in the school yard – which the romantic Hillyard called the Quad; he was our chief Greyfriars addict – and Wizam and I started a fight which drew a good crowd until a prefect separated us. Bailey, one of the 'train boys' who travelled to Penge, invited me to a new sensation. The tunnel between Sydenham and Penge is very long and he allowed me into his compartment where we opened the door and rode through the tunnel terrifying ourselves with the door open. But fame fades away. It also corrupts. I sat down a month or two later to write an account of my emotional sensations while listening to our neighbour playing Sibelius. It was a disaster; Callaghan, the frightening master of Remove B, my next form, covered it with insulting marks, gave me O for it and scribbled 'Cribbed from Ruskin and badly assimilated'. In fact it was pure Corelli again.

CHAPTER NINE

I was rushing downstairs at school because I was late for the parade of the Cadet Corps which I hated, when one of my puttees came undone. I tripped and fell down the full flight of stairs. A hot pain shot into my foot and I fainted. A master came to help me and told me it was nothing; my ankle was not broken, but I had sprained it badly. A boy wheeled me on the cross-bar of his bike to West Dulwich Station and then took me home. I bathed the foot and Mother put a cold compress on it, and I lay, aching but happy in the thought of a week or so's holiday from Mr Callaghan.

My father was home on one of his visits that evening and called me into his study. I said I could not get upstairs. 'You can get up easily,' he said. I put on a great act in getting up the stairs.

We rarely went into his study for it was uninteresting. We were used to the small bookcase, the sacred gate-legged table with an art needlework runner on it, the engraving of Daniel in the Lions' Den, and a fading photograph of the Mother Church of the Christian Scientists in Boston. There were piles of un-opened American periodicals on the table and a small collection of morocco bound books. Father rarely used the room himself.

'Now,' he said. 'I want you to understand there are no accidents in God's kingdom. You think you have sprained your ankle, but it says in the Bible that we are all the children of God, made in his image and likeness. How can you believe that a good omnipotent God would let one of his children sprain his ankle?'

The argument floored me.

'I suppose not,' I said. 'But . . .'

'I have purposely not told you anything about this, but I expect you have heard I am a Christian Scientist. I have no wish to force my religion on you and perhaps you prefer to believe what your mother believes, but I will tell you about it and then you can make your mind up. Christian Science can heal your so-called sprained ankle this very moment. In fact it is healed now, for nothing has happened to it. That is simply a mistake.'

My father then explained to me the doctrine of Christian Science. If I agreed that God was Good and Infinite and Omnipotent and had created Man in his image and likeness then there was no place where evil could possibly exist. Evil was an illusion, generated by the five senses. They were unreliable.

'Your eyes tell you that railway lines meet in the distance, but that is an illusion; they do not meet. You believe you can see a swollen ankle, but God can't see a swollen ankle, and nor can you, in reality, for since you are made in his image and likeness, you can only see what He sees.'

My father said that if I wished he would demonstrate this to me by treating me in the Christian Science way, at once. I agreed. He closed his eyes and began the process I afterwards understood as 'knowing the Truth' about me.

I was very moved. I had often hated my father but this first moment of intimacy with him was good. I felt that I was going to be cut off from him no longer. And that there would be other good results. If what he said was true, the quarrels would stop in the house, we would see more of him, he would take us to his Christian Science church, we would have some friends, for we were not allowed to have friends to the house. Anyway, in Bromley, we knew no one except the organist next door.

His eyes opened. He said:

'You are healed. I want you to walk to school tomorrow. You'll find in the morning that you can.'

And then he slipped one of the periodicals on his desk out of its wrapper and said I could read it. It was the *Christian Science Sentinel* and it contained not only articles, but a number of testimonies of healing of all kinds of diseases. He opened another wrapped. It contained a newspaper the *Christian Science Monitor*. I discovered it had a literary page. I resented being sent back to school but I was impressed by being taken into my father's confidence and of hearing about his religion properly – for until then we had no real notion of what it was and why he made the startling statements he often shouted in our home.

I woke up next morning and my ankle was still bad. He made me walk to the station and then walk to school from West Dulwich. I was in great pain. In a few days it gradually got better – which is not surprising for doctors recommend walking on a sprained foot. At the end of the week my father said I had had a startling proof of the truth of Christian Science teaching. I did not think I had but I set about reading the works of Mrs Eddy. There was a great deal I could not understand but the fundamental teaching was that life was a dream – how many writers had said that! The novelty, the dramatic and beneficent nature of the doctrine, exalted me, the hatred, sins and defeats of my life seemed to melt before my eyes.

'You believe what your father does?' my mother asked, peering suspiciously at me.

'I do,' I said and explained to her. She had lost an ally.

'I can't fathom it,' said my mother. 'I keep on having these whitlows. It's cruel. Look at it.' She held up her poisoned thumb.

Underlying my conversation to Christian Science was a desire for friends and the fact that this church had a Sunday School to which one could go until the age of twenty, was a strong attraction. The Sunday School met in a pretty house, the church services were held in a light and pleasant hall. The sect was cheerful and business-like: the notion of original sin had vanished, so had guilt. We were all good. It is true that evil was said to be an illusion caused by malicious animal magnetism, a mysterious yet unreal force that did its best to influence the mind and particularly 'worked through sex' whatever that meant. But the evil was not in ourselves. One became as guiltless as any atheist, and I have never since been able to regard the doctrine of original sin as anything more than an intellectual convenience, though it is more than forty years since I went into a Christian Science church.

It is natural to have religious emotions in adolescence and – except for the very few who have a religious vocation – it is well for it to be short. The influence of Christian Science on my father's life and upon us was eventually dulling and even tragic; for although doctors now speak with mild tolerance of the usefulness of its belief in the influence of the mind upon the body and are amiably amused by their patients who dabble with both medicine and faith, in order to be on the safe side, the occasional healings or even the many tragic failures to heal are not the important aspect of this religion. The real objection is to the impoverishment of mind, the fear of knowledge and living that Christian Science continuously insinuates; the futility of its total argument and its complacency. It operates like a leucotomy that puts the patient into an amiable stupor. A debased form of New England Transcendentalism, Christian Science spread easily in New England in the general pessimism that followed the Civil War; it was one of the symptoms of the decay of the vigorous New England culture. William James treated it gently in his *Varieties of Religious Experience* because of his psychological curiosity; but he understood it was an enfeebled form of Emersonian metaphysics; and, in fact, my interest in it was sustained by the discovery of Emerson's writings. How clearly now one sees the sage, drifting as he grows older, in two directions at once; up into the thin upper air of a beautiful but nebulous metaphysical persuasion and down into the cult of success. The heirs of the Transcendentalists were businessmen; they blandly denied the reality of matter in order to justify themselves in raking in more and more of it.

To England, Christian Science was brought by one or two aristocratic ladies, heirs of that small evangelical movement which had caught the consciences of the upper classes in the eighteenth century. The new religion was a resource for those who could not face late-Victorian doubts: the mixture of religion (without theology) and of supposed science smoothed over the troubles caused by Darwin and Huxley; its optimism accorded with the continuously growing wealth in England. The religion appealed to the ambitious lower middle-class and also to the insensitive and organizational among the blander uppers. It solved so many problems of public conscience: there were nice women who would go down to the slums, watch a hospital train packed with wounded go by at Bromley Station, look at processions of unemployed, close their eyes, 'Know the Truth' and go away convinced that they had helped to 'heal' the situation. Their complacency was naïve and sentimental; they were indignant if you suggested that they had closed their minds to reality, for they regarded themselves as 'true' revolutionaries, and indeed had to put up with a lot of ridicule and attack. This stimulated them. Most of them had belonged to the traditional churches and were glad to be free of the tragic implication of the Christian myth and its cult of suffering. There was something Quakerish about them. It is characteristic that they had a daily newspaper which reported no crime, no accounts of disaster – though the war was a problem – in which the general tone was liberal and which for years had some of the best foreign correspondents in daily journals; its literary pages were unadventurous, but many good English and American writers contributed to them. The gap between the tone of this paper and the material of their purely religious papers was great: the difference between literacy and amateur moralizing.

Most of all, I was attracted by this newspaper: the *Christian Science Monitor*. To one as little educated as I was, it was an educator, for it was imbued with that unembarrassed seriousness about learning things which gives American life its tedium but also a moral charm. In Europe the standards have been high for the few, the path of education has been made severe. If we learn, if we express ourselves in the arts, we are expected to be trained by obstruction and to emerge on our own and to be as exclusive, in our turn, as our mentors; willingness and general goodwill are – or have been until very lately – despised. There were, in fact, better popular educators in England than in America, but a paper like the *Monitor* made my interests sound easier. In reality the gaps in the *Monitor* – as I came to know when later on I wrote for it – were preposterous. It was good about foreign politics because no Christian Scientist and no American – at that time – was very interested in them.

I thought of Christian Scientists as living in a dramatic and liberating illumination. It was natural that I should be attracted to this religion. Its idealism and novelty appealed to one who had scarcely ever been to church but had lived in a house filled with religious echoes and disputes. I had been brought up as a Christian without being taught very much of what Christianity was. It was nothing but words. This new religion was *taught* to me. Father had a natural attraction to all quacks and to any crank – outside the political – who was mellifluous.

But how was it that I, with all my literary pretensions, did not see that Mrs Eddy was a loose thinker and a very bad writer; that scarcely one of her sentences followed from its predecessor, that she blocked in long strings of big words like Soul, Principle, Substance, God, Good when in doubt; that her books were a rambling collection of assertions and jumbled quotations from the Bible? How was it – after all the jokes at school about 'artful alliterations awful aid', I could stand a phrase like 'Meekly our Master Met the Mockery' . . . and many more like it? Or not laugh out loud at 'Thou are right, oh immortal Shakespeare' whom she showed no signs of having read except in a book of quotations? It is astonishing how faith makes one shut one's eyes; or how willingly the intelligence takes a holiday from intelligence. Why, at least, did the language of the King James's Bible not preserve me? The answer to that is simple: *that* language appeared to me not of this world, a spiritual utterance and not a language at all. After all, why had I swallowed the Bible and believed that the Israelites were superior in spirit, history and culture to the Greeks, the Medes and Persians, peoples far more gifted and enlightened?

Fortunately, nature asserted itself. I was soon leading a double life. I believed, yet did not believe, very comfortably, at the same time. The believing part of me was the simple idealist; also the insubordinate youth was vain of belonging to a sect that was often ridiculed. It appealed to my vanity to belong to a peculiar minority and I did not notice that we were a mild and tepid group who had cut off our noses to spite our faces. More than the nose: I was to discover among my co-religionaries that we had become as dim as eunuchs.

What began to save us was our family egotism. From our mother we had inherited an eye and ear for comedy, from our grandfather and father, a gift for irony and sarcasm.

All sects have their jargon and Father, eager as an advertising man is for slogans, had picked them all up and lived by them. We soon saw that we were supposed to go through the fundamental process of 'knowing the Truth' about this or that person or situation. For example, the truth about a burglar was that he was not a burglar but a child of God, who had seemingly taken to burglary because he had failed to see that he had 'abun-

145

dance' already, for did not the Scriptures say 'Day by day, the manna fell.' Or, rather, a hymn said that. A phrase that infuriated Mother. If I 'knew the Truth' about Mr Callaghan, that child of God, he would stop insulting my English; or if I knew the Truth about my father's violent opposition to our inviting friends to the house, or to my desire to be a writer, he would stop these tyrannies. I tried it, but was haunted by the danger that I was transforming Mr Callaghan and my father, without their permission. Suppose they, or indeed I, became transfigured, would it not be unnerving? I was handing out dangerous haloes. It seemed far too risky to know the Truth about oneself. But many of the good people – though mostly the bossy ones – in the church that met at the Town Hall were knowing the Truth about each other right and left. And even more, they were enjoined to 'voice' it when it was opportune; it was constantly opportune and rarely complimentary. Father 'voiced' very often to a Mrs E, who 'voiced' back. Not to 'know the Truth' was a certain way of 'letting Error into consciousness' – I have since discovered that this, like the word 'problem', is a common Americanism: perhaps, after all, Christian Science is a normal product of the middle-class American ethos. One of the ways of 'letting Error in' was to 'outline' the desire we were 'working', i.e. praying for. It was right to 'work', say, for a better job; but it was 'outlining' to say what precise job you wanted. Father never 'outlined' that he wanted £15 to pay the quarter's rent and stop a writ being served: he worked for 'supply', i.e. the infinitude of God's blessings, a fatal thing for his character; he would always have been better off with the Finite. Instead of 'outlining' you let God's will unfold'. Hence the delays in sending us to school, the refusal to take a family holiday: and eventually, Father took to allowing his manufacturing and sales to 'unfold' and sat in his office, gazing at estate agents' offers in a dream that at last became stagnant, then corrupting and finally pernicious. Still, when something did 'unfold' one had 'made one's demonstration', i.e. demonstrated the truth of Christian Science. If anything went wrong in the lives of any of the church members – Mr X was still stone deaf, Mr Y losing his job, Mrs X still walking on a club foot – Father would snort that they 'had not made their demonstration'. We had a sad example in our own home: Mother – in refusing to have anything to do with this religion, and becoming more and more a worn-out nervous wreck – was obviously not going to make her demonstration. But what could you do, Father would ask? It's no good casting your pearls before swine. We let a great deal of Error in, in our home.

Sunday was the worst day for Error. It began early with my brother and me standing in the scullery and cleaning the boots and shoes of the family. We did the younger children's first, then our own and then moved on to a long display of Father's. This was an anxious task for, when they were done, we would have to take them up to his bedroom where he examined them, pair by pair, and often sent us back to do them again. He was vigilant for specks of cunningly disguised mud; and he always turned the boots over to see if we had blackened and polished the instep between heel and sole.

This was a preparation for his rising and dressing, a long business. Once or twice he was asked to take the collection at the church and then he was in a state only to be compared with that of an actor on a first night. His lotions and perfumes made the air heady, as he changed from shirt to shirt and went through his collars minutely examining them. Mother would send us up to spy to see 'how your father's getting on'. At last, on these occasions, he appeared downstairs, in a tail-coat, a waistcoat discreetly outlined by a white, piqué under-waistcoat, and a pair of trousers of astounding and tigerish stripes. He wore a winged collar, a silk stock, a pearl tie-pin, and a button-hole. On his feet were spats.

'Beat,' he would call, in the voice of one getting ready for sacrifice, 'brush me.'

Mother, dressed anyhow, came out of the kitchen, and going down on her knees would brush him, working upwards to the summit. He stood there like some exotic, tropical plant that perhaps needed watering.

It was our duty to go to church with him and not to the Sunday School, on these special Sundays. On the way, except to mutter words like 'Keep your feet up', once or twice, he scarcely spoke, from fear of spoiling his entrance at our tabernacle. He so outshone the other sidesmen that they backed away and he walked up and down the aisle between the chairs with all the polish and *savoir-faire* of the perfect shopwalker. Sniggers – we were annoyed to hear – came from one or two of our friends, and ladies nodded ironically to each other.

'The guv'nor,' Cyril muttered, 'has overdone it.'

He had. Yet, if anyone of that crowd appeared to be the image and likeness of the Divine Mind, we felt, that man was our father. We kept our eye on him, our excess of glory, as Mrs Norman (the first reader) read out the first words of a passage from the King James's Bible and the second reader (Mr Gordon) responded with what were called the 'correlative passages' from Mrs Eddy which had little or no relation to the Biblical passage, and which were of impenetrable verbosity. They held our attention for a while because, I now suppose, they appealed to that self-satisfaction which is born out of straining to find meaning in the meaningless.

After the service everyone chatted happily. Father stood apart as a rule, on the look out for Error and as the congregation was mostly female, there was a good deal of it about, from his point of view; but generally his view, and mine, was that we had had a refreshing contact with the Absolute. We walked home but the voyage down from the Absolute to the Relative is tricky. Mother would be in her usual state of fighting with the kitchen stove.

'Walt, look at this brute. Look at the smoke.'

'Letting Error in,' muttered Cyril.

Mother spoke of the stove as of a horse kicking up its legs.

'Push the damper,' said Father.

'You expect me to slave . . .' Mother began. She was a talented wrecker of Sundays. Father changed his clothes and from this moment the day went to pieces.

Why, I asked, did this happen? Why did Eternal Harmony vanish so quickly? Mrs Norman and others would have said we were being 'handled' by malicious animal magnetism; others, 'higher up in the movement' would have said we were being 'handled by Rome', for it was well-known to advanced students that the Roman Catholic priesthood sent out spells of witchcraft especially upon Christian Scientists; many a 'problem' was made difficult because the jealous Jesuits – highly trained in

148

these things – were sending out anti-prayers to frustrate us. Having escaped from the dead hand of theology, we found ourselves eager for magic and superstition. This disturbed me, but Mrs Norman told me not to worry about that now and asked me kindly how 'the writing was getting on'.

'Desire is prayer' are the opening words of *Science and Health with a Key to the Scriptures*. I was nearing my sixteenth birthday: I was desire in person, frantic, stiff with it. To sit in our Sunday School faced by several pretty girls was an ordeal. I could not take my eyes off the breasts of Mrs Murstein, our teacher, a Rubens-like woman who wore her blouses so low, in the fashion of the time, so that the tops of those rumbustious globes were easily seen, indeed positively offered. Her rich lips, her faint moustache, her forty-year-old but innocent doll-like eyes destroyed me as she explained to us that the true meaning of 'to commit adultery' was the 'mixing of incompatible elements' – an example was adulterated food. I had read fortunately a popular book that told me masturbation would *not* affect my health or drive me mad; but my burdened state was too much for my modesty. At Alleyn's, someone would pass the word along that 'old Johnson' was playing pocket billiards and so was Fatty Brown; the whole of Remove B was as stiff as monkeys. Cook, the new French master, made jokes about it, which was a relief. But, at that age, one cannot get it out of one's head that one is, if not unique, at least visible in this villainous and muscle-bound state. I hated to go into shops where girls were working because of it; yet I could not stop myself trying to catch up with girls in the street. In Sunday School I sublimated.

'Still, still with Thee when purple morning breaketh,' we sang the hymn, but as fast as I sublimated, so the sublimation increased the desire and, as I sang, I was in bed with holy Eileen or Doris or Isabel singing in the row in front. I dared not look up from my hymn-book at the pretty girls and my eyes sought out plain and ugly ones; but the disadvantages of this was that the pretty girls looked coldly innocent and the plain ones were more eager to respond. One could only cling to Mrs Eddy's mixture of sentimentality about 'trysting' and her severe teaching – and St Paul's – that sexual intercourse was something to 'overcome' in the interests of something higher. One clung. One believed. Yet every instinct told one that the doctrine was ludicrous; and the result of it was that my desires were perverted in their fantasy. Dreams of sadism, of terrible sexual sacrifices on altars, of torture by machines, haunted my pious head; so that when I hear of some maniac tried for crimes of sexual perversion I think there, but for the Grace of God, go I. But it is not by the Grace of the Christian Science God or any other, that I have escaped.

Certainly fear of scandal or disease were responsible for my chastity for many years. I might dream otherwise, but chastity was a pride. The possibility of becoming an artist of some kind seemed small, but it seemed also to depend on it. I should lose command of my whole self if I lost it, and that would be the end of the force that made me want to be an artist. At school, when the boys said they had girls, I knew they wanted to settle down in little villas where they lived, in jobs like their fathers' job, marry, have children. The thought repelled me. To go from family life into family life again, seemed to me tragic; for myself, a death. To be alone – I told my mother – was the ideal; to be unhappy was inevitable. But there was one infallible resource: literature and art.

Mother looked mockingly at me; I could see the alarm and the humour move over her face, and then her expression settle into something stonily accusing.

'I never heard anything like it in me natural. You are going to be a very wicked man,' she said. And covered it up with: 'I can't make head or tail of any of you.'

I found many things to interest me in Christian Science. It introduced me to Emerson, Thoreau, Hawthorne. I was rather snobbishly shocked to see Mrs Eddy had admired Whittier, a namby-pamby poet. To keep me occupied the following year Father made me translate a Christian Science pamphlet into German; the smattering of German metaphysical terms interested me. The religion sounded better in German. I had a bad month with the origin of evil, because, to my dismay, I defeated several older members of our church in my inquiries and arguments. There was alarm about my doubts: I was handed on from eminence to eminence, and eventually to a visiting Christian Science lecturer. The young are surprisingly decent and tactful; I agreed with what was said, but I did not believe a word of it. Any fool could see this error and I was a worse fool than most, but I let the matter slide. There were more important things than the question of the origin of evil on my mind.

A more serious concern for me was the attitude of my co-religionaries to literature and the arts. Clearly art prolonged the errors of the senses, the greater the art, the greater the error. The word 'death' for example, was never used by Christian Scientists; one 'passed on' for one never, in fact, died. Similarly descriptions of battle, illness, 'inharmony' etc., were banned or had, at any rate, to be so framed in 'Suffer it to be so now' as to be emasculated. Insofar as Shakespeare or Homer approached Christian Science beliefs they were considered good, yet sadly lacking. It was disappointing to see that Christian Scientists were quick to 'give up' things. They gave up drink, tobacco, tea, coffee – dangerous drugs – they gave up sex, and wrecked their marriages on this account, and it was notoriously a menopause religion; they gave up politics; they gave up art but, oddly, they did not give up business.

Mr Graves gave up music; he looked back lingeringly at his passion for Beethoven. He would play a little but reflect that it was hard to see which part of the music came from the Divine Mind and which from Mortal Mind. Mr Hotchkiss, the lawyer with big feet, occasionally took a glass of wine, but he had given up reading Russian novels: there was something fleshy in Tolstoy; a Miss Humphrey had given up the National Gallery; for though the pictures (she said) were works of genius, it was waste of time now to consider anything but the images in the mind of God. There was almost unanimous feeling against a couple called Fitzgerald who had not yet given up socialism. Many sympathized with a Mrs Merton, a lady of large, low duck-like breast which she bore before her like a personal tragedy: her husband played in amateur theatricals and wanted to leave the bank where he worked and go on the stage. So far nothing had 'unfolded' and Mrs Merton conveyed to her friends the reason for this. So did he to me: he was one of those lost middle-aged men who confide in everyone.

'Victor, I know what's holding me up. I'm carnal.'

Also he was a chain-smoker. Everyone was sorry for Mrs Merton because she had a carnal husband.

It seemed to me that if I approached the Divine Mind on the subject of literature, I would have to give it up or – and this is what generally happened in our religion – I would be allowed to start and then I would find I had risen above it and leave it. However, Father came down from London one day and said that in Hollywood many actresses were Christian Scientists. That was a long way off; in England people took a less cheery attitude to the religion.

Such was my state of confusion in the autumn of 1916. I went to my room at the top of the house in the evenings to read Macaulay and to see if I could get a sight of the large lady lodger in the house opposite, undressing. I gazed at my own naked body in a mirror and could, at mere thought, make my organ stand upright; how surprising I looked. What was the Divine Mind going to do with this? I tried to write but could think of no subject. I sat in the laburnum tree at the bottom of the garden, feeling the lift of its boughs in the wind, imagining I was flying or sailing. More than once in that tree I shut my eyes and tried to divest myself of my mortal senses and mind and, in a few empty seconds, waited to be filled with the Divine as the mystics, I discovered years afterwards, tried to experience a unity with God. Sometimes I seemed on the point of this union, when a car hooted or my mother called and I came sulkily down. I did not know then that my methods were dubious: I ought to have felt conviction of sin, I ought to have mortified my body; alas I liked my body. But one afternoon in the laburnum tree, where I had taken Molière's *L'Avare* to read, I *did* have a convincing experience. The pleasure of finding that French was getting easier to read, the pleasure in the sparkle of words in that comedy, suddenly made me hear a voice. The voice said 'You are a sceptic.' It was my own voice, but speaking as I had never heard it before. I closed the book, climbed down the tree and stood on the lawn longing for the sensation to remain, for someone to tell it to. Even as I longed, the beautiful sensation faded; but I had had it and I felt older.

An event – innocent in appearance – soon showed that I had

been 'letting Error in' on a serious scale. It was announced that Grandfather and Grandmother Pritchett were coming down from Yorkshire to stay. Mother set about cleaning the house from top to bottom, for she knew the old lady would open every cupboard in it. The larder was cleared, for Grandma would bring two large boxes, one containing a week's baking of her best bread, cakes and pastries; the other a couple of geese from Appleton. Mother prepared two stewed rabbits – no other meat being available in war-time – and my brother betted that he would be given the heads, because she disliked him. So prepared, we waited for the three o'clock train, when my father (who had slipped away from his aircraft factory) brought his parents down. They did not arrive. Nor at four. Nor at five. We had no telephone and could not ring up my father to ask for news. Not until eight o'clock did they arrive. Into the house walked Grandmother, white-faced, in pain, holding one hand to her chest, and leaning on my father's arm. After her came Grandfather, his right arm in a sling and his head and hand bandaged, and one eye blackened. Once a soldier, he now marched in wounded like a true soldier. The train they had travelled in from Manchester had come off the rails and their coach had struck a bridge. They were scarcely in the house before a reporter came to interview them. The next day we were proud to see for the first time Granda's name in the papers.

Manchester Express Derailed. Minister Injured.

It is to misunderstand our family to think that this drama passed off entirely in anxious questions, affection and condolences; within a half an hour Grandmother, Grandfather and Father were shouting in angry argument across the table, about God and 'that Eddy woman'. Grandma, for once, was on her daughter-in-law's side and said she doubted but what Father wouldn't drive Beatty 'to go elsewhere'. She was appeased by serving the rabbit. 'Eh, Cyril, ah'd forgotten you,' she said, when we were all served except him. And she gave him the head of one of the rabbits.

After the meal talk became serious, about trade, the war, and so on, while Grandmother told how Father had given her the

best handbag in his showroom and said 'Has he given you one?'
'Yes' said my mother and went to get it and showed her. The old
lady was upset.

'Eh, Walter you gave Beatty a better handbag than you gave
your own mother.'

'Here, take it,' said Mother.

'Eh, ah think ah will,' said the old lady. And did so.

Grandfather said:

'How old's Victor? Fifteen? And still at school?'

I gazed expectantly at the man who I thought was a friend to
my hopes.

'Put him to work,' said my grandfather.

So one is betrayed. I could not believe it. Everything I hoped
for collapsed in that minute. Tears came to my eyes.

'There's three more mouths to feed,' my grandfather said.
'You must start earning.'

How was I to face the boys I knew, boys to whom I had
boasted and before whom I had unwisely glittered? How was I
to face Mr Callaghan? Where was the School Prize for French?
To despair was now added shame. If Ginger could have seen me
then what a triumph for him.

In fact, at school, everyone envied me and Callaghan said:

'Just as well. You haven't done much good here. What are
you going into?'

'The leather trade.' For so it had been decided.

Callaghan gave one of his delighted sniffs.

'Nothing like leather,' he said over his shoulder, as he waltzed
out of the room under his rusty gown.

My boyhood was over.

CHAPTER TEN

WHY the leather trade? Father had met a man who belonged to the Chamber of Commerce and who had said he knew a firm of Leather Factors that had an opening for an office boy. Begin (he said) at the bottom of the ladder, like Henry Ford. I shall not forget that spiritless January morning when Father took me to a place in the Bermondsey district of London. The one pleasant but intimidating thing was that for the first time I sat with Father in a corner seat of a First Class compartment of the train on the old South Eastern and Chatham railway. I was wearing a new suit, a stiff collar that choked me, a bowler hat which bit hard into my forehead and kept slipping over my ears. I felt sick. There were two or three city gentlemen in the compartment, smoking pipes; my father presented me with a copy of the *Christian Science Sentinel* and told me to read it while he closed his eyes and prayed for me. I disliked being seen with this paper. He prayed as far as Hither Green – I opened my eyes for a glance at a house which had been torn in half by a bomb in the autumn raids – and then he leaned across to me and, not as quietly as I would have liked, for the city gentlemen were staring at us, he reminded me of the story of the infant Samuel. Father was becoming emotional. To me the situation was once more like the sacrifice of Isaac.

'When he heard the voice of God calling, Samuel answered "Speak Lord, thy servant heareth." When the manager sends for you, I want you to remember that. Say to yourself "Speak Lord . . ." as Samuel did and go at once. It's just an idea. You will find it helpful. I always do that when I go to see the Buyer at Harrods.'

I had thought of myself as growing up fast at school. Now, under my bowler hat, I felt I was sinking back into infancy. At London Bridge, where we got out, a yellow fog was coating the rain as we went down the long flights of sour stone stairs into the malodorous yet lively air peculiar to the river of Bermondsey. We passed the long road tunnels under the railway

155

tracks, tunnels which are used as vaults and warehouses convenient to the Pool of London. There was always fog hanging like sour breath in these tunnels. There was a daylight gloom in this district of London. One breathed the heavy, drugging, beer smell of hops and there was another smell of boots and dog dung: this came from the leather which had been steeped a month in puer or dog dung before the process of tanning. There was also – I seemed to be haunted by it at the critical moments of my childhood – the stinging smell of vinegar from a pickle factory; and smoke blew down from an emery mill. Weston Street was a street of leather and hide merchants, leather dressers and fell-mongers. Out of each brass-plated doorway came either that oppressive odour of new boots; or, from the occasional little slum houses, the sharp stink of London poverty. It was impossible to talk for the noise of dray horses striking the cobbles.

We arrived at a large old-fashioned building and walked into a big office where the clerks sat on high stools at tilted desks. The green-shaded lamps were lit. A hard bell struck over an inner door. 'Speak Lord,' I instantly murmured – and a smart office boy who had given a wisp of vaseline to his forelock took us to the office of the head of the firm.

This ancient gentleman was like God himself – Grandfather and all Victorians would have recognized him. He was a tall, massive, hump-shouldered man in his late seventies, with a waving mat of long thick white hair which had a yellow streak in it, and a white beard. He had pale-blue eyes, very sharp, a wily smile and an alert but quavering voice. He was the complete City gentleman of the old school. My father and he were courtly with each other; the old man was soon on to the slump of the 1870's when his uncle had sent him to Vienna for the firm and where (he slyly said) he had got the better of a competitor because of his knowledge of German. He said he was glad to hear I was a church-goer, for he himself held a Bible class every Sunday; and his secretary, an old woman like my grandmother, taught in Sunday School too. He mentioned his eleven children, four of the sons being in the business. My father said I was good at French. The old gentleman suddenly snapped at me:

'*Assez pour tirer d'affaires?*'

I was bowled out and could not speak. The old gentleman grinned kindly. We were interrupted by a sugary, languid tinkle on the old fashioned telephone that stood in the middle of his large desk. It was really two desks joined; it had spawned some odd side-tables and was covered with papers, letters and periodicals. I watched the bent knees of the old man rise, then his back heave up, then the hump elongate itself and finally a long arm with a powerful and shaking hand on it stretched across the wide desk and reached the telephone. The quavering voice changed now to a virile, barking note, the mild blue eyes became avid, the teeth looked the teeth of a lynx. His talk was brisk and commanding: when it was over he sank back in his chair and gazed at us as if he had never seen us before and, panting a little, said:

'The *Arabic* has docked with 4,000 bales.'

His knees went up and down under his desk feeling for a concealed bell, and the office boy came pelting in.

The room, I saw, was like a studio under a dirty glass roof, and was supported by iron pillars here and there. In two corners of it were two more crowded desks and against one of the walls was a large Victorian fireplace. The smoke of the coal fire mingled with the fog that had entered the room.

I worked for four years, until I was nearly twenty, at the leather factors, starting at 12s. 6d. a week and finishing at 18s. 6d. The firm was one of the most important factors in the trade. Other factors, it was said, were merchants on the side, a lack of probity which the firm denounced: we – as I quickly learned to say – sold on commission only. We – it turned out – were the agents of a very large number of English tanners and fellmongers, also of large sheepskin tanners in Australia, of hide merchants in general and dealt also in dry-salted South American hides. More rarely, and reluctantly 'we' dealt in Moroccan and India dressed leather and woolled sheepskins. There was more money in the raw material. A large part of this stock was stored in the warehouse attached to the office, but also in the docks, in the wharves of the Pool of London and in the cold storages. The firm also dealt in tanning materials: oak bark, shumac, myrabolams and tanning extracts. The correspondence came from all over the world and was heavy; the size of the cheques the firm paid out astonished me; they ran often into the thousands; all of them bearing the large, spidery, childishly clear signature of the old gentleman. It was incredible that a firm in such shabby, old-fashioned offices should be so rich.

The premises were opened at 7.30 in the morning by an old clerk called Haylett who wobbled in fast, lame and gouty, but always wearing a flower in his buttonhole. He was one of those gardeners of *The Waste Land*. He was satiny pink, fat and very bald and went about singing bits of music-hall songs or making up words. He then went over to the warehouse and let the workmen into the warehouse. One of these, a young, feeble-minded man, cross-eyed and strong, would lumber down to the safes and carry up a load of heavy ledgers which he set out on the various desks. Dust flew out of them. His name was Paul – he, like one of the carmen, who was known as Ninety, because it was the number of the house where he lived – had no surname. Paul lived with his mother and was very religious. When he had put down his ledgers, Paul would advance upon Mr Haylett and say his usual morning greeting in a toneless voice and unsmiling:

'Well, my venereal friend.'

To this the gay old Mr Haylett replied:

'Good morrow, good morrow, good morrow.' And add one of his made-up words: 'Hyjorico', and shake with laughter. Paul, who wore a heavy leather apron, lowered his head and looked murder at Mr Haylett, and went off on his bandy legs, waving his clenched fists dangerously.

At eight we office boys arrived and often saw this scene. The other boy whose name was Les Daulton had to teach me my job. He was a weak-voiced, fair creature, as simple as Paul and also famous for his comic mis-pronunciations. Offices – like my mother's shop in Kentish Town of the earlier generation – depend for their life on repeated jokes. Goods were often collected from Thameside quays: Daulton always called them 'Kways' and the clerks concentrated on getting him to say it. Daulton gave a simple smile. He knew he was a success. Once we had arrived Mr Haylett went to the W.C. in the basement where he sat smoking his first cigar and reading the paper; Daulton and I followed him down, taking with us the packs of rubber sheets which were used in the copying of letters in the letter presses, and soaked them in the wash-basins. This done, the boy took me out with the local letters that had to be delivered by hand. We went down to the hide market, to the tanners and leather dressing firms and then came back to our main job: answering the Chairman's bell. This bell was fixed outside Mr Kenneth's door, in the main office, and snapped in startling, rusty and panicky agitation.

'Boy. Bell,' Mr Haylett would call out in panic, too.

'Speak Lord, Thy servant heareth,' I murmured. One of us would jump off our stools and go in to see what the old gentleman wanted. Sometimes he handed us an urgent letter which had to be copied, but often his knee had pressed the bell by mistake; or he had forgotten he had called us and he gazed at us blankly with the lost, other-worldly eyes of an old man.

Occasionally the bell was rung from another desk in Mr Kenneth's office. This was the desk of another old man, Mr James, Mr Kenneth's brother, well-known to be the fool of the business and never trusted with any serious matters. He wandered in to 'work' at eleven or so, wrote a private letter to Lord This or Lady That – for he was vain of aristocratic acquaintance – and would then shuffle out into the main office, calling out 'I'm going to get me hair cut' in a foggy, husky voice. Sometimes he would wander into the warehouse and watch the bales of leather swinging on the crane.

'Coming in or going out?' he would ask, putting on as much of a commanding air as he could manage, considering his voice and the absurd angle of his pince-nez glasses which were held lop-sided on his nose by a piece of black ribbon.

Under his foolishness Mr James concealed the character of an old Victorian rip and he was terrified of his pious brother Kenneth. Mr James's only work was to hand us our wages every Saturday in a sealed envelope. I was warned that he would slyly pay me too much the first time – another Victorian trick – to test my honesty. Sure enough he did; he gave me fifteen shillings instead of the agreed 12s. 6d. and I had to go through the farce of explaining there had been a mistake. The expression on his face was one of immense self-congratulation at his cleverness. We liked Mr James because his daily hair-cut took place at a smart Bar near London Bridge. Everyone envied his life of folly. We indexed the letter books, putting the number of the previous letter written to the firm at the top of the flimsy page in blue chalk. This indexing took us a large part of the day, for we, as well, had to see the customers at the counter, answer the bell, and begin copying the next crop of out-going letters. Late in the morning, Mr Haylett, our boss, would go off on a round of messages in the City, carrying shipping documents, contracts, cheques and so on, and would return about 3.30, rosy in the face, smelling of cigars and scent.

'Where's he been, the dirty old man. Up Leicester Square. Lounging in the Leicester Lounge,' the other clerks would greet him enviously.

Les and I, in the meantime, went out to lunch together into the Boro' to someone's Dining Rooms, a good pull-up for carmen, near the Hop Exchange. Upstairs we ate the same food for the next year, every day; either steak and kidney pudding followed by date or fig pudding, or steak and kidney pie followed by the same. The helpings were heavy; the whole cost 8d. but went up to 10d. the following year. I was afraid of London and especially of the price of things and it was pretty well a year before I had the courage to go into the Express Dairy Café under the arches at London Bridge Station. We walked back to the office past Guy's Hospital. The clock crawled from 2 to 2.5, from 2.5 to 2.10 in the tedious afternoon. At four we had a quarter of an hour's break for tea up in the housekeeper's kitchen, I having been sent across to a little cake and tobacco shop for sugared buns. Relays of clerks came up for tea. We sat at a kitchen table looked after by a cross woman called Mrs Dunkley or – as she sometimes wrote it – Mrs Dunkerley. The clerks munched their buns and made sly remarks about how much she stole, about her corset, her bottom, what she did with her lodger, and built up fantasies about her sexual life. She (like Daulton) could be cornered into saying one of her classic sentences such as the one made to Mr Elkins, the dispatch clerk:

'Ho, Mr Helkins, I dropped the Heggs.'

Among the clerks there was the weedy lewd and sarcastic Mr Drake, a sandy-haired man who invented the day's dirty jokes and backed horses. At a desk under the long iron-barred windows, sat a respectable puffing middle-aged man with a dirty collar, the shipping clerk, his desk a confusion of bills of lading, delivery orders, weight slips. An inaccurate and over-worked man, he was always losing important documents and was often blown up by one of the angry partners, the sons of Mr Kenneth. There was Mr Clark, a dark, drawling defiant figure who looked like a boxer. He was the invoice clerk. He would stand warming himself by the fire, unmoving, even if the head cashier arrived, until the clock struck nine. If the cashier glared at him, Mr Clark stood his ground and said: 'Nine o'clock is my time.'

The arrival of the head cashier set the office in motion and something like a chapel service began. He was a tall, grizzled, melancholy man who stood at his desk calling over figures to an assistant, like a preacher at a burial. He was famous for his sigh. It was a dull noise coming from low down in his body. 'Um ha ha,' he said. And sometimes he would call to an idling clerk:

'Press on, Mr Drake.'

'Press on what?' Mr Drake would mutter.

'Your old woman,' from Mr Clark.

'I did that last night,' sniggered Mr Drake. 'The air raid upset her.'

'Sit on her head,' called Mr Clark.

Conversations that were carried across the office in penetrating mutters. The head cashier's stomach noise pleased everyone. If he left the office for a moment, it was ten to one that Mr Haylett would mimic it and bang his desk lid up and down, like a schoolboy.

About nine arrived the only two women employed in the main office – there were five sacred typists upstairs. These two women were quarrelling sisters. Women were in the post-corset, pre-brassiere period and it was the joy of the office to exclaim at the jumpings, bobbings and swingings of a pair of breasts. One lady combined a heavy white blouseful with an air of swan-like disdain.

'Things are swinging free this morning, do you not observe, Mr Clark?' Drake would say.

'Do you fancy fish for lunch?' Mr Clark would reply, nodding to the prettier sister.

The elder girl raised her nose, the pretty one shrugged her shoulders and pouted.

Hour after hour, the cashier and the swan carried on their duet.

'Feb. 2 By Goods. Cash £872 11. 4.'

And the swan answered:

'£872 11. 4.'

'Comm. and dis. £96 16. 2,' intoned the cashier. 'Um, ha, ha.' The mournful sing-song enchanted us.

At 9.30 the 'lady secretaries' arrived. They were the secretaries of the partners, their little breasts jumping too and their high heels clattering. These girls were always late.

'The troops stay so late,' sniggered Mr Drake. 'How can a working girl get to work?'

As the day's work went on, the foremen in leather aprons would come over to the office from the warehouse. They were responsible for different kinds of leather and they usually came over to settle matters arising from the chief problem of the leather trade. Most of it is sold by weight, but leather can gain or lose weight, depending upon the season and the weather. The men in the warehouse despised the 'shiny arsed clerks with their four ten a week'. Sometimes Bermondsey life would break in on us. The kids would climb up the wall and, hanging on to the bars of the office windows, would jeer at us. A clerk would be sent to drive them off, but they picked up stones and threw them at him or spattered our windows with horse manure. But often the clerk could not get out because they had tied up the door with rope. If a boy was caught and got his ears boxed, the mother would be round in a minute, standing in the office and shouting she wanted 'the bleeding fucker' who had hit her Ernie. The mothers were often hanging about in the pub next door, feeding their babies stout or a drop of port to keep them sleepy.

We worked until seven in the evening. On Saturdays we left between two and four, this depending on the mail. In the evenings I went home from London Bridge Station. In *The Waste Land* T. S. Eliot wrote of the strange morning and evening sight of those thousands of men, all wearing bowlers and carrying umbrellas, crossing London Bridge in long, dull regiments and pouring into that ugly, but to me most affecting, railway station which for years I used. I was captivated by it as I suppose every office worker is by the station in the great city that rules his life. Penn Station in New York, St Lazare in Paris, Waterloo, Paddington and Liverpool Street, are printed on the pages of a lifetime's grind at the office desk. Each is a quotidian frontier, splitting a life, a temple of the inexorable. The distinction of London Bridge Station, on the Chatham side, is that it is not a terminus but a junction where lives begin to fade and then blossom again as they swap trains in the rush hours and make for all the regions of South London and the towns of Kent. The trains come in and go out over those miles of rolling brick arches that run across South London like a massive Roman wall. There were no indicators on the platforms in my day and the confusion had to be sorted out by stentorian porters who called out the long litanies of stations in a hoarse London bawl and with a style of their own. They stood on the crowded platform edge, detected the identifying lights on the incoming engine and then sang out. To myself, at that age, all places I did not know seemed romantic and the lists of names were, if not Miltonic, at any rate as evocative as those names with which the Georgian poets filled up their lines. I would stare admiringly, even enviously, at the porter who would have to chant the long line to Bexley Heath; or the man who, beginning with the blunt and challenging football names of Charlton and Woolwich would go on to comic Plumstead and then flow forward over his long list till his voice fell to the finality of Greenhythe, Northfleet and Gravesend; or the softer tones of St Johns, Lewisham, and Blackheath. And to stir us up were the powerful trains – travelling to distances that seemed as remote as Istanbul to me – expresses that went to Margate, Herne Bay, Rochester and Chatham. I saw nothing dingy in this. The pleasure of my life as an office boy lay in being one of the London crowd and I actually enjoyed standing in a compartment packed with fifteen people on my way to Bromley North. How pleasant it was, in the war years, to stop dead outside Tower Bridge and to see a maroon go off in an air-raid warning and, even better, for a sentimentalist, to be stuck in one of those curry powder fogs that came up from the river and squashed London flat in its windless marsh.

One listened to the fog signals and saw the fires of the watchmen; there was a sinister quiet as the train stood outside the Surrey Docks. And when, very late, the train got to Bromley North and one groped one's way home, seeing the conductors with flares in their hands walking ahead of the buses, or cars lost and askew on the wrong side of the road, and heard footsteps but saw no person until he was upon you and asking where he was, one swanked to oneself that at last one had had a load of the traditional muck on one's chest.

The thing I liked best was being sent on errands in Bermondsey. They became explorations, and I made every excuse to lengthen them. I pushed down south to the Dun Cow in the Old Kent Road, eastward by side streets and alleyways to Tower Bridge. I had a special pleasure in the rank places like those tunnels and vaults under the railway: the smells above all made me feel importantly a part of this working London. Names like Wilde's Rents, Cherry Garden Street, Jamaica Road, Dockhead and Pickle Herring Street excited and my journeys were not simply street journeys to me: they were like crossing the desert, finding the source of the Niger. London was not a city; it was a foreign country as strange as India and even though I knew the Thames is a small river compared with the great ones of the world, I would patriotically make it wider and wider in my mind. I liked the Hide Market where groups of old women and children hung about the hide men who would occasionally flick off a bit of flesh from the hides: the children like little vultures snatched at these bits and put them in their mothers' bags. We thought the children were going to eat these scraps, but in fact it is more likely – money being urgent to all Londoners – they were going to sell them to the glue merchants. The glue trade haunted many busy Cockney minds. Owing to the loop of the river, Bermondsey has remained the most clannish and isolated part of London; people there were deeply native for generations. Their manner was unemotional but behind the dryness, there was the suggestion of the Cockney sob.

'What'll y'ave? Lovin' mem'ry or deepest sympathy?' the woman in the shop asked when I went to buy a mourning card for one of our office cleaners.

I would pass the Tanners Arms and wonder at the peculiar

fact that the owner had a piece of tanned human skin 'jes like pigskin'. The evenings came on and a procession of women and children would be wheeling their mattresses up to the railway tunnels or the deep tube station to be safe from the occasional raids. I would see other office boys wearing their bowler hats as I wore mine: we were a self-important, cracked-voice little race, sheepish, yet cocky, regarding our firms with childish awe.

But my work was dull. The terrible thing was that it was simple and mechanical; far, far less difficult than work at school. This was a humiliation and, even now, the simplicity of most of the work in offices, factories and warehouses depresses me. It is also all trite child's play and repetition and the correcting of an infinitude of silly mistakes, compared with intellectual or professional labour. Most people seemed to me, then, and even now, chained to a dulling routine of systematized and tolerated carelessness and error. Whatever was going to happen to me, I knew I must escape from this easy, unthinking world and I understood my father's dogged efforts to be on his own, and his own master. In difficulty lay the only escape, from what for me seemed to be deterioration of faculty.

The dullness, the long hours, the bad food, the low pay, the paring away of pleasure to a few hours late on Saturday afternoon, the tedious Sundays brightened only by that brief hour at the Sunday School – all these soon stunned and stunted me in my real life however much they moved me to live in my imagination. I accepted, with the native London masochism, that these were hard times and that this was to be my life. London has always preferred experience to satisfaction. I saw myself a junior clerk turning into a senior clerk comfortable in my train, enjoying the characters of my fellow travellers, talking sententiously of the state of affairs in France, Hong Kong and Singapore and, with profound judiciousness, of the government. Over the years one would know these season ticket holders – perhaps not speaking to them – as well as the characters in a novel. Sometimes there was an oddity – the man who read Virgil as he travelled up and down. And there was always, for diversity, the girls who knitted for the soldiers and read novels. There was also the pride I felt in being enslaved in a city so world-famous, in being submerged in its brick, in being smoked and kippered by it. There was the curious satisfaction, in these months, of a settled fate and the feeling that here was good sense and, under the reserve, humour and decency.

But the office was brutalizing me. One morning I arrived and began teasing Daulton, the other office boy. He was slow and childish. I was trying to make him say: Parson's Kway. He would take that from a clerk but not from an equal. He saw an enemy and flew at me. It was delightful: it was like being at school again. We were soon rolling on the floor and I was laughing, but he, I saw, was savage. Old Haylett wobbling up from the W.C. found us dishevelled in the dust. He put a stop to it and Daulton, trembling, began to cry. What had I done to him? He was afraid of getting the sack. Haylett took his side. So did the clerks. Daulton was their joke and treasure. I was spoiling it. When the cashier came he called me over and I said we were only 'having a game'. 'You have upset Daulton,' the cashier said gravely. 'I am surprised at a boy like you wrestling with a boy of that type. You went to a better school than he did.' And I who had thought that Daulton and I were fellow victims! Daulton gave me a look of pompous disapproval and wistful reproach after this. The matter went on being debated by the cashier and the clerks, and I saw that I was in serious trouble. It was discussed with one of the partners. I became scared when he sent for me and came away incredulous. I was to be promoted. I was to go into the warehouse and learn the trade.

My life became freer and more interesting at once and I scarcely spoke to Daulton after that.

The firm was run by Mr Kenneth whose chauffeur brought him up from the country at ten. Mr Kenneth came in burdened like Abraham and went, knees bent, in a fast aged shuffle, like a man stalking, to his office where he was soon ringing his bell. About the same time his four sons arrived, four quarrelling men between thirty-seven and fifty years old. The firm was a working model of that father-dominated life which has been typical of England since the Elizabethan age and perhaps always, for we must have got it from the Saxons and the Danes. In the Victorian age, with the great increase in wealth, the war between fathers and sons, between older brothers and younger, became violent, though rather fiercer in the middle-class than among manual workers where the mother held the wage packet. Until 1918 England was a club of energetic and determined parricides; in the last generation the club appears to have vanished altogether. So, in their various ways, Mr James, Mr Frederick, Mr William and Mr John, active and enterprising City men, were at war with each other and attacking Father when one or other of them was in favour. Mr John the youngest and most genial, was the only one to regard the fray with grinning detachment. He sat on the opposite side of his father's desk, unperturbed.

Mr James was the eldest, a precisionist and cultivated and intelligent man; he dealt in heavy leather. Mr Frederick, handsome, dashing and hot-tempered, whose eyes and teeth flashed operatically, was in foreign hides, a very speculative market; he lived in a fine house in Regent's Park; Mr John drawled a shrewd and lazy life among fell-mongers and raw pelts; Mr William, to whom I fell, had an office on the warehouse floor and dealt in basils and skivers, i.e. tanned sheepskins. On this subject, under his teaching, I was to become an expert.

The British merchant has the reputation of being a deep and reserved, untalkative fellow, slow to act until he is certain, not easily deceived and a shade lazy. The four brothers entirely contradicted this legend, except in one respect: they were not easily deceived. Reserve they had none. They talked and shouted their heads off, they exposed their passions, they were headlong in action, as keen and excitable as flies and worked hard. Mr William was the most emotionally self-exposing of the brothers. He was a sportsman who had played hockey for England, a rather too ardent and too reminiscent golfer and extrovert. Owing to a damaged knee he was rejected for the Army during the war. His emotionalism annoyed his brothers. He would come into the office crying out: 'Father hates me. James has been telling Fred . . .' and so on, a wounded and sulky man. What their differences were I don't know; but they were strong enough to break up the firm when the old man died.

I had often known the chapel-like groans of the main office to be interrupted by a pair of these storming brothers who pranced in a hot-tempered ballet. There had to be a peacemaker or catalyst and there was.

When I described the arrivals at our office there was one figure I did not mention: a dandy called Hobbs. For some reason he was not called *Mr* Hobbs and these were the days before people called anyone but a servant or a workman by Christian or nickname. The voice in which Hobbs was addressed was reverent; it might have been used to a duke who had, for some reason, condescended to slum with us all; it was a tone of intimacy, even of awe. He was on simple, equal terms with everyone from the old gentleman down to the boys. One finds his type more often in the north of England than in the south, and indeed he came from Leeds and had a faint, flat weary Yorkshire accent. His speech was plain but caressing. He had walked into the business, in his deceptively idle way, some years before and discreetly appointed himself to be the brains of the firm. To everybody and to me especially, he was the only person to whom I could talk. He was a man of about thirty.

One saw him, a tall thin figure, a sort of bent straw, but paddling down Weston Street early in the winter mornings, in his patent leather shoes, his fur-lined overcoat reaching to his ankles, his bowler hat tipped back from a lined forehead and resting, because of the long shape of his head, upon a pair of the ugliest ears I have ever seen. His little remaining hair rose in carefully barbered streaks over the long, egg-like head. A cigarette wagged in his mouth, his face was pale, seamed, ill and amused. Hobbs was a rake and his manner and appearance suggested days at the races and evenings at the stage door of the Gaiety, and the small hours at the card table. He looked as if he were dying – and he was – the skull grinned at one and the clothes fluttered about a walking skeleton.

Eyes bloodshot, breath still smoking gin or whisky of the night before, he arrived almost as early as the office boys in order to get at the office mail before anyone else saw it. He memorized it; he was now equipped to deal with all the intrigue, quarrels and projects. By some nervous intimation he knew whenever a girl came into the office and he smiled at them all and his large serious eyes put them into a state. To all, at some time or other, he said 'Darling, I'd like to bite your pretty shoulders.' Except to the dragon, the old man's secretary, who often handed out religious tracts. She saw in Hobbs, no doubt, an opportunity for rescue and he deferred to her and started reading a line or two of the tracts at once while she was there and making expert comments on a passage in Exodus or Kings, so that the old lady began to blush victoriously. Girls liked to be caught in the warehouse lift with him for he instantly kissed their necks and looked their clothes over. His good manners overwhelmed Mrs Dunkley-Dunkerley in her kitchen. All office work stopped, even the cashier stopped his call-over of the accounts, when Hobbs went to the telephone and smiling at it, as if it were a very old raffish crony, ordered a chauffeur-driven Rolls to collect him in the evening and pick up one of his girls to take them to dinner at the Ritz. The partners listened to him in fright, wondering aloud about his debts, but would soon be confiding in him, as everyone else did and be angling for his advice.

'Look what Father has done. James has told Father that Fred ...' – Hobbs who always wore his bowler hat in the office and was the only one who was allowed to smoke, nodded and listened with religious attentiveness. The appearance of physical weakness and dissipation was a delusion. The firm chin, strong coarse mouth, the rapidity of mind, were signs of great nervous strength. The partners were gentlemen of the cheerfully snobbish kind. Hobbs was an intellectual from a provincial university who had read a lot and was a dilettante. His brain was in a continuous and efficient fever. If trade was slack and he had no business or customers to deal with, he'd go round the office and, with a smile that they could not resist, would take the clerks' pens from them with a 'By your leave, laddie' and do all their accounts and calculations in a few minutes while they gaped at him. Their lives were ruled by having to work out exasperating sums as, for example, 3 cwt. 2 quarters 9 lbs. at 3s. 4½d. per lb. less commission and discount of 3½ per cent. He could do scores of sums like these in a few minutes. Or, for amusement, he would tot up the head cashier's ledgers so fast that this sorrowing and very pious man would look over his glasses with admiration and momentarily forgive Hobbs his obvious debauches. With the workmen he was the same; he got them out of the laborious messes they made of their weighing slips, gave them racing tips, was knowing about prize fights and once in a while would buy them a drink in the pub next door where he was well known. Where was he not well known!

'Out of the great kindness of your heart, duckie,' I've heard him say to the barmaid of a discreet hide-out near London Bridge, 'would you give me a rather large gin and French?'

I had to work with Hobbs and soon, infatuated, I dressed exactly as he in white coat and bowler hat, pushing it back over my ears in helpless admiration of him. I had to sit with him and keep the Epitome Book a summary of the hundreds of letters that came in. I have always been prone to intellectual disaster. For years I thought this book was called the Opitomy Book, for I used to think of Epitome as a three syllable word.

I was enraptured by Hobbs. For a boy of sixteen is there anything like his first sight of a man of the world? I was enraptured by London Bridge, Bermondsey and the leather trade. I liked its pungent smell. I liked watching the sickly green pelts come slopping out of the pits at the leather dresser's down the street, I liked paddling among the rank and bloody hides of the market; I would cadge the job of cutting the maggots of the warble fly out of a hide in our hide shed. I liked the dirty jobs. I wanted to know everything I could about leather. Gradually, literature went out of the window: to be a leather factor, or, better still, a country tanner was my dream. I spent my days on the seven floors of the warehouse, turning over dozens of calf skins with the men, measuring sheepskins and skivers and choking myself with the (to me) aromatic shumac dust. At home the family edged away from me: I stank of the trade. With my father and me it was a war between Araby and the tanpit.

The leather trade is an interesting trade, for skins and hides are as variable as nature. At certain seasons, in the breeding season, for example, the skin will be hard and 'cockled'; heavily woolled sheep like the merinos drag the surface of the leather into ridges so that the body of some old man seemed to lie under my measuring ruler. Some skins are unaccountably greasy and have to be degreased; others may have heated in the hold of a ship; yet others may have been over-salted by a tanner who perhaps hopes when the temperature rises, that they will pick up moisture and weight. After a time one could tell from which town and county of England any skin came and from which tannery, for each tanner had his own methods, his peculiar waters and style. The names were cheerful: skivers and basils, shoulders, bellies, split-hide bellies and butts – the animals seemed to lie ba-aaing and lowing, as one looked at the grain of the skins for their quality or their defects; to see which could be dyed in red or green, say, or which – owing to the flaws in the grain, would have to be dyed in the cheaper black. There was change in every bale that the crane lifted off the vans and heaved into the 'gaps' where the men chalked the tally on the walls. And change in the human scene too. On market days, many of the tanners came to the office. They came mainly from the small towns of England and the variety of character fascinated me. A brash bearded fellow in a cowboy hat who came roaring in and shouting that we were 'a lot of stuckup London snobs' and his money was as good as ours; the trembling pair of elderly black-bearded brothers from Dorset who stood together, shoulders touching, like Siamese twins and had the suspicious and dour look of conspiring lay preachers; the flash Welshman; the famous sole leather man from Cumberland; the sad country gentleman tanner from Suffolk; the devastating fashionable tycoon who was making a fortune, wore a monocle, was something to do with Covent Garden Opera and introduced me to the name of Flaubert.

In due time I was sent down to the wharves of Pickle Herring Street or the docks, to make reports on damaged skins that had been dropped into the river, or on thousands of bales which had come in from Australia. A literary job: as the bales were opened for me in these warehouses that smelled of camphor or the mutton-fat smell of wool or rancid furs, I wrote in my large book, an estimate and a description. It was curious to open a bale from the ship or barge alongside and to see, as one got to the centre of it, that it was blackening with heat and at the centre, charred and cindery. When I grew up and read Defoe's *Complete English Tradesman* I knew the pleasure he felt in the knowledge of a trade, its persons and its ways. If I knew nothing else, at the end of four years I was proud of my knowledge of leather. It was a gratifying knowledge. During the last war I had to spend some time in shipyards on the Tyne and the Clyde and the passionate interest in a craft came back to me; and although I was then an established writer, I half wished I had spent my life in an industry. The sight of skill and of traditional expertness is irresistible to me.

My absorption in the leather trade went to comical lengths. Father had bought a fat encyclopaedia, second hand, and dated 1853; I discovered in it a full technical account of the tanning process. I decided to tan a skin myself. I got a small tank, brought home some shumac and then considered the process. First I had to get an animal and then skin it: then, either by pasting it on the flesh side with a depilatory, or letting it heat to the point of decay that is not injurious to the skin, I would have to scrape off the hair. There were superficial skins to remove. I would then have to place it in the proper liquids, having first transferred it for a time to a tank of fermented dog dung in order to soften it. And so on. The difficulty was to find an animal small enough. Our dog? Our cat? One of our rabbits? The thought sickened me. A mouse? There were plenty in the house. I set a trap and caught one. But it was pretty and the prospect of letting its skin sweat and removing the fur with my fingers repelled me. I gave up the idea.

In my second year in the trade, in the summer holiday, I hired a bicycle and went up to Ipswich, stopping at a country tannery on the way. It belonged to the sad gentleman farmer. He gave me lunch and I showed off to his pretty daughter. After lunch he took me round the tannery. This was the life, I thought, as I walked round the pits: to be a country gentleman, marry this nice girl and become a tanner. There might be some interesting erotic social difficulties of the kind that occurred in *John Halifax, Gentleman* by Mrs Craik, a novel that fed my daydreams at this time. The pits were laid out like a chequer board and we walked between them. I was in the midst of this daydream when I slipped and I fell up to the neck into the cold filthy ooze of the pit. A workman hooked me out on his pit pole before I went under, for these pits are deep; I was rushed to a shed, stripped and hosed down. Stinking, I was taken back to the house, and dressed up in an assortment of clothes, including a shooting jacket much too large and a pair of football shorts belonging to the tanner's ten-year-old son. The nice girl had left to laugh in her room.

This was my baptism into the trade; now I think of it, the only baptism I have ever had.

I was happier in my hours in the leather trade than I was at home; and strangely, I believe, the encouragement to think again of being a writer came from people in the trade. One or two of the customers saw the books I was reading on my desk and I discovered that many of these businessmen knew far more about literature than I did. There was the tycoon with his Flaubert – whom I did not read for years – there was Beale, the leather dresser, who recited Shakespeare at length, as we went through the skivers on the top floor; there was Egan, our foreman, a middle-aged and gentle man with a soft voice who, in between calling orders to the men and going over his weighing slips, would chat to me about Dickens and Thackeray. Once a month he would get blind drunk for a few days and then return, otherworldly and innocent, to have a bookish talk. There was a leather belting manufacturer who introduced me to literary criticism. They were amused by my naïvety; but when they got down to their business affairs with Mr William and the watching of the market, I realized that although I knew a lot about leather, I knew nothing about trade and money, and that the ability or taste for making it was missing in me. Beale, the Shakespearean, showed that to me. He was a man of fifty who had inherited his business and was always in straits and was rather contemptuously treated in the trade because of his incompetence. He took me round his works and looked miserably at the rollers that came down from their arms, striking the skins, with a racket that he could not stand. 'Keep out of it,' he said. 'Unless you know how to make money, it is no good.'

Hobbs sat or dangled from his high stool and said 'Journalism's the life, laddie. You read too many classics. You ought to read modern stuff. Journalists are the bright lads. What about W. J. Locke?'

I saw it at once when I read *The Beloved Vagabond*, *The Morals of Marcus Ordeyne* and *Septimus*, that Hobbs had modelled himself on Locke's gentlemanly, Frenchified Bohemianism.

A bottle of wine, a French mistress was his ideal – often realized; at any rate he had soon established one of the new women who came to the firm, the widow of a French soldier, in his flat. There was Thomas Hardy, too, he said, and Arnold Bennett. So I threw up the classics and took to the open (French) road with Locke as a successor to Stevenson; and a precursor to Belloc. I had discovered the writers I really admired: the travellers. I bought most of the books I read, and had done so at school too, by spending my food money on them. I gave up the Dining Rooms and the Express Dairy; instead in the lunch-hour I bought a bar of chocolate or a packet of biscuits and a book for a few pence at a shop near the arches at the station, walked across London Bridge and went on lunch-hour tours of the Wren churches – to the organ recitals at St Stephen's in Walbrook and St Dunstan's in the East and to St Magnus the Martyr in Billingsgate. I knew I should admire the Wren churches but they bored me. The classical Italian beauty of St Stephen's in Walbrook seemed cold to the clerkly follower of Ruskin; cold and also – to a dissenter – moneyed and even immoral. The elegant St Mary Woolnoth and even St Magnus the Martyr and its carvings, seemed to me as 'worldly' as the boardrooms of banks. And in Southwark Cathedral I had an experience of the 'mechanical' worship of the Church of England. A young clergyman sitting at a harmonium in one of the aisles was teaching another the correct intonation of

'The Lord be with you'
and the response
'And with Thy spirit'
which they repeated dozens of times, trying to get it right. Now I could admire; then I scowled like a Bunyan at 'vain repetitions'.

The one real church, for me, was St Bartholomew's. I visited these churches as a stern cultural duty, but also out of a growing piety towards the London past. The pleasure was in the organ recitals held in the lunch-hour. Lately introduced by our neighbour to Sibelius and Rachmaninoff, I now was entranced by Bach's fugues. This taste was literary and due to Browning; all my tastes were conventionally Victorian. The monocled tycoon who had revolutionized the tanning of sheep-skins, heard with horror of my unfashionable ideas. I seemed irredeemably backward and lower class and the cry of the autodidact and snob broke out in me in agony 'Shall I never catch up?'

I soon knew the alley ways of the city and intrigued to be sent to Ministries in Westminster. I ventured into Fleet Street and stared longingly at newspaper offices. Often I longed to be in love; but I was already in love with London, and although too shy to go into pubs – and hating anyway the taste of beer – I would listen to the rattle of dominoes among the coffee tables of the Mecca as far north as Moorgate, and obscurely feel my passion. I even walked from Bermondsey to Westminster. To love, travel is almost the complete alternative; it is lonely, it is exhausting, but one has lived completely by one's eyes and ears and is immolated in the world one is discovering. When, at last, I did find a girl, all we did was dumbly walk and walk round London Streets till I dropped her at her office door. When I read books of the glamour-of-London kind, I was disappointed with myself and tried to whip myself up into a glamorized state, for I could not see or know what the writer knew; but a London of my own was seeping into me without my knowing it and, of course, was despised because it was 'every day experience'.

One summer morning when I was on the heavy leather floor of our building, I heard the impudent whistle of Atterbury, the foreman of the floor. He was a cross-eyed, jeering little fly, known to everyone as Ankleberg.

'I got a nice birthday present this morning,' he shouted. 'My old woman give it me. Somethink I coulda done without. Same as last time, same as time afore that – nine bleeding times! Another bleeding kid. And no lie either.'

He had an accusing manner.

'Know what the woman next to her in hospital said to the doctor? "E's never off me".'

Ankleberg stared and, then, he shouted with laughter and went off looking like the devil. He was the man who let me have a go at cutting maggots out of some cow-hides in return for loading a van with them.

'Here Ankle,' said his mate but coming over to me and opening a wallet. 'This is what you want.' And showed him a packet of French letters.

'Dirty bastard,' said Ankleberg. 'You'll get some poor girl into trouble.'

Our talk was stopped by a curious sound of pumping and hammering going on in the sky and we went over to the gap. The sound was gunfire.

'Stone me, it's bleeding Fritz,' said Ankleberg.

Up we went in the warehouse lift.

'Nine little hungry mouths,' said Ankleberg on the way up. 'What d'you make of that, son?'

We got on to the roof. Not far off, high in the sky over the Tower of London and coming westward were a dozen German aircraft. They looked like summer gnats in the clear sky and around them hundreds of little cherub-like bursts of anti-air-craft fire were pocking the blue. Sudden bursts of bomb smoke came stepping along the Thames towards St Paul's, where black and green clouds went up from the roofs: and then, down our way the aircraft came. In the street people were watching the planes, most of our staff were there and they ran indoors when a bomb fell; some said on a printing works in Newcomen Street near by, or in the Boro'.

In a minute or two the raid was over. I was looking at the fires near St Paul's. I tried to ring my father. There was no answer. I got permission to go and see if he was all right; but in fact I was longing to see the damage. It was, for those days, startling. A flight of aircraft had bombed London for the first time by day. Over London Bridge I went down the steps by St Magnus the Martyr into Billingsgate and saw the street walls of several houses and wharves had been stripped off, carts were overturned and horses lay dead among the crowds. The pubs in Bermondsey had filled with women pouring drink into them-selves and their babies as I left; it was the same in Billingsgate. Outside a pub at the Monument, on the very spot where the old fire of London had started, one of those ragged and wild-looking women street singers with enormous plumes in her coster hat was skirling out a song, luscious with Cockney sentiment and melodrama: 'Cit-ee of larfter, Cit-ee of tears'. I kicked my way through little streets of broken glass in Little Britain and, passing the stink of burning chemical works, reached my father's office. The flames of the fire were so hot that he and I could not stay on his roof.

I went down to Alleyn's School one Saturday. The war became dispiriting, dragging and hungry. The casualty lists stretched half-way round the school hall. Appleyard the captain and cross-country champion was killed. Stevens with the strong glasses and the smutty mind had been washed off his ship in the Atlantic. Lake, our best cricketer had lost an arm and would not bowl again, gentle Pace had been killed. Appleyard's death chilled me. For days I could think of nothing else. He had been so far above me, the hero; and, yet, once seeing me across the street, he had waved to me.

Cycling on Saturdays in the country, I was obsessed by the trench war and I spun along, converting the countryside into a battlefield. Every hill, every bridge and road became part of an imaginary war game. On summer nights when the wind was blowing gently from the south, we would sit on our lawn listening, as I have already said, to the murmur of the barrage from across the Channel, hour after hour. Sometimes I went home by Charing Cross and would arrive at the station when a hospital train arrived and men unrecognizable and covered from head to foot in trench mud and weighed down with filthy kit got off it, while the bloodily bandaged wounded were being hustled into scores of ambulances. The flower girls threw their flowers in after them. Romantically I saw myself going to the war and was depressed because I was too young, yet I was terrified too. It was all a daydream, of course, for if I had had more spirit and had been a less sickly-minded animal I might have got through by lying about my age. Many tough boys did. I was a small, thin, genteel and timid sentimentalist, dreaming the idea, afraid of the fact. By 1918 the reality came nearer. I got my father to apply for me to get into the Royal Flying Corps – it is strange that I did not apply myself, but it would not have occurred to me to do anything without my father's permission. I had no will except his; only my secret will. And anyway he told me – and I believed him – he would have to 'see a man', it would require weeks of negotiation, I was not yet eighteen. There was also, he pointed out, the spiritual side of the matter. If the Divine Mind wanted me to go into the Flying Corps I would undoubtedly find myself in it. We must not 'outline'; we must wait for a 'demonstration'. I must do my best by not letting 'Error into consciousness'. To do that I must stop seeing 'that girl' he had heard I'd been seen out with. I had met one of the Sunday School girls on the train and – with reckless daring – I had been to tea with her, and sung the war-time song while her sister played the piano:

> God send you back to me
> Over the rolling sea.

Father was horrified to hear that I had a girl.

'Soon,' he said, 'she'll be calling you "her boy". A man in my office has just had to pay out £400 because his young son got a girl into trouble in his office. I want you to know I haven't got £400. I warn you. I made a great mistake myself. I married too young. A girl *has* to find a boy – that's, well, it's her trade, her living. I want you to stop that, at once, d'you hear. If you want to know about love, read what Mrs Eddy says.'

I was sunk in morbid thoughts and fancies, muddled by ambitions, sexual desire and boredom. Life at the leather warehouse was a relief but my infatuation with the trade was fading. I bought a deep winged stiff collar in order to look like Sir James Barrie whose photograph I had seen in a magazine called the *Bookman;* the effect was spoiled by a large bleeding spot on my throat, a spot I picked away at, so that it lasted for most of a year; at times I thought I had caught anthrax from a cattle sore in the hide shed and saw an early death. As I have said I had no interest in buying and selling, but I enjoyed the characters of the people in the trade. Story after story walked into the warehouse and I entertained my mother (and sometimes my father), with them when I got home.

Occasionally in the relations of these people I saw analogies with the relations of my father and myself.

There was an old red-faced coster, an angry and effervescent little Cockney who dealt in cheap loads of chamois skins, sometimes only two inches long, the torn off pieces, almost worthless, which he sold to the 'sponge' trade. Men like him, who had begun life by pushing barrows often made a tidy fortune, bought a slum house or two and became men of property. He lived in an alley called Wilde's Rents. He made state visits to us twice a year with his son, looking at every little piece and muttering.

'What's the bloody use of this? Rubbish. Let's have a look at the other bale.' And he would turn on his son and say, 'What's the bleeding idea, bringing me down to look at this lot?'

The son, a weedy and pale, dressed-up young man of thirty-five, would cringe and wince and make a curious sound, like 'Tit-tit' with his teeth. After the father had denounced his son several times he'd turn to me and say, admiring, 'He's educated up like you, a proper little toff.'

The next day the father would send the son on his own. He came sniffling and tit-titting, a young man, terrified of his father who indeed looked as though he'd bite your leg like a dog. The son had literary pretensious too, but of a political kind. He was a book-learned Anarchist.

'The European *bourgeoisie* is destroying itself,' he confided to me. 'Did you ever read Kropotkin? Tit, tit, tit. The Russian?'

Oh, not another writer!

'Marx?' he said.

Well, I have read about the Russian revolution in the papers.

'We've had nothing but propaganda for years,' he said.

For ten days, first father and then son came in, until at last Mr William would shout at the father:

'Come on, you old rogue. What's the price? 4s. 6d.?'

'Four and six, you're out of your bleeding mind – I wouldn't give a tanner. It's a waste of my time, isn't it, Dick?'

'Tit. Tit. Tit. We'd never sell it, Father,' said the obedient son.

'Sell it!' cried the old man. 'Wouldn't get it home. Couldn't give it away. I try to teach this boy the business and what happens? Dresses himself up like a toff, he doesn't know his arse from his elbow. Well, Dick, what d'you say. What's it worth?'

'Tit. Tit. Tit. I wouldn't touch it,' said his son.

'Hear what he says?' said the old man triumphantly. 'What did I tell you?'

In the end a bargain was struck; Father blew his chest out and paid for tons of this stuff in dirty pound notes, with a last battle about how much off for cash.

'Never had a bank account, no not me. Where would I be now if I'd had a bank account – I'll tell you. Down the drain! I seen it. What he calls' – pointing to his son – 'bloody capitalism'.

'That's it. Tit. Tit. Tit.'

'See what I mean – doesn't know he's born. Come on, son, you let your old dad be twisted again. I'll never train the lad, he thinks he's bought the street.'

On one of his visits the son went on about Anarchism.

'If he had the orders,' he said to me, 'I say *if* he had the orders, a true Anarchist would even kill his father and mother. You've got to follow the logic of it.'

'Would *you*?'

'Wait a minute – I said *"If he gets the orders"*. If they come, well – tit, tit, tit, you've got to admit the logic.'

The pair seemed to parody my life.

The war ground to a stop. On Armistice Day, people say, London went mad. I saw nothing of it. Some in Bermondsey didn't believe it and took their mattresses up to the tube or the arches, just in case. There was a bonfire in the yard at Guy's Hospital and a fireman's helmet was stuck on top of the statue there. We got off an hour earlier, but Mr Kenneth worked late. Father was late home too. He had celebrated with Miss H at the Albert Hall, singing 'Land of Hope and Glory', and he had his wallet stolen. He was rather pleased, as if he had done an extra something for the country.

CHAPTER ELEVEN

Now the war was over Father was exuberant. He had always had bounce: in the last two years he had bounced up high. Being away from us, in Hertfordshire, had freed and rejuvenated him. Mother said getting away from Miss H had done him good too.

We sat long after Sunday meals while he spoke to us about his new life. He had lodged in a pretty country inn. He told us, in a bashful poetic way, what he had had for breakfast and for dinner and what fine houses there were in the country near by – houses with barns and stabling, billiard rooms, a cottage for the staff: he wanted one. He had (he said, lowering his eyes modestly), joined a riding-school. He had fallen in love again, this time with a couple in the handbag trade, real live wires. They drank this new drink: cocktails.

Did you have one, Dad? we asked. He may have had one, just out of politeness – Sportscar or Sidecar, oh yes and a White Lady, too, he said. He did not drink alcohol – we never had even a bottle of beer in the house – but he did keep a bottle, he said, of 'Chartroos' in his office in case a customer came. Grandfather and Mrs Eddy had kept him off drink; in fact he had drunk nothing since his twenties when he had had a calamitous bottle of Guinness on a rough sea on the way to Belfast. He was proud of this crime later on in his life when he gave us a glass of gin.

The war had changed everything. The stuffed, quilted and cushioned Edwardian age had gone; the age so soft for the bottoms of the comfortably off, so mean and bitterly exacting for the struggling, small man, so wretched for the poor. The old family and personal businesses were being shaken – the quarrels of those brothers in the leather trade were a symptom. The new order was appearing in the great organizations like the aircraft firm. At first when he went to work there, Father was a mere letter stamper in the Registry which was in confusion. He could not bear disorder, so, always with an eye cocked for opportunity, he discreetly promoted himself. And then went on promoting himself. But he was not, by nature, an organizational man; he scorned the intrigues by which one gets a 'title', creates a small empire, conquers other empires and is finally at the top of the organization, protected by secretarial outposts. Father's technique was different. He cultivated a look of owning the place, and sailed up alone to the position of general meddler. 'I prefer to do things personally.' His life as a salesman had taught him to start from the top.

The artist in him must have died at this time; and was succeeded by the impresario. From the way he told it, he seems to have converted himself into a Maskelyne and Devant — we had apparently often sent him, at our expense too, to these magic shows and he gave us exciting accounts of them. One had the impression that a curtain went up in the aircraft manufactory, that a soft explosion of pink flame and smoke was heard, and there stood Father, the magician, creating scores of new offices, typing pools, drawing offices, executive suites and board rooms; and, what was more important, ordering furniture on a lavish scale for them. Carpeting and linoleum he must have bought by the square mile. He was pursued by all the nabobs of the furniture trade. He purred from one to the other, in chauffeur-driven cars. There was always something of the chairman and mine host about him — he had the proper waist measurements and courtliness — and he was soon dropping names so high-up in government and in aviation that Mother's underlip began to shake with fright, and the rest of us choked at the sound of them. He brought menus back from Claridges and the Ritz and went over the dishes for our benefit. We were proud to have him eat on our behalf and admired the new sad look of the gourmet under his eyes.

Our salesman had become one of the great buyers; and he did not forget us in this new occupation. There had been many periods in our lives when our various houses had no stair-carpets and when neighbours complained of the clatter we made on our boards; wardrobes, cupboards and chests were unknown in our bedrooms. Now everything changed. Father was apt when buying something, to order two of it; so we now doubled up wardrobes and chests. We had two grandfather clocks for a while, also two pianos. Out of a local hotel which was getting rid of its out-of-date furniture cheaply, Father got an enormous sideboard from the main dining-room. Our mahogany, walnut, rosewood and deal stood staring at one another in a state of orphaned acrimony. They obviously had been happier elsewhere and seemed to show it. We looked like a sale-room. My mother was not forgotten. New cleaners and polishers came in and a peculiar thing called an O'Cedar Mop. This gift, she put away in a cupboard, going every now and then to look at it and swear at it, as if it were yet another woman in her life; and I think my brother who was mechanically minded, thoughtfully broke it. Mother was one for mat, knees, a pail of water and a scrubbing brush.

It was only fair that Father should think of himself sometimes. He did not obtrude this upon us. Trips to Bond Street kept him supplied with pieces of old silver, bowls, salvers, cruets, and engraved and crested objects, which he privately took up to his bedroom and modestly concealed among his pants and vests. Mother used to note this and go through his underclothes on the quiet to see what new treasure was there.

The words of the Christian Science hymn return to me.

> Day by day the manna fell
> Oh to learn that lesson well.

This was undoubtedly the lesson of the war. The Divine Mind had shown Father not to limit his thinking. The ominous words came out one day:

'I can't breathe. I feel I can't breathe.' And the expression on his dark face was so agonizingly sincere that we were all affected.

Now the war was over it was a shock for him to come back to work full time in a small business which had modestly survived. The busy and economical Miss H had seen to that. Mother wished Miss H had married. Father went pale with anxiety when she said that. It remained for him to take note of the changed times and demands and to go off and see his old customers. One of his first acts was to buy a large quantity of heavy brocades at a high price. Miss H became angry. The price fell at once and for the first time in its history, the firm showed a loss.

'Accountants can prove anything with figures,' Father said and dismissed the matter.

Father considered the new situation in his business. Miss H told him that they must have orders. Father said, No. First principles first: he must have Right Ideas. One of these was a larger showroom and workrooms, large premises at a corner, where the world could see them. In the next few months, he brought home the plans of several likely places and we cleared the table quickly so that he could spread them out. In these schemes he was frustrated by the cautious Miss H who was getting stricter with him. She reminded him that he was not manufacturing aeroplanes, but cushions and tea-cosies, and novelties. Father said that you could not limit the Infinite. He retreated all the same, and fell to designing a trademark or symbol for his products.

'We'll ask the Professor to design one since he's always telling us what a brain he's got.' (I was the Professor.)

He decided on one of his own designs: the simple letters SP, after that the words: 'The Sign of Quality'. He walked about the room saying it aloud. It was poetry to him – but should the S be entwined with the P?

Frustrated in his desire for larger premises, Father moved to the dream of getting a larger house.

There was an urgent reason for buying a larger house. We were chocked with furniture and now, secretly – it took a couple of years for the secret to come out – he had bought a grand piano and it would have been impossible to get it into any of our crowded rooms. Yet, if the Divine Mind had manifested itself in the form of a piano, this Mind would inevitably supply a place for it to go into. He was obliged to store the piano until accommodation for it 'unfolded'. Often, when he sat studying our dining-room, he must have been trying to fit this secret piano in; and, in fact, we were more often asked to help move the furniture round – mother's pastime.

'That old sideboard is a devil, Walt,' she would say – her only criticism of these games.

In his office while Miss H did the Day Book on the other side of the partner's desk and the typist clattered next door, Father sat back reading the estate advertisements in *The Times* and

Country Life – 'getting ideas for the Christmas trade', postponing the annual trip to Glasgow until it was too late.

Brooding on this Father said that my brother Cyril had better leave school, for it was now my sister's turn for secondary education. My brother, who hated school, loved my father even more for this gesture. It was a step to his ideal: to work in the Business. The eager boy who did not like Christian Science as much as I did was hurt to hear that the 'Divine Mind has not yet shown the way'.

But the Divine Mind did deliver a motor-car: a Sunbeam. My brother who was a good mechanic, was appeased. It appeared at Christmas. Mother threw the Appleton goose off its dish on to the dining-room floor this Christmas lunch-time, shouting: 'There it is. Eat it.' And, giving a hysterical scream, locked herself in her bedroom. The two youngest children cried. Three hours later, about four o'clock, when she was calmer, we all sat down and did eat it: mother trembling in an armchair, while we, annoyed with her, began to jeer at her. She sent looks of fear and hatred at us. Eventually she grew happier and an atmosphere of exhausted melancholy and remorse softened the room; Father brought out Sir James Barrie's novel *The Little White Bird* and read it to us with feeling; tears appeared on his cheeks when he got to the sad parts about the lost woman, and he loved the pages about undoing the 'little braces' of the strange boy and putting him to bed. After supper my brother and I played chess. We had a board but no chessmen; but we used nuts and bolts and cog wheels from a Meccano set instead.

We were a problem. I told lies about what I was doing. I was going to be a writer, but carefully said I was going to be a schoolmaster; I said I was reading when I was really writing. I said I was going out with my brother when I was really going to see a girl. Cyril and my sister were, by now, helpless stammerers. Only our youngest brother appeared to be frank and normal.

My stammering brother was denounced for being idle. He wanted to be a ship's artificer, then an engineer; Father blew up and said he could not afford the training, so the boy sneaked off and got a job in a garage. Father said it was all he was fit for, then made him leave the job. In the end my brother bought a very loud cap called a gor-blimey and went for secret joy-rides on a friend's motor bicycle.

For some reason this was the only boy allowed into our home; in fact he could not be kept out of it. He arrived in the evenings and sat with us, nodding at us and staring at us and saying nothing but occasionally murmuring private jokes with my brother. The boy was called 'Curly'. He was one of those youths with big heads and rusty voices who are born middle-aged and at sixteen look about fifty. He rarely shaved, his face was covered with eccentric, curly yellow bristles, often very long; and he had many bloody pimples. We gazed at Curly and he at us; he was covered all over, you could guess from his hands and face, with a dense golden fur and he smiled out of his personal, rather pubic, forest, looking at us with wet eyes. He looked like an ageing dog, perhaps an Airedale. He worked in a gasworks which made mother scream with laughter.

'What are your duties?' Father asked once.

'Let the kids smell the gas,' said Curly. 'When they've got colds. Their mothers bring them in and ask for a smell of it on the way to school.'

Sentences like this were not brisk; they came out slowly a few syllables at a time and were broken by long elderly sighs and meditative intervals.

Curly became important to me later on: I wrote a portrait of him.

Now my father had a motor-car, my brother was very necessary to him, for Father could not bear a drip of oil or grease on his own hands; my brother liked oil. Father was a fanatical car polisher and washer; or rather, a watcher of my brother's washing and cleaning. The car affected Father's temper and he needed someone near on which to vent it. My brother enjoyed this.

Before Father got into the driver's seat, he did 'his work' and 'knew the Divine Mind or Love' was 'the only driver'. We soon saw that the gifts of the Divine Mind were purely metaphysical; the Divine Mind was the most dangerous driver I have ever known. It hit banks, tore off the sides of hedges, chased pedestrians, scattered people about to get on buses.

'Dad, careful, you nearly hit him.'

'Don't look round,' shouted Father.

He backed clean through the end of his garage and one day on the Dover road caused a brake load of ladies to tip into a ditch; they were sitting on chairs, the chairs slid down to the side of the vehicle and one or two somersaulted out. The angry outing stood and waved their fists at him.

'Stop! Stop! Someone may be hurt,' my brother said.

'Don't look round. Don't look round. There's a law against charabancs with loose seating. I shall report them to the police,' my father said.

The car had cost a good deal. He drove it to central London one morning, taking with him an elderly and important draper and my brother. Passing by way of Dulwich, at a pleasant speed, Father shot straight across a dangerous cross-road and was hit broadside on by a steam traction-engine coming fast down the hill and was rammed into a fence. The Divine Mind, I must say, saw to it that no one was hurt – no one, that is, in the family – and out my father got and wanted to fight the driver of the traction-engine. Mother said in the evening:

'Where's that car?'

'There's something wrong with the engine. I had it sent back to the works.'

'Just like his mother, so particular, never satisfied,' said Mother, for once deceived.

The wreck was replaced by a dark-blue Daimler of archaic design; it rose, in steps from its bonnet, like a couple of boxes at the opera. So distinguished was it that it was rarely driven more than the distance between the garage up the road and our house.

I used to sit up in our attic bedroom looking down at the car and hating it. The white roads of England were vanishing: the suburbs were eating into the country. The stink of oil and petrol were already spreading. Lanes that were once deserted, were now fouled by people and machines. My old complaint returned: why had I not been born in the days of Wordsworth or Coleridge? The England of the Georgian poets had gone. It had scarcely existed, but was a last minute artifice created by them, in order to stave off the contemplation of what was really happening. I had bicycled out to country inns and had seen, for myself, that the Chesterton and Belloc pubs could not have existed for fifty years. Yet I willingly joined in the fantasy and began living the sentimentalist's double life. I never learned to drive a car – the refusal was neurotic and one of the many errors of my life.

Under the blurting excitability of adolescence was the sense of exhaustion, hopelessness and failure. I seemed to have no will and to be dragged down, as if by the reeds in a deadly green river, by dreams, and caught in the sexual miasma. The enforced chastity of youths was one of the poisons of that time; but, in fact, I supported it, for only by its curious ferocity could I concentrate on what I wanted to do. Suddenly I had an enormous success; so it seemed then. It now seems pathetic.

There are pretty public gardens of sunken walks and rockeries under tall trees, next to the Public Library in Bromley. Once or twice, on some holiday, I would sit there for a while, on a fine morning, listening to the chatter of old men sitting on the benches, or reading *Pitman's Shorthand Weekly* – for I believed all writers had to know shorthand – or looking at some potted article on French literature which told me what the Pléiade or the Three Unities were, for in France more and more seemed to me my salvation. In France I would make up for my lack of education.

'Tell me one thing that makes you think it would be a good thing to go to France' Father would ask kindly. I could not say I wanted to be free.

'It's different.'

'What is different?'

'Well, a street is called a "rue".'

'Is that all?'

I could not explain what an immense strange world lay in that word 'rue' and that words in themselves meant so much to me. Like a small brush-stroke among a million on a canvas a word seemed to me more alive than anything living.

The beauty of the garden was a torture because I could not find the words in which to describe it; and I would get up impatiently from my seat and start walking about fast, trying with a word to catch what I saw, and in vain. I would be seized by a breathless sensation for a moment or two when something real – that is to say some definable vision – would seem to be there, but the moment passed; I would fall into the dreamer's exhaustion and ennui and a feeling of meaninglessness. This has often dogged me in my life; there are palliatives but only writing and sexual love have enabled me to stand it.

I left the gardens in this empty state and went to the Library. I had read all the periodicals and so I stared at the notices. In panic I could feel the minutes passing away and then I saw the notice of a University Extension Lecture on Milton. Such are the dramas in the lives of young prigs – I was mad to go to it. It was agreed at home that I could go to it if my brother came with me.

We set off at the dangerous hour of 7.30 and parted at the corner of the street, he to the garage where Curly's motor bike was, I to the lecture.

The desire for learning in Bromley was strong. There was a large audience. The lecturer was a young woman with rimless glasses, an icy, cutting and donnish voice, who looked as pink as if she had just got out of a cold bath. She sliced the air above her respectful audience among whom, distantly, I saw Mr Hotchkiss from our church, backsliding among Milton's theology. He was covertly letting Error in. Now, at the end of the lecture, we were firmly told to submit papers on the conjunction of the Renaissance and the Reformation in Milton's art. A discussion would be held the following week, after the second lecture, on Spenser.

That week I wrote and posted my essay.

I do not remember what I said in that paper, but I do know that I had started to be interested in unusual words, in the search for the *mot juste* – as it was then called. I chose words for what I called their intensity. I wanted to be terse and exact. I wanted each word to burn into the page. My pen tortured the paper.

I posted my essay and went to the second lecture, a dreary business. My brother and I were not allowed to go out separately in the evenings. The second evening, by arrangement, he crept into the Public Library to suffer the last five minutes of Spenser. At the end we heard the lecturer discuss the Milton papers; anxiously I hoped mine would be discussed. It was not. But suddenly I heard the lecturer say, there was one paper in a class by itself, an outstanding piece of writing, obviously by a professional writer, and announced my name.

'Vic!' said my brother, giving me a punch that nearly knocked me off the seat.

'Me?' I thought I must be dreaming. I got the paper back. She had been talking about me. I took the paper home and read it and re-read it until I knew it by heart.

Now there was no doubt. I could write. My brother announced the triumph at home. Mother looked terrified of me. Father said apologetically:

'It's a great pity you had to leave school. I am sorry about it. You ought to go to evening classes. The way will be shown.'

'Well, you just write up to one of these Polytechnics, don't you?' said Mother.

'That's enough advice from you,' said Father.

'Well that's what poor Frank used to say.'

'It's not what Frank says, it's what the Divine Mind says,' said Father.

The effect on my life was immediate. I needn't go straight home from the office. I could go on to the Polytechnic in Regent Street. I was able to spend evenings alone in London. I walked from Bermondsey as a rule, over London Bridge and then by St Paul's, Fleet Street and the Strand and Piccadilly to Oxford Circus. I ventured into Soho and thought, in my innocence, that there was something sinister in those restaurants where the curtains were always drawn. I got the *Writers and Artists Year Book* and sent my essay on Milton, in the course of the next months, to a large number of papers and reviews; even to the *Leather Seller's Gazette*, announcing I was in the trade. Milton came back regularly and getting filthier and filthier.

Father got impatient about this. He opened all letters that came to the house, read them and handed them to whom they belonged. In this way, he knew about my girl and had instantly forbidden me to see her or write to her again. This led me to pick out one of his, open it and read it. It turned out to be a threat of Court Action if some debt was not paid. I had expected a storm, but the revolt failed.

'Just another circular,' Father said and threw it away and added:

'I see you are sending articles to papers. You can't afford to waste money on stamps and envelopes like that. You'll have to learn to live within your income. How much do you earn? Eighteen and sixpence? If you can afford to spend all that on stamps, you can afford to pay your mother more towards your keep.'

Now the current was in my favour. I had found one or two listeners in Bromley and, released from the need of silence and evasion at home, I must have amused them but they were good enough not to show it. Mr Hotchkiss who had given up Tolstoy for Mrs Eddy, drifted back to his Tolstoyan days and, considering my case, said that he too had had little education, but that there was an alternative: travel. He pointed that out to my father. Rich Mrs Flaxman, an exalted Norwegian with beautiful eyes, spoke of 'glorious Ibsen' and Rome and asked me to tea to meet her daughter. I tried to be in love with this dark, thin, nervous, lonely girl who snapped at me in a rich girl's way. I had a bad accent. I used to walk past her large house and past the house of another exquisite half-German girl on summer evenings, hoping to see them but I never did. And there was Mrs Norman, a busy and sprightly little woman, very outspoken, whom Father 'had to put in her place' several times, especially once when she caught him with me on the steps of the church and called out, dramatically, 'Loose him and let him go.' I was very attracted to Mrs Norman whose marriage was so happy that I half wanted to turn my parents out of the house and move Mr and Mrs Norman in. She used to wear a small white ermine necklet. Father's reply was the worst thing you could say to a Christian Scientist: 'Be careful. You are being handled by Rome.'

But I did not really want listeners. I needed the sight of a fellow recalcitrant and I found him. He had been living next door but one for years, without my knowing that he was exactly the friend I needed.

Any morning in the summer, people walking up the road would hear the sound of a piano being played. Ringing out and enchanting in its accomplishment, the sound went across the gardens, into the trees, over the road and into the fields. People opened their windows and stopped to listen. Often a delivery van would stop. Mother would stand on the kitchen doorstep. The notes of a Beethoven concerto would be struck with shameless authority and passed like a crowd of crystals into the suburban air.

'That's Frank again. He's got the windows open,' Mother said. He was a boy prodigy – it seemed – who had played in Vienna, Paris and Brussels since he was a young child. At seventeen he was a well-known professional pianist. He was French.

At home we had the impression that Father was ashamed of Mother; it may be that he was wrapped up in himself and his religion in these years; but he certainly kept his own friends from the house. 'I don't want people to see how we live,' he said. But if neighbours dropped in – which was very rarely – they were soon laughing their heads off with Mother. Frank and his French family, who were intellectuals, loved her tales.

'This town stinks, Mrs Pritchett,' Frank said to her and would start mimicking the local refined accent.

'Oh, Frank, you wicked boy.'

I took to going to Frank's house when he was practising. He had a puddingy pale face, strong short-fingered hands and wore his hair on the long side and had a musician's fur-lined coat.

We used to go out on Saturday afternoons into the town.

'This place stinks. It has a horrible smell,' he said. 'Look at these people, how they smell. They make you sick,' he called out as we went through the shopping crowds. 'The whole of England makes you sick. I hate the English – low, ignorant people.'

And he would stop and make loud vomiting sounds over the gutter.

On top of everything else the Bromley people were Protestants; he was a Catholic, the only religion that cared about art. One day he said:

'You go to that church where they don't believe in the Devil. You are a fool.'

'No, I don't believe in the Devil.'

'I've seen him. He haunts this town. He's dressed in red. He's a living person. Let's go out and you'll see him.'

192

We used to go on long hate walks, looking for the Devil. We would give up.

'He's at Sunbridge Park, I expect,' he'd say, looking at his watch.

I was refreshed by a boy who lived in his imagination and by his arrogance. Once or twice we walked round the Bromley shops, Frank making belching sounds, especially in the music shop.

'They are all ignorant and stink. Listen to the voices of those terrible girls behind the counter.' 'Ow nao we' event got eet in stock' he would call out as he went to the shop. 'Nao there's no call for Mowzart.' And then he would start making his vomiting noise or stagger about saying 'I'm going to faint. I'm going to faint' and we would leave. I sniggered, and he shocked me, but with every shock I felt a load being taken from me.

'In the war, when the air raids were on, I screamed all the time,' he would say petulantly. 'Didn't you hear me? I hate the Germans, I hate the English.' We used to talk like this in his garden while he pushed his pretty little sister on the swing. His mother was kind and gave me courage to talk French at tea.

'Why wasn't I born into an intellectual family?' I used to think when I left him. Their peaceable affection for one another astonished me.

At last, I thought, I have seen genius. I knew I had none, but Frank said I must have, because I, too, knew this was a stinking town. He and I were alike; our kind of egotism had its rights. After I was twenty I never saw him again for neither he nor I were much in England. He grew up to a distinguished career. Childish though he was, he seemed older and richer in experience than I. I saw why: he lived by the discipline of his art.

Another rebel was my cousin Hilda. She was many years older than I – born, my mother always mentioned with dreamy pride, on the same day as the Prince of Wales. Hilda, as I have told, was the daughter of my mother's sister in Ipswich. She loved my father and mother. She adored especially my father and teased him; my father's dignity went out of the window.

At school, Hilda fell in love with a learned girl called Violet. Hilda had a wild ugliness. Violet was rich, Violet was a beauty,

Violet was a rebel. She cared for nobody, men were wild about her; and all that stuffy old Presbyterian, Hilda's stepfather, could think of was how to separate the two girls, chiefly because Violet had made Hilda High Church. The two girls were threatening to become Catholics.

'My dear Aunt – I'm intoxicated by incense.'

Father's jollity went when he heard this.

Violet and Hilda had worshipped the suffragettes, of course, and had set fire to a pillar-box at Felixstowe – so they said. Mr Bugg was upset by this. He regarded himself as one of the City Fathers.

When the war came Hilda and Violet went to work in a munitions factory and came down to see us. Violet was a dark beauty with a long sensuous mouth who astonished me by asking Hilda:

'I suppose *nobody* lives here,' referring contemptuously to Chislehurst, Bromley and Bickley. 'All business, I expect.'

I realized that not only ourselves but these large wealthy neighbourhoods were beyond the pale to fashionable society and that Hilda and Violet belonged to some distant unattainable social set. When they left, Father and Mother whispered about them; they were, we gathered, leading loose lives. Father said severely that it could lead to only one thing. It led to something else. Telegrams, doctors, a Swiss sanatorium: Hilda had a haemorrhage at her factory. She had inherited the disease that had killed her father.

She was sent home, but ran away to London. She was going to set up house with Violet again. She worked on my father to persuade him to battle with her stepfather. She wanted money. She arrived looking gay and fierce, her eyes hollowed, her skin reddened, laughing at us all.

'You must stop that smoking, Hilda.'

'Why? I've still got one lung left.'

'Oh Hilda, don't dear, don't.'

It was a painful visit, but for me memorable. For years I had admired Hilda, but she had treated me as a child; now an unbelievable thing happened. I was allowed to go with her to a concert given by American Negroes who had come over to sing Spirituals' – it was their first visit to London. We had lunch at an Italian restaurant in Soho – until then I had had neither the courage nor the money to go into one, and we talked about the war poets. She and Violet knew Robert Nichols and Sassoon. Hilda, though surprisingly kind and making me feel grown up, evidently thought my literary day-dreams were idle. She took me into Hachette's and bought me a selection of Victor Hugo's poems and inscribed it with this quotation:

Seul le silence est grand, tout le reste est faiblesse. A smack in the eye.

I worshipped Hilda after this. Compared with her the Bromley girls were dull. I longed to talk to Hilda but she, I indignantly saw, was on my father's side. When I murmured about him she passed it off as if I were suffering from a well-known illness.

'I can make Uncle do anything I want,' Hilda said. 'He is a dear jolly man. You're lucky to have such a father. I adore him. I love him more than any man I've ever seen, except my own father.'

A strange remark: her father had died before she was born.

'Tilly is a famous name. My father came of a family of admirals who fought with Nelson. There was a famous Comte de Tilly who wrote Memoirs. I will get them for you.'

She leapt into romance about the melancholy facts of her father's life behind the counter at Daniels of Kentish Town. She appealed to my father on this point. She was a large young woman and flopped on to my father's knee and knocked the breath out of him.

'It is true, Uncle, isn't it?'

'You've got Beattie's imagination,' he gasped.

'Aunt,' she cried. 'You're marvellous. What did my father call you? Ecirteab Nitram.'

And they all laughed until Mother had to leave the room, crying 'Oh, it's like your father, poor Frank.'

And then, the following year, a terrible thing happened. She came to see us again. She was now feverish and ill. It was in the winter. The fogs were grey.

'Open the window. Let me sit by the open window. No, I'm very well as long as I sit by the window.'

She had run away from Ipswich after a violent quarrel with

her stepfather. She had come to my parents for money and for help again.

'You're ill,' my mother said.

'Don't voice Error,' said my father sternly. And to Hilda he said: 'If you would know the Truth through Christian Science you would get your healing.'

He was very stern and she was taken aback.

'Don't be cross with me.'

'I am voicing the Truth,' said my father.

'I am well now. There's nothing the matter with me if I sit near the window. I'm sorry if it lets in the fog. You see, I don't believe it's the Truth. Mrs Eddy was a very ignorant woman, she took drugs herself. Why did she die?'

'That's what worries me, Walt,' said my mother, taking courage.

'There you are, Uncle. Aunt can see it's a fraud. And so cruel.'

My father became angry.

'It is you who are showing your ignorance, Hilda,' he said. 'I won't have you deny the omnipotence of Divine Love in my house. You have been very wrong.'

'Uncle darling, you have never talked like this to me before . . .' she said.

'It is time you knew the Truth. Go back to your father.'

'You want me to go back to Ipswich to that mean hypocrite. I came to you for help.'

'I cannot help you, but God can,' said my father.

Angry words were spoken by my father. Hilda had fits of coughing.

'Close the window,' he said.

'No,' shouted Hilda. 'It will make me ill. Open it.'

And then Hilda sat with my mother on the sofa and sobbed on Mother's shoulder.

'Did you hear him? He has broken my heart. Why has Uncle changed? His religion is not Love, it is cruel, Aunt, cruel. I can't speak to him. Aunt, he was never like this when I was a little girl. Victor, you don't believe this, do you?'

I could not speak. I did not know what I believed, but I was afraid to speak before my father. And this was a 'scene' among the elders and we had had so many in our house that I could not bear them. I longed for peace.

We all went to bed and the next morning Father went off early to his office. Hilda came down to look for him and to say good-bye, but he had gone. She could not believe it.

'He will never see me again, Aunt,' she said. 'And he never said good-bye.'

She was indeed heartbroken. She left us. In a month she died in her stepfather's home, defeated.

The choir of Negro singers we had been to hear were all lost at sea, that year; their ship was one of the last to be torpedoed.

CHAPTER TWELVE

I COME to my last eighteen months of the leather trade and my last years at home. The wounded soldiers dressed in bright blue hospital clothes, were fewer now in the street. At one time they had often seemed to outnumber the civilians; at the office the demobilized men returned. There were gaps which Hobbs talked sadly of; but those who came back were sunburned, healthy-looking and wore new clothes. They looked like a race different from ourselves. They did not fit easily into the office. One or two left very quickly. Their experience had set them apart and the effect was to make me feel childish and cut off; this feeling lasted for some years. A youth needs the friendship of men a few years older than himself; they act as a buffer between himself and his elders. Many of the serious personal and public troubles that occurred in the next few years ended badly because of the slaughter of a generation.

In a few months after their return, the new men lost their sunburn, they got married, their clothes became shabby, their faces were thinner and more anxious until in the suburban trains they were indistinguishable from the crowd. It was not until the war books appeared eight or nine years later that young men like myself knew anything about these older ones.

But the end of the war started a number of erotic episodes in our office. Girls looked suddenly like posters, for they wore coats made of army blanketing, patterned with gaudy squares; and they showed their ankles. One afternoon Flo, one of the younger, bouncing and innocent secretaries who was engaged to be married, talked in a low excited voice – telling me to go away – to a big, red-faced dispatch clerk home from the Navy, a man as soft as a sweating Frankfurter. They were whispering about an Anglican pamphlet on sexual intercourse. He had the missionary temperament; he and his fiancée, I heard him say, undressed in his lodgings in Bromley on Sunday afternoons and lay naked and innocent beneath an army blanket reading together what one of the bishops had said. His fiancée who came to pick him up at the office one day was a huge six-footer too – a passive girl with a big milky face who seemed to low rather than speak.

Flo's large blue eyes shone and her blushes were deep. Hobbs came into the room and the dispatch clerk scurried out. Hobbs looked wearier in these days, the deep lines of his face gave it the set smile of the comic mask.

'Don't be selfish, duckie,' he said going up to Flo and adroitly pulling at the low neck of her blouse and looking inside. 'Don't save it all for *him*.'

Flo was by now a trained flouncer out of rooms. Hobbs hummed a tune.

'You can have the Latin Quarter, laddie,' he said to me with a sigh. 'Give me Saturday night in Manchester. Ask your father to let me give you a night out up West. What are you reading? Maurice Hewlett – he has a richer style than Locke.'

Hobbs did not take me up West; instead he took a temporary telephone girl, a pleasant married woman. She was the second to leave the firm to settle for a time in his flat in Parliament Hill. He arrived one morning early and putting a stool near the counter snapped his gold cigarette case at the staff, including the cashier, as they came in, saying, 'Got you'.

The cashier moaned and almost wept at the dissolution of Hobbs. An hour later, Hobbs went over and did the cashier's books, chatting as he added up, about his brother who was training for the ministry.

About this time, Mr Clark, the sullen invoice clerk, took his pretty assistant up to the chamois room. It was a small warm room with a U-shaped alley between the bins of chamois leather that reached to the ceiling. The clerks were not supposed to leave the office for the warehouse without good reason. Clark, always defiant, before the amazed eyes of all the office, snapped his fingers at the girl and off they went, she pitter-pattering obediently along, up the stairs, into the wobbling lift and up to the room.

'I've got a query,' he said as he left the office.

'Four skins short – ' Mr Drake, the lewd one, said.

Like the term 'belly splits' or 'let's have a look at the flesh side,' this was a daily office joke.

'Hobbs, Hobbs,' moaned the cashier. 'I don't like a young girl like that being in the warehouse . . .'

'Quite, sir, certainly, sir. I have to go up anyway.'

In a few minutes he came back with the girl who in a minute or two was followed by Clark. The girl was sent to work at another desk. And Hobbs and Clark sat opposite to each other, staring into each other's eyes. I brought a stock book to Hobbs in the middle of the stare.

'I've been in this trade twelve years and one thing I have learned is that chamois comes off on a girl's skirt,' said Hobbs.

'You bastard,' said Clark with one of his rare smiles. 'Just in the nick of time.'

'Don't mention it. He saved others, himself he could not save. You owe me a drink.'

The cashier groaned his private gratitude to Hobbs and Hobbs being a thorough man, took the older sister for a ride in the warehouse lift. A ride with Hobbs was always an experience and she came back with a dreamy look in her eyes. She said to the cashier that she thought poor Mr Hobbs worked too hard and sighed that she had told him he ought to have sea air. She said this in a loud dreamy voice.

'It is a shame,' she said. 'He can't get away because he has to nurse his mother. She is an invalid.'

The quarrelling sisters became reconciled after this.

I sometimes had to write a letter for Mr James, Mr Charles's eldest son and the most cultivated partner in the firm. He was married to a Frenchwoman and he recommended me to read Balzac and explained the French family system to me. He was a neat, silver-haired man, soft in voice, precise in speech. He really gave me these letters to write as an exercise. I worked most of one morning on this letter and being known for bad handwriting, I re-wrote it several times and took it to him. I stood waiting and looking at his new secretary. She had lovely dewy eyes and one of them quivered, almost with a wink, as she smiled with a terrible lack of innocence at me. She was very small. She leaned towards me for her pencil and as she did so I could see her breasts in her low blouse. I gazed helplessly at them and she, pleased by the effect she was having on me, looked up. In these few seconds Mr James had taken out his pen which had green ink in it and was saying:

'Why is it, I wonder, you never dot your "i"s?'

And was dotting them in green. He turned to look at me, I was startled by his voice. I couldn't speak. I began to sway, the room seemed to spin.

'He's fainting,' said the girl archly.

I was. I clutched at the desk. Mr James jumped up and held me. Quickly the colour came back to my face and I was stuttering and blushing.

'Have you been smoking?' said Mr James to me with a sly glance at the girl.

'I don't smoke, sir,' I said.

Mr James let go of me, gave me back the letter and sent me away. A delightful laugh came from behind the frosted glass of his door after I had left.

In October, when I had my annual holiday for a fortnight, my brother and I hired bicycles and went up north to York. We were met at the station by Uncle Arthur who had his bicycle with him. With his trousers bagging over his clips and his broad black beard brushing his handlebars, he raced us across the city, pausing for us to admire the sight of the Minster in the darkness and the curious effect of the apostles frozen in the great doors and the gargoyles looking as though they were going to spew down on us. Great Uncle Arthur's wife had come into a small sum of money and they now lived in a little suburban house, lined with gaudy carpets and smelling of new furniture. The famous toad had gone from the kitchen. His butterflies and insects had gone and so had his cabinets of birds' eggs. He himself still put on his white apron and knee-pads and went about hammering, but he had retired and there was a change in him. His sons and their wives were kind and prosperous.

The miraculous cure of Cousin Dick by Christian Science had caused a split in the family, particularly among the sisters. The miracle was a victory for the Bibliolaters, which put Uncle Arthur in a bad position. It shook his atheism and looking around for new ammunition he drifted first into theosophy and then – or so it sounded – into spiritualism. He had done this under the influence of a friend called Evans, a signal-box man.

Uncle Arthur had given his stuffed swan to him and he would slink off to this friend's house on Saturday evenings and do table-turning with him, the swan looking wretchedly on. This was a decline. Uncle Arthur read Burton no more, but he said he would get Evans to show me a bundle of Burton papers; he and Evans had got through to Burton, several times, 'on the other side'.

We went on to Aunt Lax on the Moors. She was put out because she was in the middle of Wesleyan celebrations, so we stayed with the blacksmith, the happiest man I think I ever met. There was a tent for teas on the common and there I met my first writer. He was a burly middle-aged man, in battered leggings and was the reporter of the local paper. He took notes of peoples' names and seemed to know everything that was going on in the world. Everyone thought him important. I followed him around hoping to get hints from what he said.

When we got back to London we found ourselves in the middle of a Yorkshire quarrel – it lasted up there for a good ten years – which had been started because we had been obliged to stay with the blacksmith and not Aunt Lax who felt she had lost face in the village. For once, Father took our side about this; he had no opinion of his Yorkshire relations nor they of him – the ideal Yorkshire situation, decorated with 'plain, honest' words. Uncle Arthur, the rebel, repeated many times his decisive phrase, 'Circumstances Alters Cases' but the affair grew and grew until it absorbed old differences about money and became open war. No one was on speaking terms.

At home our own obsessions had changed. My brother was now the centre of attack; my father was merely sarcastic to me, saying things like 'How is Professor Know-all?' or 'What is in the superior mind of my sentimental son?' His sarcasm was often, I think, a form of shyness. My brother was more vulnerable than I.

It has always been a puzzle to us but, Father and Mother had decided early on that my brother was backward, lazy, easily led astray, like my father's brother who had been sent to Canada and had become a remittance man. I was still Cain-ish; he was still Abel-like and all heart. I see from photographs that I am thin, small, look ill and have a melancholy smile; my brother is stronger, taller, jaunty but wistful. He is wearing a gaudily striped cap with peak unclipped – imitated from the caps of subalterns in the war – and is standing by a friend's motor bike – Curly's I expect. He is good-looking; his hair is carefully greased by a hair oil we have invented: a mixture of olive oil and eau-de-Cologne, so that we smelt like two young scented salads. His heroes are people who have been in the war – ex-captains, ex-majors, delight him; they are the successors of the 'knuts' of early boyhood, for these are 'out' now. 'Hellish lads' have come in and will lead on to 'blokes' and 'chappies'; the 'birds' of three or four years back have given way to 'flappers' and 'little tarts'. He is no good at school; his gifts are in his hands. He has my father's craftsmanlike patience, mingled with a love of splash. It is he who has done all the practical work – such as putting up the ultra-modern chicken house in the garden. And he will drop anything for the sake of my father. This love has been his trouble; he has been bullied and jeered at, and for years he has been a bad stammerer. The one thing he wants to do is to work with my father in his business. Father accuses him of being a rich young idler who thinks that all he has to do is to step into his father's shoes without working.

Naturally my brother decided to exploit his bad reputation. He said he wanted to go to sea. (This was a genuine ambition: after twenty years in business, my brother joined the Navy as an able seaman at thirty-eight years of age in the last war; he had carefully toughened himself for the job. It was a romantic fulfilment.) A common sailor! My father was indignant. 'Poor Frank buried in the South Atlantic,' groaned Mother. No, said my brother, he wanted to be an artificer. Father asked if we thought he was made of money. But the postman's son opposite had become an artificer. Well, said my father, if you prefer to be a postman's son, go and live with the postman. Father was in a fix but made a lucky discovery: my brother was now over the age when artificers began their training. Procrastination had paid off, for the moment. Now my brother said he would be an engineer. Since he was ignorant of mathematics and other necessary things, he failed. What was to be done? He went off and worked in a garage and came home smeared with oil. He moved to the loading bay of a motor works and became a loader, but was sacked from that.

'Dad, what about my job?' he would say, hungry for affection.

The request ended in protests, speeches and 'unfolding'. There were violent scenes while Father was doing his Income Tax returns.

The miserable, stammering boy went off to the Public Library to read the Situations Vacant columns and came back with suggestions that led to more storms. Suddenly, no doubt to win my father's affection, he went after a job in Father's own trade, a silk firm. He got the job and Father was not very pleased: it looked like an outflanking movement. Within six months, the firm (which was French), sent my brother to Lyons to work in the factory and to learn the trade. Father could not believe the outrage: it was one of the best firms in the trade. To punish my brother he sent him off without money and for six months the boy half-starved on the low wage and bad food of a poor apprentice. He came back after six months, exuberantly happy, Frenchified and covered with a rash. He arrived at the front gate on a Sunday morning just after Father got back from church. Father stared at him in fury.

'Your train arrives at five.'

'I came by the earlier one.'

'You can't have done – that is for first-class passengers.'

'I came first class.'

'You travelled first class,' cried Father. 'What d'you mean by that? Where did you get the money?'

'The firm paid.'

'You're not asking me to believe that one of the biggest firms in the trade allows its factory hands to travel first class?'

'The manager told me.'

'He was joking.'

'He came on the same train.'

'You didn't have the impudence to travel with the manager?' shouted Father. Now they had advanced to the lawn just inside the gate of the house. Mother was standing at the door, listening to the rumpus.

'Oh dear, what's he done?'

'Only from Calais. I met him in the lavatory on the boat. We came to London together.'

'You used the same lavatory as the manager?' screamed Father.

'Walt, what is it?' cried Mother.

'Look at his face,' said Father in disgust.

'The filthy hound has been going with prostitutes,' moaned Father. 'He has got a disease.'

We stood on the lawn gazing at the delinquent.

'You'd better get inside,' said Father wretchedly.

The rash was the effect of bad food, but my brother had enjoyed himself. He was soon showing Father he knew more about silk than my father did and – height of social dreams – had lunched often on Sundays with the British Vice-Consul – a 'hellish' lad my brother murmured to me. Father contained his jealousy: on the Monday my brother would be sacked for his presumption.

'I cannot understand your lack of judgement,' he said. 'You go to the same lavatory and then – it's past belief – you travel in the same first-class compartment to London with him.'

'He asked me to. He doesn't speak English.'

'What! You little fool, every Frenchman speaks English!'

On Monday morning my backward brother was promoted.

Father was sad. He could see what it was. His son, his own son, preferred to work for a Frenchman rather than for himself.

'I shall go and see him,' said my father indignantly. 'They are not paying you enough. You must give your notice.'

His jealousy was violent and it was sad. He began tapping his fingers on the table and Mother watched those fingers.

'You see, dear,' she said to my brother. 'The business couldn't afford to pay you what these French people pay, Dad has a difficult time.'

Father lifted his hand to silence her.

Father's dislike of fact and love of drama was a misfortune for it made him unjust to himself. He was a poor man, not as well-off as he pretended to be. At its most successful, his business had a very small turnover. Once more our Micawber had become a disarming borrower and was encumbered by

205

debts. He loved saying sentences like: 'The loan has my personal guarantee' in a grand voice; and it must have seemed to him that the guarantee doubled the amount of money available.

Mother said loyally 'Dad never gives up.' His dreams were his courage, even though, in the end, they totally perverted him. He was too proud to say that his income was small; also his eccentric interpretation of the Christian ethic made him increasingly believe that behind all the human sources of money, there was the great investment house of God pouring out wealth. He believed this was literally true; and he referred people who sought to get their money back from him to the Divine source. In these spruce and clean-shaven days, Father got up at 6.30 when my mother brought tea to him. He dressed in dark clothes, grey or navy blues, wore a low stiff collar and a knitted silk tie. His shining black hair was going a trifle grey at the ears, his complexion was dark and fresh, he had a benign-looking double chin, his brown eyes were deep set. He smiled as he came towards you, but paused for a frown of quizzical rebuke when you spoke. He carried his great weight without effort. His sleep, he said, was dreamless; beyond a rare cold, he was never ill in his long life. He charmed. He was a being who could have been patented and was almost an ideal. It was a great pleasure to be with him in restaurants. And when, in years to come, humiliation and disaster fell upon him, he never admitted it. In his sixties, his seventies, even in his eighties, he was always planning to start up again and had indeed to be restrained from grandiose schemes. The solution was to take him out to an expensive lunch, and the pleasure he took in it made our hard hearts melt. It is true he would say afterwards that we were on the road to ruin; but his main criticism of me was that I 'limited' myself and did not 'think big'. The odd thing is that he did not really do so either. When he left his dreams for the facts, he was small in mind and easily trapped by petty details.

Right up to the day of his death in his eighties, none of us children could settle our view of him. It was simple to call him the late Victorian dominant male without whose orders no one could think or move. It was only partly true that he was a romantic procrastinator, egotist and dreamer, for he was a very calculating man. Sometimes we saw him as the unchanged

206

country boy, given to local shrewdness and gossip. (He loved the malicious gossip of his church and his trade.) Sometimes we saw him as a pocket Napoleon, but he never even tried to obtain the wealth or power he often talked about. His mind was more critical than creative and he was appalled by criticism of himself. He would go pale, hold up his hand and say, 'You must not criticize me.' He sincerely meant he was beyond criticism and felt in himself a sort of sacredness.

A clue was given to us, too late, after his death, by Miss H who had long ago broken with him, as people did. She knew our quarrels well. The central passion in his life, she said, was for his children. Yes – that, I now see, was true. He was in many ways far more female than he was male. He was one of those fathers who are really mothers; he had a mother's primitive, possessive and jealous love and indeed, behaved as if he and not our mother – who was not possessive at all – had given birth to us. He wished to preserve us for himself. He could not bear us to be out of his sight.

From his own words about his childhood as a favourite child under a severe father, it was obvious that he lived in constant anxiety about food and money – he ate enormously, as if to make up for early hunger – and, as so often happens with anxious people, his anxiety led him to obtain power wherever he could. He was a man of immovable self-will. He was female, again, in his long-headed disingenuousness in obtaining money. Both my brothers eventually worked for him for a while and both quarrelled with him and left.

Before the final catastrophe Father bought a new house, quite a large one, and the secret grand piano came out of hiding. I saw my sister playing The Moonlight Sonata on it while my youngest brother tried to drown the sound by playing a ukelele. But this was years ahead when my nearest brother, the backward one, had become a startling success in the silk trade and was earning a large income, more than the whole family put together. Indeed, Father adroitly wheedled the money out of him to pay for the grand piano.

Christmas 1919 came and we had our annual reading of James Barrie, also of a satirical story about business called *Letters of a Self-Made Merchant to his Son* by Pierpont Morgan Junior.

Mother called for the short stories of W. W. Jacobs which she loved and I read them. She thought Barrie sentimental, but a few lines of Jacobs would make her pull her skirts up to her knees as she sat in front of the fire and cover her face with her hands as she laughed.

'I say, old duck,' Father often said, when she sat laughing like this, 'we can see your bloomers.'

For Mother there was no funnier word than 'bloomers' in the English language and she was off again.

I looked in the library for more works by Barrie and made an important discovery. It was a novel about journalism called *When a Man's Single:* in it a clever journalist explains to another the art of writing short sketches. It was a simple revelation. Twenty years later when I read H. G. Wells's autobiography I discovered that Barrie's book had taught Wells how to become a professional writer. It taught me instantly. Indeed the writers who really helped me to start as a writer were not the great; they were W. J. Locke, Du Maurier and Belloc, who whispered to me to go abroad; I saw myself as a mixture of those three, out on the open road with Stevenson's donkey, and Barrie, the shrewd Scot, telling me how to write about it.

But the strain of the last few years, the stunned boredom and torn emotions, were too much for me. Coming home by slow train one evening and changing trains at Grove Park junction, I was sick on the platform, got home somehow and collapsed. The post-war flu epidemic had caught me. I fell to the floor. My father was as frightened as I was and luckily a doctor was called. I scared everybody by saying I was a kipper being cut in half. (This was true. I had been smoked by London and was split in two by the family quarrels.) I do not know how long I was in bed, but one morning, thinking I was well, I got up and fell unconscious to the floor again.

The illness was a long one and the end of it was that I did not go back to the leather trade. I spent a pleasant couple of months sometimes bicycling in Kent, but often going long country bus rides with my mother. We used to go to the inn at Westerham and eat chops and have a glass of shandy. We did not talk at all about her woes or the Business, but about her childhood or the people we saw about us. They were all funny to her. At home, my father regarded me with respect: the leather firm had paid my salary and given me £10 as a present. I had told them I was going to Paris. They said I could come back to them when I wanted. I heard something odd about myself at the leather factor's. Apparently, when asked to do something, I always said 'Just a sec' and went off to do something else. Now I had £20.

'If you're careful you could live for a month in Paris and then we'll see,' Father said. I could not tell him or my mother that once I had gone I would never come back.

But now I stood on the platform beside the Boat Train at Victoria with my father. Portly and almost sumptuous, he had several times asked where I had distributed my money and my ticket and I was moved because I could see he was moved. We were distracted by two Italians as dark as earth, a grey-haired oldish man and another of about thirty. They were held, wrestling and swaying in each other's arms, and they were howling with grief, the tears drenched their faces as they rocked in shouting agony and sorrow and, if they paused, it was only to get breath to rush at each other again with cries that outdid the stamping and steaming of engines and the shouting of porters. Two large women in black stood by them silently approving the display of the two men. It has often struck me since that it would have been better for my father and me, especially as we too felt strongly, to have purged ourselves of our anxieties, hatreds and conflicts in the manner of these two Italians: my father would have found it easier than I, but I whose eyes were soon full of tears in those days when I tried to speak to him, would have fought for pride's sake against it.

On my side it would have been impossible to howl. I was happy. I was excited. I was setting myself free. After Paris I saw myself turning up, shabby, weatherbeaten and speaking whatever patois was desired in remote inns, in remote countries, in remote mountains. I would have arrived, of course, on foot. As it was, on the Paris train I was wearing a boater with my school colours on it, a ginger-coloured tweed jacket, flannel trousers and a classy pair of tony red shoes – the latest colour – bought wholesale in the trade.

The train to Paris moved off. There is a small white farmhouse near Dunton Green in the Westerham Valley and nowadays when I come back from the continent I look at it incredulously. It and I are still in existence. For on this first Paris journey I remembered all the bicycling trips of the last months on which I had often passed this farm and was so homesick that I wanted to go back; but once out of home country my mood changed. By Ashford, where dozens of locomotives sat smoking, I had forgotten; and at Dover the white-hot flash of the chalk cliff and the sight of the silky blue sea set me free. I got a smut in my eye early on the crossing for I stood on the top deck eager to get my first sight of the dunes of Calais, but this bad luck was cancelled by a heartening incident. A young man with flopping fair hair, with heavy shoulders and a broken nose was standing there too, looking for France. He stepped back and trod with all his weight on my foot. He murmured and went off. It was Carpentier, the famous French boxer. How right I had been: to know the great world one must go to France! On the French train I drank wine for the first time in my life: it was vinegarish I thought, but I was committed to liking it. It was disappointing that there were no Frenchmen in the compartment. There was an elderly Englishman. He asked if I was going to Monte Carlo. He was a clergyman. I was soon showing off about myself and telling him I was not at all the Monte Carlo type and how eager I was to see the spire of Amiens cathedral. Ruskin, I pointed out, had written about it. The clergyman said Gothic inevitably appealed to the disorderly minds of the young, was ramshackle in comparison with classical architecture or with Italian baroque and made some discreet religious inquiries. My careless answers puzzled him. He spoke of how one was baptized into Christ.

'I haven't been baptized,' I boasted.

He was upset.

'I beg you, I beg you, to get that put right. A small matter, easily attended to, but most important!' he said. We stopped talking. He sat in silence. It was obvious that I was an uncouth and swollen-headed boy. After a while he spoke again. He asked my name and then hopefully put a question that bowled me out.

'Are you by any chance a connexion of the Gloucestershire Pritchetts?'

I was affronted to hear that there were other families with our name and then I saw I was being introduced for the first time to one of the openings of the English class game. The failure to be a Gloucestershire Pritchett – evidently a remarkable clan – dogged me for several years. The clergyman's doubt increased. When he heard I had not been to a Public School or to the University he was lost and he fell into a self-congratulatory silence. A mystery had been solved. As for myself, my new life as a young man had begun.

Except for a night or two when passing through London, I saw very little of England for seven years. I could not bear the sight of it. For two of these years I worked first in a photographer's shop off the Boulevard des Italiens. Then, starting off from the Square du Temple, I traipsed for a year from one paint shop to the next round Paris, selling glue, shellac and, for a hungry period, ostrich feathers and theatre tickets. I became a foreigner. For myself that is what a writer is – a man living on the other side of a frontier.

MIDNIGHT OIL

Whence is thy learning? Hath thy toil
O'er books consum'd the midnight oil?

— JOHN GAY

CHAPTER ONE

THIS is the year of my seventieth birthday, a fact that bewilders me. I find it hard to believe. I understand now the look of affront I often saw in my father's face after this age and that I see in the faces of my contemporaries. We are affronted because, whatever we may feel, time has turned us into curiosities in some secondhand shop. We are haunted by the suspicion that the prayers we did not know we were making have been only too blatantly answered.

I have before me two photographs. One is, I regret, instantly recognizable: a bald man, sitting before a pastry board propped on a table, and writing. He does little else besides sit and write. His fattish face is supported by a valence of chins; the head is held together by glasses that slip down a bridgeless nose that spreads its nostrils over a moustache. He is trying to find some connection with the figure in another picture taken fifty years ago. He knows that the young fellow sitting on the table of a photographer's in Paris, a thin youth of twenty with thick fairish hair, exclaiming eyebrows, loosely grinning mouth and the eyes raised to the ceiling with a look of passing schoolboy saintliness, is himself. The young one is shy, careless, very pleased with himself, putting on some impromptu act; the older one is perplexed. The two, if they could meet in the flesh, would be stupefied and the older one would certainly be embarrassed.

The embarrassment is the subject of this book. To write about one's childhood is comparatively simple. One's life has a natural defining frame. One knows who one is; in childish egotism, one supposes people have a relationship only with oneself. But after the age of twenty, the frame is uncertain, change is hard to pin down, one is less and less sure of who one is, and other egos with their court of adherents invade one's privacy with theirs. One's freedom is inhibited by their natural insistence on themselves; also, the professional writer who spends his time becoming other people and places, real or imaginary, finds he has written his life away and has become almost nothing. The true autobiography of this egotist is exposed in all its intimate foliage in his work. But there is a period when a writer has not yet become one, or just having become one, is struggling to form his talent and it is from this period that I have selected most of the scenes and people in this book. It *is* a selection, and it is neither a confession nor a volume of literary reminiscences, but as far as I am able I have put down my 'truth'.

I am not sure whether I should describe myself as an egotist or an egoist. The distinction is subtle and important; I am forced to use the personal pronoun and would do anything, if I could, to avoid it in a book like this. I am not a public figure. I would almost prefer to use the pronoun 'we' rather than 'I' – and I do not mean in the editorial or royal sense – and there is a strong argument for doing so. For a writer is, at the very least, two persons. He is the prosaic man at his desk and a sort of valet who dogs him and does the living. There is a time when he is all valet looking for a master, i.e. the writer he is hopefully pursuing.

When, at 20 I got out of the train in the early spring of 1921 at the Gare du Nord, I was all valet: the master was no more than a wish or a dream and it would be a long time before the two would be united to each other. To find the writer, the valet had decided that he must break with his family and with everything and everyone he knew and go to France – a common opinion in the Twenties. In my case this would be a remedy for what I foolishly thought was my fatal disadvantage: lack of education. I had little romping notion of 'seeing the world'; in a disorderly way I quite seriously wished to be taught. The petty aspect of the drama could be detected by the anxious way I kept on touching three of my pockets as I followed the porter who was carrying my heavy leather suitcase to the barrier. I had £20 divided between them. This sum, one could tell from my frightened eyes, had got to last forever and the word 'forever' was like a sustaining tune running through my head. If it did not last forever, I would be back in London with my tail between my legs; back on a stool in the leather trade. They used stools in those days.

Two things stick in my mind when I look back upon that arrival. First, the sight of the Sacré-Coeur on its hill just before the train got in. White and Byzantine, this prosperous church looked like some harsh oriental bird with a large eye just below the dome – as it appeared in the afternoon light – a hard eye that cynically regarded the sins of Paris and made no comment. The second sight was alarming – until I got used to seeing it all over the walls of Paris: the huge word *Défense* followed later by the words 'Loi de' and some nineteenth century date. I would have to live carefully.

The bid for freedom was not as bold as I needed to think it. I would not have got away so easily if a Mr Hotchkiss, a member of my father's church in Bromley, had not happened to be in Paris doing the books of an Anglo-French company. He met me at the barrier and carried me off in a taxi while the Rue Lafayette rocked alongside, and the disturbing dome of Sacré-Coeur reappeared up the hill in side streets. We arrived at the Hotel Chatham. I was a little ashamed that Mr Hotchkiss carried a Baedeker. He was a man with heavy plodding boots and a long face, like Louis Jouvet's, who knew his way about. He had the not uncommon English art of pretending to be stupid and then giving a shy, comic side glance; a dry affectionate fellow, but with his cranky side. He stayed at the Chatham because English painters used to stay there, years before. He used to be a Tolstoyan. He had given that up now, but I had seen the complete Works in his house and I had one memorable chat with him in Bromley about Russian literature; when I left I wished, for a while, that he were my father. The idea had to be dismissed: his wife was a shouting woman (from South Africa, I believe) who sounded as if she were calling the cattle in. You could hear her far down the street where no one shouted. We used to say 'There goes Mrs H calling the cattle off the veldt.' If she caught me coming back from the station in Bromley she would make me carry a pile of broken boxes containing damaged fruit she had bought cheap in Covent Garden; and, on our way, her quick eyes would look for bits of wood in the street or in people's front gardens. If she saw any she would give one of her shouts and make me run in and get it. Very humiliating if you were wearing a bowler hat. She was a good-natured woman, but economical. Her husband was a frugal man too. We dined at Duval's that evening. Mr Hotchkiss told me that the Duval restaurants belonged to the Paris of Arnold Bennett. They were safe respectable places and, he said, inexpensive. The waitresses were middle-aged women who wore long starched white aprons that came up to their chins, and had been chosen for their plain faces. Here I saw my first pepper mill, ate my first *omelette fines herbes*, drank my second glass of wine. Mr Hotchkiss drank a glass, too; he would not have dared to drink a glass in Bromley in the presence of a member of our sect. It was forbidden. He carefully calculated my share of the cost of the dinner at Duval's and I admired his scrupulous behaviour. My father would have largely put the amount down to expenses and charged someone else for it, in a generous way, which would lead to trouble the next day. But Mr Hotchkiss went one better. We got out into the Rue de Rivoli where I took in yet another breath of the Paris night air. It was like one's first cool smell of the sea, but a sea made lightly of Gauloises, coffee, scent and Castrol. As we stood there a lady of the French Red Cross who was collecting money for the French wounded in the 1914 war, shook her tin at us. Mr Hotchkiss's big droll eyes went dead with patriotism.

'Noos avons no blessays ah noo,' he said and walked off.

'Money is all they think of,' he said.

Fifteen years later when my father's business went bankrupt, my father shrewdly called in Mr Hotchkiss to 'wind up' the firm and when the job was done refused to pay him the usual fee on the grounds that they belonged to the same church. Mr Hotchkiss, who had admired my father for years, could not believe this betrayal and wept when he told my brother about it. Soon after the poor good man died.

I was shocked by the accent of Mr Hotchkiss. I was already an accent snob, hot on vowels and the French 'r'. We walked back to the hotel and outside a gaudily lit shop-window a girl accosted us, my heart raced, my body iced and then became boiling hot, for she looked like a pink-faced angel with eyes like blue crystals. Her eyes and voice made my skin prickle.

'Did you see that girl?' I said, swaggering, putting on an air of experience, to see how she would affect a member of our church.

'You'll see a lot,' he grunted. I had grown a year older.

My father's friend lived for tasks. In England, in his spare time, he liked making brass rubbings of the tombs in Norman churches. On our second day I went up in his esteem by saying I must find a cheaper hotel to live in. Eagerly he found me a much cheaper hotel near the Champ de Mars and then we went to the Invalides and, reading from the Baedeker, looked down at Napoleon's tomb. He discussed Tolstoy's opinion of Napoleon and Napoleon's Paris. He was a good guide.

I was sure that my father would have told Mr Hotchkiss that I was being sent to Paris for a few weeks to 'learn the language', and go into the textile trade. So I told Mr Hotchkiss that this was not so. I was going to stay 'forever' in Paris, or at any rate I was going to travel from country to country all over the world, and that I intended to be a writer. Mr Hotchkiss said thoughtfully that this was exactly what I should do.

'But father is against it,' I said.

Mr Hotchkiss thought a long time and then said: 'You should do what you want to do.' The next day, after taking me up the Eiffel Tower, Mr Hotchkiss left.

In our family, as I have told, we lived an isolated life. No friend ever came to the house, not even Mr Hotchkiss. Father always said he had no time for people. We had to ask permission to see our friends and that was rarely given; and if it was, we had to dress up in our best clothes. 'Is your own family not good enough for you?' was the piercing question. My earliest pleasure was therefore in being alone; and to be alone in Paris, knowing nobody, was an intoxication; it was like being on the dizzy brink of knowing everybody. I felt I was drinking the lights of the city and the words I heard spoken by passers-by. After Mr Hotchkiss had gone I walked to the Place de la Concorde and there by the bridge in the shade of the warm trees looked over the stone wall into the river. I was instantly under a spell. The water looked still yet it rustled like a dress. I had never seen water and stone in such pleasant conversation, the stone moonish, shading to saffron like the cheese of Brie, the water womanish and velvet. My solemn young eyes were seeing order and feeling united. I was so moved that I could feel myself grow into a new being. I repeated to myself my vow – for I was at the vowing age – never to leave France and I was so entranced that tears came to my eyes. I walked from bridge to bridge along the Seine, past the acacias, the poplars and the planes that leaned with a graceful precision over the water, each tree like the stroke of a painter's brush. The orderliness of the trees, the gravely spaced avenues, rearranged my mind. My English feeling was for Wordsworthian nature; here nature had been civilized. I was shocked and converted in an hour and though later in life I have often lapsed, the conversion has remained. It was exasperating that I was followed by a couple of boys who jeered 'Look at the Englishman, oh yes, oh yes' – exasperating because at school I had won a prize for French but could hardly tell them I had read Molière, Bernadin de Saint-Pierre or Balzac: that given time I could tactlessly recite from Victor Hugo's *Les Châtiments*, beginning with:

Waterloo! Waterloo! Waterloo! morne plaine!

and was in the middle of Anatole France. It was annoying. Language and the sound of words had been my obsession from childhood; the pursed or the open subtlety of French vowels, the nasal endings, the tongue slipping along over silk and metal, the juiciness of the subjunctive, made my own lips restless. My ear was good, if my grammar was bad. As I walked I repeated to myself the names of the shops; *quincaillerie, boulangerie, bouquiniste*, even the horrific words *voies urinaires* plastered over the buildings, and any phrase I overheard. But the word that had an overwhelming beauty for me was *cinquième*: my room was on that floor in the hotel. What significance *cinquième* had! Its meaning was liberty.

I did have two introductions to people in Paris. My father had had ambitions to enter the perfumery trade and in fact he had once set fire to the top floor of his premises in Middle Street while experimenting with essences, boiling them, I suppose. Anyway that narrow street was soon glorious with fire engines: a District Call he boasted when he came home bandaged. He had given me an introduction to a scent maker and also to a Christian Science lady. The scent man lived in the Faubourg Poissonière. He asked me to lunch at his flat. (I was to spend nearly two years in Paris, but I think I was briefly invited only three times to the house of a French family). This gentleman had a reddish moustache and lived in a spacious and dowdy place of polished floors and gilded furniture. The floor polish had a sickly smell. All the family were at lunch. His wife, a cheerful woman, stood scooping out soup at the end of the table and passed it on to her two daughters, their husbands, her son and the rest of us. One of the sons-in-law was a young officer in the army, full of wine and butter. He was in uniform. They were all shouting and laughing most of the time, especially at me. I could not understand much of what they said and my grammar made them throw down their table napkins and shout with merriment. At every half sentence they corrected my genders. I was unlucky enough to defend myself by saying I had trouble with my *gendres*. Screams of laughter. Lunch was a withering lesson at school.

The father stopped them at last and said:

'There is only one solution. You must get a "sleeping dictionary",' and this started the warm-eyed girls off again.

'Do you know what that is?' the father asked me.

'Yes.'

'Ah,' shouted the soldier. 'He is making progress already.' This started the girls again.

After lunch the son took me into a small salon with gilt cabinets in it. He was a pale boy with red hair and a large Roman nose.

'My father is right,' said the son. 'My mother arranged a mistress for me.'

I heard my voice say coldly 'We do not do such things in England.'

I was astonished by my hypocrisy.

'Don't you believe it,' the soldier said. 'I was with the English during the war.'

I couldn't bear the condescension in the son's long naked nose. His voice seemed to come down it. One of the young daughters overheard us and said to her sisters:

'Il est féroce, cet Anglais.'

But the city was evidently made for me. It was built for Art and Learning whereas my London was built for government and trade. At home I was a tolerated joke, 'the professor'. One foggy morning when I'd been with my father in Cheapside, he had stopped to talk to a customer in the textile trade who asked what I was going to do. My father said:

'He says he wants to be a journalist.'

The man replied:

'Give him a copy of Compton Mackenzie's *Sinister Street*. That will cure him.'

Because of this I have never read that famous novel.

In Paris, I thought, a conversation like that could not take place. Here one was driven into displaying a talent. One would even be mocked for not doing so.

And how the streets and gardens of the city *helped*: the names were an encyclopaedia of French history and classical instruction. In the parks the statues of heroes and goddesses, busts of painters, dramatists and writers declaimed among the nursemaids and the children and shared the place with the birds. In the next few days the old age that had rounded my shoulders in London – the James Barrie–Edmund Gosse stoop – slipped away from me.

The Christian Science lady lived near the Champs de Mars. She was a pleasant woman, busy and contented in the knowledge that she had had the final revelation about God and man, particularly on the practical side. I met her carrying a long roll of French bread under her arm into her house. A sort of virginity had been restored to her in the crisis of middle age. It turned out that she had once been married to a Frenchman, a problem which had been successfully prayed away to another address. She had lived in Paris most of her life. She took me out to lunch in Passy at a pretty and very private garden restaurant which, she said, was unusual among Paris restaurants. The owners were noted for their moral standards and cleanliness. We ate in the garden and I was given a glass of Vichy water. This drew out the buried Calvinist.

'The war was the final manifestation of French decadence,' she said.

('Manifestation' was a word often used by our sect. It was followed by another favourite: 'Mesmerized').

'They are mesmerized by sensuality. Their food is the cause of it – cooking in butter, the sauces, apéritifs and above all their strong coffee and wine. These stimulate their sensual appetites and make the French the most unspiritual race on the earth. They are far from God as we know him "through Science".'

I said I liked sitting in the cafés.

She corrected me: 'French people of good family *never* go to cafés.'

This lady was kind but one soon came up against a blank wall in talking to her. The effect of these opinions was to make me want to eat more sauces and drink more wine. I kept quiet about this, but went with her to the Christian Science Meeting because there, she said, someone might know of a job, for my £20 was running out; to stay in France I would have to earn my living. She said the editor of a Paris newspaper was an admirer of the *Christian Science Monitor* and very interested, as they said, 'in Science'. I was astounded. What influence our religion had. My doubts must be wrong!

Every small experience played on my wavering mind. The meeting of twenty-five people was held on Sunday morning in the room of a small dancing academy for young ladies in a genteel quarter. The waxed floor, the large black framed mirrors on the wall, the piano rather chipped with its ill-tuned notes would send my mind wandering through the prayers and readings to the imaginary Mademoiselle counting out the steps: '*Un, deux, trois, quatre – attention Marie-France*' in some refined Edwardian tinkle. Even our First Reader, who read the Lord's Prayer in the primmest of good French, sounded as if he belonged to the eighties of the last century rather than to 1921; and indeed, young and American, he suggested as many polite Americans did at that time, a society fixed in the past. The sensation of joining a previous age of gentility was a novelty to me who had been brought up in vulgar England and in a family where manners were unknown, where everyone shouted, and no one had any notion of taste, either good or bad. We lived without it. And after the meeting, the amount of bowing and hat-raising that went on suggested a social life which I was entering just as, of course, it was maddeningly on the way out. Too late. Too late. I longed, for my first two or three weeks in Paris, to be in this sense a bourgeois if only to have something to give up.

In Paris the congregations were gayer and slacker than ours in Bromley, for they were a mixture of tourists glad to be out of England or America, business people, or French and Italian Protestants who said it was a liberation to get away from the Lutheran and other churches. They seemed to be the happiest people on earth: the Divine Mind fizzed like some harmless *vin mousseux* and stimulated the yes-yes-yes of the Americans. One or two of these had started or inherited small banks in the United States which were booming, and the Divine Mind had so arranged it that in Paris one got more and more francs for the dollar every month on the falling exchange – an exchange that fell because of the decadence and sexual indulgence of the French, their obsession with food and wine, their neglect of plumbing and the disastrous fact of being Latins with the long, now happily decayed, influence of the Roman Catholic Church behind them. It amuses me to read nowadays that the twenties were a decade of wit and licence. I had fallen not among sinners, but among the good.

I told everyone I spoke to that I wanted to be a writer. Or a painter. I had brought a box of water colours with me. Two men in the group took this very kindly. One was the Reader – whose French was so good – a well-off, handsome and ascetic American of about thirty-five; his father was a small banker, who had lived in Paris before the war.

'I was an abstract painter.' He smiled wearily at his folly.

'Can I see your pictures?'

'No, I've given it up.'

Abstract painting was on the right lines, he said; it was more 'mental', less of the flesh and the senses than the traditional thing. It alarmed me to hear he was one more of those intelligent men who had given up literature and art for our religion. Shyly, tolerantly, he looked back on those mistaken Bohemian days. My resistance to the idea of becoming a purely spiritual being hardened. Still, he forgave me for hankering after the life he had, with evident struggle, put aside. He was a fanatic beneath his irony and gaiety. He had mortified the flesh. There was a rumour that he had attained the ideal and lived in a state of blessed virginity with his wife.

The other man was totally different: a gaudy and fleshy Americanized Londoner called Shaves. He sang louder than anyone else when the hymns started. I shall have more to say about this touching and ludicrous man who, when he laughed, looked like someone shouting in agony for help. He was in his forties. Once in the street after the meeting he could not hide his relief – he was made to go to church by his wife – and started to bawl out bits of opera while his wife and three young children tried to stop him. He was unquestionably common.

> La, la, la, di, da, dah! Oh my old coat
> My old coat tried and trusted

' – Know it? Bohême! Cecil Chavasse, Metropolitan Opera, New York. My father. Ever hear him? What a voice!'

He scrutinized me. I'd never heard of his father. He gave me his look of vulgar appeal, then he committed a crime. Christian Scientists are told not to smoke or chew tobacco for Mrs Eddy belonged to the tobacco chewing age in the U.S.A. Mrs Nathaniel Hawthorne had felt as she did about it. Mr Shaves pushed a cigarette into a small holder, stuck it at an angle of forty-five degrees in his mouth and sailed off under his straw hat like a Cockney tripper at Southend. His wife put on the Christian Science smile of seeing and hearing no evil.

Nothing came of the Christian Scientists. After three weeks my money was nearly gone. I was desperate. I tried to get jobs on English newspapers. In a fatuous moment I went to *Le Figaro* and asked the girl at the desk, as best I could, if I could get a job as a reporter. I tried banks, tourist offices. I read with bewilderment French advertisements. Then one evening of panic I saw an advertisement in the Paris *Daily Mail*; a photographer wanted an assistant. I could hardly sleep that night. I brought the full force of Christian Science prayer to work. A success! At eight the next morning I rushed off to the place on the Boulevard des Italiens. It was a photographer's shop. The manager said: 'I suppose your parents sent you over to study?' 'No,' I said. 'I have to earn my living.' I got the job.

I was a good young man, but the good have their dubious moments. I went to the nearest Post Office and sent a telegram to my father. I knew he would be pleased. But it was also a message of defiance. Letters had been coming from him every other day, advising me to make a daily list of my expenses, asking what I was doing about my laundry, and so on, pointing out that I must, when in doubt, refer any detail to himself and the Divine Mind; and from then on there would be half a page on its operation, on the need to make the most of this experience until I came home, to see what would 'unfold' for me in a few weeks. He had a very neat hand which ran one word into the next so that his letters were like one long sentence. I was not to regard these letters, he said, as lectures. A letter came back at once in answer to my telegram, asking me to say whether the photographers were a sound firm; was the salary paid by the week or month? The advice to put down my daily expenses was repeated. He always did this himself and, I believe, this was one of the reasons for his chronic insolvency. The mere act charmed him into extravagance. These letters touched me, but my weeping days were over and I was angry. I sent him a rude letter saying I did not want his advice every day, and that I was quite able to manage my own life. This must have hurt him and – so unreasonable is guilt – I felt guilty in standing up for my independence. But not for long.

I started work on a misty morning. The shop was in an arcade and was the Paris branch of an English manufacturer of photographic plates and papers. At first I had thought the boss was French, for he had the black long curly moustache and frisked-up hair of a French barber of the period and wore a tight little jacket and boots with high heels. In fact, he was a London sparrow brought up in Marseilles. His sallow skin looked as though it had been painted with walnut stain and he spoke French fast but with an entirely English pronunciation. His 'combiangs' and 'ker voolay voos' raced through the tongue of Molière like a rusty lawn mower. He pointed out that on the small salary he was paying me I should have to leave my hotel and find a cheaper room.

That morning, I saw that my job was a come-down after the leather trade. First of all, the situation of the shop was wrong. Du Maurier, Murger and W. J. Locke and Anatole France would have dropped me if they had known I was earning my living on the Right Bank within five minutes of Thomas Cook and the American Express: that I was in Paree and not Paris. My mind split: here I was copying, in pencil, lists of stock on half sheets of flimsy paper, hour after hour, in the dark back office of the shop, but my other self was across the river among the artists. The other people working in the shop were, first, the salesman: he was a heavy, black-haired, scowling young Highland Scot, a handsome man with grey threatening eyes and a very soft voice. He had run away from home at fifteen and, disguising his age, he had fought in the artillery in the 1914 war. He was a broken-nosed Army boxer, too. Towards the end of the war he had been blown off his horse and received a chunk of high explosive in his bottom and spoke of this with gravity. He had married a French woman and I imagined a pert little midinette: but one day she stood in the arcade outside making signs to him and I saw she was a plain, short woman, middle-aged and enormously fat. They lived in Montmartre and he spoke of her cooking reverently. He was a magnet to all the women who came to the shop. They became helpless or frantic at the sight of him; he would stand close to them and look down into their eyes, unsmiling, and speak in a low voice, with slow, pedantic deliberation.

The rest of the staff were a nimble little guttersnipe from Montmartre called Pierre, and a gangling, hot-faced Breton. I was the clerk: they were messengers and packers. I checked the stock in a store-room opposite the shop and packed as well. After a month, when suddenly my awkward French became fluent, I had to serve the customers and deal with the dozens of Cash on

Delivery forms at the Post Office. By this time, if the boss had left, I had to type out short letters to the customers, on an old English typewriter. I bought a book on French commercial correspondence. I was the hero of Pierre, the Montmartre boy, who jumped about as he watched me type with three fingers and helped me salt and pepper the letters with the proper French accents.

The customers were mainly from firms of photographers in Paris, but many came up from the provinces bringing with them – to my mind – all that one thought of as the provincial bourgeois. Madame Bovarys came in to see the Scot. Their voices – and his – would drop to murmurs. Sometimes the two would disappear into the street together and the Scot would be away for half an hour; the office boys, particularly the Breton, danced about him when he came back trying to get details out of him. What was she like in bed? The male photographers had an artistic appearance which I admired. They wore hard-crowned black hats with wide brims and a loose black bow dangling from the collar. I longed to dress as they did, but the artistic dress was beyond my income.

For some time I was the office joke. The French boys could not pronounce my name. I became Monsieur Shwep or Machin-Shwep, occasionally M. Victor and their clown. We all got on well. There is that picture of me standing by the counter of the shop, wearing the tweed jacket and flannel trousers – a uniform unknown to the French in the twenties for most Frenchmen wore black then – and my juvenile grin. I grinned most of the time for I was careless of the future, living from day to day, free to do as I pleased. I became finally acceptable to the French boys when in the evenings we left the shop and all walked arm in arm along the Boulevard practising the girl auction invented by the Breton.

'How much to sleep with this one? A thousand, five hundred, a hundred, twenty, ten?' they shouted as the girls came towards us.

One day I had a triumph.

'M. Shwep – how much?'

'Twenty-two francs fifty,' I said.

They were ravished by this superb office joke. Twenty-two

francs fifty was the well-known price of one of the photographic papers we sold. How easily the office humorist is born.

But the Scot was the hero of the shop. It was he who was worshipped as we trailed after him to the bistro round the corner. His unsmiling face imposed. His drinking amazed. His betting at Auteuil and Longchamps was famous. We marched back to the shop after lunch, the Montmartre boy singing:

> O, O, O, O, O!
> Monsieur Mac boit pas d'eau.

The boss was frightened of the Scot, who towered over him. Mac's gestures were as slow as his speech. His arm came up as if judging for an uppercut when he talked to the boss, whose eyes began to flutter and his feet to edge back. Sometimes, when one of the Madame Bovarys came in to the shop and the magnetizing stares and monosyllabic invitations began, the boss would come out to stop them, but his courage always failed; and with ceremonious impudence Mac would say that in view of the importance of the lady as their best customer from Lille or Dijon, he thought he would go out for half an hour with her for a drink. One lunch time when we were at the bistro and he was talking to the barman about some horse-race or other, one of his women (who could not get a word in), became annoyed. She made a dart at his flies and pulled his cock out. The Scot turned slowly to her with admiration. He buttoned up and our procession marched back to the shop; Mac went straight to the boss and in the sad manner of some old Scots preacher he told the boss what had happened.

'I thought it might be advisable to warn you about the bistro,' he said, 'in case you should find yourself in a similar situation.'

I left my room on the *cinquième* at the hotel. I now lived in a cheap room at Auteuil, a fashionable quarter, but my room was in the poorer part of it, where servants, shop assistants and small employees lived. I had given up trying the Latin Quarter, for thousands of Americans had swarmed in and put up the prices. I had been forced to reject a tiny room in the Mont St Geneviève because the place stank. In Auteuil I found a good cheap room on the ground floor in the flat of a war widow who went out to work every day as a charwoman. She was a sad woman in her thirties who came from Tours, and she was very religious, a strong Catholic, and very proud of the pâtés of her region. A priest used to bring her little boy back from school at the weekends: nuns visited her. The flat had two rooms. Mine was nearly filled by a large bed and a washstand and looked out on a yard and dirty wall.

When she was at home Mme Chapin wore a black overall from chin to feet and felt slippers. She had a lamenting voice and sounded like one of the Fates. On Sunday mornings, usually when I was naked and washing in cold water, for there was no bathroom, she would come in with my laundry and stand there telling me bits of her life.

'Oh, that filthy war,' she would say again and again. 'My husband would have been the chief mechanic at the garage if he had not been killed.'

Paris was a wicked city of heartless people, she would groan, as I tried to cover myself with the little wet towel. And there was a good deal of 'Such is life', in my mother's fashion. Madame Chapin worked for a rich cocotte up the street.

'A life of luxury – but with women like that, a false step, a suspicion, and the man who keeps them throws them into the gutter.'

On Sundays she dressed in her best black and now her face would seem rounder and her yellowish eyes would become warm and seductive. Her pale, dressed-up little boy would stare at me.

'Ah, my son,' she often said to him. 'Look at the gentleman. He works. Work – follow his example, my son.'

And they would go off to Mass. I got to know Madame Chapin very well.

'I feel safe with you,' she said after a month. 'It was not the same with my Polish lodger. I never felt any confidence with him, but with you it is different.'

I was hurt. One Sunday, when Christmas came, she came in dressed up in her black as usual with her boy. She was going on her annual visit to her sister who had come to stay at the Ritz. This sister was a kept woman and lived with a motor car manufacturer. The rich sister gave her discarded dresses to sell and the boy was given a book or a toy. When Madame Chapin came back she fell back on her stock epitaph, standing still as stone in the doorway, in her mournful voice:

'With those women, one false step . . .'

She seemed more like a man than a woman to me.

It did not occur to me until forty years later that this annual visit would make a good story. I moved the two sisters to London and, in the manner of writers, changed or added to what I could guess of their characters. I gave Madame Chapin a husband. I think that what prevented me from writing the story before was my knowledge of her real life. It was not until I had given her an imaginary husband and transferred her to another place that she took on the reality of a fiction that I think dignified her. It is part of the function of the novelist to speak for people, to make them say or reveal what they are unable to say, to give them a dignity, even the distinction of being comical though she was not comical in my story. But in those Paris days I could not easily think of what to write about, and I did not know that the creative impulse is often ignited when scenes and people from the almost forgotten past are struck like a flint against something from the present. Her one happiness was knowing the 'saintly Brothers' who took charge of her son.

At lunch-time I usually ate a crusty roll and butter, and by six o'clock, after the long wait in the queue at the Post Office with the parcels, I was torn between hunger and the whole of Paris. I walked down to the Tuileries, crossed the Pont des Arts into the Latin Quarter and then began a torturing study of the grocers, the butchers and the menus of restaurants. I was reading Rabelais by now and his joy in the belly, his lists of sausages and pâtés and his cries of 'A boire', half fed me. The sight of snails, cheeses, garlic sausages and the oily filet d'hareng, worked on me until I had to give in. In the next two years I ate my way through the cheap streets of Paris. I sat alone, read or watched people. I was no longer a shop assistant when I left at six o'clock. I became a gifted student, a writer, a painter 'studying life'. The noise of these restaurants made me happy. I had no friends, but the crowd seemed to be my friends. There was a stout, shouting fellow in a place in the Rue de Seine whose voice was

233

rich and greedy: he had a peg-leg and when he came in he used to unstrap it and hand it to the waitress who stood it in the corner. Now where in London, I thought, would you see a sight like that? Afterwards I sat in cafés in the Boulevard St Michel and watched the students at their game of squirting soda water at one another and joined in their singing:

> Ton honneur sera perdu
> Commes les autres
> Tu feras ma pauvre fille
> Comme les autres font.

One day a sewage cart passed and the students rushed from the café, took off their hats, and with bowed heads walked in funeral procession behind it.

I discovered that the artists met in the *Rotonde* and *Dôme* at Montparnasse, and there I sat over a glass of coffee or beer for the rest of the evening, hoping that some of their genius would rub off on me. Once, there was a violent thunderstorm. I had switched from Rabelais to Plato. What with the lightning, and the wine inside me, I was exalted. After these speechless evenings I would walk across that part of Paris, through Grenelle, to the room in Auteuil, and I would either go exhausted to bed or sit up trying to write, while my landlady groaned in her sleep in the room next door.

Most writers begin by imitation. I had the examples of Stevenson, Chesterton, Belloc, and – for his practical hints – the clever short sketches of Barrie. In French there were the essay-like writings of Anatole France. Naïvely I supposed that these writers were all learned men who had read enormously at the university and that until I had read pretty well as much, I would not be able or even entitled to write at all. I passed my Saturdays looking over the bookshops of the Boulevard St Michel or the boxes of the bouquinistes. I saw that I had not only English literature but the whole of French literature standing between me and the act of writing. Books were cheap. I was used to going without a meal, if necessary, to buy them. I bought indiscriminately. I had got a history of French literature; then the Rabelais; Balzac with his gluttonous appetite for the names of pieces of furniture, door knockers, lamps, the names of trades and products, pushed me to the dictionaries, but the *Contes Drolatiques* were cheerfully licentious; at any rate, in print, I would be a sexual adventurer. I read Lamartine, Vigny and witty Beaumarchais: out of duty to my dead cousin Hilda I read Victor Hugo *and* the Pléiade; I mixed the sermons of Boileau with the titillations of *Manon Lescaut*; Chateaubriand was given up for the adulteries and seductions of Maupassant, or the ballads of Villon. What could I possibly get out of such chaotic reading? How far did my understanding reach? Not far at all, but I did seize the nature of these writers in some of their pages, for something stuck in the confusion of my mind as I sat reading by the light of Madame Chapin's oil lamp. The row of books along the high fly-blown mirror over the marble mantelpiece in my room got longer and longer and the smell of the lamp was made aromatic by the smoke of Gauloises.

There was another reason for hesitating to write: a love of painting, the old hang-over from Bartlett's days at Rosendale Road School, and *Modern Painters*. I spent afternoons in the galleries and stood unnerved by the pictures of the Post-Impressionists in the shops. The smell of paint itself excited my senses. I gazed with desire at the nudes. The attraction of painting was that a work could be instantly seen – no turning of the page – and each brush stroke 'told' to the eye. I lived by the eye: the miles I walked in Paris fed the appetite of the eye above all, so that I could imagine everything in the city was printed or painted on me. One warm Saturday I took my water colours to St Cloud and sat down to paint a group of trees. Other painters, stout men with beards, were painting Cézanne-like pictures of Prussian blue avenues. I squeezed and dabbed my paints and after a couple of hours got up to study the running muddle I had made. I was angry with my incompetence. I sneezed. The grass was damp and within an hour I was down in a café trying to kill a heavy cold with hot rum and lemon. It lasted a dreadful fortnight in which I moved to Russia and read *Anna Karenina*. My career as a painter was over; but, all the more, pictures seemed to tell me how I ought to write.

The question was – what to write about? I found I simply

wanted to write anything. I used to go and look at the Sorbonne: obviously I was not a man of learning. I gazed at Racine's face: dramatic verse was beyond me. I had read that one writes because one has something to say. I could not see that I had anything to say except that I was alive. I simply wanted to write two or three sentences, even as banal as the advertisement on a sauce bottle, and see them in print with my name beneath them. I was at the bottom rung.

Suddenly I had a stroke of luck. I saw in the Paris New York Herald a note asking their readers to send in jokes. I realized I had been giggling for some weeks over one. After an hour or so of struggle I wrote it out. I had been standing outside the Opera with a young Englishman I had met, studying the playbills. He said: 'Let's go there tomorrow night.' I said: 'We can't. There's nothing on.' He pointed to the notice. 'Yes, there is,' he said, 'they're doing Relâche.' I sent this to the paper. The next day it was published with my full name and address underneath it. (I resented that they put in my address, exposing me as an amateur.) They did not pay me. This was my first published work. I kept it a long time. It taught me one thing. If one had nothing to say one could at any rate write what other people said.

I was unable to progress from this point. I went back to the English writers I then admired: the Georgian poets, people like Stevenson, Chesterton, Belloc, Max Beerbohm. What was their common characteristic? It was obvious. They walked. Even Max Beerbohm had walked one morning. Walking started the engine inside them and soon came the words: but they walked on the 'open road', not simply about city streets.

So, when the weekend was fine I took to the road. Paris was small in 1921. It ended at the fortification where the Metro stopped. There were not a great many cars about and I often walked out to Saint-Cloud, to Saint-Germain, to Versailles, and to Marly; and once, on a longer holiday, to Chartres, to see the blue glass and the withered kings. I came back white with dust and with a full notebook. I was being Stevenson without the donkey, or The Beloved Vagabond, with knapsack, garlic sausage to eat in a field by the roadside or at some cheap restaurant where, sweating and tired, I found my head spinning wtih the wine I drank. (*A boire!*) I think I was never happier. On longer journeys – to Pontoise and Poissy – I came back by train. Later on I found a young Englishman who came into the shop one day and talked about a writer called Lytton Strachey. My friend worked at the Bourse; we went on a tramp in the Bellocian tradition. We made a vow. We vowed we'd cross the Loire. We walked to Orléans and crossed the river. The country was dull, the pavé roads were straight and monotonous, the villages were not pretty: in the nights the bullfrogs barked in the pools of the plain; the wide river bed of the Loire, when we came to it, was all stones and the water had dwindled to little pools between them. We were twice pulled up by astounded gendarmes who thought we were tramps and asked us why we didn't take a train. We said it was '*pour le sport*', a phrase that was just coming in. 'You are mad,' they said as they got back on their bikes, with that heavy swing of belts and leggings, and continued the interminable moralizing of the gendarmerie.

This young man was intelligent. He too felt liberated by being in Paris and hated that he had to go back into the family stockbroking business in London. He was a more sensible reader than I: he introduced me to the works of the new writers: Keynes, Roger Fry and Clive Bell. I envied him because he had been to an English Public School; he envied me for wanting to be a writer. I said if I could not manage to be a writer I would still not return to England. He said I was right. He added he had an uncle who owned a mine in Morocco and that the uncle might give me a job as a Labour Manager there. On and off, after that, I would see myself dressed in breeches, gaiters and open-necked shirts by the lift of some rattling mine. I was always weather-beaten in these pictures. This dream became so real to us that he wrote to his uncle who wrote back and said, alas, he had sold his mine. Another fantasy of ours arose because he had acted in *A Midsummer Night's Dream* at school: we called ourselves Pyramus and Thisbe, a joke that seemed side-splitting to us. When he laughed his wide mouth curved up almost from ear to ear and his eyes closed into long curving slits. He was very shocked by the screaming greedy frenzy of the brokers at the Bourse, a noise that could be heard streets away, even in the Boulevard des Italiens. After we had been friends for some time, an American at the Christian Science Meeting said:

'I suppose you know he is Jewish? I thought I ought to warn you.'

This was my first meeting with anti-semitism. I did not know he was Jewish; but it made me reflect that, especially in my school life, the only boys who took my desire to write seriously were Jewish.

But what was I to write about? My collected works were on the little bamboo table at Madame Chapin's. There was my major work, done three or four years back: three pages on the Reformation and Renaissance meeting in the works of Milton. There was half a page describing the clock in our dining-room at home. There were two more half-pages on my brother's hairy friend and another two on a man in the leather trade who was always quoting Shakespeare as we turned over the sheepskins on the warehouse table. And there was my latest work: the joke. I must hurry. I have already told how I had read in Barrie's *When a Man's Single*, that the thing to do was to write on the smallest things and those near to you. There is a straw caught on the window ledge. Will it fall or will it stay? There was an essay, he said, in things like that. What was nearest to me? My room, Madame Chapin groaning next door. Nothing there. And then, by a trick of memory, my mind went back to my first room in Paris. There was a barracks near my new room and at night I would hear the bugle, as I used to hear the bugle at the Champ de Mars. The beautiful word *cinquième* sounded at once in my head. My nights there came back to me. I set about evoking the rough blue cloth on the table, the attic window, the carpet worn by so many predecessors till it was as thin as a slice of ham, the bugle call, even the notices on the door: 'No strangers in the room after eleven', and 'After eleven a supplement for electricity will be charged': and how the light flicked off at that hour. I began to write. Madame Chapin's groans supplied a tenant for the room next door at my old hotel. I wrote for two hours. On other nights I re-wrote several times. I added some sentimental moralizings.

At the photographers I stayed late and typed the thing. I sent it to a London paper and not to lose time I finished two more and sent them. They went to two weekly reviews – the *Saturday Westminster* and *Time and Tide* – and to the *Christian Science Monitor*. There were weeks of iron silence. Then, within a month or two of each other, the three papers accepted them. There! It was easy to be a writer. Outwardly cool and with a curious sense of being naked and exposed, I hummed inside with the giddiness of my genius.

I cannot describe my shame-faced pride. There was no more 'I want to be a writer'. I was a writer. Editors thought so, I told the boys and the Scot at the shop. The Scot had his nation's regard for the written word. The wet-mouthed Breton gaped and punched me in the back. Pierre astonished me. He was always picking up Montmartre songs and about this time his favourites were one about the rising price of Camembert, and a topical one about Deschanel, the Prime Minister who had fallen out of the train on his way to the lavatory, a song with a chorus of innuendo:

> Il n'a pas abîmé ses pyjamas
> c'était épatant, mais c'était comme ça.

He stopped and put on a small act:
'M. Shwep, the great Balzac,' he sang and danced around me. He had picked up the name from the street. At this age boys knew everything.

I told Madame Chapin. She congratulated me, but hers was a face of little expression. Mournfully, after reflection, she said the man who kept the woman for whom she worked was a journalist. I could not tell her how her groans had helped me to write and I felt, when I saw her, how strange it was when she stood bringing in my shirts, that part of her led a ghost life in what I had written. She asked to borrow the first article. She wanted to show it to the priest who came on Saturdays with her boy.

239

A week later the priest returned it.

'Ah,' he moralized. 'At that time you were on the *cinquième*. Now you are on the ground floor.'

There was, to judge by the amusement in his eyes, another meaning to this sentence; like every Frenchman he loved a *nuance*. I read and re-read this article again and again and then, as happens to writers, I was impatient with it and disliked it. I had my first experience of the depression and sense of nothingness that comes when a piece of work is done. The satisfaction is in the act itself; when it is over there is relief, but the satisfaction is gone. After fifty years I still find this to be so and that with every new piece of writing I have to make that terrifying break with my real life and learn to write again, from the beginning.

Sometimes when I wanted to hear English voices I went to an English tea room in the Rue de Rivoli. The place was crowded with tall pink Englishmen in light grey herringbone suits, their summery wives and pig-tailed daughters. I was sitting there one day when a man of about fifty with a foppishly drooping moustache and a very correct out-of-date appearance asked if he might sit at my table. He appeared to be a Frenchman. I was being very French by now and I was abashed when he said a few things in English. His grey eyebrows were brushed up, his large eyes rolled mockingly: under his moustache large, wet wolfish teeth were showing.

'Are you on holiday?'

'No,' I said.

'Ah,' he said. 'Then you are at the Sorbonne.'

'No,' I said. 'I live here.'

I was always proud to say I *lived* in Paris.

'Ah' – again. 'Your family live in Paris?'

'No, in London. I work here.'

'How interesting,' he said. 'May I ask what is your occupation?'

'I work at a photographer's shop.'

The waitress came up and he said to her 'I shall have a *mille feuille* and a cup of tea,' and to me he said:

'I am an Inspector of Schools in England. It's a great bore. I have to get away to France. England is intolerable, don't you find?' he said. 'Why did you choose photography?'

'I didn't.' It never took long for this to burst out – 'I am trying to be a writer.'

He ignored this and now began cornering me in the English fashion. Where did I live in England? Where did I go to school? I told him.

'Oh, Alleyn's school. I inspect it. I know the headmaster. A grammar school,' he said severely. He put his head on one side; his teeth and eyes became playful.

'And so you are going to be a writer? What are you reading? May I see?'

I was reading *La Rôtisserie de la Reine Pedauque.*

'Ah, Anatole France. A failure, don't you think?' he said. 'Do you like it?'

I said I did.

'But it's pastiche,' he said. 'He gets it all out of books. Horrible man. He really is second rate. So affected. His style is beastly.'

Anatole France second rate!

'He only wrote one good novel – *Le Lys Rouge.* Do you know that? That has form – nothing more.'

I tried to think what 'form' was. All I could remember of this novel was the chapter in which the lover sees the pink nipple of his mistress's breast through her thin chemise, an incident that put me in a desperate state one hot afternoon in the Rotonde café. In England a girl had once let my hands play with her breasts and she had said 'You are a funny boy. Why do you do that?' This was nothing to the scene in *Le Lys Rouge.*

'Yes,' I said. 'I've read it.'

'It's his only book. One used to see him – but no longer. Not after the Madame X business. Really he behaved appallingly. We're not on speaking terms,' he said. 'A mean little bookseller! – but what do you expect?'

Good heavens! He knew Anatole France! Here I was, in the English tea room, and with one who was at the centre of French literary life.

'When one remembers what she did to get him into the Academy and he treats her like that!'

His eyes appeared to be denouncing me too.

'And you admire his work!'

'And what is he – what are you going to write?' he said. 'A novel? I never read English novels. Hardy, George Eliot – unbearable,' he grimaced with suffering. 'I only read French novels. Ah, not a novel. Then – what?'

The word 'what' presented me with an endless wilderness. I, the one true friend of Anatole France, blushed and was wary. I began to hate this man's foolish moustache and his feline manner. I now played my trump card.

'I have had an article accepted by the *Christian Science Monitor*,' I said. 'And by two Reviews.'

The effect was awful.

'Oh,' he said, as if he had got me pinned down at last. 'You are not a follower of the Eddy, are you?'

'My father is. I am,' I said.

'But, my dear boy,' he said sharply, 'you have horrified me. Why? Don't you know – well, I mean, the lies! She died drugged to the eyes.'

It was not in the official *Life*, but people said this.

The awful thing about his horror was that it was playful. But now he became stern.

'I must tell you,' he said austerely dismissing me, 'I am an Anglo-Catholic. Do you know what an Anglo-Catholic is?'

I had heard of this religion.

'Never, never,' he said, as if speaking of the intellectually unspeakable, 'confuse that with the Roman Catholic.' He paused. 'Promise me.'

'Oh no,' I said. I remembered now that I had once been to an Anglo-Catholic church with my cousin when I was a boy in Ipswich. She had put on such airs during the service about my ignorance of ritual. This was the time when she said she was going to marry an earl: the church, the smell of incense, instead of the smell of peppermints and hair-oil that came off the Dissenters I knew, made me feel I was among near-earls. I was uncomfortable. Until that moment I had been in love with my cousin. It was very humiliating. I could never get into the right set.

'You should read other writers,' he said.

I was on my mettle. I picked out ones that sounded impressive. 'I've read Montesquieu,' I said, 'Boileau...'

He said, nodding with grim mockery: 'And you are going to be a journalist?'

I was being stripped of all my pretensions and I could see he was amusing himself by drawing me out. I did not know how to stop him. It occurred to me that he was the devil. I did not want to be reduced to nothing. I hated being questioned. I said something about having to get back to the shop and got the waitress to bring me my bill. I was getting my money out of my pocket when he said:

'I would like to ask you a favour. I always ask it of people I like. I have enjoyed talking to you. Will you let me look into your eyes?'

I was too startled to refuse.

'Ah no, wide,' he said.

'Ah,' he sighed. He shook his head. 'It's a virgin. Charming. You mustn't mind if I call you "it". I grew up in Italy. It's an Italian habit. Do you come here often? Perhaps tomorrow?'

'Sometimes,' I said. I was in a rage.

'I have a great friend who is a journalist who might help you. I might persuade him to come and meet you.'

I got away. He had made a fool of me. I was furious that he thought I was a virgin. So I was – but he did not know how far I had gone! I walked sulking up the Rue de Richelieu to the shop to hear the blessed words: '*M. Schwep. Combien pour coucher avec?*'

The next day I did not go to the tea room. I wanted vengeance and in the evening when a prostitute stopped me in the Rue Stanislas while I was looking at a bookshop window and said, 'Will you come with me?' I said coldly 'What for?'

She was taken aback.

'What! You do not know what for?'

'Oh *that*! It doesn't interest me,' I said. And walked away.

'Dirty swine!' she called after me.

After that I felt I was even with life.

243

I recovered. I went to the tea room the following day. After all, he knew Anatole France.

He was sitting at the same table.

'I hope you didn't come yesterday. I was not here. I have been having the most awful trouble, really it is too shocking. I just come to Paris for ten days and my whole holiday is ruined.'

He raised his hands and stared at me accusingly.

'Ruined!' he said.

'Disaster!' he said.

He contrived to look older, even more out of date. His eyes stretched, until I thought the eyeballs would shoot up to the ceiling and that he was commanding me to watch them go.

'One expects nothing of human nature – but of a lifelong friend!' He still accused.

Slowly the eyeballs came down from the ceiling and he considered me.

'Will it tell me its name?' he said.

The crushing 'it' business had begun again, but I could now laugh inwardly at the word.

'My name is Ralph,' he said. 'Do you know how to pronounce that? If you are going to be a writer you must pronounce it correctly. Rafe. Say it.'

'Rafe,' I humoured him.

'Never, never, never Ralph. That is middle class. Will you remember that? Rafe. Now perhaps we can be friends?'

I made a note of this.

'Rafe Shaw.'

I have changed the name. But it was a plain name. I had not read Burke's Peerage, but I read the newspapers. I could see heavy black headlines. I could see columns and columns about a scandalous action for divorce. A small hyphen connected the name Shaw with another enormously territorial, dotted with tiaras and coronets, that swirled from mansions to castles, from embassies to yachts, from grouse shoots to palaces. Mother had said at the time, upset: 'It's a good thing poor Queen Victoria is dead.'

Mr Shaw said nothing about this, but we were soon in and out of the embassy in Rome when he was a boy.

244

'Ah, Victor, the Italians have heart!'

What had happened to 'poor Oscar'! The dreadful Queensberry would be 'in-con-ceiv-able' in Italy. The Shaws were an aristocratic tree shedding its leaves in all capitals from Petersburg to Athens; in Rome they had bloomed; but the ashy appearance of Ralph and his occupation showed that one branch had been, as it were, struck by lightning. Yet think of my case. I was rising. First Anatole France; now High Society!

'It is going to be a writer,' Ralph said irritably. 'In human nature it will find the depths. There is nothing more dreadful than seeing the character of a human being changed by money. But dreadful! A friend for life suddenly inherits two millions. Two million pounds. Oh yes. Left to him by the richest Duchess in the world. And it ruins him.'

On a wage of thirty shillings a week I struggled to show despair.

'It's happening now. In Paris. A life-long friend. I was going to bring him to meet you. But I couldn't. He has destroyed his character. I can hardly bring myself to speak to him. Victor, he has become suddenly *mean*, a miser. Avaricious. A millionaire and he won't spend a penny. One is expected to pay for his lunches, even his cab fares. He cheats porters and waiters of their tips – there are scenes everywhere – all over Paris. It is horrible. After twenty years I cannot bear to be with him. I told him I shall stay at the Récamier. I simply cannot bear to see what this has done to him.'

There was one of those curdling pauses and then the eyeballs shot up and when they came down, they rolled.

'And, Victor, he has married!'

I have never heard the word pronounced with more disgust.

'A widow. A second-rate singer. I am asked to dine with them tonight. I doubt if I can stand it. I tell you this because, of course, he belongs, dear boy, to the profession you wish to adorn.'

I was glad of the 'you'.

But the 'it' returned.

'One could arrange perhaps for it to meet him,' he said, 'but one couldn't bear to, not at the moment. One cannot stay in the room with her. She stinks. She stinks like a polecat.'

245

'Stinks!' he said.

'And they keep the windows closed,' he went on. 'Think of me tonight.'

And he got his bill and carefully counted out coins from a little purse.

'And now,' he said, 'it must go back to its photographers and tomorrow to the solaces of Mrs Eddy. I am going to London on Tuesday. Will it have dinner with me on Monday?'

'Yes,' I said. After all, I was sorry to lose contact with High Society.

'Ralph,' he corrected me.

'Ralph,' I said.

'Remember. We are friends.'

On the Monday I called for Ralph at his modest hotel. The vulgar bells of Saint Sulpice, he said, deafened him. We took a tram to a place beyond Saint-Cloud. The forest was carved black by the full moonlight. We dined in a garden and scores of nightingales were sounding like bells in the trees.

'Now I must give it a reward and tell it the full horror of the pole-cat. An intelligent man, a scholar, grovelling before a grasping creature like that! Imagine being in bed with her, Victor! Now, tell me what it did. Now why did it go to the Sainte-Chapelle? What a place! Did it go with a girl?'

'No,' I said.

'I think it ought to meet some clever girls. I wonder now. The Shaw girls are in Paris. They're staying at the Embassy.'

He considered me. As I say, I read the papers. Whatever the Shaw girls did was in the papers, usually on yachts, in night clubs, getting engaged and getting disengaged. Articles on the Bright Young Things always mentioned them. They wore very little.

'Yes,' he mused. 'No. I wonder. Very good for it. They've got brains. But no,' he went on. 'It wouldn't do. All they think of is horses.'

We sat drinking Burgundy, and over the brandy High Society drifted away on the air. I was glad. The Shaw girls terrified me. As they drifted off, Ralph said suddenly:

'Yes, I can see why you like France. I wonder if you are the short Mediterranean type? No, I think not. The head tells one everything. Turn your head sideways. I wonder . . . would you allow me to touch your head. I want to measure it.'

At this he put a finger on my forehead and then the fingers of his right hand upon the back of my head.

'Ah, as I thought. The long flat-topped head – Celtic. Yes, it is a long-headed Celt. Not a trace of the Anglo-Saxon. It's name is Welsh.'

I had often been told that; but my name is Teutonic.

'Long-headed Celt. Will it allow me to follow an Italian custom and kiss it?'

I could not move; I was also a little drunk. I saw the large eyes close and the damp moustache brushed my cheek as it passed and he kissed the top of my head. I sat speechless.

'Well, we must get our tram,' he said.

I had scarcely heard of homosexuality. As far as I knew there was none at school. So Ralph's kiss seemed to me insulting and ridiculous. I put on a stupid, sulky, stolid look. The tram bumped into Paris. We said Good-bye.

In the following year he wrote me one or two short, schoolmasterly notes; and once or twice he came to Paris for a week or two and I would have lunch with him; but he made no more Italian gestures. He did not ask about my writing. I enjoyed his scandalous tales and his stern remarks about literature. He was my first aesthete. When, after two years, I left Paris and was passing through London on my way to Dublin where I had got a job as a newspaper correspondent, I called on him at his flat in Lincolns Inn. I did this out of curiosity, but also because I wanted to show him I was not now as naïve as I must have once seemed.

He came to the door of his chambers wearing a black velvet jacket and looked at me like a cross aunt dealing with a rude nephew. He told me it was very ill-mannered to call upon people without first writing to ask if I might do so. I knew this, and I suppose my rudeness was, in a clumsy way, a young man's revenge. Still, he allowed me to come in. The walls of his flat were yellow with the backs of hundreds of French novels. The place was elegant. With him was an already celebrated young actor who was having a success in a Galsworthy play. I had evidently interrupted a long joke, for they resumed it. It was about a woman sex-maniac who was on trial, and, running through the alphabet, they were inventing perversions. When he heard of my job in Ireland he did not congratulate me.

I left with the actor who had to go to his theatre.

I never saw him again nor did he or I write. A few years later I ran into the actor who said he had no recollection of meeting Ralph. No one had. When I was fifty I met the two Shaw girls. They had never heard of their relation. They had both married authors. I began to think Ralph did not exist. Perhaps he was a kind of Corvo. He is one of the mysteries of my life in Paris; the only certain thing is that he was an Inspector of Schools.

CHAPTER TWO

Now I could speak two kinds of French fairly well. The first was polite. On my free Sunday afternoons I used to sit on a hard upholstered chair and have conversations about literature with a severe and very old French lady in Auteuil. She was a friend of my landlady's priest and approved only of the greatest writers – Racine and Corneille – who were correct in style and in morals. She pulled me up at every sentence and I had to be wary of the grammar and pronunciation I had picked up from Pierre and the Breton at the shop. A mild phrase like 'Sans blague' annoyed her. My afternoons with the old lady were painfully polished exercises.

My desire to appear to be French took an extravagant turn. For a long time Pierre and I had admired each other's footwear. He wanted me to send to England for some shoes like mine. I admired his boots.

'Let's swap,' I said.

We measured our feet and, one evening in the shop, we swapped. He wore boots laced to the top from the small, black patent toecaps. The boots had yellowish uppers that looked like a pair of old banana skins and very high, small, black heels. Tipping forward in his boots – which pinched a bit – I was forced out of my natural rushing walk into a small mincing step. I was very much struck by this when I saw myself in the mirrors of shops. The next thing was to get a wide-brimmed black hat with a round crown of the Bohemian kind worn by the photographers. On a youth as short as I was, these hats looked like umbrellas. I could not afford them. I settled for one with a high crown, pinched in the middle at the top, black and with a wide-ish brim. It made me look tall – more hat than suit. A pipe was the next thing. I would pass a shop in the Boulevard St Michel where there was a pipe with a ten-inch stem. I used to visit this pipe nearly every day, yearning for it. At last I got paid for one of the articles I had written and bought the pipe. I filled it with rough French tobacco which blazed up like dry hay, and I was soon sick in the street. This long pipe was impossible out of doors, for it was easily jogged down my throat if someone bumped into me; and it nearly dragged my teeth out. I returned to cigarettes: *Gauloises* or an English cigarette called *Pirate* which blistered my tongue. I smoked all day long, except in the shop. I took to doubling and trebling the usual amount of coffee I drank because Balzac had done this. On my way to the shop I passed his house in the Rue Raynouard which reminded me of this; and there was another reason for drinking more coffee. I wanted to get a dark complexion. I had seen a man of thirty-five or so sitting on the terrace of a café; a tired, cynical boulevardier who had the dark olive look I wanted. His hair was receding. I cut a chunk of hair on the left side of my head to get this superb effect of a dissolute life.

I began to go to cheap cabarets. There were two popular places in Montmartre called Le Ciel and L'Enfer. In L'Enfer one was greeted by a smelly young wit dressed as the devil who mocked each customer. I slipped in behind two middle-aged women and so escaped his joke. But to the ladies he shouted:

'Oh, *voilà deux nourisses de Saint-Germain-en-laye-en-lait*.' This joke came out every time I went there. I picked up a lot of songs and swapped them with Pierre.

'You can see M. Schwep has a mistress,' said the Breton.

'I have,' I said.

'Where does she live?'

'In my quarter. Auteuil.'

'That is chic.'

They were awed.

'Is she English?'

'Yes.'

'Ah,' said the Breton, giving me a slap. 'You come from Great Britain. I come from Little Britain. We understand each other. You're cunning; you've kept it very quiet.'

I had invented this, of course.

That summer the Bohemian crowd in Montparnasse had thinned. They put on fisherman's shirts in fisherman blue, or loud red and white checks and went off to the South of France. I could not afford such a journey, but in September when my fortnight's holiday came, I took the train to Rouen. My brother came over from London with a friend. I had longed to sleep à *la belle etoile* in the manner of Stevenson. I warned my brother and his friend of this, but they arrived in Rouen wearing bowler hats, without knapsacks, ground-sheets or blankets. The hats disgusted me; I made them leave them in the railway cloak-room. A heavy lunch, beginning with oysters, and washed down with cheap wine, put us in a better temper. The friend wanted to get to Paris, but we forced him to walk northward. We were aiming for Dieppe. An hour or two after leaving Rouen clouds piled up, then a heavy rain came on as we got to a large forest where we sheltered. We sat under trees eating bread and sausage and then pressed on into the forest. Soon the wet darkness came, the footpaths confused us, and we had to find our way by striking matches that went out almost as soon as they were struck. The expedition was losing its high literary quality and soon sank to the coarse level of *Three Men in a Boat*; for when we decided to lie down for the night my groundsheet and blanket had to serve for the three of us.

So our night passed in a vulgar struggle with the blanket: now my brother pulled it his way, and the other youth pulled it off both of us. The rain, spouting through the trees, came down on us in lumps. At about three in the morning we could stand this no longer. We got up, and finding a path we groped mile after mile, until daylight when at the edge of the forest we could smell apples. We were among the Normandy orchards and dogs barked at us. But no one was about. The rain stopped, the sun came out and we found a lane and staggered along it. We fell asleep as we walked, like drunks; we had to hold one another up. Eventually we gave in and lay down on a wet grass bank by the roadside.

Two hours later we woke up: we found we had rolled off the bank and were sleeping in the road. One of Maupassant's peasants croaking along with a wagon had to stop to get by us. He did not say much. I was shabby, but the respectable clothes of my brother and his friend, though mud-spattered, must have saved us from suspicion. The fine rain came on again. We went through a sodden cornfield to a river where we got out of our clothes and stood naked among the boulders waist deep in rushing cold water; then we wrang out our clothes, dried ourselves on our shirts, and went on to a village. No villagers were about, but there were carters at the inn: we wisely drank a lot of cognac. My companions wanted to stay, but I was fiercely for the road; we found another village inn kept by a decent couple. Seeing an advertisement for a drink called *Amourette*, we plumped for that. The landlady dried our clothes and gave us a huge meal with two bottles of Normandy cider. Strong as Devonshire cider is, Normandy cider is much stronger; it flowed into us as innocently as lemonade and suddenly made us incapable. The man and his wife couldn't stop laughing at us and the end of it was that we slept in a bed that night.

The roads of Normandy are exposed, hedgeless and boring. We slept out again, in a field and once in a barn. Outside Dieppe we visited a castle from tower to dungeon; in the town we guzzled, but slept out on a cliff outside. I tried to make coffee on a methylated spirit stove and when we lay down we spent a cold night watching the lights of the fishing boats in the Channel. Then, for several days, we walked back to Rouen by some roundabout route through some pretty places. I enjoyed this journey, as a young animal does, but except for games of billiards with village people in the inns and a dance with some railway workers and their girls, the expedition was not up to the standard of Borrow, Stevenson and Belloc. There were no heroic invocations or poetic jollities; only grunts and wondering if our money would hold out. Jerome K. Jerome, as I say, haunted it. It worried me that as a traveller I was evidently tame. I also saw that to travel well, one must travel alone.

The secret of happiness (they say) is to live in the imagination. I had many imaginary lives, building up every day and dissolving at night. I lay in bed reading, occasionally putting a date on the page of say *Le Père Goriot* and wondered what I should be doing in years incredibly far ahead – say 1930 or 1940. A strange woman with large dark eyes and wearing a long red velvet robe used to console me sexually. I fancy she must have been an idealized version of that disturbing secondhand-clothes dealer my family had taken us to see in the Edgware Road when I was a boy. She had worn red velvet too. Late one night, having waited in a café near the Etoile for the orchestra to get round again to the Danse Macabre by Saint-Saens, I walked up the Avenue Hoche. Two girls jumped out at me and one called out:

'*Où allez vous, M. le Marquis? Où couchez vous?*'

'*Chez la Marquise,*' I said, shooting up into High Society, this being near the mansions of the Avenue Hoche. What wit! I was a marquis.

And I *had* found a marquise, a young girl. At any rate, her mother was having a quarrel with a Baroness, an Italian-American. This girl was training in Paris to be an actress. I met her at the time of my acquaintance with Ralph Shaw: and my tales about him went down well with her mother who was very snobbish. ('Who were his people?' she kept speculating.) Our meeting had a headlong, unreal quality that lasted throughout our friendship. I had not been near the Christian Scientists for some time (one or two complained that my breath almost knocked them down with the smell of wine) and I found they had moved their meeting-place because their numbers had trebled. The new meeting place was a fashionable night-club off the Champs Elysées, which was closed on Sundays. Two or three of the few men in the congregation used to go there at eight in the morning to remove the tables and the bottles, open the windows to get out the smell of wine and stale tobacco, and turn about twenty *Gravures Libertines* to the wall. On the platform where the band had played the night before, the Readers now read from Mrs Eddy and the Bible, in that curious game of swapping texts which dissenting Protestants play.

Here I saw a graceful, but militant, well-tailored woman with straw-coloured hair come in with a girl so strange and exquisite that my eyes filled with tears. Her body was slight, but she had a fine forehead and black hair that had the soft gleam of oil in its waves. Her long eyelashes hung over large blue eyes and she had very heavy short eyebrows. She wore a big bow in her hair so that the effect was of being half-girl, half heavy-headed, thin-legged butterfly, rather than anything human; yet the artifice was not complete. Her lips and her round chin could hardly keep still for amusement. As the two passed where I was sitting

253

I could see the maddening dark hair of her armpits under her sleeveless summer dress and there was a breath of musky scent that put me in a frantic state. It melted into sadness for I had the sensation (when she sat down two or three rows in front of me and I gazed at every move of her shoulders) that she had passed into an unattainable foreign distance. The older woman – her mother, I was to find out – could not have been more than thirty-seven. She was a pretty woman, with a small decided chin and the proud collected eyes of a cat, and all through the service she kept turning to look at her daughter's hair and her face, as if the girl were some adored doll. Afterwards, a middle-aged Italian was talking to them and gazing as intently as I was at the daughter and the mother looked at him mockingly as if she were saying: 'Yes, of course, you have fallen for her. Everyone does. Isn't she dazzling? I invented her. You're not dangerous. But she is. She's mine.' And, indicating the rest of us with a nod, 'How she shows up these awful people.'

I went away desperate. I had heard the mother's voice: they were rich, inaccessible English.

The next Sunday I went again in order to suffer. But, after the service the mother was caught up in a conversation with a grand and sullen looking woman, and the daughter was alone. I was impelled by a force I did not know existed in me. I worked my way through the chairs to her. We looked at each other. I smiled. She smiled. I knocked over a chair. She laughed. We started talking fast. She had a low warm voice and everything that came spitting out of me made her laugh more. I had an inspiration. I pointed to the pictures with their backs turned towards us.

'I wonder what's on the other side of those pictures. Shall we try to see?'

'Oh yes.' Enthusiasm!

'Come along.' I dared her. 'I'll turn one round.'

'Please!' she said.

We made our way to the wall. I reached for a picture. It was very large and I could not turn it more than a few inches; a heap of dust fell into my eyes.

'You see!' she said. 'You must not get so excited. You *are* funny.' Funny: the word haunted my efforts with girls. I was in love. And – I could not believe it – we instantly seemed to be living in each other's eyes.

Her watchful mother came smiling towards us and I put on my best behaviour.

'We wanted to look at the pictures.'

'And he got covered in dust,' the girl said.

We walked out of the building, talking. I was determined not to let them go. They had heard about this church from 'the Baroness' the mother said. They had come, the mother said, to have a word with her. She asked me questions in an unusual, drawling voice, looking me up and down. I was wearing my French hat, but I had put on my best suit.

'Where are you having lunch?' the mother said, suddenly. 'Are you free today?'

It was a miracle. We walked into the Champs Elysées and once she turned to her daughter and murmured:

'The Baroness was impossible,' she said.

'Poor Mummy,' the girl said in a sorrowful voice and slowly shook her curls. And to me:

'The Baroness is dreadful.'

I was in the middle of a play.

'We come from Mexico,' the mother said in a grand, drawling voice. The Baroness: Mexico: High Society.

We went off to a flat they had rented in the Rue Notre Dame des Champs that looked down on the Bal Bullier.

'I have brought Judy to Paris because she is going on the stage. It is possible, of course, nowadays, for *ladies* to go on the stage,' Mrs Lang drawled on.

'I am going to be a writer,' I said.

The girl clapped her hands.

'You will write plays for me!' she said.

The mother smiled at me.

'Isn't she a child?' she laughed.

By four o'clock that afternoon, in the impetuous laughing way of strangers who meet outside their own country, we had told one another what is called 'everything' about ourselves. It was in fact a meeting not of three people, but of six – ourselves and our fictions. I have said that it was like being in a

play, but really it was more like being in a puppet show. The
girl was her mother's doll.

'You shall be cousins,' said the mother when she had questioned me about my family. (I had, I must admit, moved them
up in the world.) 'He must be part of the family, mustn't he?
You must call me Tia, that is Spanish for Aunt. Jolly good pals.'

There was a man-to-man touch about Mrs Lang.

'Oh yes,' cried the girl to her mother. 'He's like your pony,
that wicked pony of yours who took you to assignations.'

'Really Judy!' said Mrs Lang. 'Assignations – what a word!'

'Oh, but he did! It used to stand under mummy's window
waiting for her to climb down and dash off to marvellous
parties.'

Mrs Lang said fondly: 'You can't remember. You were only
six in Puebla.'

'It was the only way she could get out,' said the girl.

I saw Mrs Lang galloping across the landscape, in the moonlight, to some hacienda. It was a thrilling sight.

'Married to that brute' – the brute was her elderly husband –
'when I was sixteen, it was the only way. Her grandmother
was Spanish – look at her hair,' said Mrs Lang in her offhand
way.

Whenever I saw Mrs Lang after this I imagined her on a wild
horse. Her life seemed to come out of a novel. The 'brute' had
been shot in the Revolution – 'a good thing too' – and here she
was fighting to get her money (for he had a big estate) out of
the Mexican government. They had refused to hand it over;
but now, after years, they had promised to pay up and so she
had come to Paris. I was captivated by Mrs Lang, especially by
her strange straw-like hair, her cold eyes and her lazy laughing
manner. I could see her sitting in her Mexican house, which had
once been a convent. She gets up and sticks a hat pin into a
scorpion (or was it a tarantula?) that is going to drop on Judy's
bed. Some nights a dozen hat pins impale the bodies on the
wall. In the morning the maid collects them. I saw Mrs Lang
get a revolver out from under her pillow and shoot at the hand
of a thief that comes stealthily round the handle of the door
one night. Was it a thief or was it the ghost of a nun? Mrs Lang
was open-minded but she was (she said) a devilish good shot.

I left the house at five and walked down to the Boulevard Saint Germain, then along the river, all the way to Auteuil, but I seemed to float. What I had so often dreamed had magically happened. I was in love, and although Judy and I had done nothing but laugh together, surely she was in love too? I was to meet them the next evening at a small restaurant. No one was happier than I to be able to lend Mrs Lang fifteen francs towards paying the bill: she had foolishly left her purse in her other handbag. This evening Mrs Lang told me that Judy was engaged to be married – engaged since the age of twelve: but the marriage would not take place until she became an actress.

'They'll give their eyes for her,' the mother said. 'The moment the lights go up . . .'

'Glorious lights, Puck!' Judy exclaimed. That was the name they gave me: they hated Victor as much as I did.

'She will make a fortune.'

'Oh yes! And you will be famous and write a play and I will act in it,' she said again.

Engaged? For a second time I was jealous, but dismissed it. We had years before us.

So began – what? A love affair? Hardly. The sketch or outline of a love affair. A fantasy. I could never quite bring myself to believe Judy was human. But when the Breton at the shop had asked if I had a mistress and I had said 'Yes' it was Judy I was thinking of. After leaving the shop I would hurry up to the flat and would hear of her dangerous career. She was seeing theatre managers in Montmartre, of all places; or she was having tea with that Italian; or considering posing as a model – 'but only for the face,' Mrs Lang said. How reckless the rich English were. And then Judy's talk was a mixture of mischief and the unbelievable. She would say, 'Monsieur began to get – you know? Hot? He looked awfully hot.' Or Monsieur wanted to make 'assignations' or was 'a bit *gallant*.' And to me 'Your heart is like one of those hotels, you know?' And the mother said proudly 'Isn't she dreadful?'

Where was I? Hadn't I read this somewhere – in Wilde? Was she an *ingénue*? Now, when I think of our chats and our walks, I understand that Mrs Lang and her daughter were both acting

Edwardian roles. The mother could have appeared in any of the plays of the period.

The comedy of it all excited me and my vanity was flattered when men turned to look at Judy as we walked down the street. I discovered I was a natural flirt – as the word then was – and since the word 'gallant' was a favourite of Mrs Lang's, I was as gallant as anything with her daughter. A new faculty: what a pleasure it is to discover this when one is young and coming out of one's shell. And there was a darker side to this: I feared the accusations, the solemnities, the jealousies of adult love. I was 'in love' with a girl who was really a child, though she was older than I. Was I a child, too? The doubt was wounding.

Paris had put a spell on me. Mrs Lang and Judy were part of that spell. Mrs Lang often had to go and see someone or other about her Mexican affairs (she said), and Judy and I were left in the evenings or on Saturday or Sunday afternoons to ourselves. We wandered along the Seine, laughing and inventing fantasies. One afternoon we went out to Saint-Cloud and sat in the park. The girl started collecting snails from the grass and we put a wall of stones round them.

'Look at our children,' she said.

She said this at the moment when I was wondering whether to break the spell and kiss her. There are *voyeurs* in Saint-Cloud on Saturdays. I could hear one crawling on his hands and knees nearer and nearer to us. I got up in a temper and found the man.

'How dare you spy on us!' I said.

A sullen man stood up.

'Who is spying? I have as much right to be here as you.' My imagination and temper went up in the air together.

'I shall report you to the British Ambassador for molesting his daughter.'

'Go on!' sneered the man.

I can't think what made me say such an absurd thing. I advanced upon him and he walked backwards from me swearing. I watched him till he went off.

'What was he doing?' Judy said.

'They spy on lovers.'

It was the nearest I came to saying I loved her.

'Whatever for?' she laughed. 'You were very funny.'

We went back to my room. This agitated me. The sight of the big double bed was like something large and human, and we behaved very respectfully before it. She looked at herself in the big mirror and for long afterwards I used to remember her face reflected in it. I had bought some cherries and we threw them into the branches of the tree in the yard so that they looked as if they were growing there. Madame Chapin came in. She was delighted my 'cousin' was. so pretty: and often asked about her eagerly. I had gone up in Madame Chapin's estimation and she became almost fond.

What puzzled me was that the desire I had felt for Judy when I first met her would vanish when she was present; it was only when she was away that it returned.

I was now – mysteriously to me – the chief acknowledged, imaginary lover of Judy among her friends, who were mostly students, and I had no rivals. It was agreed that we were both extraordinary and I certainly played on that. There was only one critical figure: this was a tall Danish girl who took an austere interest in Judy and me. She had straight hair and green-ish eyes and was a big-boned girl who lived with a professor's family and was writing a philosophical thesis. She was the daughter of a sea captain. Those greenish eyes gazed at Judy and then at me greedily. One week-end we all went off to Fontainebleau together, taking a cheerful English youth with us. We walked through the forest, but he and I walked faster than they and so the girls were far behind most of the day. We stayed in a cheap hotel. The moon came up, the nightingales belled all night and I could not sleep. I shared my room with the young man who made a whistling noise when he slept. The girls were next door. I longed to be with Judy and lay tortured by the moonlight and the nightingales. The next day the girls were always together and I was jealous. Judy had to go home when we got to Paris and I did not go with her. I was left with the Dane.

'I thought you always went with Judy.'

'Not always,' I said.

'I think you should have gone with her,' she said. 'She is unhappy.'

I could guess the cause of Judy's unhappiness: the habits of the adventurous Mrs Lang. The Mexican stories were true, but the Mexican money was a dream. The puzzle was to know whether Judy understood that her beauty was being used by her mother; knowing that it attracted us all, the gambler took to borrowing money from everyone Judy met. The Baroness had been at the beginning of this career. Now, I, who had had a struggle with an overwhelming father, saw Judy in a similar case. The Dutch girl soon told me the rest.

'We both love Judy,' she said. 'We ought to tell her. She must get away from her mother.'

'I am not in love with Judy,' I said.

And I wasn't. The nightingales singing all night had sung it all away.

'Judy is sleep-walking and so are you,' said the girl.

So love turned into fascination. Mrs Lang, keeping up a fight for her dream, forgot about Mexico and took a job as a governess. Judy went from family to family looking after children. When she had time off I would go to fetch her. I felt great tenderness for her, but she would not speak of her troubles. Then, in a bad crisis in their affairs – for Mrs Lang quarrelled with her employers, usually about some slight to 'an English lady' – they moved to (of all places) the Avenue Hoche, my marquis street.

I went there and a butler at the front door sent me to the servants' quarters. There, in the ironing room and treated with the contempt the French keep for the inferiors, the mother and daughter were living. We went out to a cab drivers' restaurant. The following week the mother went to work with a family in Dieppe, leaving Judy with me. I was living in her day-dream; she was living in mine and, taking my opportunity, the disciple of Belloc and W. J. Locke made her walk most of the way to Triel down the Seine. It was a hot, happy day. I remember the smell of hay and drinking wine and eating lunch under a tree. I remember I fell asleep for I was woken up by Judy laughing at me. We traipsed on to an hotel at Triel and there I wanted to stay with her; but we were tired, I had just enough money left to take us back to Paris by train. So I said nothing. In fact, having been paid for two of my articles and having, unfortunately, boasted to Mrs Lang about it, the clever lady had soon got most of it out of me.

The next week a message commanded Judy to join her mother in Dieppe. I saw Judy off at the Gare Saint Lazare. We were not sad. We still seemed to be living in each other's eyes. At twenty one is light-hearted. It had all been gayer than love. A lesson, too: altogether Mrs Lang had had from me what seemed the enormous sum of £10.

CHAPTER THREE

Now when I look back on the tragic figure of Mr Shaves I see he was not a born banker. He shared a corner of the bank with three other men. The other clerks looked like repressed rips, especially when they talked to women at the counter. Shaves was an indigestible pudding of suppressed virtues. The other clerks wore black or dark grey suits; he wore either a cocoa brown or grey one with holiday stripes on it. There was a buttonhole in his jacket. His glossy, buttery hair frisked in curls of grey at the ears, he had a smoker's stained moustache; and very often he sat sideways at his desk lost in the sheer wonder of gazing at his trouser legs, his coloured socks and his shoes. Only by an effort of will, recollecting his duty, would he suddenly sit straight at his work. Then he put on an absurdly mean expression.

Shaves was short and had puddled impudent eyes; he looked vulgar. His powerful voice had made the worst of American and English speech. I learned my first American phrases from him, leading from 'Whad d'ya know?' on to 'I'm through' and 'I can't make it.' Hollywood made them current in England eventually. He was a rumbustious English patriot who saw himself, after twenty-five years in the United States, fighting a dogged one-man war against that country.

'Jesus,' he would say, 'you can have Paris and New York. I'm through with them. I can't take them.'

The bank was a 'whore-shop'. In twenty-five years he had picked up every cliché going in suburban America. When he cashed my first cheque, he said:

'You're a writer? You come from Bromley? Whad d'ya know! I was born in Lewisham.'

He spread his arms: I thought he was going to embrace me. He had found what he was longing for, an ally.

'This'll interest you,' he said and from the counter he took a circular. On it was printed 'The Boulevard Players Present

Fanny's First Play by George Bernard Shaw.' Among the cast of players was Basil Chavasse.

'I'm playing Gilbey,' he said. 'Ever seen it? That's my stage name.'

'No,' I said.

He was indignant: then he lit up. In the next quarter of an hour he ran through his favourite scenes. One I was to hear time and time again:

'Remember how it goes – Gilbey says:

' "We've done what we can for the boy. Short of letting him get into temptation of all sorts he can do what he likes. What more does he want?" And Doris comes back with "Well, he wants *me*!" Can you beat it?'

In the middle of this, Basil Shaves had passed my cheque, collected the money himself and gave it to me.

'He's a Britisher,' he called around to the office.

He asked me to come and see the Shaves family in Neuilly.

The Shaves lived in a small villa, built in a mixture of red brick, yellow brick and dotted with tiles; it looked like a coloured crossword puzzle. There was a high noisy iron gate with spikes on top – French suburbanites fortify themselves – and as we crossed the pebbled stretch to the steps between dusty shrubs, Mr Shaves said:

'See that? No grass. You never see a decent lawn outside of England.'

There were two very young children. Mrs Shaves was a short woman with a heavy blob of white hair and a duck-like bosom which she seemed to carry about as if it were a personal tragedy. She made a soft noise like a carpet sweeper when she walked. There was a slender fair-haired daughter with her mother's pretty blue eyes and delicate voice, a child of nine. There was also a son with exactly her boyish pouting lips. The family gathered protectively round the husband and father. They laughed as he darted at once to a piano in the sitting-room the first time I went there, banged out a tune, and wagging his head from side to side, started to sing. His voice had some quality that brought home the London streets. He swung round on the piano stool and called to me:

'Pagliacci – know it?'

Mrs Shaves said : 'Basil's father was a singer.'

'Chavasse, Cecil Chavasse, Metropolitan Opera House, New York.'

He had told me this when we had first met.

'Victor is too young,' she said tenderly.

Shaves was annoyed that I was too young. His mean look came on for a moment.

'Basil's father. Chavasse was the stage name,' his wife said.

'Berlin, Vienna, Brussels, New York, all over America. Australia. Italian opera,' said Basil Shaves.

One of those marital interludes of competitive story-telling began.

'It was after the Australian tour that he brought Basil and the family from London to New York,' Mrs Shaves said complacently.

'I was twelve.'

'All the famous singers used to come to my father's house.'

Mrs Shaves said : 'That is how Basil and I met.'

The Paris furniture, she took care to explain, was not theirs. All her best French furniture was at her sister's in New York.

'Her father was a connoisseur,' said Mr Shaves, admiring her family.

'My mother was French,' Mrs Shaves said, in a distinguished way.

'Yeah,' said Mr Shaves. There was a reverent pause and then Mr Shaves switched back to *his* father.

'Cecil Chavasse,' he said. 'A tragedy.'

'A tragedy,' said Mrs Shaves in a firm voice.

'After the Australian tour he was billed to sing in Chicago. It was in December. Jesus, can it be cold in Chicago! The inside of his coat froze. He got laryngitis, his voice went. He couldn't sing. The voice went like that.'

'They got a specialist from Vienna,' said Mrs Shaves, in her refined hoot.

'It went on for months,' said Mr Shaves. 'He never sang again.'

'At the height of his career,' said Mrs Shaves. 'That's the trouble with the theatre. A little thing – and you're finished. At fifty-one.'

'It was terrible for Basil,' said Mrs Shaves. 'He was only six-teen. At that age you are impressionable. And for the family – his mother and two sisters.'

'Father always lived,' said Mr Shaves. 'We were at the Waldorf – suddenly, not a cent. He was a spender. Champagne dinners, open house, and,' Mr Shaves lowered his voice, 'there were women. We were down to living in a couple of cheap rooms in Brooklyn,' Mr Shaves said.

Mrs Shaves shook her head sadly.

'They put me into the bank. I wanted to be an actor,' said Mr Shaves. 'The Rooters were looking after my mother. Her sister,' he jerked a proud thumb at his wife, and said with awe, 'married a Rooter.'

I was lost.

'Bankers. Own the bank,' he said. Mr Shave's awe increased and he gazed at his wife.

In all the time I knew Mr Shaves his astonishment, his pride and his despair at having pretty well married into the Rooters always came out. He had married above himself. Mrs Shaves was high above him – socially, intellectually, morally : *she* could have married a Rooter, too, instead of an unsuccessful clerk. He had ruined her.

We sat down to a meal. When Mrs Shaves brought the casserole to the table and steam rose from it, Mr Shaves said :

'Victor understands what I mean. He's a writer. I ought to have left the bank. I'm an actor.'

He looked at the food as if it were part of a plot against him.

'I ought to have starved,' he said. He was accusing us of preventing the starvation of an artist. The children lowered their eyes and giggled.

After dinner Mr Shaves went to the piano, singing out a few lines from an aria and then changing to another and another.

'Do you sing?' he called to me. 'Come on. I'll find some-thing.'

'I can't sing.'

'You've never tried. Here, how about this? Cutts of the Cruiser What-not. Know it?'

'Oh Basil, please not that. Haven't you a French folk song? I'm sure Victor would like that,' said Mrs Shaves.

Mr Shaves stuck a finger in an ear, burrowing there, in thought.

'Basil,' said Mrs Shaves.

He pulled his finger out of his ear. He had vulgar habits.

'Come on, all of you.' And he banged out a tune and sang:

> I'm Cutts of the Cruiser What-not
> A cruetty salt of the sea ...

He paused. 'That's good – a cruetty salt.'

> When homeward bound
> My old ship runs aground
> I love it – I shriek with glee.

Soon he forced all of us, except Mrs Shaves, to sing it.

When I left Mrs Shaves said to me: 'I am so glad Basil has found a friend.'

A tussle was going on in the Shaves family. It had begun in 1914 in New York when the war broke out. Firmly kept away from the theatre by his wife and his relations, he now saw his chance. He became violently patriotic, went off to Canada and got himself into the army; he expected to be sent to London. Instead he was sent to the weariest of the campaigns in that war: the stalemate in Salonika. His age was even then against him: something in his appearance, the moustache, no doubt, suggested Bairnsfather's Old Bill in the shell-hole; but Shaves was an old Bill in the regimental kitchens throughout this war. When the war was over he went back to New York and the bank. He got his wife to pull strings with her relations and to get his transfer to London. No American in 1919 wanted to go to London. They couldn't believe him. They sent him to Paris. His wife may have had a hand in this: Paris was far from Shaftesbury Avenue. Mr Shaves admiringly agreed but set about getting his transfer to London. Mrs Shaves thought his part with the Boulevard Players would divert him from this. On the contrary, it aroused his desire to throw up everything for the stage. How complex are human manoeuvres: to get Mrs Shaves out of Paris he conveyed to her that he was exposed to moral danger there. Paris was a sink, the office was a brothel.

Once I stayed the night in their house and when we went off to our jobs in the morning it was touching to see his wife and his children standing on the doorstep to see him off. Their smiles were anxious, protective and wistful, as they saw the breadwinner light up his cigarette and under the halo of smoke go bravely out, his shoulders wagging, to face the sins and temptations of the wicked city.

These things came out in my occasional walks with him when I ran into him on the Boulevard.

A walk with Mr Shaves was always embarrassing. Once out of the bank he looked like a tourist doing 'gay Paree', with a foolish smile on his face. He waltzed along, humming a tune out of one side of his mouth. His cigarette holder went up and down according to his moods. What I dreaded was that he would stop walking; for when a thought struck him he would start to sing – as he thought – quietly. 'La, da di da, la la,' a bit of Italian opera; if it was a favourite bit, he would go on far more loudly, making a sweep with his arms. 'La di da di plonk, plonk, plonk da–a–a–a–', in some finale and utter his common phrase: 'Figaro – know it?' Or 'Tosca – get it?' We would continue our saunter. But sometimes he stopped with indignation: his moral nature gave him his mean expression.

'See that? No, there. That waiter looking at that woman – mentally undressing her. Victor, that's what I can't stand about this place. I've got to get my transfer.'

Yet if a pretty girl passed us, his face would become dreamy:

'Look at those breasts,' he would say.

But if the girl happened to look at him he would put on a stern look; if she looked at me, he would say, warning me:

'They're brazen.'

Outside a newspaper kiosk near the Palais Royal when, in a fit of showing off, I had stopped to buy *Le Crapouillot*, a gossippy paper about the arts and the theatre – he started spouting his favourite lines from *Fanny's First Play*, the ones about the cockatoo. He was running over the scene with Knox. I have looked them up.

My Uncle Phil was a teetotaller. My father used to say to me Rob, he says, don't you ever have a weakness. If you find one getting hold of you, make a merit of it, he says, your Uncle Phil doesn't like spirits but he makes a merit of it and is Chairman of the Blue Ribbon Committee. I do like spirits; and I make a merit of it, and I'm the King Cockatoo of the Convivial Cockatoos. Never put yourself in the wrong.

He came out strongly with the last lines:

'Convivial Cockatoos, Victor! Can you beat it?'

A load of tourists were going into the hotel there. One or two looked cross because they thought he was shouting at them.

'What I've got to show is the change in Gilbey's character,' he said and he walked worrying under the arcades of the Rue de Rivoli.

The bond between us, as he saw it, was that we were fellow artists, both at the beginnings of our careers.

I did not see much of him and then, in August, when so many shops and restaurants put up their iron shutters that the streets look blind, and when the Seine has its white August gleam, Mrs Shaves's sister, the genuine Rooter, came over from New York, looking like something out of a bazaar. She soon put on the fashionable tawny, orange make-up and became parrot-like – Mrs Shaves never had more than a dab of powder on her face – and took the family off to Britanny, leaving Mr Shaves behind. I saw him sagging in the Café de la Paix. He was lost without them all. This brought out his confessional side. One Saturday afternoon we walked together. A walk with Mr Shaves was like walking with someone undressed. We paused in fascination at Maxim's. What wickedness went on there! Up the Champs Elysées we strolled under the trees. We came to a stop at a café opposite Fouquet's where we sat and where his look alternated between the showy and the agonized. The quickness of his fantasy and its sudden extinction gave one the impression that he was shady. He was not. He was tormented. Enthusiastically tormented. There was his enthusiasm for the affection of the two sisters. He sunned himself in it, congratulating himself on being adjacent to it.

'I have a lovely family,' he said.

But a cloud came over the sun. The sister-in-law had taken the whole family to Fouquet's to dinner the night before their holiday.

'I ought to have starved. Father starved when he was young.'
This theme returned.

'I ought not to have gone into the bank.' This lead on to 'ruin'.

'I could not ruin them.'

Looking for money in his wallet, he found a photograph.

'She' – he showed me his wife's picture; she was a slender young woman at that time – 'could have had anything she wanted. I have ruined them already.'

There was remorse in this but out came the sun again, and his foot wagged faster and he hissed a tune and rolled his head from one side to the other, in time with it, happily. It was, I gathered, a kind of coup to have 'ruined' someone who was almost a Rooter, a liberation.

He said: 'The Thousand Islands – ever heard of them? You haven't heard of the Thousand Islands? Well, whad d'ya know! On the St Lawrence – that's where we spent our honeymoon. It took me six months to break the hymen. It all dates back to that – then the war – I was away. I came back. She wants something higher, Victor. She says I'm holding her back from God. Her sister's the same. That's my problem – I can't make it. I'm not pure, Victor!'

He looked at me with dreadful appeal.

'I sometimes undress and look at myself in the mirror. I get a funny pleasure out of looking at myself.'

'Tolstoy used to do that,' I said.

'What – Tolstoy the writer?' said Mr Shaves, amazed.

'Yes.'

'Well, whad d'ya know!'

He became furtive. 'You know – the way my hair grows, everything about my body – interests me. I sometimes sit in a bus and imagine everybody there without a stitch on – nude. No kidding. I enjoy it. You say Tolstoy was like that?'

He sat like some steaming nudist beside me. He had put on weight in the last month or two, he said, his chest was over-developing; it worried him. Do men get like women? It was funny the pleasure you get from scratching your backside, almost like going to bed with a woman. That was why the Rooters got him into the bank: he'd got into a small touring company going to Detroit when he was sixteen and a girl in the company was very kind to him. The company was broke and she let him lie beside her, naked, in her room. No, he never touched her. They just looked at each other. Innocent. But the family found out and got him back to New York; he was too obviously following in father's footsteps.

Mr Shaves, in confessions like these, would seem to swell. He was the Flesh, a man encumbered by his physical person. He saw the very pores of his skin through a kind of sensual magnifying glass: I often saw him hold up his hand and look at it with secretive wonder. Even in his walk, the roll of his gait, one could see he was bewildered by the obligation of carrying this warm throbbing load of flesh and tissues around, singing to himself as he went (I suppose), to distract his mind from it.

I sometimes saw Basil Shaves sitting at lunch-time with friends in one of the cafés on the Boulevard des Italiens. He had the gift of admiring his friends. He was casting himself for their lives. One day he called to me as I passed. I went to his table.

'This is Victor, he's a writer,' he said.

I met a tall talkative Englishman, with sandy sidewhiskers, a military type; and a silent burly Frenchman. They said they were in the shellac trade. The Frenchman asked me, in French, what I was doing. Fatal question to a young man like me: I told him, at length.

'Tell him about that office boy, and Mac. Go on,' said Shaves. 'Tell him about your father,' Shaves said. I had an audience. The listening Englishman said to the Frenchman: 'Just what we want, don't you think?' And to me: 'Do you want a job?'

The Frenchman nodded. At the end of half an hour I found myself in the shellac trade at double my salary, employed as a commercial traveller. The minds of business men – as Walter Bagehot says – live in a sort of twilight: the Englishman had taken me on because he had read Maupassant; the Frenchman because I had never played Rugby football. He had been one of the first to introduce Rugby football to France.

The Englishman had been a Staff Officer during the war. He was a bookish man, a connoisseur of pictures and would-be

Bohemian. His voice was icy and excitable. The Frenchman was dour and quiet.

The office – I was glad to find – was far from the despised Grands Boulevards, in the old Temple quarter on the edge of the Marais and the old bourgeois Paris of Balzac. It was in a small seventeenth-century building in the Rue Vieille du Temple. The staff were a grumpy French virgin who had been educated in an English convent and who soon needled me about the looseness of English morals; and a sad French salesman called Leger, an anxious, penny-counting man with a large family. He and the typist believed I was the son of a rich Englishman who had put money into the business and despised me. They were shocked by my light-headedness. He and the typist had a facility for hackneyed quotations. They talked like a French edition of the *Reader's Digest*. When I told Leger about my writings he said – but with sinister overtones:

'Le journalisme mène à tout.'

The girl said, with disapproval:

'I see you are a follower of Montaigne rather than Pascal.' She said that the English boss was going too far in discounting bills and putting unsold goods down to a varnish maker who had some connection with the firm; and by her look I saw she thought I was in the manoeuvre. Her tale was nonsense. The girl was in love with the boss who could not bear her. She tried to interest him by putting on a sulky look and saying men were always pinching her breasts in the Metro. I tried to smile away her sulks first of all; then I tried to dazzle. Another failure. I fell back on bickering; she liked that.

The job in the shellac and glue trade was very suited to me. It was more interesting than work at the photographers. I was out of the office all day, calling on ironmongers, paint makers, furniture shops and sealing-wax factories, all over Paris and the suburbs. The glue buyers would hold my sample of glue up to the light, then they would give it a lick as if it were toffee. 'Yes, very good, but we've got plenty.' I never sold any glue, but we had interesting conversations. I always carried a book with me; some wanted to know what it was, and it was surprising among these tradesmen to find how many had views on Balzac, Hugo, Dickens and so on. I had a pleasant afternoon with a sealing-

wax man, chatting about *Manon Lescaut*, a tale that put me in
an erotic daze; he bought nothing, but twelve years later, when
I was a known writer, I came across my old boss in London.
He had given up shellac in the 1929 crash and was running
three pubs near Leicester Square, and told me that the sealing-
wax man had become one of the firm's best customers. I don't
think this was true: my boss had the romantic belief in his
own intuitions. I scarcely tried at all, for I was writing one or
two more sketches and thinking of nothing else. The typist and
Leger were scornful when I came back without orders every
day.

The opportunity to go, with a purpose, into innumerable
streets and corners of Paris, particularly in the old part where
the big middle-class houses had been chopped into rooms for
tailors, printers, cabinet makers and all the petty trades – had
for me the excitement of real travel. And, since I carried with
me my little rustling samples of shellac, I felt I had a working
right to be there. I strongly wanted to belong to this world of
small trades. A man who made varnish became a human being
to me. I would admire the way he fingered the flakes of shellac
or studied my copal gum. My boss was an enthusiast and was
sure that I was just the bright young man the business needed;
so did the French Rugby player. They took me out to smart
restaurants. In spite of the story of my violent difficulties with
my father – for I was always talking about this – the boss, I
found, had convinced himself that, handled the right way, my
father would buy me a partnership in the firm: he saw money
in me. Nothing could possibly have made me present my father
as a man willing to pour out money on his son: rather the reverse. Like so many Englishmen, like myself indeed, the boss
was a day-dreamer. Carried away by what I told him, he in-
stinctively reversed it to suit his dream. In time he saw there
was no hope in me and he became doubtful. He was a hard-
working man and was surprised that I would not work on
Sundays.

Presently there was a disaster. Leger, the salesman, had had a
temporary triumph. He had sold a large quantity of copal gum
and he sat working out his commission to the last centime.

But the copal (it turned out), was adulterated with gravel

and quantities of cinder and dust; there was a row. The stuff –
tons of it – was returned to the yard of the varnish manufacturer near St Denis to be sorted. The salesman, who was nearly
out of his mind, was told to sort the stuff and I had to work
with him.

The week was hot. It was a long way to the factory, which
was in a street that might have been painted by Utrillo. Leger
told me to get there at seven in the morning. He was eager to
get the job done. I managed to arrive on the first morning at
half past seven, but the following days I found it hard to wake
up and I was an hour or more late. The tons of gum were
stacked in a yard against a wall and looked like a heap of grey
marbles. Our task was to shovel the gum and pass it through
sieves: a cindery dust fell through and often left large stones
which we had to throw out. We sieved and shovelled until six
or seven every evening. The dust choked us, sweat soaked us
and, all the time, Leger was muttering about the swindle and
groaning about his commission which diminished with every
shovelful. He groaned about his wife and family and the
recklessness of the boss and sneered when I came late: 'You
don't care. Your father's a rich man.' The drains of the neighbourhood had gone wrong and gangs were digging up the road
for half a mile and the air was sour with the stink of cess. At
midday we went to a rough restaurant where the roadworkers
crowded in. We sat down at long tables. The labourers shouted
and swore, swallowed their food and then, having drunk a
bottle of wine apiece, fell asleep, some of them with their faces
in their plates. They looked a savage lot, most of them, naked
to the waist. There was one from Marseilles who bawled out
the sailors' word for red wine: *Encore du pousse-au-crime.*

Back to work we went in the long afternoons. At the end of
the day, Leger and I stripped off our filthy shirts and went to
the pump in the yard. I pumped water over Leger's back and he
pumped it over mine. One or two women from the factory
came to jeer at us.

After a week of this the heap wasn't much smaller. We got
careless.

'Leave the stones in,' shouted Leger in a rage.

We got used to the jeering girls. Leger uttered a few well-known proverbs about women – not relevant to our situation. There were two or three more women every day and they came nearer to us. Their jeers became dirtier.

'Want to push your trunk upstairs?' a big one shouted at Leger.

'Whore,' shouted Leger.

It was a mistake. He had just stripped and was under the pump. The big woman strode forward, got a quick grip of his trousers at the back and pulled them down his thin, hairy legs, to his ankles. The women screamed with laughter. Leger thought I had done this and, blinded by water, grabbed a bucketful out of the trough and emptied it on me.

It soaked me and, seeing my state, one of the girls copied the big one, pounced on me from behind and the fat one pulled down my trousers too.

'Look at his little toy,' the big one called out.

The owner of the factory had heard the shouts and found Leger and me trying to pull our sodden trousers up. The women ran off.

Leger behaved badly about this. He was getting his revenge. We sat steaming and soaking in the bus going back into Paris, which was crowded with workers.

'They pulled his trousers off,' he called out, indicating me to the passengers in the bus every now and then, as new passengers got in.

Worse, he told the boss, and said I had started the water-throwing. He said he would rather finish the job himself. I was always late.

'What indecency,' the typist hissed at me in the office. 'Like all the English. I know what the English girls at the convent were like. I've seen it with my own eyes.'

The boss had lost money on this transaction and saw that after all these months I had sold little. He said he would give me one more chance. He was buying a consignment of ostrich feathers and I was to sell them in the Faubourg St Honoré.

I felt insulted and mystified by this new job. Everything connected with the dress trade depressed me. I liked the dirtier occupations. But feathers! A world of women! The milliners and dressmakers, I found, always seemed to be at the top of

high buildings. Some stout or waspish woman would either
shut the door in my face or tell me no one used ostrich feathers
any more now. One said cuttingly 'Go to the Folies Bergères.'
I gave up trying. Leger was sarcastic and so was the girl. The
boss had forgotten his loss and had had a sudden success with
shellac. 'Nothing as usual?' he said, with a short laugh, to me.
A distant look came on to his face. He wondered why on earth
I was there. I was sacked. He gave up ostrich feathers, too – the
final insult.

I left the office frightened by my situation, but also in a
temper. I trudged glumly a good deal of the way to the Boulevard St Germain where the lights were brighter, and suddenly I
realized I was free. I had a month's money in my pocket. I felt
the abandon of the workless. My sexual instincts, distracted by
the anxieties of having to earn my living, came undeniably
alive. I made a reckless decision and the sight of Sacré-Coeur
on its hill had a curious part in it. I have told how, when I first
arrived in Paris, it seemed like some evil and exotic bird regarding the city with cynical eye and frightening. Now it frightened
me no longer: I felt it connived with me. The erection sym-
bolized one thing only and blatantly. I found myself looking
into the windows of pharmacies. I was working up courage to
buy a packet of contraceptives.

The bother was that I knew only the slang words for these
objects. My first attempt was at a small shop of the shabby
kind. The assistant came to the counter, but I was unable to
speak to him because of his face. He had a red nose with white
pimples on it; he looked sly and horrible; his condition (I
imagined) being the result of some sexual disease. I quickly
changed my mind and asked for a headache cachet and when I
got outside I threw it into the street. I walked on looking for a
larger, less unpleasantly intimate shop. The next shop had
several women in it. I moved on. At last, after passing and re-
passing the door and making a cautious study of the assistants
in a larger shop, I went in. They wore white coats and looked
like an impersonal priesthood. But when one of the men asked
me what I wanted my aggressiveness turned to nervousness. The
French language became jumbled up in my head and vanished.

I stammered out 'French letters'. The young assistant was puzzled. I tried one or two more slang names in a voice that was scarcely a murmur. The assistant was mystified. Another and older assistant came up and said 'What is it for?' In the state I was in I could not tell him, except in a way that was meaningless. He listened and then suddenly he said: 'In the second drawer.'

A package was brought out and carefully wrapped up. I rushed out of the shop.

The experience exhausted me and indeed my sexual desires. I took the packet home and put it in my wardrobe. Slowly a strange feeling of power, of being at last at one with the world, came over me; indeed it was so strong that I forgot the packet itself and never thought of taking it out with me. It was a sort of hidden capital. Its immediate effect was to make me start writing again and to think of living by writing only.

CHAPTER FOUR

FROM the beginning my efforts succeeded. I wrote an account of the walk to Orleans; also a portrait of one of the *bouquinistes* on the quays. I went to see the old man and his wife in their attic in the Rue de Seine. These articles were accepted, soon published and paid for. I went on to an article about Chartres. This also was accepted. Although I wrote each one three or four times, I found them easy to write and, for a while, was proud of them.

When I read memoirs about the Paris of the Steins, Sylvia Beach, Joyce, Hemingway and Scott Fitzgerald, I am cast down. I was there. I may have passed them in the street; I had simply never heard of them. Nor had I any notion of what they were trying to do. I had really carried my isolation in England with me. One evening I did see a number of young people walking up the Boulevard Montparnasse with a thick, blue-covered book, like a telephone directory. They went to the *Dôme*, the *Coupole* or the *Rotonde* and sat there reading. I asked a young Irishman whom I sat next to at the *Dôme* what the book was. He was dressed in green and wore a cowboy hat. He was surprised to be asked such a question. The book, he said, was *Ulysses*; for years 'everyone' had been waiting for this great moment. He allowed me to read the first page; its adjectives and images annoyed and flustered me. (In fact it was a good five years before I could bring myself to read the book.) I did not know that I was living at the centre of a literary revolution. I was an outsider, and younger than the writers and painters who were becoming important; and if I *had* known, I would still have been under the delusion that before I could know anything about modern literature I must catch up with the old. When I did hear of Tristan Tzara and Dada, I was angry because he was smashing up a culture just as I was becoming acquainted with it. The only artist of importance I talked to was the sculptor, Zadkine. He took me to his studio for half an hour and I stood there in a crowd of primitive African totem poles, twelve feet high. I was speechless and came away lost.

There was a great difference between the American crowd who swamped the Left Bank at this time and the handful of Europeans; the French avoided this international circus. The Americans belonged to the generation who, for the first time in their history, had made a mass exodus from the United States. Always alert for the new thing, they arrived in gangs, dressed up in gaudy shirts and played the Bohemian part. They had a lot of money and took over cafés and restaurants and hotels. They drank heavily and brawled, which shocked the French. They boasted they had bought Europe. But one or two of them were sensitive and seriously encouraging. If I said I was 'trying to write', they enthusiastically announced to their friends that I was 'the writer'.

I became friends with an American painter and his wife. He was a frowning slow-thinking man of forty whose face was sullen with inner struggles that he could not get out except in sentences like 'What a painter wants is a place near a good whore-shop – like Van Go or Says-Ann,' or in blasts of boasting. His hair stuck up in spikes and his blue eyes seemed to be bursting with tears he could not shed: he was of German origin and very sentimental. The sight of me brought out the worst in him. Europe was finished. The Americans had won the war. Europe was shit – a favourite word. America was the largest, the richest, the only country that believed in democracy and peace. The English accent was sissy. We were all homosexuals. What was wrong with us was our servile class system: there were no class differences in America.

He was a living proof of the opposite. He had married a Virginian of superior family. He boasted of this and he resented it at once. The unsure, the ugly part of American character – I have often found – is very near the surface. But he was decent and had the American virtue of seeing everything as a possibility. He was laborious and slow, but when his wife said I was a promising writer that was enough. I was *doing* something. One day, he said with awe and almost affection:

'Hold it. You just said an epigram.'

His wife was long-nosed, ugly and bony, but very intelligent

278

and attractive. She thought and spoke the things her husband could not get out. He said that my writing needed an illustrator. He would do sketches to illustrate my articles and he'd see if the *Monitor* would run a series. He knew the paper. The editor was coming to Paris. The editor arrived. I met him as he was leaving his hotel. He paused on the steps. He was a gay fellow with a white beard.

'I like your stuff. I'll take ten more with those drawings.'

I walked away. Ten. Guaranteed. I was a commissioned writer, not an amateur any longer. No more leather, photography, shellac and glue. The dread that I had no talent at all, a dread that kept me awake at night, left me. The hotel was in the Faubourg St Honoré, the scene of my wretched attempt to sell ostrich feathers. I looked into the windows of jewellers, hosiers, tailors, perfumeries; wealth seemed to coat me. I went to an expensive shop that sold luxurious stationery, tooled blotting pads and so on. I went in and ordered a hundred engraved visiting cards, taking care in choosing the print. Afterwards I went to the Café Weber and ordered a bock.

Now my life as a professional writer, and the last six months I was to spend in Paris, began. It is true that if I had moved among cleverer and more instructed people I would not have been so late in developing an original imagination. And there is always the danger that people who work hard become blinded by work itself and, by a paradox, lazy-minded.

Since I no longer had to be at a shop or office between eight and nine, I lay in bed until eleven o'clock in the morning. I was, I suppose, making up for years of doing work I did not like. I lay in that wide and lumpy bed at Mme Chapin's until I was woken by the siren at the Fire Station near by. Then the life-long panic of the writer's life began. A whole day free, yet eaten by the anxiety of having to write something: the day of false starts, torn up paper – how I grew to love tearing up paper. And then there was the reaction against the task: to write little sketches of places, how feeble! How could it be important to go to Amiens, to Pontoise, to the stamp market on the Champs Elysées? I was nothing but a hack. And then I had no 'adventures' – an old complaint. In trains people talked of little but the price of food, the cost of living, or told stories about their illnesses and families. A writer ought, I felt, to know about 'low' society, but 'low life' is as hard to discover as High Society is. The *Monitor* certainly would not publish anything about the whores prancing about the hotels of Les Halles, with their red dresses, slit up to the thigh, and their hard voices shouting at the draymen below. If I nosed my way up to a *clochard* who had kipped down on one of those iron plates on the pavement where the warmth from the central heating comes through, near the Gare d'Austerlitz, I never got much more than a grunt out of him. The paper would not like that, unless I made him a picturesque character amusing to tourists. And Americans in 1920 loved the picturesque. I began to get the suspicion that I was hired to leave half of life out. Perhaps my discontent was spotted by the editors, who are no fools in matters like this. My first two articles appeared at length: the others were cut to little more than a dozen lines of caption for the pictures.

When I wrote my articles I showed one or two of them to the Danish girl who had been Judy's friend. It had been a joke between Judy and me to call her Hester, for she had a slow, considering manner which (we thought mischievously) went with her height. To our surprise she liked the name. It made her stern and truthful face soften with a yielding pleasure. I used to meet her at a café near the Palais Royal, because she often went shopping on the Right Bank. Her dissertation was done and she was waiting for her parents to take her to the South of France and then home. Hester read and spoke English exactingly well. She was taller than I and this, and her seriousness, made me show off to her; but when we sat down, on the same eye level, we were friends and she stopped snubbing me. In fact, she had the Danish gaiety with other people, but doubtfully with me. She had a good head, a straight nose and long, narrow hips and big bones. But girls turned into something else when I looked at them. In Hester's face I saw libraries and lecture halls and the philosopher Malebranche – I had not heard of him up till then and have never heard of him since – on whom she had written her dissertation. I also saw mountains and fjords, though there are none in Denmark which, she crossly told me many times, was flat. I could even see her father, the sea captain, to whom I gave a fair beard; twice she had been to Canada in his ship. How healthy, free and confident she was: I was half angry with her for this. I cannot think why, but I was especially angry because her father was a sea captain. I felt a strong desire to get her off the sea. The sea made me sick. Only the pink inside of her long mouth when she laughed – which was not often – saved her, in my eyes. It reminded me that she was a girl.

I cannot remember our conversations. She told me, of course, about Malebranche: that has gone too; but I remember attack-him. She said: 'Why do you exaggerate?'

or

'That is superficial, isn't it?'

or:

'I read what you wrote. Your writing is unequal. You will have to learn to say what you think.'

or:

'Be careful. You will lose your integrity.'

or:

'I don't understand your attitude.'

These phrases stick in my mind. She also quoted Shakespeare to me. 'To thine own self be true ...' Suppose, I argued, the self was criminal or amoral? I was divided between admiration and awe of her. She said I lacked moral seriousness. I cultivated the lack of it with her. Look how I had treated Judy! Hester was very moved when she mentioned Judy and especially about that time at Fontainebleau. Nothing would convince her that Judy and I had not been lovers and when she said this, there was a change in Hester's face: her eyes became large and greedy.

I gazed at her and thought of the package in my room.

On the 14 July she agreed, to my surprise, to come with me to the general dancing and soda-water-squirting along the Boulevard St Michel. She squirted soda water at me: that was an advance. A party of us danced in the streets. She had un-fortunately brought her professor's son to whom I recklessly said something about Racine. He snubbed me. I puzzled Hester by dancing with a pretty Hungarian girl who could not speak French, English or German, so we had to make gestures that Hester assumed were intimate; and they were, because words were not obstructing us. I still see the sadness of her eyes when, in the end, I took Hester to her lodgings. Hester was silent: she did not believe the story that the girl and I had no language in common. When we got to the professor's house, I made an excited gesture and asked Hester to come to my room. My landlady was away. But, either because I shouted this, or she was too tall, she appeared not to hear me. We shook hands and I left. I trudged back, all the way through Grenelle, and got to bed tired out.

The next day in the streets, people looked pale and ill. In the bar near my room the barman had not shaved and a woman was trying to put her hair to rights by a mirror.

Once more Hester and I met at the Palais Royal. The Hungarian girl was on her mind. Her next remark was baffling: she insisted Judy had told her I had slept with her.

'Tell me the truth,' she said.

'But it is the truth,' I said. 'I haven't.'

And then I saw what had happened. I gave a yell of laughter at Judy's fanciful mind. Of course! I had fallen fast asleep under that tree on the hot day of the walk to Triel. Hester was put out.

'Babes in the wood,' she said.

She did not like being laughed at.

To talk about love is to make love: Hester and I were nervous of each other. I kept tapping the ash off my cigarette into an ash tray as we talked.

'I wish you'd stop that,' she said and put the ash tray out of reach, but I touched her hand as she did this. She took her hand away quickly. The marble-topped table between us seemed to become six foot wider and to heave like the sea. In the pit of my stomach I could almost hear the voice of a man choking and trying to speak and recasting the same question again and again.

Then Hester said that if what I said about Judy wasn't true, I had slept with the French girl at the shellac office. The voice in the pit of my stomach came blurting to the surface.

'I haven't slept with any girls,' I said.

'I don't believe you.'

I recast my sentence in negative form. I could think of no other.

'I wish I had slept with *you*, but you're going away ...' There, I had got it out at last. I was startled to see Hester's pink face go dead white. A lot of words must have come out of me after that for I saw a satisfied look on her face.

'I have often wondered about you,' she said. 'I don't do that for the asking. I'm engaged to be married.'

I got up. 'I've got to go,' I said coldly, because I'd given myself away. I called the waiter and paid him.

'No. You can't go like that,' she said. 'We must talk.'

'Good-bye,' I said. She got up too. I went to the door. She called to me. I did not turn round but went blindly out, bumping into some man who was coming in. Once in the street, the strange thing is that I felt hysterically happy. The glass case in which I had been living was smashed. I raced down the street and got into the Metro. I only feared she might be following me. When I got home my larynx ached as if my voice had ripped it.

I decided not to see Hester again; the more I reflected on what I had said and her reply, the less clearly I remembered it all; and even now, my memory must have made the incident bleaker than it was. I suppose I am drastic because what I am really remembering is the uncouth figure I cut; also, I had fallen back into my defensive habit of expecting disappointment and unconsciously preparing for it. This has some connection with the idealizing of women, picked up from Victorian novels and punishing myself for it. And then, conceit is all the stronger in a young man who is afraid of love. I was sulking.

For two or three days I tried to work. Then I gave up and went to Montparnasse. There as I walked up the street from the station I heard a sound well-known to me. A man was spitting and hawking a little way ahead of me. I knew him a little. He was a thin middle-aged American and a terrible bore. My desire for punishment must have been strong, for I hurried to catch him up. At other times I had often turned down side streets to avoid him.

Percy was a journalist who wrote fashion articles for American papers. As a bore he belonged to the race of the soft-voiced interminable and insidious, who catch you with a note of sympathy and then shoulder you into walls or trap you in doorways.

Like the air, Percy was always moving from one place to another; and, again like the air, he was invisible until you suddenly saw his face looking down into yours, a pale face stamped by pock marks that might have been the off-prints of faded conversations.

He stopped now at once when he saw me. After twenty minutes he said: 'Do you want to come along to the hotel? I'm meeting Fraser there.' I did not know who Fraser was, but I was so low that I went.

Percy was distinct from everyone else in this gaudy quarter by his quality of being the Invisible Man, for he wore a dim grey office-going suit, a stained trilby hat and walked in rapid vanishing little steps. He usually had the remains of a cigar on his lips. He lived in a poor hotel room at the corner of the Rue de la Gaieté. It was an hotel used as a rendezvous for lovers. He was bound to go into a long tale of his running war with the manager about the noises of fornication in the night. Percy had the Calvinist's obsession with the 'whore house', though he was a pious man who played the organ for the American Methodists on Sundays: an extension of his own monotone. He was an old Radical who hadn't been in the United States for twenty years and he had been a reporter in one of the Balkans wars. I think of him as one of those lost eighteenth-century Utopians who stray from country to country but who have caught from Longfellow Hiawatha's mania for detail. In Greece he had been imprisoned; and he brought to Paris that fear of foreign police which is so often buried in the guilt that haunts expatriates. Yet Percy was a saint of kinds, a soft touch for all 'the boys and girls' of the quarter. Broken painters, girls who could not pay the rent, always went to him. He was always doling out small sums of money. If any painter was carried off drunk or starving by the police, Percy was down at the station to rescue him at once. The only work of art he admired was 'The God damn great Cock', which the admirers of Wilde had erected over his grave in *Père Lachaise*. He was sad because the French police had covered it with a tarpaulin.

We skipped along to Percy's hotel and climbed to the top floor.

Percy spat once or twice into his washbasin in his small room. He was reminiscing about Trotsky. Shortly Fraser turned up, a red-faced and suspicious little Cockney mechanic.

'Aren't we going to do anything?' said the Cockney, uneasy about my being there.

'He'll watch us,' said Percy.

'We do it most Saturdays,' the Cockney said.

They got out a light round table and a pile of manuscript in single-spaced typing for me to study while they got going. Table turning was their bond. They were chasing spirits on the other side. They were secret agents between the living and the dead.

'We've had Hamlet three weeks running. You couldn't stop him,' said Percy. 'There it is.' He handed me a bundle of manuscript.

They put their hands on the table. They waited and waited. It was a grey day and rain came on.

'Nothing there,' said the Cockney.

'Ah, there's something,' said Percy. 'He's trying. Maybe it's Hamlet again. Perhaps he didn't finish. Is that you, Hamlet?'

No answering knocks came.

'Hostile presence,' said the Cockney, indicating me.

'Perhaps I'd better go,' I said.

'No,' said Percy. 'They're about.' He got up, made another spit into the washbasin and picked up the papers. 'We've had Julius Caesar. We had Bismarck. George Washington.' One or two Greeks had poured out their monologues.

'Perhaps they want you to join in,' Percy said to me. So we all sat with our fingers on the table. Occasionally there was a slight move, but nothing happened. I thought of my great Uncle Arthur, the cabinet maker, in York, who had upset the Bible-reading branch of my Yorkshire family by getting through to Burton, the author of his secret Bible, *The Anatomy of Melancholy*, with a signalman who was a friend of his in that city.

'They get like that,' said Percy. 'They get sulky or something.' We had to give up the séance. We passed the rest of the afternoon listening to Percy who read us pages and pages of literary material from the other world. Occasionally a fretful woman would turn up in the complaining notes of all the speakers who seemed to live in another version of Montparnasse. I think this woman was his mother. We were listening to a minced up instalment of Percy's autobiography.

When I got back to my room there was a note under my door. It said:

'Where have you been? I called this afternoon. I am terribly worried. I have some news I want to tell you, Hes.'

Victory, of course. I do not propose to tell in all its detail what happened between Hester and myself in my room when she came to it. Our encounter was helped because I had only one chair in which she sat for a short time and dabbed a few softening and attractive tears from her eyes. The thought thundered in my head that I was on the point of holding in my arms the serene author of a dissertation on Malebranche, a philosopher (she had told me), who had written a work entitled *De la recherche de la Vérité*. There was a bit of rational protest when we had got to the hooks and buttons. I excused myself and took my package into Madame Chapin's kitchen. I opened it and made a terrible discovery. The priests of the pharmacy either out of cynicism or malice, had sold me a box containing twenty pills for the liver. I searched for hope in the 'directions', in four languages. I read the list of chemical content. I had not taken a pill of any kind for years and had no notion of what any medicine outside of a cough mixture was designed to do. I knew little about contraception. It occurred to me that these pills must be the things the French used, perhaps having esoteric knowledge of the action of the liver upon the sexual organs, and in a sudden fit of faith and superstition I swallowed one, indeed to make sure, swallowed two. Recklessly I went back to Hester, but the sight of her pulling a garment over her head and the long white back of a living woman who was an image no longer, brought me to my senses and made me tell her of the disaster. She did not understand and half-undressed and sitting on the bed asked to see the package. She read the directions carefully.

'Is there something the matter with your liver?' she said.

'No, it's not that,' I said and had to explain again. She said in her advisory voice, that she never trusted things like that.

She said: 'You must take it back to the shop. You must get your money back.'

'I couldn't. I've taken two.'

'Well it's their mistake,' she said, and pulled the garment back over her head. The Sorbonne, the lecture halls, the libraries, the imaginary fjords of Denmark vanished as I looked at her and all I can say is that, after some grapplings and false rammings, during which she talked fractiously, nineteen to the dozen, down went Malebranche and the captain of the ship. I looked down at her and saw two tears on her smiling face.

We went out and walked tenderly by the river where the lights were going down like spears into the water. Hester suddenly stopped. For the first time I heard her laugh out loud. She stood there laughing her head off, she was nearly doubled up with laughter and clung tottering to my arm. She could not stop.

'And you took two of them!' she said. 'I've just seen what you were trying to tell me.' And off she went again. Passing people were astonished by her. She recovered.

'I'm sorry. Why are you looking so sad?'

I wasn't sad. To make up for her laughter she said very seriously:

'You may not realize it, but your ideas have influenced me a lot.'

My ideas! What ideas? I had only one: terror that she would be pregnant. The philosopher Malebranche returned to reassure me. She had one or two young men, it seemed, in Denmark who were interested in him and her; and she said she knew how to look after herself. We sat closely in a restaurant and twice during the meal she put down her knife and fork and laughed like a Viking. People said: 'Americans!'

In the next five days, which were all we had, I said she must break her engagement. She frowned at me tenderly. Her parents arrived: the captain had come to the surface. They were taking her for a spree. The Captain had a tuft of fair hair on his chin (I saw), when we all met at the professor's and it made me gaze at Hester. Her small tuft had been fair, too. But the captain,

who did not speak French, cottoned on to me and said roguishly
that if only they had had time, he would have asked me to show
him Paris.

'I will write,' said Hester in the dark hall of the professor's
flat. We shook hands. Her hands were long. It was awful leaving
her. But I noticed as I went away how every man, woman or
child I saw seemed more real to me. The whole of Paris ceased
to be a dream and became alive. I had so often heard or read
of the disgust and guilt of sexual love; I realized I had never
believed these tales and now never believed them again. But
often as I walked about I would look at the faces of women
hoping I would see something of hers, and at every corner for
a long time I had the illusion that only a minute before she
might have turned down there.

I went on a wet day to Amiens and wrote about it, but slowly
luck turned against me. My money was running out. Mrs Lang's
promise to pay me back came to nothing and I could not get
payment for my articles. There was – I heard – a lawsuit
going on in the holy city of Boston: I knew nothing of the
delicacies of the religion, but it seemed that the Divine Mind
had split in two and – in the general phrase – someone had let
Error in. Both parties were accusing each other of witchcraft, a
common accusation among the congregations as I was soon to
find out. In practical terms, the *Monitor*'s funds were frozen.
Fortunately Madame Chapin stayed on in Tours and I could skip
paying the rent.

I was back in my fear that I should have to leave Paris and
go home. I was saved by one more cheque from a London review, but after that things went very wrong. A time came when
I had to sell back my books, first one at a time, then two at a
time: for two volumes I could get a cheap meal. So two by two,
the row on my mantelpiece got shorter and shorter.

I wrote to Hester, but the letters became fewer. At last one
came from Cape Town. She was going to be married. She had
emigrated. And then I heard no more. Geography, that I loved
so much, had swallowed her up.

I went on selling my books: off went Balzác and Boileau,

Maupassant, Vigny and Hugo, to be converted into soup, noix d'agneau, a cassoulet, ham sandwiches. I was soon down to an anthology of comic verse and Rabelais. I stuck to that; it was expensive.

Poverty makes one morose, envious and lethargic. I had a special hatred for small vans delivering food. I grazed off the menus outside restaurants. People eating there struck me as sordid and dogs as unnecessary. I developed lingering habits if I met an acquaintance to see if I could cadge a meal. I was far too proud to borrow from some of the Christian Scientists I knew, but from whom I had drifted away; and my father's habits, as I have said, had given me a fear of debt.

Madame Chapin came back. I evaded her. The good woman said nothing but, noticing that I did not go out in the evenings and sat eating a sandwich only, she got into the habit of bringing me a bowl of soup and invented a tale that she had brought back some pâtés of Touraine. The thing that reassured her was to hear me typing; but I had nothing to type, and if I heard her coming from the kitchen to my room I would start typing anything that came into my head to deceive her.

I sold one of my suits, a grey one. At last I ate my last book. The injustice of being forced to this sacrifice made me give up my principles. I would have to borrow for my next meal. The enterprise made me brash, and I began to feel contempt – contempt for my victim, whoever he should be. I arrived outside the *Dôme* and there he was – Percy, of course. I hadn't seen him since the séance.

'Where have you been?' he said. 'I haven't seen you since the 14 July. Fraser and I have been worrying about you.'

My grin was ravenous.

'Could you lend me two francs?' I said. I explained my dilemma. I joined the long list of his charities in the quarter. The saintly bore paid for my dinner and gave me two francs more.

When the benefits of this feed had passed off in the next two days I was tempted to become one of Percy's regular following of beggars. After all, the tradition of debt for writers was an honourable one. I could not humiliate myself to rich friends:

only to Percy whom, in my heart, I despised. The old puritan pride which had stiffened me had become shady and hypocritical.

Soon I had only a few centimes left. Perhaps Mrs Lang or the paper would pay? Perhaps there would be a letter? I searched all my clothes and my room, even under the bed, looking for one more dropped coin, but there was none. In the next six days I ate half a small roll per day. Hunger excited my imagination. What would it be like to starve? I got interested in my sensations, in the rumblings in the empty cave inside me, in my giddiness and my dashing indifference to traffic – for I seemed to be flying when I crossed the street. I talked to myself loudly as I walked. To go out by day was tormenting, for one saw people who had eaten; it was better to go out late at night when no one much was about in my neighbourhood. One night I went out just to look in at the door of the nearest café bar. Rain had set in heavily. I had no coat and the cold rain thrilled me. More suffering! I just stood, letting myself get soaked. I had once been in this bar with a young pianist who used to play Coleridge Taylor to the sharp daughters of a French Protestant clergyman in Asnières – a scene from André Gide I recognized later in life – he puffed like a steam engine as he thumped out the piece: he had gone back to England but, in a mad way, I half expected to see him come puffing out. Instead, a ludicrous thing happened: a tipsy young student went into the bar, casually picked up three hard-boiled eggs from the counter, dropped them one by one on the floor and marched out shouting:

'*Ils sont tous morts les amoureux.*'

The world had simply come to a grotesque end: I walked home down the Rue Raynouard, past Balzac's house. I thought of him scrambling through the trap door when his creditors came after him. I stopped outside two closed warehouse doors where I had once seen a procession of five rats run out and disappear into a hole further down. One could eat rats. I was fascinated by this idea. It was nearly midnight when I pushed the button of the outside door, shouted 'Chapin' as I passed the lodge of the concierge whom I could see in bed, through his little window, and splashed across the courtyard to my room.

Madame Chapin had not gone to bed. She was waiting up for me: she had never done this before. There was enough light in the little dark passage for me to see there was a change in her, or, perhaps in my exhausted state every thing and every person looked unreal and half-dreamed. I could see her white nightgown under a black overcoat – it was a cold time of the year – and her hair was drawn back from her forehead which looked broader and paler, showing two fine lines across it, and the hair was let down in two long plaits at the back. She looked severe instead of placid; the plaits made her look like a fierce schoolgirl and her voice had changed. We always addressed each other as Monsieur and Madame.

'Monsieur, I must speak to you.'

Then she saw I was soaked with rain; it was squelching out of my boots and on to the floor she so often polished.

'Look at my floor. Get your shoes off,' she said sharply. She pushed into my room ahead of me and lit my lamp.

'And look at you! Your jacket! Your trousers!' Sharp fingers gave a pull to my shirt.

'And your shirt! Get them off.' She opened the wardrobe.

'Where is your other suit?' she turned and accused.

I had, of course, sold it.

'At the cleaners,' I said.

'Get your pyjamas,' she said, and picking up my boots, as I took my jacket off and my belt, she left the room with a prim and huffy look I had never seen before. It was strange (I thought afterwards) that Madame Chapin, who came into my room every Sunday when I had nothing on and had to grab for a towel, seemed to think now there was something unspeakable about seeing me undress. A new, threatening formality had come between us. I was afraid of her and got into my pyjamas and dressing-gown – the one my mother had given me on my twenty-first birthday. Now Madame Chapin came back.

'Where are your books?' she said, looking at the empty mantelpiece. 'And your typewriter?'

'There!' I pointed to the side of the wardrobe. I had hung on to that.

'Ah!' she said. If that had gone I think she would have screamed. The sight of it calmed her. She said, as I stood there, dazed, 'You have always been frank with me. You are not like my Pole. I have a right to know – are you leaving me?'

Oh dear, the rent! But she did not mention it.

'If you are leaving me, I have the right to a month's notice.' When she said 'the right' her eyes became bright with anxiety and I, in my weakness, could not stop grimacing as if I had St Vitus's Dance; instead of a sentence a noise that was like a yawn came out of me.

'No,' I tried to say.

Well, what was it? Had I been drinking? Drinking! My voice squealed when I said I hadn't.

'Get into bed,' she said. 'You are ill. Oh, my God.'

And out of the room she went again. I heard her groaning in the kitchen; it was a relief to hear her return to her familiar lamenting voice. Presently she came back into the room with a bowl of soup.

'Sit up and eat that.

'You can't deceive me,' she said. 'I've seen it for a long time. What has been happening to you? I've seen you've not been eating. God, if your poor mother knew.'

She watched every spoonful go into my mouth. I was slowly able to stop grimacing. She went to get a glass of wine.

'I'm not afraid to give you this. It is good wine from my village.'

I drank it and when she stood questioning me in the next half hour I was liable either to mumble or to shout. It was a struggle, for her eyes didn't stop staring. The rent, I thought, was in her eyes.

'I'm waiting for my money to pay the rent,' I said. 'There has been a delay.'

I had to stop my tears when I said this, but she was evidently lost in suspicion.

'Where is that beautiful suit?' she said again.

In wine out came the truth.

'I sold it,' I said.

'You sold it! And the money for that beautiful story?' She was terrifying.

'Which one?' I was confused.

'The one I showed to the father.'

'I lent it to a friend,' I managed to get that out.

Madame Chapin looked suddenly older.

'Oh no you didn't,' she said. 'I know young men. You are like my Pole. Oh God, you threw it away to sleep with some *fille*.'

'I didn't,' I said.

I didn't realize I had shouted the words. The shout made Madame Chapin straighten and step back.

'I've seen the sheets,' she said and the beginnings of mockery ran along her lips.

'You poor young man,' she said. 'I suppose you gave it to your pretty cousin.'

'No. I lent money to her mother!' Then, thinking this would be an advantage, I told her the whole story. Out came the Mexican Revolution, the wild rides on the hacienda, the pistol, the dreadful husband. Madame Chapin was caught and carried away by it. As I got to the end she was turning to the mirror over the mantelpiece and looking at herself; then she remembered me and said:

'The rich! That's what those rich women are like. They are worse than kept women. At least *they* give something for their money!' And added: 'Her mother!'

I thought I made it better by confessing that Mrs Lang was not my aunt.

'That,' said Madame Chapin drily, 'I knew well, young man.'

There was no more to say and she came to the bedside to ask me if I wanted more soup and took the bowl, and that would have been the end of it. But the bugle went off at the barracks, clearer and harder as if it were in the room itself, because of the wet night. You could picture the man with his chest out and his cheeks swelling. Madame Chapin gave a jump and dropped the soup bowl on the floor.

'Oh my God!' she cried out, and put her hand to her breast. She stood there trembling. She leaned against the wall. 'My heart!' she said weakly and panting. Suddenly she snatched my hand and pulled it under her coat to her breast.

'Feel my heart. I am choking. Can you feel it?'

Her heart was indeed thumping, but I could feel her breast. Her hand was holding mine hard there. Her breast was not, like Hester's, the small breast of a young woman.

Madame Chapin hesitated and took a long breath.

'Soldiers. That filthy war,' she said sadly pushing my hand away. And then, sighing, she picked up the bowl from the floor. She considered me.

'In the morning I will lend you five francs,' she said in a tender voice. 'Get something to eat before I come back from work,' she said.

She came in the morning and put five francs on my table and left.

All day I could feel the roundness of Madame Chapin's breast, but I forgot it in the afternoon because a miracle happened. I had eaten, and then I went along the Boulevard des Italiens looking into the cafés where Mr Shaves often sat after lunch with his friends. He knew many people in business and in the theatre and he had said once or twice that he'd keep his ears open for news of a job I could do. He was there looking bumptious and pleased, his cigarette holder sticking up in the air under a lilac halo of smoke. His socks, which were in blue and yellow stripes, showed at the ankles and joined in his joy of life. When he saw me his smiles went.

'Where have you been?' he said. 'People have been asking at the Church.'

I didn't tell him much. He didn't appear to listen. One of his friends said to me: 'You've lost weight. I wish I could.'

I joined them nervously and I saw in Mr Shaves the mean, shrewd look of his that usually followed his loud laughs. He said that when his wife came back in a week's time they'd ask me to a meal. He kept staring at those boots of mine that had belonged to Pierre; they were worn down and shabby beside his and when I left I felt he was watching me. I did not realize that Mr Shaves was regarding me in a day-dream of envy; that, in a sense, he wanted worn-out boots like mine. I took the Metro back to Auteuil; with food inside me I was wondering if I could write an article on starvation.

Madame Chapin was out, but there was a letter on the floor. It contained francs to the amount of £15, a large sum in those days. They came from the young Jewish abstract painter – the one who was no longer an abstract painter – who said he and his wife were concerned that I had not been paid for my writing and I needn't hurry about repaying the money. It came out eventually that Madame Chapin had been up the street to talk to the old lady with whom I sometimes had my excruciating French conversations on Sundays; this woman knew the painter; and that Mr Shaves had telephoned to the painter also and said I looked in a bad way. I went up to Montparnasse, ate an expensive meal, including the largest plate of *cêpes provençales* I have ever seen; nowadays, they would kill me. I paid Percy back the money I had borrowed. He was so astonished that he lost his power of monologue and went off with disappointment in his face, discerning perhaps that I showed signs of ceasing to be one of his clientèle. He had the Bohemian's scorn.

I went back to Madame Chapin's. She was in her long black overall once more. She looked older than she had the night before when she had held my hand against her breast. I paid her rent and we resumed our formal conversations, I thanking her for her kindness and she saying that she had always had confidence in me.

This experience must have exhausted me, because I tired of Paris. The enchantment had gone. Basil Shaves's play came on at last after three postponements. I went to see it with Mrs Shaves and her children. There was a large audience in one of the Paris Salles. From the moment the rigged-up curtain rose and Basil came bounding on and shouted at Mrs Gilbey:

'Here's a nice thing. This is a b . . .'

Basil Shaves was a success. All his vulgar mannerisms were there: his habit of boring his finger into his ear, his scratching of his armpit, the wagging of his shoes when he sat admiring the shape of his leg, the looks of hurt, meanness, absurdity jumped into his face; he looked outraged yet cunning, virtuous yet dubious. The casting was perfect. Basil Shaves was there to the life and yet was morally and physically, Gilbey. He was so pleased with himself in the part that, like all amateurs, he could not help glancing at the audience half-way through his longer speeches; but that look was one of wonder at himself.

There were good notices in the English papers and one in a French paper. He and the woman who played Doris – I had met her once with some of his friends in the Café de la Paix, a thin, dark woman with intense worried eyes, were the stars. 'A tragedy,' he had said to me at the time. 'Married a French actor who left her with two children.' This scandal of the theatre made him regard her as a very superior woman. 'Can you imagine it, in an office like ours? The men round her like flies. Why not another slice off a cut loaf?' Mr Shaves could be very crude.

It was not long after this that Mr Shaves sent me a note saying there was a job for me if I would take it. An English company he had mentioned at least six months before was coming to play Shakespeare. Hébertot had taken them on. The great Hébertot! I went to see him. He received me as if I had come from an embassy. He was nervous of not getting an audience. The job was to canvass the English and American colony and sell blocks of tickets. The good thing about it was the high pay which could be collected every evening at the box office. I took on the job.

My last efforts as a salesman were as poor in their results as my earlier ones had been. Happily Hébertot did not notice this for a long time. I bought books again and a green velour hat with a wide brim. It was in a shop window and I used to visit it every day dreading it would be sold, until I could risk the expense. The hat was my religion. I decided that I would go to London and see if I could get the money I was owed or if I could get a job as a Paris correspondent; I knew that it would be stupid to stay in Paris. I had met too many Frenchified Englishmen. For two years I had lived thoughtlessly from day to day. I could not go on like this. Still – clinging to a last hope that I still might see more of the world – I left my luggage behind with Madame Chapin and went back to London.

Before I left I heard bad news of Mr Shaves. It came from a man who worked with him at the bank. The husband of the woman who played Doris, and who had been acting in America, had come back with some large scheme for starting a new show in Paris. Mr Shaves had always been fascinated by this man whom he had never met: he had 'ruined his family'. The sight of a ruiner, coming at the time when Shaves himself had shown that he could act, must have turned his head. As easily, as dreamily, as he had cashed my first cheque, he cashed a couple of large ones for this man. They bounced. American banks do not forgive the wandering mind. Shaves was sacked. I saw him at his café.

'I have ruined them,' he said. 'The bank has fired me.'

'I heard,' I said.

I can only describe his appearance as haggard, but ecstatic.

'I've got my chance,' he said. 'We're going to London, too.'

What did I get out of my two years in Paris? Freedom above all, and the love of it has never left me. Self-confidence, too. I had rebelled successfully. I could stand on my own feet. I had another language, so I could now become two persons. I had had a large amount of time for reading; it was a small capital. I had learned to be absurd, was willing to see what happened to me. Above all, I had had pleasure, a thing suspected by the calculating, constrained and anxious lower-middle class from which I came; to whom, all the same, I owed the habit of working hard. I was in the simplest way happy. My only dread was that I would be forced back into the world I came from.

And what did I get from France itself? I have known French people far better, their character, their literature, their arts, since that time and have even written about them. It has been hard not to smuggle in some of this later knowledge here. What I gained, lastingly, was a sense of the importance of the *way* in which things are done, a thrift of the mind. I also began to see my own country – a very powerful one at that time – from abroad; and I felt the beginning of a passion, hopeless in the long run, but very nourishing, for identifying myself with people who were not my own and whose lives were governed by ideas alien to mine.

CHAPTER FIVE

ON the train out of Paris I did myself well in the restaurant car, sitting opposite a middle-aged man who dropped his food down his waistcoat. Bunches of hair grew out of his nostrils and ears and when he spoke he did so with puffs of kindly importance. When he told me his name I knew he was a celebrated political writer; long articles of his appeared in *The Times* and even longer ones in the heavy monthly Reviews that still survived from the nineteenth century. He bathed in opinions, telling me that certain remarks of his had upset Clemenceau, affected the Treaty of Versailles and caused trouble in Poland. The belief that they have re-directed the course of history and agitated Cabinets is (I found in due time) chronic among political journalists. He congratulated me on writing for the *Monitor*. He gave me his card. I pulled out my French one. Something about him made me feel I was a man of the world, yet he disappointed me. Young men are snobs. He talked loudly and effusively and everyone in earshot became aware of his importance. With growing malice, I watched him splash more sauces on his jacket. Not to be thought less a man of the world than he, I unwisely drank a glass of Benedictine which I didn't really like. I have not done so since; for at Dieppe a strong wind was chopping up the water in the harbour and once we were out on a very rough sea, I was sick down the side of the boat. The oily odour of that liqueur hung about me for weeks afterwards. For years I used to be sea-sick in the Channel, the Irish Sea and the Bay of Biscay and sometimes thought of Hester's father.

At last, with patriotic English joy, I saw the white cliffs through the storm and, with disgust, smelled English cigarettes and beer at Newhaven. I saw the pink, masked faces of my humbugging countrymen. I felt the prison growing round me as the quiet English train passed through Bromley to Victoria. It would have been more sensible to go from there directly home, but there was an unwritten law in our family that his sons must show themselves to their father first in Middle Street, off Bartholomew Close, and travel down with him. He was still the master mind. I went up the stone stairs of his small factory which was a building of fear to me, into his spotless and lavender-scented showroom and he stood in his white dust-coat at the other end. For years all of us were anxious about the set and mood of his face when we met him.

'You are late,' he said.

It was his usual greeting: the unfortunate man, so feminine (or was he such a Yorkshireman?) in disposition, could not resist putting himself in a position of advantage. He fed on the creation of guilt.

'Where is your luggage?' he said.

I explained I was going back to Paris. He stepped back. His face took on at once his look of incredulity and insult, though I know he was glad to see me and I proud to see him. His affront turned to annoyance. I thought he was going to be sick. My clothes were shabby, I was wearing the awful green velour hat with the wide brim, the Montmartre boy's worn-out black and tan high-heeled boots. How sons appal their fathers! When I spoke he looked puzzled and then angry. I easily pick up accents and I had a marked French accent which I exaggerated. Inevitably we took a cab – one of the few surviving growlers – from Bromley Station. By the time we got home my father's struggle with nausea and affection broke down.

'I wish you'd stop gesticulating and shrugging your shoulders and raising your eyebrows all the time, like a Frenchman. You've got lines on your forehead already. You look like an old man. And I can't understand a word you say, your voice going up and down like that.'

Mother was gay and reckless: 'He always raised his eyebrows, Walt. He takes after Gran's brother Gill.'

This was an unhappy remark. That long dead relation's only skill lay in the dashing way he drove a fishcart. Mother's connections were vividly low.

I forgot to say that over my French boots I wore spats: they were too large but they covered the holes in my socks.

When I said that I had left all my things in Paris, because I had only come over for a week or two on 'journalistic busi-

299

ness', my father could not speak. My mother anxiously defended me, but she was as worried as I was. Then she said: 'Give him his letter.'

Father went out of the room for it and gave me a letter that he had, of course, opened and read. 'It's to you from a girl,' he said. 'A girl called Judy. Have you been writing to a girl? Have you been seeing this girl?'

My father could put a criminal emphasis on words like 'this' and 'girl', 'letter' and the word 'seeing', an emphasis so sexual that it made one grow hot.

Judy had written one of her large theatrical scrawls in purple ink, and after wishing me a happy birthday she had added one of her silly lines:

'Dearest Puck. I hope you haven't forgotten our children.'

'What is this about children?' said my father.

'Yes?' said mother, 'You haven't . . .'

Those children were the snails at Saint-Cloud. There was nothing from Hester.

There was, I soon heard from my mother's frightened whispers – she was secretively changing the subject – the usual difficulties in the 'business', but these were glossed over. 'Let's be happy,' she said. For, eventually, after a very un-French meal of mutton chops burned black and mashed potatoes, my father expanded. He had fallen in love again – with a new house. Sometimes he called it a 'shooting box' or a 'hunting box', words that evoked the life of a country gentleman for him, dreams of field sports and air. The child of the Yorkshire moors still longed for air. He would be buying tweeds, knicker-bockers, perhaps guns. Mother said drily:

'We go there every Sunday. Oh yes!'

And so they did. They picknicked in the garden of the aban-doned place while father talked of the woods, the songs of the birds and the moorlands of the north. He missed the heather. On Sunday, we all went to the 'shooting box' for me to give my opinion. Mother sat in the back of the car, a Sunbeam, with her hands over her eyes, moaning 'Are we there yet?'; just as in thunderstorms, with her head under a cushion, she whimpered 'Is it getting lighter?' There were the usual remarks about the Divine Mind driving from my youngest brother, who was about twelve or thirteen, as we grazed a bank or two. When we got there mother groaned to me that, being a London girl, she would be driven 'out of her natural' by the loneliness and was upset by the amount of the fare to London, the 'shooting box' being another twenty-five miles 'out'. The place was less eccentric than stark. It was nothing but a kind of superior bungalow built of brieze. The owner had built on a bathroom a couple of yards from the main building. You had to make a dash for it, sheltered only by a glass roof. The thought of father making a short skip in his pyjamas in the open to the place in the mornings, made us laugh; but to mother, the whole thing seemed dissolute. Her mind quickly ran to the indecent.

'I mean, Vic, if you wanted to . . .'

One of her characteristic unfinished sentences.

The affair had been going on for the best part of a year, as these things did with father; but the crux of the matter was waved away. He hadn't the money. And mother, in her dishonest manner, pretended to be upset. Miss H would not let him take money out of the business. We were on the edge of one of our great family quarrels.

My father who had been so opposed to my becoming a writer was impressed by my one or two successes in the English weekly reviews, but most of all by my getting two or three things published in our sacred paper, the *Monitor*. (I ought to have said that he had paid for my typewriter.) His opposition, from the beginning, had everything to do with his wish to be in command of what all his children did. He was enraged when my brother, the following year, bought a third-hand motor car and then sold it for another; powerless, he made a subtle effort to get hold of the cheque, saying it would be 'better if it passed through my bank'; (One knew, once passed in, it would never pass out), on the excuse that my brother should not become extravagant.

Father was distressed by the quarrel in Boston – it had ended in the death of the American editor who had been 'handled' by 'animal magnetism' – for Boston was a holy city to him. He wanted to go and have a row with the London editor in his office. I said I would deal with him. I went to the office in the old Adelphi Terrace.

The odd thing about the *Monitor*'s London editor was that he was not a journalist. Mr Bassellthorpe – as I will call him – was a tall brotherly Englishman. He was masterful, shy and forgiving in manner. I was in awe of him. He was the first famous Christian Science lecturer I had seen; a top figure in the movement and well-off. Background: Quaker family, Charterhouse and Cambridge. His voice was kind and suggested some warm beverage. His accent notoriously puzzled American audiences when he spoke to them of the 'pah of prah'. He was embarrassed by his present difficulty, but said he could only ask me to be patient. My work was good and I would soon be paid. He put me on to H. M. Tomlinson who wrote about books for the paper and who also worked with Leonard Woolf on the most distinguished of the weekly reviews, *The Nation*. Their offices were a few doors down the street.

I had never met a well-known writer before. I had read Tomlinson's book on a voyage to South America, *The Sea and the Jungle*, which many critics thought equal to any of Conrad's writing about the sea; also his books on the Pacific Islands and the Thames. He was an adventurous traveller. His prose was elaborate; he used strange adjectives, words like 'obsidian', strenuous metaphors and dilated and pessimistic generalizations about human fate. He was pertinacious with *le mot juste*. His manner of writing was admired in English journalism of the distinguished kind. Here is a passage from the powerful description of a small ship in an Atlantic storm:

The ship would roll to that side, and your face was brought close to the surface of the bare mobile hill swirling past in a vitreous flux, with tortured lines of green buried far but plain in its translucent deeps ... The hills were so dark, swift and great, moving barely inferior to the clouds which travelled with them, that collapsing roof which fell over the seas, flying with the same impulse as the waters ...

One reads of:

The foundered heavens, a low ceiling that would have been night itself but that it was thinned in patches by some solvent day.

For longer than I ought to have done – for it was not *my* style – I tried to write like that. *The Sea and the Jungle* is a mixture of rhetorical and plain narrative and a minor classic in the genre of bad voyages; he knew sea life. One can explain Tomlinson's manner, especially his pessimism and afflatus, from his own life. He saw experience as a stoic's punishment. A wharfinger's clerk, beginning in the humblest newspaper work, he projected himself as a sort of defeated but irrepressible Napoleon against 'the powers and presences'. His prose might be traced back to Carlyle, to Browning's verses; certainly to Meredith and Stevenson. At the end of the century, writers like Henley and Belloc took it up and it entered journalism though C. E. Montague and the *Manchester Guardian*. Leonard Woolf scarcely mentions Tomlinson in his autobiography, though he worked with him every day; there was scorn for images among the lucid Bloomsbury rationalists, though not in Virginia Woolf.

My interview with Tomlinson took no more than a minute or two and on the stairs outside his office. He was a stocky, dogged man with a flattened nose and very big ears and he wore the wharfinger's bowler hat; and he was quick with the over-worked journalist's bitter phrase.

'I'll tell you what to do. Go back to Paris. Who the hell wants to work in this damn country, in the state it is in. Hang around the Chambre des Deputés and the political cafés. Pick up what is behind the political gossip. Hardly anyone knows how to do this. Get under the French skin.'

'I'm not interested in politics.'

In Tomlinson one was up against the 1914 war in person. Too old to be a soldier, he had been a courageous war-correspondent, embittered by the horror of trench warfare. *The Nation* had supported the 'conchies' and had published the indignant protests of Siegfried Sassoon and Robert Graves after the losses on the Somme; and Tomlinson was willing to serve on a poorly-paying review like *The Nation* in order to keep the public conscience alive. To him, I was one of the soft pups of the new decade; and it is true that those of us who were too young to be in the 1914 war felt at a loss with the men who had been in it. We were far less grown-up; and they rarely had

anything to say to us for the next few years. They clung together; in any case, the distance between a young man of
twenty-one and one in his late forties is enormous. It takes
years for the distance to shorten. Not until the war novels came
out in the late twenties – one of them by Tomlinson himself –
was much said about the realities of that war. The *other* war
interested us more; the war of what was called 'the new
morality' against the old; and the Russian revolution.

I moved on to the editor of the *Observer*: J. L. Garvin.
Fleet Street used to produce histrionic editors. I found Mr Garvin with his head in his hands, as if writhing in a prophet's
agony, conjuring up thought, and it was a long time before he
could raise his head to look at the anxious youth before him. He
uttered at last:

'I do not believe in the present. I live in the future, months,
years ahead.'

I sympathized as best I could. At last, the moment he had
been conjuring came out:

'Go to South America,' he pointed to the window. 'That is the
continent of the future. No one knows anything about it. Go
there.'

'Not, however, for the *Observer*. He had glanced at two of my
articles!

Presently Mr Bassellthorpe paid up and asked to see me. What,
he said, did I know about Ireland? Almost nothing, I said. All I
knew was that the Irish Treaty had been signed and that, as was
foreseen, the Irish were fighting one another. The Four Courts
had been besieged, several of the leaders of de Valera's revolt
had been shot. Griffiths had died, Michael Collins had been
killed. Sickening. The war was dragging on. Why, I did not
know.

Mr Bassellthorpe smiled with relief at my ignorance. The
readers of the *Monitor* in Boston and Ireland, being mostly
Protestant, were in a state of civil war themselves. Wasn't the
Roman Catholic Church one of the manifestations of animal
magnetism? I might be just the young man (Mr Bassellthorpe
thought), to describe how people in Ireland lived their ordinary
daily lives, despite the civil war. He pondered. At last he risked

it. Six articles, he said. £25 the lot, to include expenses. If I succeeded I might become the paper's Correspondent in Dublin for a year. The existing one, a woman, was causing the paper trouble.

Mother groaned when I got back to Bromley and told her the news, for that day another murderous Irish ambush was reported in black headlines in the evening paper.

Only the *Monitor* (which was really more of a daily magazine than a daily newspaper in those days), and had great prestige among liberals in the United States – and only Mr Bassellthorpe who, as I say, was not a journalist, could have sent a young man as untrained and innocent as I was, to Ireland. And only an American paper, with the American impulse to ask no questions and give anyone a chance. I had never been in a newspaper office. I did not know how one gathered news. I did not know that one could actually call on a government office or a politician. I thought it wasn't allowed. I knew no one in Ireland. My only interest was in describing scenery and I considered myself very bold if I introduced a human being into it. Countries existed for me only for their literature, and now I found myself faced with the life H. M. Tomlinson had suggested to me and which I had rejected.

I went back to Paris for my belongings. I wrote to Hester boastfully: there was no reply. I walked with confidence through the ever-growing crowds of artists in Montparnasse, keeping my ears open for Percy's hawking. Sure enough, I heard it. *I* stopped *him* – the reversal of our old relationship. He gaped at me. I could see he could not believe I was there.

'Where have you been?' he said. 'We've all been worrying about you. How did you get out of Germany? We tried to get through to you. We heard you'd been beaten up by the police.'

They had got out the table.

'You came through. You said you were in Coblenz, in danger, appealing for help. We kept on trying and you came through clearly. You said they had shot you dead.'

He was puzzled but not upset by my death nor was he interested in my survival.

'It must have been someone else,' I said.

'No,' he said. 'It was you. I've got the script.'

There is no arguing with a man's religion. It is tempting to an old man to play with the idea that there was something symbolic in Percy's words and to say 'Yes, he was right. My youth had gone.' What had really passed was careless happiness. I had crossed a line and henceforth I would know happiness, but I would also know pain.

I went to my room and looked at it for the last time. I shook hands with Madame Chapin. She had, to my eyes, become suddenly much older as she said good-bye.

CHAPTER SIX

On a misleading sunny day on the first of February, 1923, I took the train from London to Holyhead. In a heavy leather suitcase I carried a volume of Yeats's poems, an anthology of Irish poetry, Boyd's *Irish Literary Renaissance*, Synge's Plays and a fanatical book called *Priests and People in Ireland* by McCabe, lent to me by a malign Irish stationer in Streatham who told me I would get on all right in Ireland so long as I did not talk religion or politics to anyone and kept the book out of sight. Unknown to myself I was headed for the seventeenth century.

The Irish Sea was calm – thank God – and I saw at last that unearthly sight of the Dublin mountains rising from the water, with that beautiful false innocence in their violets, greens and golden rust of grasses and bracken, with heavy rain clouds leaning like a huge umbrella over the northern end of them. My breath went thin: I was feeling again the first symptoms of my liability to spells. I remember wondering, as young men do, whether somewhere in this city was walking a girl with whom I would fall in love: the harbours of Denmark gave way to Dublin Bay and the Wicklow Hills. The French had planted a little of their sense of limits and reason in me, but already I could feel these vanishing.

Once through the Customs I was frisked for guns by a Free State soldier with a pink face and mackerel-coloured eyes. I got out of the local train at Westland Row, into that smell of horse-manure and stout which were the ruling Dublin odours, and was driven on an outside car with a smart little pony to (of all things, in Ireland!) a temperance hotel in Harcourt Street. It was on this first trot across the city that I had my first experience of things in Ireland not being what they seem. I have described this in a book on Dublin which I wrote a few years ago. The jarvey whipped along, talking his head off about the state of the 'unfortunate country', in a cloud of Bedads, Begobs, God-help-us-es, but turned out to be a Cockney. The Cockney and Dublin accents are united by adenoids. Cab drivers are, perhaps, the same everywhere.

It was now dark and I went out into the wet streets. Troops were patrolling them and I was soon stopped by a patrol and frisked once more. More friskings followed as I got to the Liffey. It was enjoyable. I didn't realize that my green velour hat from the Boulevard des Italiens with its wide, turned-down brim, was an item of the uniform of the I.R.A. I went straight to the Abbey Theatre. In the shabby foyer, a small middle-aged woman with grey hair and looking like a cottage loaf, was talking to a very tall man. He was unbelievably thin. He seemed to be more elongated by having a very long nose with a cherry red tip to it. The woman's voice was quiet and decided. His fell from his height as waveringly as a snow-flake. The pair were Lady Gregory and Lennox Robinson. He took me to his office for an hour and then we went into the theatre. To an audience of a dozen or so people (for the Civil War kept people away), the company were going through the last act of *The Countess Cathleen*, in sorrowing voices. They went on to the horse-play of *The Shewing-Up of Blanco Posnet*. Both plays had caused riots years before when they were first put on. Now the little audience was apathetic.

Soot came down the chimney in my room at the hotel when a bomb or two went off that night.

The spell got a decisive hold of me in the next two days as I walked about the comfortable little Georgian and early Victorian city, where the red brick and the brown were fresher and less circumspect than the brick of London. The place seemed to be inhabited only by lawyers and doctors. The mists of the bog on which it is built softened the air. Complexions were delicate, eyes were alive with questions. As you passed people in the street they seemed to pause with expectation, hoping for company, and with the passing gaiety of hail and farewell, with the emphasis particularly on the latter. There was a longing for passing acquaintance; and an even stronger longing for your back to be turned, to give a bit of malice a chance.

The Civil War was moving to the south west; now de

Valera's men – called with beautiful verbal logic the 'Irregulars' – had been driven out of Dublin. I had seen the sandbags and barbed wire round the Government offices and the ruins of O'Connell Street; now I took a morning train in cold wet weather to Cork from Kingsbridge, the best of Dublin's monumental railway stations, a station that indeed looked like a fantastic chateau. A journey that normally takes two or three hours, took close on fourteen, for at Maryborough (now called Port Laoise), we stopped for the middle of the day, while they got an armoured engine and troops to escort us. I had seen pictures of these extraordinary engines in books about the Boer War: I suppose the British had dumped a lot of them in Ireland. One of the exquisite pleasures of the Irish (I was soon to find out) is pedantry: a few of us, including a priest, left the train and went into the town for a drink, sure of finding the train still there after a couple of hours. It was. It gave a jolt. 'Are we starting?' someone asked.

'Sure, we haven't started starting yet,' the porter said.

The afternoon faded as we went across the bogland; at Mallow it was dark, and there we got into cars to join another train across the valley. The viaduct had been blown up. We eventually arrived in Cork in a racket of machine-gun fire. I hesitated. But the passengers took it for granted and a barefooted urchin who took my case said: ' 'Tis only the boys from the hills.' The firing went on, from time to time, into the small hours, and patrol lorries drove up and down. One stopped at the hotel and after a lot of shouting and banging of doors, a posse of soldiers came into my room, got me out of bed and searched the bedding and my luggage. They looked respectfully at my books and one of them started reading a poem of Yeats and said if I kept to that I would be all right.

Cork is a pretty city, particularly in the dappled buildings of its riverside quays and estuaries. By this time my mind was singing with Irish poetry. I went out into the countryside to see how Blarney was surviving the revolution. It was surviving in the best of its tradition. I plodded round with a farmer whose chief ejaculation was a shout of 'Blood and hounds', when his narrative needed it. It often did. Back in Cork, I went to the theatre where Doran's touring company were playing a different Shakespeare tragedy every night: my earliest experience of *Macbeth*, *Othello* and *Hamlet*. Doran's company had been slogging away in England and Ireland for years. He himself was a sturdy man with a huge voice. He hogged the plays of course, and put such a stamp on his roles that it was pretty well impossible to distinguish Hamlet from Macbeth, or Macbeth from Othello. The Theatre was always packed. When Hamlet said his line about everyone being mad in England, the whole house cheered. I had gone with a commercial traveller from Kerry, who came back to the hotel and then he and one or two other commercials recited Shakespeare to one another for the rest of the evening. I couldn't understand a word the torrential Kerryman said, but Shakespeare was tempestuously Elizabethan in a Kerry accent.

I travelled across Tipperary to Limerick, arriving there in one of those long soft brown and yellow sunsets of the West, with the white mists rising from the Shannon. The Celtic twilight was working on me. I sat up drinking with a satanic engineer; and, thinking it was about time, I tried that night to write one of my articles. I found that after two or three whiskies my pen swept across the paper. When I read the thing in the morning, I saw it was chaotic and I tore it up. That is the last time I ever wrote on alcohol.

Limerick was in an edgy state. It had just been relieved of a siege and there was still a crack or two of sniping at night. There was a strike on at the bacon factories; and there was an attempt to start a Soviet. I went to see the committee and politely took my hat off and made a small French bow when I went into their room. The leader told me to put my hat on: they had finished, he said, with bourgeois manners. We had a wrangle about this because, although I am shy, I am touchy and argued back. We had a rapid duel of sarcasms. He was one of those 'black' Irishmen one occcasionally comes across; there was another, a waiter at the hotel in Limerick who threw a plate of bacon and eggs at a customer. He was a big fellow who looked murderous every time he came into the dining room with a plate.

There occurred in Limerick one of those encounters which – looking back on it – I see as a portent. I found there a very serious young Englishman, in fact a Quaker, who took me to a house inside the town. As we climbed up on an outside car, he whispered to me not to talk on the long ride out because, he said, his situation was delicate. He had caught the Irish love of conspiracy, even the whisper. When we got to his house he told me he had been in the fighting against the Sinn Feiners, but had lately married an Irish girl. I think he had been in the Auxiliary Police. Except for having his tennis court shot up now and then, he said, when he and his wife were playing in the afternoons, there was not much trouble now. The English have stubborn natures but, I saw, could get light-headed in Ireland. Into the sitting room, which was furnished in faded Victorian style, with pictures of lakes and vegetation on the walls and the general Irish smell of rising damp, came an elderly woman wearing a wig of black curls and with a sharp, painted face; and with her a pale little girl of twelve – I thought – one of those fey, unreal Irish children with empty blue eyes and untidy russet hair. She looked as if she had been blown down from the sky, as, in her tiny skirt, she sat bare-legged on the floor in front of the fire. She was *not* a child of twelve; she was the Quaker's wife, and very excitable. The shooting, she said, livened up the tennis and they were afraid for the strings of their rackets, because in these times you might have to send them to Dublin to be re-strung. A brother-in-law came in, a man who sat in silence breathing sociably, as Guinness after Guinness went down. I gazed from the old lady to the girl, from brother-in-law to the ascetic looking young Quaker soldier, and could not see how they could be together in the same house. In how many Irish families was it to seem to me that the people had all appeared accidentally from the wheel of fortune, rather than in the course of nature. The old lady chattered about balls and parties, about Lord this and Lady that, about the stage – was she an actress? In her wig, paint and her rings, bracelets and necklace, and her old-fashioned dress of twenty years before, she was nimble and witch-like. Indeed, she got out a pack of cards and told my fortune. I dropped the Queen of Spades. She sprang on it with glee:

'You will be surrounded by women who intend to harm you.'

I walked back to Limerick late, feeling, as I was so often to do in Ireland, that I had stepped into a chapter of a Russian novel. The smell of turf smoke curled among the river fogs and I was not sure of the way in the dark. I waited for a shot or two, for the Irregulars liked to loose off at night to keep the feeling of war alive, from behind a friendly hedge. There were no shots that night. It was an eerie and pleasant walk, like a ghost story told in the dark.

I went on to Enniskillen, the border town, all drapers, hardware stores and useful shops, brisker in trade than the towns of the south, a place half Orange, half Catholic. The Town Clerk, a twentieth-century man, was the kind who enjoyed the comedies of fanaticism, but the jokes rippled over the surface of the incurable seventeenth-century bitterness. It is often said that Irish laughter is without mirth, but rather a guerrilla activity of the mind. I was stuck in Enniskillen for another cold wet Sunday when the only other guest in the hotel was a glum commercial traveller from the English Midlands, a man with one of the flattest minds I had met up to then. Careful with his money, too; his father was an undertaker and the son used the motor hearse at the weekends to give his girl a ride. He was to be – from my point of view as a writer – the most important man I met in Ireland, but it took me ten years to realize this. I wrote down every word of his I could remember.

I look back upon this Irish expedition with an embarrassed but forgiving eye. I see the empty mountains, the bog and the succulent marshy valleys, the thin, awkward roads, through a steam of strong tea. The sun came and went, the rain dripped and dried on my hat. I stuffed with fried cod, potatoes, potato cakes, scones and butter as I read my Yeats and Synge; the air, even when cold, was lazy and I couldn't get up until eleven in the morning. I was thick in the head, with no idea of what to write about until, in despair, I was driven to write flatly everything I saw and heard. The 'everything' was a torture for I discovered that places overwhelmed me. Every movement of light, every turn of leaf, every person, seemed to occupy me physically, so that I had no self left. But perhaps this means I was all self. It was with a conviction of failure that I sent my first four articles to the paper and sat staring into a 'jar' of

Guinness. I was dumbfounded to get a telegram from London saying my articles were excellent.

Alas, I have seen them since. They are very small beer. They are thin and sentimental; but here and there is a sentence that shows I was moved and had an eye. They were signed by my initials and that is why from then on people dropped my Christian name – to my relief – and I was called V.S.P. or R.S.V.P. My literary name developed from this. I preferred the impersonal, and to have added the 't' of Victor to a name that already had three, and was made more fidgety by a crush of consonants and two short vowels, seemed ridiculous.

In this short trip I had easily rid myself of the common English idea that Ireland was a piece of England that for some reason or other would not settle down and had run to seed. I had heard at school of 'the curse of Cromwell'. I ardently identified Irish freedom with my own personal freedom which had been hard to come by. A revolutionary break? I was for it. Until you are free you do not know who you are. It was a basic belief of the twenties, it permeated all young minds and though we became puritanically drastic, gauche and insensitive in our rebellions against everything we called Victorianism, we were elated.

I became the Irish correspondent. It was momentous. I had a career. This was no time for living the dilapidated day to day life I had lived in Paris. And there was the religious question: I had lapsed in Paris where I had been the average sensual young man. Now I found myself employed by the paper from whose religion I had lapsed. It seemed to be my duty to reform. The shadiness of Puritans! I threw my last cigarette into the Liffey, gave up drinking wine, beer and whiskey, though my tastes there were youthfully moderate. I was really more austerely the Romantic idealist than Puritan for I soon found the Calvinism of Ireland – scarcely buried under Irish high spirits – distasteful and indeed dull; my nature rebelled against it.

I lived in Dublin in two periods and I write now mostly of my first year there when, far more than in Paris, I lived in my imagination. When I re-read nowadays the German court episode in Meredith's *Harry Richmond* and of the ordeal through which Meredith's young romantic passes, I recognize something close to my Irish experience and indeed to other experience in my youth; like Stendhal, Meredith is outstanding in his observation of easily inflamed young men.

If Ireland moved me, it also instructed me. As a political education, the experience was excellent. One was observing a revolution: a country set free, a new young state, the first modern defeat of colonialism. Sitting in the Press Gallery of the Dail day after day, listening to the laughing, fighting voice of Cosgrave, the irony of Kevin O'Higgins or the tirades of the old defeated Redmond was like being at school taking a course in the foundation of states. I realized what a social revolution was, although I was (inevitably as an Englishman and Protestant), much more in the old Anglo-Irish society, the majority of whom reluctantly accepted the new regime, than among the rising Catholic middle class. I did not really know them until many years later. I was carried away by Irish sociability and nervous scorn of England into thinking I was in the contemporary European world. I was not, but there was the beguiling insinuation that Ireland was in temperamental contact with Paris and Italy and had by-passed the complex social preoccupations of industrial England. (Joyce's flight from Dublin to the Continent was an example of the Irish tradition.) The snobberies of the Ascendancy were very Colonial – as I now see – though not as loud as the Anglo-Indian, nor as prime as the Bostonian: they came closer to those of the American southern states. (There is a bond between Anglo-Irish writing and the literature of the American south.) In Ireland, shortage of capital and decaying estates had given these snobberies a lazy but acid quality; in many people there was a suggestion of concealed and bloodless spiritual superiority. English snobbery was based firmly on vulgar wealth; and a class system energized by contention and very mobile; the Irish was based on kinship, without wealth. The subject is perfectly displayed – though in an earlier generation – in *The Real Charlotte* by Somerville and Ross. Noses were kept raised by boisterous and tenuous claims to cousinage.

Ireland is really a collection of secret societies; for a rootless young man like myself, this had a strong allure. I was slow to see that I was meeting an upper class in decay and at the point

314

when it was disappearing in boatloads, from Dun Laoghaire every day; and that I was really living in a world far more like that of Mrs Gaskell's novels in the prim and genteel England of, say, 1840 to 1860 (except that old ladies had been using the word 'bloody' in company freely for a couple of hundred years). Genealogy, as one could tell from the Libraries and the number of societies given to it, was the national passion.

The easy-going life in this Victorian lagoon was delightful to me. It is often said that in Ireland there is an excess of genius unsustained by talent; but there is talent in the tongues and Irish manners are engaging. I sat in my office in St Stephens Green, a cheerful outsider in Irish quarrels, turning myself into the idlest of newspaper correspondents. I lodged with two Protestant spinsters in a sedate early Victorian terrace house in Waterloo Road, where they left me cold meat and pickles and a pot of strong tea for my supper; they popped up every quarter of an hour, if I had a young woman to visit me, to see that nothing was 'going on'. Dublin was a city so gregariously domestic that the sexes did not care to meet without other company. The English were deplored as coarse sensualists who ate too much, were sex-mad and conventional.

The pleasant wide eighteenth-century streets of Georgian Dublin were easing to the mind, and the wild mountains over which the weather changed every hour, excited the fancy. And there was Dublin Bay, so often enamelled and Italianate. More and more, I was idling at Blackrock or Dalkey, with a crowd of young men and girls, watching the sea or walking across the mountains as far as Glendalough or the Vale of Avoca or scooping a kettle of water out of a stream in the heather, for a picnic.

My mind fed on scenery. The sight of lakes, slatey in the rain, or like blue eyes looking out of the earth in the changing Irish light; the Atlantic wind always silvering the leaves of beech and oak and elm on the road to Galway, empty except for a turf cart or a long funeral; the Twelve Pins in Connemara now gleaming like glass in the drizzle, now bald, green and dazzling; the long sea inlets that on hot days burn their way deeply inland beyond Clifden where the sands are white and the kelp burns on them; the Atlantic coming in stormily below the high cliffs of Moher; and the curious tropic of Kerry. My

315

brother came over from England and with two girls we borrowed a horse and cart and went slowly across to the West and back; and in Clare, which was still in a disorganized state, we attracted the 'boys from the hills' who kept us up dancing half-sets, singing all the rebel songs and finishing up with 'Nancy Hogan's Goose'. Two young Englishmen with two unmarried girls! The scandal of it! There was a lot of talk in Dublin. I do not think only of landscape but of the wide disheartening streets of the long villages and the ruined farms of the West; and the elaborately disguised curiosity of the impulsively kind but guarded people, looking into your eyes for a chance of capping your fantasy with one of theirs, in long ceremonies of well-mannered evasion, craving for the guesswork of acquaintance and diversion.

The darker side of this was blurred and muddied and stinking; the dramatic character of the misery. In Dublin, the tenements were shocking; the women still wore the long black shawl, the children were often bare-footed. You picked up lice and fleas in the warm weather in the Dublin trams as you went to the North side to the wrecked mansions of the eighteenth century. The poor looked not simply poor, but savagely poor, though they were rich in speech and temperament. There were always ragged processions of protesters, on the general Irish ground that one must keep on screaming against life itself. There were nasty sights: a man led down a mountain road with his wrists tied behind his back, by a couple of soldiers.

I think of the story of the house close to a lonely cottage I had in my second Irish period at the sea's edge near Clifden. It was no more than a two-roomed cabin with a loft and, with the Irish love of grand names, was called Mount Freer and had once belonged to an English painter. (A pensioned-off sailor owned it.) Near it was the Manor or farm, a ruinous place of rusty gates and scarcely habitable, occupied by a bank manager from some inland town. He was very ill and was still suffering from the shock of having been badly beaten up in a raid on his bank in the civil war. He was not alone at this time. His brother, a cropped Australian ex-soldier had come over to look after him for a while. I used to go shooting rabbits with the Australian in a deserted graveyard. It had belonged, the Australian said, to the ferocious O'Flahertys, from whom the people in Galway had in the far past called on God to protect them. He was trying to persuade his dim sick brother to go back with him. If the sick man saw anyone in the road he would climb gingerly over the stone wall and dodge away in a wide, lonely circle across the rocky fields to the house. I knew the Australian well. He was a good fisherman. We used to go out and spear plaice in the sands and catch mackerel. Many a fry we had. Often I walked, as night fell, to look at the wink of light on Slyne Head, America the next parish. He told me the brother refused to go near anyone.

'The poor bloody brother, he has the idea he stinks. He thinks he's got a bloody smell on him. He'll never come near you.' His house had almost no furniture – simply a couple of beds, a table and two chairs – and if I went there, the sick man slipped away and hid in another room. Eventually the Australian had to leave and when he did the 'mad feller' as he was called cut his throat or hanged himself. Thank God I'd left before that happened.

It has been said that the Irish live in a state of perplexity. The poet Patrick Kavanagh has written that the newborn child screams because it cannot bear the light of the real world. Yet, from Shaw onwards one finds the Irish saying they are not dreamers, but are realists. Not in the literary sense of the word 'realism', but in the sense of seeing with cold detachment where exact practical advantage lies. I would have said their instincts are tribal. They evade the moral worries of settled societies and there is a strain of anarchy in them: they can be charitable and cruel at the same time. It is self-indulgent to generalize like this and, anyway, the Irish do that more coolly than we English do. But one has to make something of the way they turn tragedy to farce and farce back into tragedy; and when in the thirties I wrote a story called *Sense of Humour*, a piece of premature black comedy, which was set going by the meeting with that glum commercial traveller I had met in Enniskillen, it expressed something of the effect of an Irish experience on myself.

One of my acquaintances among the gentry class – how naturally one associates the word 'gentry' with the same class in old

Russia rather than with an English equivalent – took me down to a mansion he had inherited together with a title he detested. He was not one of the raffish, shooting kind, and he was too simple and plain a fellow to care much about the brilliant group of Anglo-Irish intellectuals who still dominated Irish life. He was a bit deaf and was thought dull – 'I hear he's a decent kind of feller.' He was by way of being a gentleman socialist, and the 'good society', in that sense, interested few Irishmen. The decent fellow had a social conscience and had to bear the curse of land-owning. It had fallen on him by accident. As a poor boy he had been sent off to Canada where he became a Mountie; in the war he had been one of the early flying men. Suddenly he came into 'the place'; he married a beauty whom he bickered with, because he refused to have anything to do with fashionable life in Ireland, London or Italy. His real taste – but as a social reformer – was for low life on the Dublin quays. After I left Ireland I heard he had sold his mansion to the nuns, as many Irish landlords did in the end (the Irish Church having a shrewd eye for property) and cleared off, at a moment's notice, without telling a soul, to America. He is now dead.

This week-end was my only experience of Irish country house life in the Civil War. It was still sputtering away when we drove off in a little French racing car with planks strapped to the side of it. This was to outwit 'the clowns' on his estate who had burned down the mill he had built – part of his practical socialism – and had dug trenches across the key roads to prevent him getting home. A true Irishman, he was more than half on their side. At each new trench we got out, put down the planks and drove across. He loved the comedy.

We drove into a large demesne. The mansion stood empty above its lake; he had built himself an efficient little villa near it. When we got in, we found the house had been invaded by 'Irregulars', who had come searching for guns and ammunition. The servants were hysterical and a parrot imitated them, calling out 'Glory be to God'. He went up to his bedroom, slid back a panel in the wardrobe: there was a good supply of untouched weapons, but girls among the raiders had gone off with his wife's riding clothes, and one of the men had emptied a gallon jar of ink over the drawing-room carpet. The raiders had found a safe in the estate office, but could not open it. So they dumped it in the middle of the lake. My host rang up the local military who put on an offensive.

'We'll send down the Terrorizer,' the officer said. The Terrorizer and his men rowed about the large lake very happily. It was a lovely afternoon. Her ladyship came down in the evening. She was a slender and handsome, dark-haired woman with fine features and an amused sparkle in her eyes and a despairing voice. She treated me very kindly, but firmly, as the social peculiarity I was, because I had not changed into a dinner jacket. (I hadn't got one.) Still, despite her high-class groans, she was an amusing and witty woman. The more snobbish she became, the rougher her husband.

'She's talking a lot of rot,' he'd say down the table, jerking his thumb at his wife. I felt, like another Pip, one of my moods of Miss Havisham worship coming on, for a caustic, mocking tongue and beauty combined were irresistible. I put on dog and burst out with a long speech about a new book of D. H. Lawrence's.

'What extraordinary things are going on,' she said. 'How very unpleasant.'

The next two days I was put through a short course in Irish country house life. We went out fox-cubbing in the rain with a lot of wind-reddened country neighbours. We got very muddy. I was never one for the sporting life. We went for a drink to a large dark house where the family portraits looked like kippers. A man was dumbstruck when I told him I didn't hunt, shoot or fish. 'What do you do?' he asked coldly. I naturally supposed this was directed at my employment. I told him I was a journalist. He looked shocked and had never heard of the paper. Trying to think of a comparable English paper, I said, 'It's like the *Manchester Guardian*.'

He stepped away making a few short sarcasms about that traitorous 'Sinn Fein rag'. In Ireland, it is nowadays, I believe, called 'The Niggers' Gazette'.

The following afternoon we went riding. I had never been on a horse before. To me the animal smelt of the leather trade. I was surprised to find that horses are warm. I gripped the reins as if they were a life line; I was jellied and bumped by its extraordinary movement. The party began to canter and I was tossed in the air and I got a fixed smile on my face. We arrived in a field to try some jumps. A wicked old trainer shouted bits of advice. I went over one or two gaps and arrived, surprised and askew, but still up. So they tried some more difficult jumps. The party hung about waiting for the slaughter. The animal rose, I fell on its neck, but I did not come off. The stakes were raised; at the next jump the horse and I went to different parts of the sky. I was in the mud. I got up and apologized to the horse, which turned its head away. Afterwards we walked and trotted home; it seemed to take hours. Back in the house, I felt someone had put planks on my legs and turned my buttocks into wooden boxes. So my life as an Irish sportsman and country gentleman came to an end. Still, I had stayed with a baronet. I was snobbish enough to be pleased by that.

I like curious clothes. Back in Dublin I stayed in my riding breeches, bought at a cheap shop in Dublin, and wore them for weeks after, as an enjoyable symbol of the Irish habit of life, until someone tactfully suggested I looked like a stable boy.

There was one seminal and lasting gain in my time in Dublin. The Irish revel in words and phrases. Their talk is vivid and inventive. They live for the story. I had no idea of what kind of writer I wanted to be, but there were many, in the flesh, to offer me a new example, and who woke something in me.

In their twilight, the Anglo-Irish, especially, had discovered their genius. Yeats was in Merrion Square, A.E. was editing the *Irish Statesman* next door but one; James Stephens, Lennox Robinson, Lady Gregory were there. And so was the young Liam O'Flaherty – not Anglo-Irish – and Sean O'Casey was working in his slum room on the North Side. There were other good dramatists and there were the gifted actors and actresses of the Abbey Theatre where I went every week. There one could see not only the plays of Synge and writers of the Revival, but masters of tragic form like the unjustly forgotten T. C. Murray, and Shaw, Ibsen and Strindberg. Literature was not to be studied or something to be caught up with, but to be practised and at once. In writing, the stories of Liam O'Flaherty excited me for he had the Irish gift of writing close to the skin of life. The best

Irish writers have always had a fine surface. They have always had élan. The writing is clear and sensuous and catches every tremor of movement in the skin of the human animal and of landscape. The prose is athletic and flies along untroubled as if language were their life. Then, the Dublin bookshops were excellent. It was in Dublin that I read Katherine Mansfield, Chekhov and D. H. Lawrence, and Joyce's *Dubliners* and hoped to catch his sense of epiphany. In 1923 the short story, like the one act play, had a prestige. I wrote my first stories in Ireland and Spain.

Living among writers who were still at their good moment added to my desire to emulate them. I had the – to me – incredible sight of the beautiful Mrs W. B. Yeats riding a bicycle at St Stephens Green; and of A.E. (George Russell), also riding a bicycle and carrying a bunch of flowers. I had tea with James Stephens one Sunday at that hotel at Dun Laoghaire where people go to day-dream at the sight of the mail-boat coming in from England, that flashing messenger to and from the modern world. This gnome-like talker sparkled so recklessly that one half-dreaded he might fall into his teacup and drown. One afternoon I took tea with Yeats himself in his house in Merrion Square.

It was a Georgian house, as unlike a hut of wattle in a bee-loud glade as one could imagine. To begin with, the door opened on a chain and the muzzle of a rifle stuck through the gap. A pink-faced Free State soldier asked me if I had an 'appointment'. I was shown in to what must have been a dining-room but now it was a guard room with soldiers smoking among the Blake drawings on the wall. Yeats was a Senator and he had already been shot at by gunmen. Upstairs I was to see the bullethole in the drawing-room window. Presently the poet came down the stairs to meet me.

It is a choking and confusing experience to meet one's first great man when one is young. These beings come from another world and Yeats studiously created that effect. Tall, with grey hair finely rumpled, a dandy with negligence in collar and tie and with the black ribbon dangling from the glasses on a short, pale and prescient nose – not long enough to be Roman yet not sharp enough to be a beak – Yeats came down the stairs towards me, and the nearer he came the further away he seemed. His air was bird-like, suggesting one of the milder swans of Coole and an exalted sort of blindness. I had been warned that he would not shake hands. I have heard it said – but mainly by the snobbish Anglo-Irish – that Yeats was a snob. I would have said that he was a man who was translated into a loftier world the moment his soft voice throbbed. He was the only man I have known whose natural speech sounded like verse.

He sat me in the fine first floor of his house. After the years all that remains with me is a memory of candles, books, wood-cuts, the feeling that here was Art. And conversation. But what about? I cannot remember. The exalted voice flowed over me. The tall figure, in uncommonly delicate tweed, walked up and down, the voice becoming more resonant, as if he were on a stage. At the climax of some point about the Gaelic revival, he suddenly remembered he must make tea, in fact a new pot, because he had already been drinking tea. The problem was one of emptying out the old tea pot. It was a beautiful pot and he walked the room with the short steps of the aesthete, carrying it in his hand. He came towards me. He receded to the bookcase. He swung round the sofa. Suddenly with Irish practicality he went straight to one of the two splendid Georgian windows of the room, opened it, and out went those barren leaves with a swoosh, into Merrion Square – for all I know on to the heads of Lady Gregory, Oliver St John Gogarty and A.E. They were leaves of Lapsang tea.

I can remember only one thing he said. We had got on to Shaw whom he disliked. I murmured – showing off – something about Shaw's socialist principles. The effect on Yeats was fine. He stood now, with a tea-pot full of tea in his hands, saying that Shaw had no principles. Shaw was a destroyer. Like lightning, Shaw flashed in hilarious indifference, and what the lightning briefly revealed was interesting but meaningless. This has always stuck in my mind, but of the rest I remember nothing except that with solemnity he pointed to the inner door of the room and said that, sitting in this room, he had experimented in thought transference with Mrs Yeats who sat in her room next door. As I say, I had seen her out on her bicycle and I have often wondered, as the eloquent mind expelled its thoughts to the wall, whether Mrs Yeats was always next door at the time. He was kind enough to walk with me to the Irish Senate near by, and I was overcome when he leant on my shoulder while he lifted a foot, took off his shoe and shook out a stone. I noticed he had a pretty blue ring on one of his fingers.

I went to see A.E. in the office of the *Irish Statesman*, the weekly review that preached cooperative farming. He was a large tweedy bunch of a man with a beard, a talker who drowned me in beautiful phrases of a mystical, theosophical kind. The walls of his office were an extension of his mind, for they were covered with golden murals of ethereal beings. He must have been the kindest and most innocent man in Ireland, for he was a slave to the encouragement of young writers. When I wrote my first story, he took it at once, kept it for two years, and almost with tears of apology sent it back saying it was crowded out. This was inevitable. A.E.'s talking overflowed into print and occupied nearly the whole paper. I sat again with both Yeats and A.E. at Yeats's house, while Yeats praised D'Annunzio and A.E. tried to argue him out of the admiration. I watched on Yeats's fireplace, for A.E. distracted himself during Yeats's long utterances by making designs in the soot with Yeats's poker.

The only playwright I knew a little was Sean O'Casey. He was still living in his tenement on the North Side, a smashed fanlight over the door. His room was bare and contained only an iron bed, a table and a couple of poor chairs. He always wore a cloth cap in the house. A fire of cheap coal dust was smouldering on the fire where a kettle was singing – a true sign of the old Ireland. On the shabby wall was a notice he had printed:

Get on with the bloody play.

He was writing *The Plough and the Stars* at this time. Again, only one thing remains of his conversation: he was angry because he said that the 'authorities' were trying to keep the poor from using the Public Libraries, on the grounds that the poor would spread their diseases through the books. I'd been angered myself by the argument when I was ten, and I had read it in a book by Marie Corelli.

323

It was my duty to go to Ulster now and then and there, after crossing the Boyne, beyond Dundalk, the political grafitti were violent.

'To hell with the Pope.'

or: 'Ulster will fight and Ulster will be right.'

or: 'Remember Derry and no surrender.'

I walked round the grey and dismal walls of Londonderry; odd to think of the most sorrowful and lilting of Irish ballads bearing the name of that ugly and raging city. I looked beyond the drizzle to the empty hills of Donegal. I went again to Enniskillen, where I met the only Orangeman I really enjoyed. He was a solicitor and a fanatic who boiled at the thought of the I.R.A. just a mile away. They tried to kidnap him. He had one chink in his armour: he had married an amusing woman from the South. The bond in Irish marriages, it struck me often, was a common interest in battle; and in the course of their frisky warfare, the wife succeeded in getting her husband to laugh at himself after one of his rages. He was telling me about the night raid on his house and how his wife, as a foolish woman would, had run to the window and beat on a tin tray to call for help, while he got out the gun he always kept under the bed.

'I always keep one up the spout. That's the lesson you don't forget in the British Army.'

But his wife joined in: 'And it went off just as he got it from under the bed. There was a crash of china. He had shot the chamber-pot.'

Belfast was detestable. The only 'decent' hotel at that time was grubby. The city is the most dreadful in Ireland. The Ulster accent, a bastard lowland Scots, is harsh, and is given a sort of comic bluster by the glottal stop imported from Glasgow. (It is strange to think that Henry James's Ulster ancestors may have spoken in this manner.) The humour is boisterous; the fanaticism is brutal and the relations between the Ulster employers and workers were rough; it was a simple matter to rouse national passions, so that social reforms were checked. The minority of the liberally minded were the merchants and middlemen; the manufacturers were more obdurate. Still, I have known genial Ulstermen. It is no good trying the southern Irish game of evasion, indirection and covert conspiracy with them, at least not with the Protestants; one has to stand firm and hit back hard. They understand that and, like plain-speakers in northern England, they grin.

I speak, of course, generally; one can always find the gentler and more reasonable spirits. One of these, whom I always went to see, was a very distinguished writer – now forgotten and lost because he buried himself in Belfast – called Forrest Reid. He was a friend of Yeats and E. M. Forster and his few novels have an element of pagan symbolism that is present also in Forster's early short stories, and reflect something of Yeats's mysticism. The idea of the ghost or revenant, some shade of a lost culture or a guilt appearing out of the past, is often found in Irish literature. Reid's autobiography, *Apostate*, describes his upbringing in Belfast. It is a minor classic, and it will stand beside Gosse's *Father and Son*. He was indeed an apostate in that awful, rainy and smoky Presbyterian city: he was a genuine pagan. He stayed there as if in hiding, I used to think. He lived alone on the top floor of a sour house, shaken by industrial traffic, and opposite a linen mill. The smoke hung low and blew into his windows, so that he had been obliged to bind his thousands of books in white paper covers: not very practical in that place for the smuts stood out on them. One passed old bicycles in the hall, then climbed stairs of torn linoleum to his bare room on the table of which there was usually a pile of novels for review from the *Manchester Guardian*, and a bone of cold mutton pushed to the other side of it. He was the first book reviewer I ever saw. He was a thin fellow and he had a strange nose, very long and thin, that tipped up suddenly like a small hook at the end. He had A.E.'s habit of poking the soot off the back of his little fireplace as if looking for secret intimations. After sniffing out politics in mills and newspaper offices, or coming back from some Orange beano at which an English politician would be trying to beat the Orangemen down before they all started singing (of all songs), 'Oft in the Stilly Night' by Tom Moore – I would make for Forrest Reid's room to hear softer and more civilized accents. It was a relief after a day with a shipyard owner. There was one to whom I spoke about Forrest Reid.

'Wratin' poetry don't drave no rivets, yoong man,' he said.

I may exaggerate Reid's isolation, for there is a decent university in Belfast and the Belfast playwright who wrote that biting farce *Thompson of Tir-na-Nog* must have been worth knowing; but it was odd to find a mystic, deep in Blake and Yeats, among the linen mills. Why didn't he go South? Perhaps because of some core of Ulster obstinacy or of family chains that are so powerful in all Ireland.

Naturally, by pleasing the pro-Free State faction in Dublin I had angered the others. The Divine Mind instructed them to complain to my paper. They even sent anonymous letters: I had thought my upper class co-religionaries would be above that. It was rumoured that I had gone off to the country with the girl who worked with me. I had, and very chastely, for the 'open road' was a chaste movement. I was called back to London. I supposed I was to be sacked.

The situation, I found, was different. By the end of 1923 Ireland, which had attracted the newspapers of the world since 1916, had ceased to be interesting. No one wanted to read about Ireland any more. And Mr Bassellthorpe – very English in this – had grown sick to death of his Irish troubles. I sat in Mr Bassellthorpe's office. He praised my work, saying however, that I must beware of getting swollen-headed. It would have been truer if he had said I had a brain but no head at all. He came nearer the truth when he suggested I had become youthfully addled. He had elected to become a father to me.

He took me to the Bath Club for lunch. I carelessly said I admired Yeats. I was surprised to find he had read Yeats thoroughly and he politely but abruptly told me of my error. The poet had the fatal Celtic tendency to sensuous mysticism, to abominations like the Wisdom of the East; he was obsessed by sex. So was Mr Bassellthorpe; his face fattened into blushes when he used this word. When we got to coffee he came out with what had really disturbed him. The Irish had never been distinguished in the visual arts, he said: I had written the notice of a picture show and sent a photograph of one of the pictures. He brought out the picture from his pocket. I forget who had painted it. It had been inspired by a line of Synge's 'And he rising up in the red dawn'. It was the back view of a savage-looking and naked, middle-aged tinker, with hairy legs, standing in a patch of bog, against a riotous sunrise. How could I like it? 'He's not even a young man' said Mr Bassellthorpe. There was no suggestion of the Ideal. I did my best to defend it in a stammering way. He said, unforgivingly: 'That is what Ireland does to the mind.'

He said he had read a line in a Gaelic poem which ran: 'What does the salmon dream?'

'A salmon does not dream,' he said firmly.

After this he became more lenient. He had talked to an Irish peer who had complained about my political writing and Mr Bassellthorpe had defended me. At the mention of peers, my ears pricked up and, in a worldly way, possibly due to the influence of the Bath Club, I dropped the names of one or two with titles whom I had seen in the Irish Senate. Mr Bassellthorpe was not going to let me get away with that. They were only Irish peers, he said, and they ranked lower even than the Scots. His thoroughly English satisfaction in placing peers socially relieved our luncheon. He changed the subject. There had been a *coup d'état* in Spain: the paper's correspondent there had died. Would I go there? He would pay me £400 a year and the paper would pay the fare.

The suggestion of Mr Bassellthorpe was tormenting. In Ireland I had wanted to be an artist of some sort, like the Irish writers I read or knew. I had day-dreamed of settling there. I remember sitting on a rock on the little island called Ireland's Eye, near Howth, and thinking how tragic it would be to leave this beautiful place. I was living – if my Irish friends were not – in an unreal world.

The torment had a private aspect. Naturally I had fallen in love again – this time with the young woman journalist who worked with me; a troublesome business because the Major, her father, detested me. He would get up from his day-long game of patience and leave the room muttering something about 'the nasty little clerk' his daughter brought to the house. I was clearly not a gentleman. And certainly had 'no money' – i.e. no private means. I had, in fact, £14 in cash. Mr Bassellthorpe's move put everyone in a panic, for I had to leave almost at once. The young woman and I had been nosing our way out of friendship towards marriage; now, in a rush, it was upon us and to the indignation of our fathers we were married soon after my twenty-third birthday.

CHAPTER SEVEN

AT the beginning of January in 1924, shortly after my twenty-third birthday, I set off for Madrid. We spent two days in Paris on the way and went up to Montparnasse. I saw no recognizable face. Had everyone been 'passing through' like myself? The Rotonde had become very expensive and vulgar. Smart night clubs were springing up. The quarter had become a tourist spot. The one or two restaurants that had seemed so pleasant to me, now looked cramped. The gleam of my Bohemian days had gone, my own Bohemian gleam with it. Even my shoes were clean. That silly notion of 'becoming French'! I was as English as I could possibly make myself. The lines of Henri Murger came back to me:

Je veux bien consenter à regarder le passé, mais ce sera au travers d'une bouteille de vrai vin, et assis dans un bon fauteuil. Qu'est-ce-que tu veux? – je suis un corrompu. Je n'aime plus que ce qui est bon.

Basil Shaves had gone to London. I knew that, because he had stayed for a while near my parents in Bromley and had made their hymn-playing piano ring with 'Cutts of the Cruiser What-Not' and Albert Chevalier songs which so cheered my mother, bringing back the olden days, that she talked and laughed about it for the rest of her life. My brother, now successful in the artificial silk trade, had got the expert in ruin a job selling stockings and ladies' underwear.

I would have liked to have heard Percy hawking up the Boulevard, to show him that I had gone up in the world; but Percy was not there. Madame Chapin had moved too. The bugle went off at the barracks opposite my old hotel, and its note did not cheer me.

We took the night train, second class, in low spirits. Marriage had stunned us. I spoke no Spanish. The only thing I knew about Spain was that it had had the Inquisition and that the Armada had been defeated. And I also had garbled memories of pictures of Granada, the scene of the novel I had written 100 pages of when I was twelve. I have written two books about Spain since that day in 1924: the first in the twenties, *Marching Spain* – long out of print – and in my fifties, *The Spanish Temper*. I shall do my best not to repeat myself, but it will be difficult because Spain was to bring about a fundamental change in my life. Until now I had picked up my education as I went along. In Spain the matter became more serious. Irish sociability had made me a careless amateur; in Spain I was to get one of those moral shocks that make one question everything one has taken for granted.

At Hendaye rain was driving out of a cold sky; across the choppy bay I saw one of those big cheese-coloured baroque churches that seem to bully the town like some shabby and portentous old bishop. The old Protestant scorn and rancour rose in me. The grass growing over the railway tracks at Irun, the battered rolling stock, rotted by use, sun and rain, the liverish faces of the silent officials who seemed so thin that the yellow straps of their green or blue uniforms were holding them together, and their exhausted laconic manner suggested people who were waiting for death with the little that was left to them: their dignity. Through France, people were as rosy as lawyers and almost buttered. Here they looked corpse-like. In the train the passengers were heavily wrapped up, glum and silent; well, it was early in the morning. One looked out of the carriage window at the driving clouds and the smear of drizzle low over the Pyrenees and the sodden Basque mountains. The rain spouted off the heavy wide eaves of the little towns. Years later I was to see people dancing in the town squares there under umbrellas. Swollen and rocky rivers flooded through ravines. Although the train was a *Rapido* it trundled along on the wide gauge that had been built to prevent another Napoleon dashing straight in from France, and stopped at every small station. Wet and silent Basques got in. Only after fashionable San Sebastian where Madrileños entered was there the dramatic parrot-like chatter which the Basques, like the Portuguese, silently despise. A youth got in playing a guitar for money between stations for a while. Another youth slid back the door of the compartment, opened his jacket wide and shouted, with a look of desperation: 'Knives?' He had six rows of knives of all sizes slotted into the inside of his jacket. No one answered.

The journey from the French frontier nowadays takes about eight hours. In 1924 it took thirteen and, in our case, nineteen, for one of the two engines broke down as it failed to get up the steep gradient from Avila into the snow of the Guadarrama mountains. But long before this, about two in the afternoon, we got out of the rain of the Basque provinces into the daylong sunlight of the tableland of Castile, here some 2,000 feet above the level of the sea.

I have described the effect of this sudden sight in *The Spanish Temper*: the slow journey through a landscape unlike any other in Western Europe, the monotonous yet bizarre landscape of flat-topped mesas that proceeded like a geometry under a clear cold sky and dry winter sun. I had never seen anything like this before. I was magnetized. The bleached yellow of the soil, sometimes changing to metallic pinks and cindery greys; the curious associations of desert harshness and serenity, especially of desert-like space and of distances that ended in wildernesses of rock; and then of sierras that seemed to be cut out of the sky as if saw-blades had sliced them, and towards which some mule team straggled along the rare roads: all alerted me. I daydreamed of getting out of the train and crossing Old Castile on foot or by mule. I recognized, though there were no windmills here, the country of Don Quixote's adventures. We slumped into towns as if the train had suddenly come upon them by accident, so cunningly were they hidden in the creases of the plateau: Burgos, Valladolid, Medina del Campo, Avila, Escorial – those names burned into my mind. On the crowded platforms families of peasants camped; it seemed that a population was patiently migrating. There is a line in one of the notebooks of Albert Camus which was made for me:

One of our contemporaries is cured of his torments simply by contemplating a landscape for a long time.

Landscape, the sight of nature, has always had an exciting yet appeasing effect on me. This landscape of Castile caught me at the right time. The landscape of Andalusia is voluptuous. Italy is richer, but here in Castile, far from the sea, one could see the bare flesh and bone of the earth.

The sight of wide stretches of country and sky liberate the mind and lift some of the load from it. When I was young, especially in adolescence and aided often by some poem I had read, distant scenes were an extension of my mood and myself, when I saw the lineament of the horizon changing to colours that became impossible to distinguish, until they became frail and transparent as they touched and broke against the sky. There, distance seemed about to speak. But, now in the Castillian scene distance was hard and taciturn. The colours themselves were harsher in the foreground and there was, above all an exact sight of shape and line. The earth did not fade into the transcendental; rock was rock, trees were trees, mountains were mountains and wilderness was wilderness. There was nothing of the 'deeply interfused'; there was something that could be known and which it was necessary to know. There was a sense of the immediate and finite, so much more satisfying than the infinite, which had really starved me; a sense of the physical not of the spiritual. I felt I was human.

There was something else besides this and beside the desire to wander, that such scenes had on me: I felt also that I was being watched and critically regarded; not so much looking as being looked at. The transcendentalist dream in which I had lived up till then came to an end – or so I believe. I was being cured. It is true that the clarity of the Castillian air which, in summer or winter, flutters against the skin of one's face, was a novelty to a northerner in whose countries mistiness and uncertainty blur the edges of objects and feelings. Here one began to see exactly. I have few recollections – though I must be wrong in this – of seeing the clouds move fast over Castile in the winter or the autumn. I remember only clouds that were still, as if embossed on the sky. I was no more than a mortal jot.

The Spanish language, which is clearly pronounced in all its syllables and all its masculine emphasis in Castile, had its effect on me and indeed intimately, before I knew a word of it, even on this journey. George Borrow calls it 'the lordly language of Castile'. I mentioned this in one of my books on Spain, but not the rather absurd personal consequence. The train stopped at

Medina del Campo and one of the porters there who, I afterwards heard, was noted for the power and beauty of his voice, called out the name in the measured and resonant manner of the region. Voice and man stuck in my mind. The name was a sentence. I was liable, in the next few years, to nightmares of physical violence in which I was attacked and defeated by terrifying enemies. Then, one night, when I was in France, I dreamed that the porter at Medina del Campo had annoyed me, telling me the train had gone when I knew it had not. I fought and grappled with him and flung him victoriously on to the line before the oncoming train. After this I had no more dreams of violence. I have heard many interpretations of this dream, especially from amateurs of Freud; but, only last year, did the likely fancy occur to me that it had some connection with a childish battle with my grandfather, a very alarming man. I once shouted at him when I was a child of five and in a temper, that I hoped he would be killed by a train at the level-crossing near Sedbergh in Yorkshire. I got a spanking. I still feel the sting of his hand. Was the station at Medina del Campo the dream scene of a revenge twenty years late, and not one of congested sexual passion?

One of the curious sights of the journey, when darkness came, was the blackness of the dark, the nearness and size of the stars, and the yellow lights, scattered and individual, of distant towns. There was no glow of the motoring age above them. Each light in a window, though it might be miles away, was distinct and itself, as if it were the signal of a person or a family.

In those days you did not make reservations at hotels – or at least I didn't. It seemed to me a loss of freedom to know where one was going to stay. Inconvenience was worth the gamble. Outside the station in Madrid, as in other Spanish towns, small hotel buses waited in charge of drivers who had hurriedly put on their hotel caps and came shouting at one. A small man, one of those Spaniards who look like little monkeys, got us; we ground and rattled over the cobbles out of the North Station near midnight to a rather expensive hotel where the central heating seemed to be puffing out thick waves of hot olive oil. I had caught a bad cold in Paris and my temperature boiled up in the night. In the morning sleet came down. A heavy Spanish meal gave me diarrhoea within an hour or two – one of the very few experiences of Beethoven's disease that I ever had in Spain though I always ate recklessly, especially of the strong dishes. The prices at the hotel were more than we could afford. I had the name of a Spanish lady in the Plaza Isabel Segunda who turned out not to be Spanish but a German who had married a lawyer. He had died a year or so before, leaving her with three young children. Our meeting was eager and mournful. She found us rooms with another widow, an Andalusian from Puerto Santa Maria, who took us in at a small dark flat on the ground floor of a street off the Castellana and there, sleepless because of the all-night banging of the bells of a church opposite and the shouts of the night-watchman who trudged the street with his lantern and javelin, I settled down to influenza and days of heavy snow.

The altitude of Madrid is above 2,000 feet and in the winter the cold is biting and the incessant wind from Guadarramas is dangerous. My first impressions of the city were gloomy. I had expected another Paris, but here the brisk and gay Latinity was missing. The people in the street, all in black, walked about with a look of long mourning about their persons: the place seemed shut in some pinched and backward period of the nineteenth century, the 'modern' itself being long out of date and sad. The cafés were feebly lit, the shops were small and dim. There was the sour smell of charcoal in the doorways, for most people cooked on charcoal, and even sat in their houses with their feet on pans of charcoal or ground olive stone; and, even so, in their shawls or coats and their knees tucked under heavy tablecloths for warmth. In 1924 the Puerta del Sol was still the centre of Victorian cafés. Barefooted children ran coughing their lungs out and poor women screamed out the names of newspapers and sold lottery tickets in the wet. One passed enormous cold churches, their huge jaw-like doors open and inside lit only by the altar candles. They seemed to me like warehouses of melancholy and death. In the mornings dozens of plumed hearses went up the Castellana; a large number contained the

334

tiny white coffins of children. At night, many of the men wore long black capes with red velvet linings, and walked muffled up to the eyes with scarves against the wicked wind. The men's faces looked anxious as if concealing a personal agony; but if a woman was walking with them, it was strange to see that she was large, strong, calm and unmuffled. The women felt no terror of the cold. At this time – in 1924 – women were not welcome in cafés. In one or two, a few blowzy-looking ladies might be seen together at the back, but the Madrid streets and cafés were emphatically for men only. They sat for hours, their feet shuffling in the litter of shrimp shells and sugar papers, staring into a glass of water, drinking poor coffee or chocolate and very rarely wine or beer.

My impression was of morose silence; yet this was only half true. The silence of a café was broken from time to time by a sharp clap of the hands: a waiter was being called. If people did talk, they shouted. The city was noisy in the pleasureless way of New York. The ruling noises, apart from clapping and shouting, were the slashing and croaking rows of mule teams that straggled across the city; and the scores of small yellow tramcars that inched along in grinding processions. It was common to see twenty or thirty of these travelling boxes jammed up in the centre and to be bumped by them as they went clanging up the narrow streets. The ostentatious Gran Via, built out of the enormous profits made during Spain's neutrality in 1914 was far from finished and soon ended in that typical Spanish sight: the vacant lot of baked or frozen soil, according to the season.

A man's wealth could be pretty accurately guessed by his size: if he was well off he had a great belly on him; if he was poor he was skinny. There was a large number of fat priests about – I had not seen as many, not even in Ireland – sitting about smoking cigars or playing cards. Madrid had little industry, the place was packed with government employees, most of them obliged to do two or three jobs to keep alive. Delay was the only serious labour. The first two words one heard in Spain were, of course, *mañana* and the shrugging *Nada* – the nearest in Europe to the Russian *Nichevo*, uttered in all shades of meaning, but rooted in indifference to all egos except the speaker's own.

As I say, these were my earliest impressions in January 1924. I was soon to change them entirely, but I record them because the tens of thousands of French, German, British and American tourists who pour into Spain nowadays – and even those who came to Spain in the thirties, at the time of the Republic and the Civil War – can have no idea of what Spain was like in 1924. Only two roads, the Carreterra de Francia and one diverted by way of Extremadura from Madrid to Seville were completely passable. There were not many modern hotels outside of Madrid, Barcelona, Seville, and at the Alhambra. The only foreigners who came were a few business men, a handful of students from England and Germany, and a few tourists who went to Seville and Granada. There were scarcely any motor cars because of the state of the roads. The trains (many of them mixed goods and passengers trains), waited while goods were unloaded and crawled for hours from village to village: and the provinces were so cut off from one another by the mountains of the country (for after Switzerland, Spain is the most mountainous country in Western Europe), that they lived, felt and spoke almost as separate nations. Madrid was a small city with only one building thirteen storeys high and the population was about 800,000.

I had brought with me the only English books worth reading: Havelock Ellis's *The Soul of Spain*, Borrow's *Bible in Spain* and Ford's *Gatherings*, written in 1840. But in Paris I had picked up a new English book at Brentano's: *A Picture of Modern Spain* by J. B. Trend, who was later Professor of Spanish at Cambridge. (I met him months later in Madrid. He was a rosy precise little man, a sweet-tempered and curate-like figure who concealed a black Protestant fanatic inside him, though that rarely came out). His book eagerly demolished the Romantic legend of Spain, created by the French, especially by Bizet's (not Merimée's) Carmen and Théophile Gautier; he also reconsidered the 'black legend' in the light of what had been written by the new Spanish scholars, polemical writers and novelists of the 'generation of '98'. They had reacted violently against the incompetence and illusions that had led to the loss of Cuba in that year.

The late husband of the German lady had grown up among these people; she had lived a long time in Spain and worshipped them – there is no other word. She was young in middle age, with steadfast face and big earnest blue eyes that easily moistened with tears. She particularly worshipped the new educationists who had sprung up, among them the disciples of Trend's hero : Francisco Giner de los Rios, the lay saint now dead. They had founded a free school in Madrid; that is to say one in which there was no religious instruction : also the *Residencia*, a modern attempt to provide a collegiate life, inspired by Oxford and Cambridge. It was run by Alberto Gimenez, the son-in-law of Manuel Cossio, the great El Greco scholar, and had associations with the historians, scientists, novelists, critics and poets – Antonio Machado and the young Lorca, still a student, with great figures like Menendez Pidal and Altamira in history; Ramon y Cajal, the surgeon; Ortega y Gasset, Azorin the exquisite essayist, Unamuno (then in exile), Pio Baroja, Perez de Ayala, and many brilliant journalists such as Luis de Araquistain who was to become a figure in the Civil War of the thirties. The Duke of Alba was their patron. They were hated by the Church and the new military dictatorship, and were the most interesting intellectual group in the country.

The widow was planning to emigrate to the United States because she had been left poorly off; but for a few months, since she knew Spanish thoroughly, she gave me Spanish lessons until I moved to another lady, also a widow, who was Spanish. I learned quickly. But mortality hung over the verbs and participles. The German lady was an exacting and melancholy teacher.

There seems to be a link between the Romantic attitude to death one often meets in German literature and the traditional Spanish cult of mortality; and perhaps my lessons and our trips with her family to the Guadarrama thirty miles away, added to my early sense of the gloom of Spain, for we had grieving visits to every house, and in the mountains to every pine tree where she had been with her husband. Her own flat was in the old part of Madrid near the Plaza Mayor, on which the severity of the past was imposed. My other teacher, I discovered, came from a fierce Spanish Protestant family, and since under most Spanish governments this sect has been vindictively dealt with – no sign of their cult is permitted on their buildings – she had the fanatic character of the persecuted. Her grandfather had been a priest of the Franciscan mission in Manila who had become a convert to Protestantism. Still, she was a nimble, gay if aggressive teacher; and her charming daughter had a far more interesting mind than the usual nice Spanish girl of the time. Both these ladies were agnostics now.

So, in a country even more obsessed by religion than Ireland, though with far greater dignity, I found myself among agnostics. After Ireland, it was indeed a relief. I may have been given an austere and one-sided view of Spain by being so close to a minority movement, but it sharpened the mind. I was beginning to have the most valuable experience of my youth and many of their ideas have remained with me. I became a humanist. Political reaction and civil war defeated these Spanish friends later. Many of the people I knew were murdered, many more went into permanent exile in France, England and Mexico. They were a tragic generation. In matters of education they were powerfully thwarted wherever possible by the Church, especially the Jesuits, and sneered at by the wealthy *bien pensants*. The accusation – that they were diabolical Free Masons and 'free-thinkers' – was off the mark as propaganda always is, but also indicates how archaic the ruling Spanish world was. The word 'free-thinker' had a bad sound in Spain, not so much because of its irreligious connotation but because it smelled at that time of France, the traditional early nineteenth-century enemy. There is more common ground between England and Germany and Spain, than between Spain and France; there is a breach with the Latin which is strange in a country whose language is closest to Latin.

I often had lunch at the *Residencia* with the students and professors from the Madrid university, one or two of whom were poets. They were men of conscience and sensibility. They tended to be poor and their domestic lives were somehow shut away. They did not hang about in cafés, but seemed to follow some scrupulous private footpath of the mind between their classes and their homes. I am trying to convey that what the Spaniards respect is, for them, in some way inviolable. Never have I met academics less incessantly pushing. Their dedication was deeply moral. Alberto Gimenez became the most diffident and yet most discreet of my guides. He was a small neat man, under forty, very dark-skinned, with a very shy quiet voice that crumbled his words in the Malagueño way and his skin, especially round the eyes, was meshed in fine lines and seemed to be filled with hundreds of years of Moorish sunlight. He helped me with books and people, in the tortuous personal manner of the Spaniards; there was that long business of finding the right combination of times and persons, so that to go and see Ortega y Gasset (to take an example), one entered a sensitive web of acquaintance before one reached him at the right moment. There was something of E. M. Forster's attitude to the sacredness of personal relationships. I tried to find out what Alberto Gimenez believed in – for the disciples of Giner de los Rios were mysterious believers: he said he would tell me but not before I was leaving Spain. This took almost two years: an example of the retreat into timelessness which is precious to Spaniards.

I knew that the followers of Giner de los Rios had been greatly influenced by the minor German philosopher Krauss. I never read him, but I have lately looked him up in the *Encyclopaedia Britannica.* He invented a system called Panentheism, a combination of Theism and Pantheism. The world and mankind are an organism. I can see why Krauss appealed to this Spanish group; first because it is natural for the strong Spanish ego to feel that it contains the universe – a mystical notion – and secondly because Krauss believed, as they did, in working from the individual to small groups of men and finally to man as a whole.

When I did leave Spain Alberto Gimenez kept his promise. I remember how mysterious his manner was. Yes, he said, he was *almost* a Kraussist. His eyes wrinkled; he hesitated and hesitated as he approached the point of 'fineness' which tantalizes the Spanish genius. Yes, he said, Kraussism – but with 'algo' i.e. 'something' mystical. What this 'algo' was I could never discover.

The disciples of Giner de los Rios were, in a way, puritans of a sunny kind and indeed there is (contrary to popular opinion

339

which has been based on the gaieties of Andalucia) an ascetic and formal strain in the Castillian character. The country of excess is also the country of abstinence. The counter-reformation was austere and the Castillian temper is open but rigorous. The disciples of Giner de los Rios lived simply; they rarely drank wine; they hated rhetoric; they abominated Generals – there were 900 Generals in the Spanish Army – and refused to go to bullfights. They had some resemblance to the Russian westerners of the nineteenth century, in their wish for a closer contact with Europe and their dislike of 'Africanism'. They believed in intellectual contacts with Europe, in studying in foreign universities. Such ideas seem harmless today for many Spanish students now study abroad; but, in 1924, there were violent polemics against the idea in the conservative press and there were severe political obstructions particularly by the extreme clerics. The idea of a university Residence outside of religious supervision was anathema. But, as Gimenez used to say, 'Wait. They will soon copy us.' And, in fact, this eventually happened after the Civil War and with money the disciples could not afford.

Some of Don Alberto Gimenez's reserve was due to a care to keep the *Residencia* out of the coarse and corrupt rhetoric of Spanish politics. The place existed precariously; there was the fear that Primo de Rivera would close it down, as a hot-bed of Left-wing disaffection, though the General was at heart a liberal-minded man and did not do so. Don Alberto wrote me a long letter twenty-five years later in reply to something I had written about his movement.

Minority work is exposed to peril because it does not offer action; because of the mistrust of the public, and the dread of stirring hatred and passions which lead inevitably to persecution, the cruelties and monstrous disorder of civil war. The reformer tends to think 'Only the élite knows how to work for the perfecting of humanity and can stop the passions of the masses from preventing a wise progress.'
Here the error is that the intelligent élite start thinking of themselves as an isolated body. They forget that they are justified in believing they are superior only when they share their faith with the masses, and that possessing the light of truth is nothing if it is not shared with all the sons of God.

The Giner group, he said, understood this.

Their minds were awake to the supra-rational (*sobre racional*) instinctive, historical life of the people, not simply emotionally, but because they knew that once they lost contact with the masses, the masses would plunge over the precipice like animals and blindly follow leaders who encouraged their lowest appetites.

The Spaniards are a mocking race, especially in Madrid. They made a good deal of fun of the puritanism of the *Residencia*; of the expeditions to the mountains which no one visited at that time, in the spirit of science or contemplation; and of the attention to Spanish popular traditions and so on. The 'disciples' were closer to a real Spain than the rich whose ideal was Paris and the Riviera.

The name of our landlady was Doña Asuncion. She was a pretty little pigeon with a crackling but gaily tripping voice and a glitter to her eyes. I stayed with her all the time I was in Spain. She came of a family of wine importers who had sent her for a while to a convent in Paris so we stumbled along in French first of all, though her French was almost incomprehensible to me owing to her Andalusian accent, a form of fast Spanish where the trick is to leave out all the consonants and to turn as many words as possible into diminutives. It is a witty-sounding speech because of the mixture of bird-like notes mixed with joking sounds that seem to come from a mouth full of marbles. The only times she became vehement were when she attacked the priests and the government. She was a simple Andalusian who almost danced with joy at her memories of Puerto Santa Maria, a paradise for her as Alfaqueque was for the typical, provincial Andalusian lady in one of the plays by the Quinteros. We were crowded in her small flat because she had three young shouting sons. Watching us closely, she saw we were cramped and discontented and she went out to find another flat in which we could spread. In a week or two, she adroitly and with every kind of cry of excitement moved us all into a larger place in Cuatro Caminos and there we stayed. The manoeuvre was a masterpiece of shrewdness and light-heartedness, a conspiracy also made possible by her maid, Fanny, a rough, good-natured girl from Alcalà de Henares with black hair at the corner of her lips. She sang songs about love and death all day long in the kitchen and could not read. She slept on the floor in a sort of cupboard alcove, as it might be the larder, in the kitchen. She and Doña Asuncion sat on little chairs in the wide empty hall of the flat which had very little furniture – a table to eat off, a dresser, a few cane chairs and beds – and there they gossiped, unless they were sleeping in the afternoons. The only thing that stirred them was the voice of the eldest son. He was the master. He must have been seventeen and did nothing much except to come out of his bedroom at five in the afternoon and shout the word 'Water' in a voice like the bellow of an indignant animal. At once, in a panic, Doña Asuncion shouted also:

'Fanny! Hot water for the señorito.'

And to her son, in a terror of obedience:

'It's coming now.'

The boy was about to shave, in order to go out 'to pass the time' with his 'friends', passing the time being a central Spanish preoccupation and 'friend' a general word for anyone. This was the only part of the day in which something approximating to the idea of a 'time' was known in the house. Lunch appeared any time between 2 and 3, dinner any time between 9.30 and 11. There was a rush to the stove; Fanny dipped a piece of rag in oil and lit the little charcoal fire with it and then fanned the fumes all over the flat with a straw fan. We were privileged: we had a paraffin stove in our sitting-room. The need for these meals took the whole family by surprise every day, as if they had suddenly woken up from a long day-dream into violent action.

Were they dreaming? What were they dreaming about? The answer is 'Nothing whatever'; incuriously and with vacant and passive pleasure the minutes poured through them like sand in an hour glass that had no hours. They were waiting for some passion, some fiesta or some purely formal request, like the son's shout for 'Water' or Fanny's floor polishing, to mark the dark. The sun shone and they were alive. If there was bad weather, their faces went greenish and stupefied. And all day one heard Doña Asuncion's long drawn out sigh, an Aye-yai-yai of content, and Fanny tried another song.

Doña Asuncion and Fanny were polite (once I knew enough Spanish to talk to them) about my interest in Spain, but they looked upon it as a sort of insanity. Spain was something they cursed as if it were a destiny; and, in fact, to them Spain was a myth, perhaps like original sin, uncalled for and unchosen. In their hearts they knew there was no such country. They were living in 'the Spains', as many as there are provinces, towns, villages and finally individual Spaniards. For Doña Asuncion only Puerto Santa Maria had a real existence; for Fanny, Alcalà de Henares.

One Saturday that first winter, when sun and ice were in the light and in the air, I walked to that little town of cold white arcades, where Cervantes was born; and where the few people about were muffled against the wind. It was only sixteen miles from Madrid and this was my first attempt to get closer to that yellowing, sharp-edged landscape. Fanny was stupefied, then she shouted in ecstasy about the fiestas of the town, the young man whom she would marry in a few years, the families there, the superb food, the beautiful drinking water; and in the end called down from her balcony to the maid below the news that I had seen 'her town'.

In the next two years we would often talk about it. At the back of her mind there may have been a doubt, for there is an undying idea that foreigners who come to Spain are 'spies' (usually French spies) 'making plans', a tradition dating from the Napoleonic invasion. Fanny was a level-headed girl with a free tongue and without a touch of servility or of malapropism in her. Like all Castillians she spoke her language decently and knew her proverbs. She lived by custom and knew who she was: I do not mean that she was stolid. I am sure that whatever happened to her (and appalling tragedy may have in the Civil War, or she may have committed savageries as both the rich and the poor did), her identity, as we call it, would have remained with her. It appears to have been built into the race. She carried herself well, with innate pride, but not of the vulgar flamenco sort. And so did Doña Asuncion. In this there was nothing to choose between mistress and maid, and that – outside

343

the *petit maître* class – was general in all classes. Doña Asuncion was not a practising Catholic.

There was little in the way of news for a newspaper correspondent to cable from Spain. And if there was anything urgent – the resignation of one of Primo de Rivera's military and naval team for example – I was certain to miss it, through incompetence. I did try to learn this part of my trade, but I had never been under a brisk editor's hand. I wrote background pieces. I was, I confess, vain of being an amateur. I never visited the Embassies and avoided the English and Americans. This was a mistake; for the British Embassy, particularly, had life-long Spanish experts. Luckily for a journalist Primo de Rivera was a lazy dictator, bent on seeing that nothing happened in the country. His chief efforts were practical: snubbing the old politicians, seeing about roads, badly needed – and crushing Basque and Catalan nationalism, a permanent obsession of governments in Madrid. I read the newspapers, hung about with South American journalists who, in one or two cases, were novelists and had been Cabinet Ministers in their own countries. I went to the international telephone office, which was then scarcely more than a corridor squeezed between a barber's shop and a café in the Puerta del Sol. The parliament was closed: I sought out the deposed politicians to see if anything was going on there. Nothing was going on. I became the 'stringer' for the *Manchester Guardian* and wrote an obituary notice of the dictator for their morgue. In the evenings I heard the day's rumours from a reporter at the Café Gijon. The story was always the same: jokes about the Generals; soon the king would abdicate because he was directly responsible for the heavy Spanish defeat in Morocco; a coup, even a revolution would occur and there would be a Republic. These events did not occur for seven years, long after I had left. The only foreign correspondent who had a true finger on the Spanish pulse was de Caux, a gentle, sceptical, lazy-voiced Hispanofil who wrote for the London *Times*. He seemed to know every village in Spain and the political bosses of every province with quiet intimacy. He wrote very well. It was a pity that he was too idle and shy to write a book about Spain.

It would have been as good and wise as Richard Ford's if he had. He was partly French, but perhaps it was because he was a fatalist that he was so close to the Spanish temper. How terrible the life of the wise is: the Spanish Civil War broke his heart, and his Irish wife, a very severe and very Catholic lady, went mad.

'How terrible,' I said when I met him again in his old age. Tears were briefly in his eyes.

'One learns that life is a tragedy,' he said. 'One can do nothing against Fate.'

He considered me gently – I was then in my fifties – and said:

'You were inclined to be a little severe when I first met you. You have changed. Everything changes. That is the only meaning of life.'

He was right. I *had* become a severe young man. I was alone for long stretches of time in Spain for my wife was homesick for Ireland. Spanish life repelled foreign women; the lives of Spanish women were strictly enclosed. And, I, too, was enclosed in my intense Spanish interests. I would spend the days and nights sitting over an oil stove in the early freezing weather, reading Iberian history, in Oliveira Martins and Altamira. I was deep in the Moors, the re-Conquest, in the Council of Trent, the counter-Reformation, gripped by a view of Europe and life itself so dramatically opposed to the one I had been brought up in.

One of my earliest efforts in reading Spanish was an auto-didact's aberration. Croce was all the go at the *Residencia*. I got a book of his essays on essences: it is I think the first book in Spanish that I ground my way through. I had scarcely heard of aesthetics, unless Roger Fry's theory of 'significant form' counts as that. As fast as I had mastered one sentence of Croce, the next one drove it out of my mind. Little notion of his argument remains with me, for I am no thinker or philosopher. But Croce seemed – and this was what kept me going – to convey that it was necessary for the artist to get to the core of his experience. I am sure now that Croce meant something far more intricate than this and probably something very different too. But I made him say what *I* thought because to strain after the essence of things had become a mania with me. I connected it with the laconic. I have noticed since how often writers totally misread when they admire. I was cheered on because I discovered Unamuno learned English by translating Carlyle – of all people – into Spanish, because he was captivated by his manner.

I come now to two decisive experiences. I have a sceptical temperament and it was a relief to me that there was no Christian Science Church in Madrid. I had grown sick of Christian Scientists in Ireland. Church services bored me. Alone at this time in Madrid, I started to read Unamuno's *Del sentimiento tragica de la vida*. The opening sentences were a violent shock to one brought up on the dilated transcendentalism of Mrs Eddy:

Homo sum: nihil humani a me alienum puto, *dijo el comico latino. Y yo diria mas bien,* nullum hominem a me alienum puto; *soy hombre a ningun otro hombre estima extraño. Porque el adjetivo* humanus *me es tan sospechoso como su substantivo abstracto* humanitas, *la humanidad. Ni lo humano ni la humanidad, ni el adjetivo simple, ni el adjetivo sustantivado, sino el sustantivo concreto: el hombre. El hombre de carne y hueso, el que nace, sufre y muere – sobre todo muere – el que come y bebe y juega y duerme y piensa y quiere, el hombre que se ve y a quien se oye, el hemano, el verdadero hermano.* *

And the agony of this man is that he knows he will die and yet passionately desires immortality. Unamuno's book contains the Spanish paradox: life intensely felt in the flesh and made whole by the contemplation of death.

**Homo sum; nihil humani a me alienum puto*, wrote the Latin playwright. And I would go further and say, *Nullum hominem a me alienum puto*; I am a man and I regard no other man as a stranger. Because the adjective *humanus* is as suspect to me as the abstract noun *humanitas*, humanity. No more of 'human' or 'humanity'; no more of the simple adjective or the adjectival noun; only the concrete noun: man. The man of flesh and bone, who is born, suffers, dies – above all, who dies – the man who eats, drinks, plays his part, sleeps, thinks and loves, the man one sees standing before one's eyes and whom one hears, the brother, in very truth a brother.

This is not the place to expound or discuss Unamuno's book. From Spaniards one gets the sense of the whole, not of the divided man. It irked his fellow liberals who were rationalists. He was dangerously personal, irrational, paradoxical, a mixture of Quixote with the mischief of Sancho Panza. His vigour enlivened. He was a Catholic, but of the independent almost Protestant Basque kind, and he even had the nerve to defend Philip II. There was a touch of Chesterton in him, a touch of the Welsh preacher too. He was an excellent essayist. From now on, after my Irish aberration, I was the man of flesh and bone.

Another writer who affected me strongly was the novelist Pio Baroja. I went up to the Guadarrama mountains to Cercedilla, and started reading his novel of the Madrid slums, *La busca*, in the train that crawled hour after hour in the rising heat of June. I had toothache. I spent the day scrambling up a dry torrent-bed and then walked for miles in the pinewoods there and came down at some small *posada* to eat a poor thin garlic soup and two 'pairs of eggs', as the Spaniards say. The light in the rough inn was too feeble for reading by; I had to share a room with three labourers and their wives, who kept the windows closed; and in the night my toothache was agony. I walked off the next day with a face blown up like a football. The heat was violent. The only diversion of the walk was half a mile of processional caterpillars as fat as my fingers, who were travelling up the road, head to tail. I killed a few; they joined up again and went on. I sat for hours in a small railway station until the *Mixto* came along. It took something like six hours to get to Madrid, shunting and unloading at every station.

So I read *La busca* with desperate concentration to conquer the pain of the abscess. At last there was an explosion in my head. I spat out a foul liquid; the abscess had burst. I don't think I have ever read a novel with such care, looking up every strange word in the dictionary. And what I discovered was that Baroja was a kind of 'essence' man. He wrote in short, accurate, dismissive sentences. His feeling was dry. His attitude to life showed an emotional indifference. He put down with a bleak pungency what he saw. His pessimism, his disbelief and his pity burned. He was an anarchist.

Baroja had written dozens of novels and was to write dozens more. They were curt reports enlivened by contemptuous opinions. I saw him several times in Madrid, at first in an old house run by his sister. He had pale blue eyes, a flour-coloured face, a short beard and wore a beret in the house. He and his brother had run a bakery when he started writing. He had a Wellsian twinkle in his eye.

I went to Pio Baroja's *tertulia*. All Spaniards like to hold *tertulias* in cafés or at home, meeting of strictly chosen friends (and an occasional stranger), always the same ones, who sit, rarely drinking anything except a cup of coffee, and often not that. Many of these were gatherings of eight or nine distinguished persons whose talk was familiar and also fantastic, but Baroja was fond of surrounding himself with very ordinary people of curious character; a doorman, a minor clerk, were among them. At five in the evening the cafés were full of such groups. There was one café of the Calle Alcala where one could see a *tertulia* of generals, another of journalists, another of politicians and so on. The Madrileños love to live publicly in small Courts and it was common at the hour of the *paseo*, between five o'clock and the late dinner, to see these groups walking up and down the street together, slowly, for hours, pausing for a long time when the subject got interesting, before settling into some café. An official would be surrounded by his friends and hangers-on. And there were always spies. The women held their *tertulias* in their houses; the men in the streets. One could see this not only in the capital, but in every town in Spain.

It was impossible to make sudden arrangements in this time-less world in which a person's daily habits were his unchanging law. You could not say 'Let us do this or that tomorrow or next week', for although there might be enthusiasm for the idea, it would soon turn out that the right 'combination' had to be found, a combination depending on waiting for the moment, not of convenience, but of mysterious collective impulse. In the meantime, one waited passively, 'passing the time', until, like a sudden fire, the impulse was ignited. It might take weeks and weeks to ignite. The instantaneous habits of Europeans struck Spaniards as an impoverished restlessness of mind.

There is a theory that the mind of the Spaniard is one where the image of an intention and the will to act on it come rarely together; but when they do, then the action is sudden and often violent. The central point of Ganivet, the writer, who first raised the question of the Spanish lack of will after the defeat in Cuba, was really the failure of the image and act to merge. One heard the word *gana* every hour; unless the *gana* or wish-will to do something visited one irresistibly, one did not do it. The famous *nada* or nothing is related to this. There is a line in one of Baroja's novels that exactly describes this state: it refers to a bird:

Parece que busco algo; pero no busco nada.
(It may look as if I am seeking something; but I am seeking nothing).

When in the thirties I came to write a story called 'The Evils of Spain', it was based on a dinner party in which we all tried, and failed, to come to a conclusion about visiting Belmonte, the bullfighter, at his estate in Seville. Belmonte was with us. The initial difficulty was in choosing our food: the matter dissolved into fantastic anecdote. The story is a very accurate rendering of a real Spanish conversation, one of those things that fall occasionally into a writer's lap; but it leaves out the problem of the visit which the collective will found unseizable. The subject vanished to the backs of my friends' minds, although they were all for going 'the day after tomorrow'. The strange thing was that the expedition *did* eventually come off a year later, when I had long given up taking it seriously; indeed I went off alone. The intention was genuine, but it was the sudden arrival of a master-personality, a sort of dictator, that took the group off on their romp. In Spain one is always waiting for a Godot or personality of this kind. Belmonte, the master-technician of the bull-ring, the thin, scarred gipsy with sharp eyes, had earnest intellectual aspirations. He listened with detachment to his future guests and, in a silence, politely asked me what I thought of T. S. Eliot of whom he had heard. He liked to keep in with 'the intellectuals'.

CHAPTER EIGHT

In the spring I went off alone by train to Seville to see the Holy Week processions. It was the first time I had been in the south. The white city smelled of roses, jasmine and orange blossom, of olive oil, anis and shrimps. I stayed in the pretty Barrio Santa Cruz listening, after the long silences of the afternoon, to the bugles of the military bands accompanying the processions of the *cofradias* to the continual whisper of feet, the trit-trot of the carriage horses. The heat was heavy. In Sierpes, streaked as all the streets were, with the candle-drippings of the *cofradias*, one saw the fat owners of the olive groves or their relatives, their trousers high on their enormous bellies, sitting stupefied by sun in the clubs. It was a wealthy city of bull-breeders and olive-growers and a very gay one, given heavily to sherry drinking. In the countryside the peasants lived wretchedly on their eternal *gazpacho*, dipping their bread into it: a poor meal, but Spanish bread is the best and most nourishing in the world. They lived in huts where the rush walls were beginning to be replaced by the flattened petrol can. There had been savage peasant risings in Andalucia – hence the hatred of the Civil Guard who really ruled the peasants. I had read and heard about it from Fernando de los Rios, one of the 'disciples'. The Anarchists were strong in Andalucia. There was a theory, which had something in it, that the Andalusian ideal was to see how little one could live on, how few one could make one's material wants, an inheritance perhaps of Arab or desert culture: happiness was in the little and the less. The wealthier Andalusians are famous for their parsimony and if their possessions are great, their way of living is usually simple. A rich man like Belmonte was certainly very frugal.

I stayed with a widowed relation – yet another in my long list of Spanish widows – of Doña Asuncion. The house was pretty and white, its balconies were hung with flowers and I was given a simple room on the ground floor, with an alcove at the far end in which the maid slept, a fat little girl who snored all night. The daughter of the house was a great beauty, the son was a doctor, busy in his surgery next to my room. (Seville is a bad place for rheumatism.) The mother was a dumpy, shrewd woman who charged me an enormous price for my board and lodging, telling me how lucky I was to find a place at all. I was indeed lucky. She was a real Sevillana, placid and proper to look at, but with shrewd, mischievous eyes. She was determined that I should do everything according to formality and custom. I must get up late, drink my coffee, and not shave until five o'clock, for the *paseo*. Before that I had eaten a heavy lunch and slept.

Afterwards, the young doctor and I were out most of the night. He was a young spark, but a conscientious guide. I wasn't let off a single procession or *saeta*. He explained all the time that Seville was the most beautiful and richest place in the world, packed with the wittiest people in Spain. Mockery and tricks play a strong part in the Sevillano's character and, of course, Don Juan's love of the boastful phrase. The doctor scored off me continually. His nerve was remarkable. To get me into the Mass at the cathedral, to hear the *Miserere* sung by Tito Schipa, without having to buy a ticket, he pushed me through a back door, with hurried whispers to figures in the darkness, until I found myself planted in the choir, only four places from the Archbishop. I felt I had been captured by the Inquisition or had got on the throne in Buckingham Palace. Between two very old priests who were going through their chants from parchment books two feet across, I stood without knowing when to stand up, sit down, pray or go through a pretence of chanting too. Thank God, I had a jacket and tie on, for dressed as I was among all the gold and purple I was a vulgar mistake, with the air of a burglar or some creature who would be arrested if caught. Worse, the young doctor had withdrawn and left me to it. I gazed as apologetically as I could at the Archbishop, wondering if I should signal excuses, or run. If he saw me he did not show it; after all, there must have been a hundred priests in the choir. Presently I was distracted by the old man next to me. He must have been in his eighties and nearly blind. He mumbled, got up and sat down in the wrong places, and was so unsteady that I thought he would fall on me. To the other side of me was another of these saints of second childhood, staggering too. The heat of the candles was strong. The encrusted gold of the choir was heavy and seemed heated too. I sweated and at last the *Miserere* burst out. It was a full theatrical performance and drove off my panic.

The young doctor and I went off to the 'Kursaal', the night club with a shocking reputation, and I saw from my *palco* the fat young bloods of Seville cuddling their mistresses, and everyone talking regardless of the singer or dancer until he comes to the crucial technical difficulty of *cante hondo*, when everyone falls silent to see if he does the thing well, for at errors in song and dance the Spaniards shout in anger.

I have often been to Seville since that time. It is a deeply provincial place. The comic spirit of the city is crude. I have seen a respectable elderly man solemnly empty a castor of sugar on to the head of his friend in a café, with careful, expressionless dignity. The *piropos* are notorious. An extremely tall woman scholar, an American, working in the Archives of the Indies in my day, was told by some road workers as she passed to 'Come back tomorrow and let us see the other half.' In the foreign colony there was an English doctor who interested me, when I met him in his old age. He was an interesting example of what I call the Maugham fallacy in sentimental travel. Maugham has a typical story of meeting a young doctor in England who is tempted to go to Seville as a doctor, but who will be obliged if he does so to break his engagement to an English girl and risk giving up a safe medical career in England. Romantically, he decides to go to Seville. There he blossoms as a Silenus and has a string of superb gipsy mistresses : his gamble is a romantic success.

The doctor in Seville was the original – or so he complained – in Maugham's story. I guessed the real story might have other aspects and I went to see him. He had a very pretty house. Now in his seventies, he was irritable.

'Stomach all right?' he said. 'Chest? No bowel trouble? You haven't been – er – a naughty boy?'

He was disappointed to hear I was in good health and looked coldly and defensively when I told him I was a writer.

'We've had them all down here – Hemingway, Maugham' – he ran off a list of popular English and American novelists, riff-raff, he said, not a gentleman among them. 'I'm the doctor in Maugham's story. I don't mind the lies – we've all got to live – but I should like to have what Maugham made out of me. All of them, for that matter.'

Every foreign writer, he said, had put him in their books. He'd been portrayed as an English spy, as an agent in the Civil War, a gun runner, above all the scandalous lover of Carmens by the dozen.

He was a pleasant bald man and there was a look of doggish contempt on him as he swelled with his importance: the fact that he was a simple doctor and yet had other selves that roamed the world.

'I don't mind what they said. But where's the economics? They made a packet out of me. What did I get?'

While we talked – and we had gone to a bar – we were being pestered by a bare-footed little girl who knew him well and who was trying to sell us lottery tickets.

'She knows me, the little nuisance. She knows I won a damn big prize in the lottery two years ago. When I hadn't a bean in the world. I tell you frankly, I've been ruined three times in this country. Sunny Spain! Spanish women! Here,' he called to the child. 'What is the most important thing in Spain?'

'The peseta!' said the child, quick as a rat.

The doctor smiled for the first time and put his hand in his pocket, but the hand stayed there.

'I've been here forty years. In the thirties the tourist traffic went in a night. If I hadn't won that prize I'd have been on the streets.'

I bought a ticket off the child and she at once ran off bawling at people getting off a trolley bus. The doctor went on:

'And remember this: when I came here forty years ago I wouldn't have touched the tourist side. We had a very exclusive colony. It was unpleasant for a man in my position, but I was forced to do the hotels – but this last knock was the worst. Not what you expect in old age. I'm down,' he said with shame, 'to treating Spaniards – the aristocracy. They're the meanest of the lot. It's like getting blood out of a stone.'

353

He had ceased to be a 'character' now. He was denuded of his fiction. Presently he said, with malice:

'What would you say if I told you who that kid was who sold you the ticket? Suppose I told you that kid is one of So-and-so's?'

The writer he named was, at that time, one of the most celebrated of English popular novelists.

'You'd say I wasn't a gentleman. You'd say I was a liar. Anyway, what would I get out of it?'

I realized when I left him that a great revenge on literature was in his docile and offended head. Marked down, watched and stalked by writers, the doctor was turning rogue. Even I might be his next candidate; indeed he was becoming a writer himself.

Usually I travelled second or third class on the Spanish trains, for there the Spanish crowd came in and were good company. Often the women travelled with a pet bird in a cage: everyone took their shoes off and when they unpacked their large thick cold omelettes, they were careful to offer it first to everyone in the carriage. At the stations, which were often a couple of miles from the towns they served, water sellers calling out '*Agua fresca*' walked up and down in the red dust of the south and the pale dust of Castile. But in 1924 I travelled back from Seville first class, for it was a fifteen-hour journey. In the next compartment was extraordinary company. There was the stout red-faced figure of Arnold Bennett, wearing a wide-brimmed Spanish hat tipped back on his head, leaning out of the window at every station and taking notes. Stretched out full length covered by a rug, despite the heat, was Lord Beaverbrook, his little monkeyish face glued to a book called *How to Understand the Drama*: and opposite, sitting in the middle of the seat with his hands hanging down between his knees in dismal boredom, was Tim Healy, the old Governor General of the Irish Free State and destroyer of Parnell, a man with the wickedest tongue in Ireland.

My Spanish journeys were many. I often went walking in the Guadarramas, to Avila and Segovia, staying in the rough inns, sometimes sleeping in the common bedroom on a sack of straw.

354

In the summer, three of us walked over the Picos de Europa from Santander, eventually coming down through the terrifying gorge of Cangas de Onis to the fishing town of Llanes, where the local youths stoned us as we walked in. Stoning was not uncommon. In this expedition I did, by accident, the longest walk of my life: nearly forty miles over two high ranges of mountains. There were no real roads, but simply wagon tracks, river beds and shepherds' paths which vanished when we got to the top of the pass and we had to guess our way down. Luckily it was moonlight when we scrambled down the last eight miles and got to a poor inn and slept in a room with a raw goat skin, stinking, drying in the only window. We lived on river trout in the inns. We were not at the bottom of the range and were so exhausted that we travelled by a rattling little diligence with a calf roped to the roof and its groaning head hanging over the side looking in at us. It was the most frightening bus journey of my life: our bones were shaken to bits and we were sick after it.

It was a pleasure to miss an English Christmas and to go off through Estremadura to Cordoba, Seville, Ronda and Granada, and then round the coast to Barcelona and back through Aragon. It was a rough journey especially in Granada, where we had to ford rivers, and in Valencia where the high wheels of the orange carts had cut ruts a foot deep in the dust of the unmetalled roads. They were notoriously the worst in Spain. This journey was done by car, and crowds would gather round us in the towns. We left all our belongings lying in it and no one touched a thing. Unlike the Italians, the Spaniards are sternly honest people. A lot of excitement was caused by the fact that my wife was driving. People shouted: 'A woman driving!' and rushed after us. In one large *fonda* where a crowd was having luncheon the proprietress rushed forward, accusing:

'Is it true that your wife is driving?'

'Yes. I can't drive.'

'Let me see your hands.'

The woman took my hands, held them up to the guests. My hands are small. She said:

'A man with hands like that could never drive a car.'

Spain was too stern to be picturesque though I suppose certain places in Andalusia and along the Mediterranean coast might have met the Victorian prescription. That coast is ruined now.

The spring rains drove in to Granada as we left and the unmetalled roads were washed away in waves of red mud; torrents rose to the bridges and flooded the ravines and valleys; the rain drove with a Spanish ferocity. It was usual for rivers to be simply wide beds of stones with only a pool or two of water in them, but now they were rushing floods that washed away the roads. At one likely spot for crossing, where the water seemed calmer, we were hailed by a group of wild looking gipsies a hundred yards away. They had posted themselves there with ropes, hoping for rescue money. They hauled us across, putting up the price high when we got to the middle. It ended in a rowdy haggle, but we got out of it. I had never seen rain so wild and so solid, rain that in fact set the soil in motion, as if the earth were pouring too. It excited me – I was not the driver! And so excited me that a few months later, when I was alone again in Madrid and was glad to be off the empty streets where the August heat burns through the soles of your shoes, I sat down at Doña Asuncion's to write my first short story. I had up till then thought of writing mainly as description of landscape. My narratives were packed with mountains, hills and foliage and I ransacked my mind for nouns and adjectives and metaphors to describe them. It is true that I had put an occasional human being in, but the emphasis was on physical description; now I had begun to put in words of talk. But since I was an attentive listener to people's words, the only talk that got into my writing was the simple, commonplace remarks they made to me. Now I had to advance to the very different task of making people talk not to me, but to each other.

My trouble was that I had no story to write. I was full of stories without knowing it. The difficulty of the young writer is that he does not recognize what is inside him. My mind really evaded any story I knew. Life – how curious is that habit that makes us think it is not here, but elsewhere. But I sat down to try because I was tiring of my life as a newspaper correspondent; it seemed superficial and I was not good at it. In my heart I despised news and was confused by opinion. But I remembered all that rain and those gipsies in Granada. I found in the newspaper some account of a gipsy quarrel. Somewhere in this I suspected there lay the most alarming thing in the world: a subject. I called the story 'Rain in the Sierra'. It was very short, but it took weeks to get it into shape. A good three years passed before it was published in the *New Statesman*. I have not read it since for I dread the prose I shall find there and I am rather ashamed of having written on the Spanish gipsy, the corniest of subjects. Still, I had begun.

Half way through my last year in Madrid I found a Civil Guard on horseback outside the building where I lived. He handed me an official document. It was a summons to appear before a military court: the charge – cabling an attack on King Alfonso to America. I had not done so, but I had written articles in which the strong anti-monarchic feeling was reported. I asked Alberto Gimenez what I should do. The important thing was, he said, to pretend not to understand Spanish and to take with me an interpreter, a man I already knew, who was a professor of medicine. He had to pass himself off as an official interpreter.

We went to an untidy back room in a side street off the Gran Via and found a collection of grumbling Colonels who were saying the whole thing was a farce. My role was to look stupid and speak French, for my professor did not know any English. The professor adroitly sympathized with the Colonels for having dug out a person as ignorant as I was. There was a long wrangle about whether a professor could legally be an interpreter, but the Colonels gave in and questions began. I understood the Colonels' questions, but I could not understand my professor's terrible French and the Colonel in charge gave me a hard look when he caught me almost answering the question before the professor had translated it. In the end the case was dismissed, owing to the confusion of the professor and myself. Afterwards, the professor was very hurt because I could not understand his French, but he saved his honour by saying I had obviously never been in France because he could not understand a word of mine.

My time was coming to an end. A General who was thought to be plotting against Primo de Rivera was being sent to exile in France. It was the only piece of real news to occur during my stay and, for once, I raced off to see the riot that was expected at the North Station, when the General went off on the night train. It was easy to find him. He was a large smiling man with two deep belts of chin. He leaned out of his carriage window and was waving to a court of admirers. The train moved off. There were shouts of *Viva la libertad!* from young supporters who were easily arrested after a scrimmage with plain clothes men. The moment of violence was heady: I dreaded I would myself shout and slunk away glad not to be arrested. I have a terror of the rage that might spring up in me if I got into an excited crowd.

This was the end of Spanish news. Primo de Rivera seemed to be there for ever. The only flutter was a revival of the Riff war and I was sent to Spanish Morocco. A gale was blowing at Algeciras and we had a horrible crossing. All the tables and chairs got loose in the saloon and piled up against the portholes, and then swept back. An army officer and a priest kneeled among the debris praying loudly for most of the journey; and the first sight I saw in Africa was the bodies of dozens of drowned mules, swollen with water, washed up on the shore. We arrived in Tetuan by a little train at sunset to the sound of rifle shots from the Riff and Spanish outposts in the hills overlooking the town.

My incompetence and laziness as a newspaper correspondent was demonstrated here. A born newspaper man would have gone in search of Abd el Krim or have pestered the Spanish military for secret information. Or he would have invented. I did find one or two Moroccans and got something out of them, and I did find myself spending a morning in one of those Moorish houses – so like Victorian tearooms inside – that are in the white-walled alleys. I remember the ballooning pantaloons of my host, his fez, his teeth. An enormous naked Negro lying drunk, dead or asleep was in the gutter outside when I left. I remember too my first ghetto, if that is the proper description of the Jewish quarter, for the narrow streets were squared off like a chess board in order that the district could easily be controlled. The old Jews stood long-bearded and wretched-looking at their doorways, among the flies and stenches of the street. I was horrified. I supposed these must have been the descendants of those who had been expelled from Spain in the fifteenth century. I had seen the battlefields of Anual, where the Spaniards had run into disastrous defeat a few years before. Everyone in Spain, especially the poor whose sons were conscripted without chance of evasion, hated the miserable colonial campaign. It was the efficient French who conquered Abd el Krim in the end. I was too soaked in Spain to find this part of Morocco understandable and when, afterwards, I was sent to Algiers, Constantine and Tunis, I felt uneasy in the first colonial state I had seen outside of Ireland. Also in Algeria I felt the guilt of being a tourist who is passing through and who is a mere *voyeur*. I still feel that. Yet there are rewards. In 1946, when I first read Camus I found that something more than a superficial knowledge of his scene had seeped into me when I was twenty-four. And, when I look at a Matisse odalisque sitting on one of those ugly Moroccan leather cushions, thick-browed and sullen, small images from the distasteful journey come back to me. I recall the insipid *couscous*; the French bourgeois lady in the tram in Algiers calling out about the Arab woman sitting near her: 'How she stinks, that Arab'; the cold stoniness of the 'bled', the steppe that lies between the hot coast and the cloudy Atlas mountains; the misery and rapacity of the Kabyles in their villages. And the occasional scenes, when one is incredulous; down the mountain path comes a chieftain-like figure out of a film, riding a pony, with a rifle across his saddle and behind him a veiled lady clinging.

My *wanderjahre*, though not my travels, were coming to an end: they had only a year to go. The paper was getting tired of my Spanish articles and invited me for a short stay in the United States. I went reluctantly, for I too was getting tired of the writing I was doing. I had been fortunate in being able to travel; but, looking back upon myself at twenty-five, I can see I was a prickly and difficult young man. I was glib and quick to see, but slow to grow; however, enlivening it is, travel has the serious defect of taking one away from the stimulus and criticism of one's contemporaries in one's own country. One is too much alone, too much the passing stranger. And then, my marriage had not gone well for either my wife or myself.

After France and Spain, Boston seemed dead and dreary, except for its spectacular thunderstorms. I hated the Holy City. The American boom was on and one could not exaggerate the complacency of a people who had been so cut off from the rest of the world by self-congratulation. The faculty of self-criticism was not yet born. Boston was not the place for seeing the Jazz Age and, in any case, I was shut in by my own frustrations. Only two journeys there interested me: a short trip when, getting lost in the forest trails north of Quebec, I spent a week or so in a lumber camp among the French-Canadian lumberjacks, bitten to death by the myriad black flies of the 'forest primeval', and a long walking journey among the poor whites of the Appalachians. I went there because I heard one could find traces of Elizabethan English. It was peculiar, but not Elizabethan. The experience became an exercise in writing dialogue: I filled my notebooks with pages of it, covertly written down in the shacks where the poor people then lived. They were docile, half-starved, long-nosed, hospitable Baptists. The men shambled about in jeans and always carried a gun, and spoke in a drawl difficult to understand. You simply knocked on a door and they took you in instantly, fed you on what they had which was salt pork, pastry, apple butter, molasses and black coffee. There was nothing else. The women married at about fourteen, had families of up to twenty children. They were inbred and, certainly, backward. I met a whole creek full of feeble and bony Pritchetts: the patriarch of the tribe said he had 'fit' in the Civil War – on the side of the North, of course. Few had ever seen a Negro. I heard no folk songs, but if there was nothing Elizabethan in the language there were grandiose names. There were Apollo and Leander Bacchus, a Beaumont Starr and Gash Alison who claimed to be a Turk. He was a legend – I never met him:

Thar haint no one the like of Gash Alison. He's the travellingest man I ever seed. Seemed like as though he jes went sportin' and broguin aroun' peddlin'. I haint seed the like of thata one. He jes' went snoopin' aroun' like you uns, peddlin', totin' things on his back and gettin' folk to take him in o' nights. He sure was the talkingest man I ever seed. He used to tell us about Canady and Jerusalem. He uster say thar haint no better water nor the mountain water in the worl'. Hits plumb pure. Thar haint nowhaur Alison haint been.

I wrote it down. The tradition of the American monologue was alive:

Nat'rally thars a sight 'o things bin writ that haint never occurred. Like ol' Uncle Durham uster say that every time a story crossed water it doubled itself. Did you ever hear of Phil Morris's defeat? That's a true 'un. Phil, like the rest of us, was in a kind o mixed-up business. Hit'd be hard to say what kinda business, it'd be with one thing and another and nothin' reg'lar. Waal, we was up in the woods and thar was snow on the ground and the country was mos' friz up. We lit a fire and Phil sits him down and offs with his boots to kinda rest up his feet. Waal, during the night, one of them boots get pushed into the fire and burned up. And in the mornin' Phil sent up a great hollerin' and had to make him mocassins out of his leggins and walk back sixteen mile in 'em. An' ever since they have called that place Phil Morris's defeat.

We spent a night in the shack of a family who had left the mountains to work in a cotton mill in South Carolina, but had been thrown out of work. I arrived on the very day they had returned to the shack they had left. It was hidden behind corn grown tall and was almost roofless. There was a husband and wife, their son and daughter and an old woman. We all slept in one room, partly under the stars, and were bitten all night by fleas. The house was ten miles from the nearest store, five miles off the wagon trail, with two rivers to ford, and the little holding was on a very steep hillside. It was in sight of one of the highest peaks in this part, with the fine name of Clingman's Dome. The mountaineers were poorer than European peasants. One saw many deserted shacks. The topsoil had gone. I find a note.

Beaumont Starr's farm. He left las' spring. Hit was too hard. Siles gone and wore out an' nothin'll grow in that thar.

We climbed hour after hour through steep woods of pine, balsam and hickory, through maple and walnut, and sometimes huge chestnuts shot like isolated grey columns out of the thickets. We climbed, as I say, from creek to creek, sometimes through woods and thin fields of sumac, michaelmas daisies and golden rod; the creeks smelled of fallen apples and once we saw a wild girl dressed only in a sack with holes for her head and arms in it, stirring an iron pot of the apple butter with a stick. The walls of the shacks were rarely papered, but when they were it was with tailors' catalogues and newspapers: and there was usually an iron stove with a pipe going up through the roof in the middle of the room, round which the men would sit on cool evenings, spitting gobs of tobacco that hit the stove with a hiss. We all jawed away contentedly. They knew we had 'come over the Waters', but geography was myth to them. Some thought France and England were in the 'next state'.

When I look at the prose I wrote at that time, I am shocked. What can be the origin and meaning of those bizarre lyrical outbursts, those classy metaphors and finicking adjectives? Here, for example, I am at the top of a mountain in Tennessee:

From our 'necket' we could see our ridge slung like a firm hammock of green from knob to knob, a blue green causeway crossing the water of sky, or broad and churned with green and chopping light like the wake of a steamer. Distantly was Clingman's Dome, with the other gray hosts, while a wide surf of cloud lay fixedly, mazedly upon them. From their highest elevation bannered a stilly chrome wash of startled light.

One must grant the passion for words in themselves: I am not ashamed of that. But what a bombardment! What is the cause of all this show of strength and aggression? Well, youth is the period of assumed personalities and disguises. It is the time of the sincerely insincere. Some of that writing was the confused expression of unsatisfied or diverted sexual energy; some of it is due to a mistaken notion that one could write as a painter painted: the visual world made a violent impact on me. But I think now that the key reason is that I was beginning to suspect the tameness of my matter, and in a rather shady way was trying to make it more important than it was. I was 'covering up'. The result is a strange mixture of the diffused, the strenuous and the coy – but why? Because I had arrived at no settled view of life. There was a desire for hardness in the twenties; no bad thing, but even hardness has to be coherent. I had a long struggle with this kind of writing. Naturally, editors were puzzled and bored. I had come out in a rash. They had had enough. Readers felt no need to watch a young writer so patently teaching himself to write at their expense. I went back to Ireland.

In my second time in Dublin, the Romance had gone. The city itself had changed. The Anglo-Irish Revival was thinning out. Yeats had left for England. Soon Sean O'Casey went. One could smell the coming reaction and the dullness of growing religious obduracy. I became aware of Irish self-destructiveness. I am not much of a roystering man and long hours in Dublin pubs, where the same stories – getting better and better, of course – go round, did not attract me much.

But I had some time to myself and Ireland did revive in me the desire to be a writer of stories. I sat down and wrote my second short story: 'Tragedy in a Greek Theatre'. It was published at once in the *Cornhill*. I wrote three more: 'The White Rabbit; Night in a Corsican Inn' and 'The Mad Feller' about the sick man in Connemara. These had to be re-written many times, but a year or so later I did find publishers for them. The *Monitor* gave me this leisure, but their saintly patience was running out: my prose was at last too much for them. I was sacked.

This was a disaster, but one of those disasters to which a writer owes so much. It was a liberation.

CHAPTER NINE

I LEFT Dublin and, after the singsong of Welsh voices at Holyhead, got into the night train for London. The love affair with foreign places was not quite over, but the heart had gone out of it. I was back in England. After the chancy sky of Ireland the English sky looked smoky and glum and the huge black Greek arch at Euston was a symbol of defeat. I was back where I had started nearly seven years before, with very little money, no job and no prospect of one. I knew scarcely anyone in London. An Irish student at the Slade had lent me his back room in Charlotte Street and when I got to it the excitement I had felt in those two happy years in Paris came back to me. I was alone. Now I could make a real beginning.

The room was separated by double doors from another used by two girls who were painters, and was large and dirty. The floorboards were bare. The place stank of mice, which scampered out of a safe where stale food had been left; the sour smell of old tea leaves came out of a sink in the corner; there was a gas ring on the floor by the cracked marble fireplace and there was a cane-seated folding bed. On the first night when I got into it the two ends folded over me and trapped me: I was still caught by the leg when I struggled out. There was a small table against a wall and a chair, and a big grey-lined box with doors to it at the side, with the name Colonel Guise painted on it – part of the travelling equiment, I suppose, of some officer in the Indian Army. The only elegance was a towel rail in mahogany. It was later claimed from me by an earlier occupant who had left it behind a few years before. I did not know that I had come to live in the quarter of London occupied by many well-known artists. I was to hear the names of the Bells, the Woolfs, Duncan Grant: I did not know anything about them.

One looked out of the back window at the low roofs of small workshops where lathes whined all day, and on a dogs' home. The dogs barked at the howling London cats half the night, and women came to windows and shouted down at them. Some threw things. In the next year or two I moved about among such rooms in Fitzroy Street and Charlotte Street, but never reached the distinction of Fitzroy Square at the top.

Most of the cement-coloured Victorian houses were let off into rooms for tailors, cabinet-makers, picture-framers, small craftsmen and as studios. Italian grocers kept stores of wine and food in the basements. The population was a mixture of French, Italian and Swiss, and Cockney. These houses usually had only one lavatory and there was competition among workers and tenants to get into it. The situation over a framer's called Drowns was made indelicate by young apprentices who sat kicking the pedestal, smoking or whistling half the morning. At night it was not uncommon to see a policeman struggling on the pavement with a man he was arresting while the small hostile London crowd stood by watching fair play. The only time I saw a crowd moved to action was when two women were fighting. One knocked the other down and made to stamp on her face, at which the men advanced and roared out 'No' and pulled the woman off. London has a deep regard for the rules. There were several cases of D.T.s. I remember a man racing along demented, driving off imaginary rats from his throat.

The houses had their special smells; one of my rooms was over a flat and cellar which seemed to be full of cheese. The Italian owner hired a Rolls-Royce and chauffeur every week-end and went off with his huge, high-tempered English wife to Southend. Returning on Sundays they had drunken rows. He was a timid old man who begged me to pay him in the cellar, where he worked among his cheeses and his wine, in case his wife should get at it. Many of these houses were infested with fleas and some of them with bugs. One Saturday I caught thirty fleas on my leg and, going out to the chemists to buy sulphur candles to kill the plague off, I was told that every chemist in the neighbourhood had sold out. It was a street of very cheap Italian and French restaurants – my lunch at Vaiani's cost 1s. 10d. I used to see Prince Mirsky there, reading for his *History of Russian Literature*. At Lossenegger's I could get a meal for 11d. Most are Cypriot owned now and are very expensive and fashionable. Bertorelli's alone retains the old Charlotte Street character; it was reckoned cheap then, but was a few pence beyond my means.

My wife had had a success at the Abbey Theatre, acting in a play by Martiñez Sierra; when she eventually came over to London she got a small part in a repertory company. Our money was running out. I applied for every journalistic job advertised, never failing to give the useless information that I was good at French and Spanish. I tried the weekly reviews that had published one or two things of mine; nothing came of it for a long time. I wrote to the editors of all the other weekly reviews – there were about eight – sending them samples of my writing. I had been reading the *New Statesman* for two or three years and I picked out a sketch of two Dublin tailors. After six months the literary editor, Desmond MacCarthy, wrote to say he could not publish it, but would consider anything else of the kind I liked to send. I was down to my last few pounds before my luck changed.

A school of languages in Oxford Street advertised for a translator. I went down Charlotte Street to the offices. A number of shabby men – teachers and translators – were hanging about on the stairs. I found a girl sitting at a typewriter and chewing gum. An elderly Greek was shouting at her. My arrival stopped the row. The Greek considered me, hissed questions, and gave me a Spanish business letter to translate. It was simple. I was taken on. I went back to my room to translate a dozen business letters from French and Spanish at the rate of one farthing per English word.

Excellent English language! It takes at least seven English words to render four from the Latin tongues and one could add a few polite forensic phrases. I made the sentences long. Back in Charlotte Street, my landlord was waiting for the rent. He was at war with many of his Bohemian tenants: there was a tale that one could palm oneself off as one of the distinguished painters if one put on the right manner. He let me off this time: the next time he was rude: the third time I was safe. I had graduated: the Greek gave me a pile of foolscap documents each thirty pages long which were specifications for the laying out of airfields in France, Switzerland and Spain. For a few weeks I made anything from £1 10s. to £4 a week. Then it all came to an end: I have bad handwriting and, impressionistic as usual, I had failed to consult a technical dictionary.

I went to see Leonard Huxley, who had published my 'Tragedy in a Greek Theatre' in the *Cornhill* Magazine. I had been paid the decent price of twelve guineas for it, and I had got another two guineas when it was published in E. J. O'Brien's *Best Short Stories of the Year*. Leonard Huxley was then in his fifties, a tall, talkative figure, a Greek scholar and Alpine climber, with fanciful grey whiskers. Like all the Huxleys he was mellifluously well-educated. For an hour or so he poured out charm, quotations and classical references very fast, and I see now that what attracted him to my story was that it was set in the Greek theatre at Taormina: he assumed I was a Greek scholar too. The subject of the story was close to me: a painter is made to turn out commercial muck by the hotel keeper to whom he owes money. Huxley turned down my next story, indeed it was never published. It was about the seduction of a housemaid in Cheshire. *Vieux jeu*, he said. His published letters show that he was very shocked by his son's novel, *Antic Hay*. I enjoyed its blasphemies and ribaldry.

The disquisitions of Leonard Huxley were followed by the languid and studied aesthetic manner of Edward O'Brien. English short-story writers owed a lot to his interest. He was an American expatriate and a mixture of the dilettante and the man of business. His fine pale blue eyes were like stones. I had up to now got on better as a writer with Americans than the English people I knew: the English seemed always to have been at Westminster or Eton or Bedales and Oxford or Cambridge. They had acquired a standard precocity. They offered me that sociable, ironic discouragement on which they had been brought up and on which English intellectual society had tested its wits for generations. O'Brien's advice was American and practical. He told me it was indispensable to meet the 'Bloomsbury Group'. I had never heard of them. I didn't even know the *New Statesman* had a connection with it. He said I must live in Bloomsbury. I was not sure where Bloomsbury was, but was too proud to say so. He also said I should live, if not in Bloomsbury, then in Clifford's Inn where very cheap rooms, once occupied by Samuel Butler, could be had. I was put off by these strategic suggestions. I know it is the habit of many young writers to attach themselves to distinguished elders, but I was too shy and too proud to do so. I left him, got a map of London and found that I lived in Bloomsbury without knowing it, or rather just across Tottenham Court Road from it. Cliffords Inn, I discovered, was fully occupied by well-off lawyers.

I did manage to write one or two very short stories for the *Manchester Guardian*, on Irish and Spanish subjects; and I was lucky with a weekly review called *The Outlook*. The literary editor was another American expatriate, Otto Theis. He got me to write one or two short sketches and he went carefully through my prose, weeding out my wildest metaphors. He and his wife, Louise Morgan, were a great help to me. I was allowed to write a review of *The Notebooks of Nathaniel Hawthorne*.

And then there was the benevolent Mr Bassellthorpe. He was worried about me and was distressed by my tastes: did my admiration for Aldous Huxley, D. H. Lawrence mean that I was obsessed with sex? I did not care to say so, but I thought sexual frustration poisoned mind and body. Mr Bassellthorpe had noticed a strain of satirical pessimism in my writing. That, he said, was natural to youth. But my pessimism was not of that kind: it was the expression of the dislike of the bland, meaningless optimism in which I had been brought up in a quarrelsome home and if my bitterness was a defect there was energy in its comic form. He forgave me, but with discomfort. I thought I might collect some of my sketches of travel and publish them in a book and he said he would help me there; in the meantime, it occurred to him there was a minor job I could do. The pay was scarcely £1 a week, but the duties were light and a writer ought to have a steady job to fall back on. Perhaps, eventually, I might review books. After one of his well-chosen lunches, washed down by a glass of tonic water, I was given the job of the Hon. Librarian to the Bath Club.

The difficulty at this exclusive London Club was that the members expected to find there a dozen or more new books every week and were always exasperated by the librarian's choice. The second was that the Club's library catalogue was years out of date and that members took out the books and didn't return them. I would have to 'chase up' the members: from their point of view, many of them hunting men, this would be like the fox chasing the hounds. There was a committee meeting once a month under the chairmanship of Lord Desborough. I had to attend.

The Bath Club was a grand place. A number of its members were racing men or the sporting rich. They were keen on erotica, so keen that a French novel called *La Garçonne*, popular because it contained a page or two on sexual penetration, had to be kept, with several others, locked in the secretary's drawer. I was not allowed to lunch at the club, except by invitation of a member. One, who was a member of the library committee, saw hope in me; he was an expert on porcelain and a man keen on getting the members off books on hunting, shooting, fishing, murder and sex and on to ceramics and cultural subjects. At committee meetings I was expected to put in a word of support. This made me suspect to Lord Desborough, a distinguished and wily gentleman of the 'old school' and a great friend of King George V. My ceramist had only to say that some antiquarian work ought to be bought, for the library, for Lord Desborough to damn the proposal shortly by saying the King had just shown him, for example, an 'awful nice' little book about wild duck with colour plates, or something of the kind. The ceramist tried once to outflank Lord Desborough by saying:

'It's a scandal. There isn't a decent Atlas in this club.' And, considering the extent of the British Empire at that time, it was.

'What do you mean, not a "decent" Atlas?' said Lord Desborough.

'I mean a really good one, where you can see the detail.' What detail did the ceramic expert want to see? The ceramist wanted to see, for example a decent map of Arabia, the exact position of archaeological sites, wadis and oases. That, Lord Desborough said, sounded like a damned big Atlas. The ceramist said, not enormously big. How big? said Lord Desborough, bringing out his guns. One you could put on a table and look things up in, said the ceramist shakily. What did he mean by a table? What size table? Like the one we were sitting at? Lord Desborough asked. It was a large table. The ceramist hesitated. 'Well ...' he began.

'Take four footmen to lift it,' said Lord Desborough. We slid off the interest in atlases and it was here that Lord Desborough played the trump card I have mentioned: that 'awful nice' book about wild duck the King was so keen on.

I had collected my sketches. Mr Bassellthorpe had a publishing friend who would like to see them – a Mr Hicks-Flannell. I went to see this sad and intelligent man briefly one foggy evening when I found him poking a low fire in his lodgings. He was sceptical. One thing about his appearance discouraged me: like Mr Bassellthorpe he wore button boots. But, unlike Mr Bassellthorpe, Mr Hicks-Flannell was lean and melancholy. He had the fated look of a bookish man resigned to the disappearance of the remains of a small private inheritance. God would never fail, would never dare to fail, to answer the prayers of Mr Bassellthorpe. He would just nod his head, acquiescing in the unassuming regularity of his views; perhaps even flattered. In an evangelical way, God was just a bit of a snob. Mr Hicks-Flannell's prayers would be treated parsimoniously, simply because they were anxious. He talked of the hopeless prospect of a collection of essays. My manuscript came back in a week. He had shown it to his partner, a Mr Eddie, who had instantly turned it down.

I was not surprised. The stuff, I saw at the second reading, was thin and scrappy. Twenty years later I met Mr Eddie for the first time in a night club. He was elderly and had given up publishing. He had retired to the seaside. He said if he had only known! 'Frankly,' he said, 'if you had only not come through Hicks-Flannell.'

This was a surprise to me. Frankness in Mr Eddie made him look shady. He was a pale, round, obsequious man with a psalmy voice, combined with the manner of the racing tipster, a man free with unction and binoculars. He dropped, from time to time, a confiding aitch – 'Icks-Flannell, for example. He chatted on. It seems that Mr Eddie could not forgive Christian Science for being issued under the imprint of a name so close to his own. He made his partner responsible for the irritation. If

Mr Hicks-Flannell brought in the MS. of a book on Greece he suspected that he was pushing it for religious reasons, so he would say (he giggled at this), that he'd just got a much better book on, say, Turkey, by an atheist or a Buddhist. The partners were engaged in religious warfare.

How did writers and painters manage to live and yet keep their independence? How did my elders, D. H. Lawrence, Katherine Mansfield, Aldous Huxley, live? My crisis was becoming desperate. I could not go on drifting. But I had another stroke of luck: I managed to sell a secondhand car I had had in Dublin for £60. My wife and I split the sum in two. It was capital.

The thing to do was to write an original book of travel. I had just read D. H. Lawrence's *Sea and Sardinia* with despairing admiration – despairing because why was he so 'inside' his subject and I so brittle, cold and 'outside' what I was writing about? Through what defect of character and especially of feeling, was I so shut in upon myself? But there was a lesson I could follow: the short, compact subject, made personal. I got maps and decided to walk from some spot in the south of Spain to the north, and to write of nothing but the walk. On the money – and to save some for my return – I had to shorten the journey. I decided to take ship to Lisbon for economy's sake and walk from Badajoz to Vigo, through a part of Spain that was little known and, in patches, was notorious for poverty. It was also the route of Wellington's armies, though that historical interest was not mine. So, taking *Tristram Shandy* with me, and fortified on the way by thrillers by E. Phillips Oppenheim which I found in Catholic bookshops, I walked across Spain.

I have described it all in *Marching Spain* – note the deliberately ungrammatical, protesting, affected title. Though I have a tenderness for the book and think some pages rather good, I am glad it has been out of print for forty years. The few people who have read it give me a kindly but knowing grin now. I don't blame them. It has a touching but shocking first chapter of exhibitionist prose; but despite the baroque writing of the rest, the mistakes of fact, and the declamations, it is original and has vigour. It is the work of a young man worried almost to illness by lack of money and by the future for a lot of the time. As he tramped along he was doing accounts and stamping out his anxieties with his heavy boots. I posed as a photographer working in the picture postcard trade. In the book I was purposely silent about knowing Spain already, because I wanted to preserve an instantaneous impression; and indeed in the stories and criticism I was to write later on in my life, the instantaneous and 'first sight' of the object has been my infatuation. Critics have noted a preoccupation with religious cranks, thinking that because of my upbringing I must have sought them out. This is not so: I had little religion left. I am always eager to listen to anyone. My first encounter, simply as I walked down a street in Badajoz, was with a group of Spanish evangelicals.

The weather was good. The sun burned. The nights were cold. I was strong. I did my twenty miles a day, slept in simple *ventas* on the stone floor after I had sat round a stick fire with the family and ate what the women fried there. The poor were more interesting than the well-off and the Spanish poor were not dull and whining. They were whole in their manliness and womanliness. I once shared a pigsty with very clean piglets. Food was very scarce. I lived on 'pairs of eggs' and bread, except in the towns where I made up for it. I found a dirty inn only once. It was in a large village, used by commercial travellers – who peddle from village to village – where the pillows were soaked in years of their old hair oil and the sheets sour with sweat. I got to the Tagus, deep and golden in its gorge, one evening and there I was badly poisoned after eating a powerful garlic stew with some railway workers at a hut on the line. I recovered after a terrible time in Palencia where, in the middle of the night, I saw the cook asleep in his cotton 'combinations' snoring on the kitchen table. I crossed the Gredos mountains and sat on the roadside talking to the travelling shepherds of the Mesta and listening to the sheep bells; then farther north the weather broke, the rain washed the road away, and I got one of my spectacular bronchial attacks. I gave up at the last stretch to Vigo, for I had grown weak; and in Vigo I had just enough money left to get a comfortable bed for a few days. The guests in the dining-room were startled by the graveyard cough which has been my pride since I was a child, and I sat all day staring at the superb bay of the seaport, waiting for the boat home, counting my money over and over again and down to one glass of beer a day. A South American on the boat went the round of the ladies lifting up his shirt to show them the scars of his operations. He had a success.

Back in London I moved from one furnished flat or room in Bloomsbury to another, taking places because people were away for a few weeks. I wrote chapters of my book, now here, now there, and managed to get bits of it published as I went along in the *Guardian* and the weeklies, and finished it in a room above the Italian grocer's in Fitzroy Street. (A good deal of this neighbourhood was destroyed by bombs in 1940: this house went too.) This room was unfurnished. I got my books out of Ireland – there were 600 by now – and a carpenter made a bookcase and also a table, to a Spanish design. I bought a birchwood chair with a high back. I still work in this chair; this furniture made me feel I really was an author. I clipped my paper to an old Atlas – I moved to a pastryboard when the Atlas wore out. Stability at last. Here I finished the book and a new young literary agent, A. D. Peters, found me a publisher at once: Victor Gollancz at Ernest Benn's. I was to be one of his notably unsalable young authors, impervious to all his enormous advertising could do for me. He advanced me £25. That paid for the furniture.

I was writing the book one steaming afternoon when in came a figure from my past: my remote past, for when one is young three or four years seem like thirty. This was Basil Shaves, no longer the rolling *boulevardier*, but fitfully playing the part of the brisk businessman and member of a Bohemian club. His state was still trance-like. My poverty jogged him into nostalgia for a minute or two. I was eating an apple and threw the core out into the street; he admired this gesture of a carefree life. After his bad luck at the bank in Paris, he was selling, as I have said before, women's wear to small shops in the suburbs of London. He had hung around theatrical agencies first of all, showing them his notices of *Fanny's First Play*, but as he apologized to me: 'I'm too old.'

373

His hair was curly grey now, he was stouter and suetty; but he still broke out into a line or two of his Italian arias. When he heard I was writing a book, his well-known phrase came out: 'Well, whad d'ya know!' He liked being a salesman. He loved his little house in the suburbs. He adored England. He was home! My brother told me that customers rang up and asked who this opera singer was. He sang orders out of them.

I promised to visit him, but put it off from week to week until one day I had a message that he was ill. I found his villa – 'my little English home' – on a new building estate where the roads were still stretches of rutted wet clay. There he was in his pyjamas and dressing gown and he showed me around. But, presently, when we sat down, he got up again and switched on the light, though it was daytime. He left the room and went round switching on the lights all over the house, came back and said, irritably 'The lights are on' and went off again and switched them all off. After that he went upstairs. His wife said he'd gone to bed; he had a temperature. But down he came, switching on and off, and said 'Hullo' to me as if he'd never seen me before. I reminded him of *Cutts of the Cruiser Whatnot*. He was puzzled. He'd never heard of it. I recited it to him.

> When homeward bound
> My old ship runs aground
> I love it, I shriek with glee.

Mr Shaves did not smile. He was dying. He had had a stroke a week or two before and had been found wandering lost in the streets. In two days he was dead.

Marching Spain appeared in 1928 and was briefly parodied by two painter friends, under the title *Reaching Slade*. The first review was in G. K. Chesterton's paper, *G.K.'s Weekly*. A whole page was given to it. The reviewer picked up his merry knife and plunged into one of his funniest feats of satirical butchery. He portrayed me as a lunatic juvenile prig, dressed in Shaw's Jaeger suiting, a teetotaller, probably belonging to the Ethical Church, given to vegetarianism, eugenics, birth control, an ignoramus in religion and a wrecker of the English language. I had upset him by an aside on Spanish pictures of the crucifixion

374

which, he said, I made to seem like a bloody morning at Smith-field Meat Market. The last was a fairish comment, for even now the cult of pictures of the crucifixion – especially the Spanish – horrify me. The sadism, so marked in Christian history and especially in Spanish history, shocks me. But I took the point, that taste and sensibility were not as strong in me as I thought they were. I know I had blustered – though not in order to attract public attention but, naturally enough, to attract my own attention to myself. It was myself I was addressing privately as if I were looking at some lost stranger.

I was not upset by the review. It was long and witty and as full of exaggerations as indeed my own book was. I have always suspected that it was written by that very original English humorist: Beachcomber; himself a stout Bellocian walker in the Pyrenees. The next review was in Leonard Woolf's *The Nation* and had all Bloomsbury's acid scorn. Crude. Small beer, they said. True enough. It was the kind of review that makes a writer wince; but I had the vulgar instinct for survival. Another reviewer reproached me for ignoring the upper class Spaniards and concentrating on the poor. Desmond Mac-Carthy's *Life and Letters* praised the book. My excesses were passed over as youthful follies and the writer ended by saying I knew the Spanish people well and that Belloc and Borrow would gladly 'find a chair for me at their table in the inn'. The reviewer of the evangelical *British Weekly* liked the Protestant tone and announced that I was 'a genius with a brain packed in ice'. I have talent, but no genius, yet the phrase was a near-miss. I *had* intended my images to have a hard, icy and brainy flash. I had always liked Meredith's 'brain-stuff' and I was growing up in a period that taught hard detachment.

The winter was cold and foggy. I was invited to a publisher's party – my first – in Whitehall Court. I knew no one there. A white-haired woman screamed at me: 'What is the most exciting experience you have had in your life? I will tell you mine. I once swam over a volcano.' One of the young partners of the firm said, looking up at the ceiling of his flat, 'This room is very high.' Another partner said, 'This room is very large.' I was glad to get out of the crush and went out into the fog to study the posters announcing Bodies Found outside Scotland

Yard, then walked back to my cheese-flavoured room in Fitzroy Street. The book sold 600 copies and was soon remaindered. Another innocent publisher issued it in a pocket edition in 1933; it was remaindered once more. Still, I was an author.

And I was an author with a contract. I was to have £25 for a volume of short stories and £50 for a novel, when I delivered them. But how in the next two years was I to live? I could not survive as the librarian of the Bath Club. I would have to be a spare-time book reviewer. It did not occur to me that there was any other solution. I was warned: 'Once you use book-reviewing as a crutch you'll be on crutches all your life. You'll never be able to throw them away.'

The brotherly Mr Bassellthorpe, so uncertain of me, so fearful of my tendencies, but so indulgent, gave me what I needed. He gave me a small regular job of sending out two or three books to English reviewers every week or so for his paper. I had also to do a review myself. I was paid £5 a week and kept the job for years. Indeed until in the thirties I wrote *The Saint* and was sacked for good. The task was easy: the paper's moral attitudes enabled it to find most of the important imaginative literature of the early part of the century unsuitable for review. Pound, Eliot, Joyce, Huxley, Lawrence were ignored. The imagination, especially the modern, upset Mr Bassellthorpe. But history, biography, politics, travel and general literature were pretty safe. Many reputable English scholars and essayists – in my time – H. M. Tomlinson, E. H. Carr, Richard Church, Harold Hobson and some survivors of the nineties, contributed. Many still do. I imagine the paper has mellowed. Even so, though £5 a week was a godsend, it was not enough and, of course, I wanted to write something of my own. I had managed to get 'Rain in the Sierra' published in the *New Statesman*. I asked to see the editor.

In 1928 the *New Statesman* was edited in a shaky building only too conveniently next door to a little pub in Great Queen Street. The review had been founded in 1913 by the Webbs and by Bernard Shaw to propagate very seriously the new ideas of Fabian socialism: its circulation was small; it had lost money for fourteen years and its wealthy backers had to subsidize it: but Fabian socialism was the rising idea. Unlike modern tycoons who wish to buy a sudden respectability and who treat journals as commercial products to be played about with and quickly dropped, the backers of the *New Statesman* were firmly dedicated. But the payments to the writers were meagre even when they were famous and there were periods of crisis when from week to week, one did not know whether the thing would close down: the pugnacious editor, Clifford Sharp, a domineering and hard-drinking man, was reckless of libel actions. The literary editor, Desmond MacCarthy, was noted for his charm and indolence and when I went to see him, he was not there. He had not been in the office for months.

I was taken to a shabby top room of the building where there was a third or fourth hand desk, a couple of chairs and a sofa with broken springs, on which people sometimes slept. The most solid object in the room was a gas meter. I met here the temporary editor, S. K. Ratcliffe, an impish middle-aged man, well known in Fabian circles and who lectured at American universities. (He was a Scottish pedant too; for years he would send me postcards of praise or blame, but making a list of grammatical and printers' errors and of incorrect punctuation. If I talked on the radio he would send a card saying, perhaps, 'Breathing rather heavy on second page'.) Now, at our first meeting, he said:

'What did you read at the University?'

'I've never been to a university,' I said. I thought I was done for.

Mr Ratcliffe bobbed up gaily in his chair.

'Totally uneducated,' he said. 'Like me. I didn't go to one either.'

That was a relief. We chatted and presently he became mischievous. He left the room on tiptoe with me and said to a very severe Cambridge girl who sat in a little office like a lavatory, 'How is he?'

The girl shrugged coldly. She was tall and stern and had corn-coloured hair.

On tiptoe again Mr Ratcliffe nipped across a passage to the

editor's door and listened; then he went in and soon came jumping out like a naughty boy and whispered:

'Go in. He'll see you.'

Clifford Sharp was a massive man, red in the face, handsome, a glaring editorial chunk, full of drink. He sloped at his desk. On the wall was a poem in large letters, I think, by Belloc:

> Thank God you cannot bribe or twist
> The Honest British journalist.
> But judging what the man will do
> Unbribed, there's no occasion to.

'You've been in Spain?' he said thickly. 'There's a book by a young man called Pritchett. Will you review it?'

'I wrote it,' I said.

He grunted with anger and suspicion.

'Well,' he said, 'Go away and talk to Mr Ratcliffe.'

Outside Mr Ratcliffe gave a skip of delight.

'I've got just the thing for you. Do me 150 words on the history of the Coptic Church. Do you know anything about it? No? That's good. Look it up.'

Ten shillings for that. A few months later I advanced to 600 words on Galdos and the Spanish novel. One pound for Galdos. The lure of book reviewing is that you can sell the books at half price – a matter that explained why one or two down-and-out journalists came in and did short notices on out of the way volumes. In a year I had moved up to an expensive *Life* of Columbus, for I had read a good deal on the Spanish discoveries and on the opening up of the Americas. These became my specialities. But once more disaster threatened the *New States man*. Clifford Sharp's drinking made him reckless. He libelled the Commissioner of Police: the paper's sponsors, the Webbs, the Shaws and Arnold Bennett had to pay up. Ratcliffe went off to America. A rolling and eloquent boon companion of Sharp's (Clennell Wilkinson who had lived in Egypt and Africa), became literary editor, a fellow with a husky voice. He had written a *Life* of Dampier. He belonged to the group of older journalists who had taken up the tavern habits of Belloc and Chesterton. He arrived in the office with the martyred look of a man whom God had heartlessly appointed to save the whisky business from bankruptcy; he had been cursed, he said, with an illness called 'waking up in the morning two double whiskies under par'. In his conversation strange protests would go off like gun fire. One I put into a story :

'Bloody white women in Africa crawling about taking photographs of poor helpless wild animals. Damn cruel. Poor animals sooner be shot – what?'

That final 'What?' softened to a husky, injured 'Wha . . .?' marked him as a surviving Edwardian. He did not last long. Sharp's final aberration – for he died soon after – was to appoint an Anglo-Catholic Fabian called Ellis Roberts. He was like a soft fat cooing priest. When Kingsley Martin became editor they soon quarrelled and he left. Kingsley hated religion.

The paper's most talented young man was G. W. Stonier, who wrote about Flaubert, Kafka and Joyce, and about films under the pseudonym of William Whitebait. Stonier, a year or two younger than I, was a sharp and candid critic with an excellent eye for the delicate and bizarre in vulgar events. He was an eccentric who came into his own in the Blitz. He wrote the only comic book I know about it. He became a great friend. He astonished us all by going to live in Africa a few years ago.

I write here of the *New Statesman's* early days. I saw little hope of more than a guinea or two now and then. For the next twenty years one had to work for other papers in order to afford to write for it. I managed to write for the *Fortnightly Review*, which published two or three short stories of mine. It was necessary to write a very long story to complete a book. Reviewing did not give me enough money for living in London and so I moved to a cottage in the hills above Marlow. I became the novel reviewer for the *Spectator*, the rival weekly which in those days was far more prosperous than the *New Statesman*. My life became a shade less precarious.

And so I became a literary journalist of highbrow tastes who lives in a country cottage because it is cheap and who divides his time between reviewing and doing his 'own work'.

In the country one is outside literary circles and I have rarely been intimately connected with them. There is a disadvantage in not being a paid-up member of a set in England, for one's continued existence is a surprise; and sets give their members publicity. But in the long run they become little parishes of mutual admiration; they corrode the independence of criticism, and the novelist or storyteller – unless he is satirical – is taken farther and farther away from the ordinary life he has sprung from. One advantage of country life is that it gives one time, for there is little distraction. One cannot pick and choose one's neighbours, and slowly, seeing them month in, month out, one sees them in the round; in the country, people reveal themselves without intending to do so. Conversations are longer and in this relaxed life it is easier to let the bucket down into the unconscious. For most novelists there is far too much opinion in cities: a little is necessary but it goes a long way.

The cottage where I lived was a little flint place about three miles up in the hills from Marlow. The nearest house was a bungalow which often changed hands and some odd specimens occupied it from time to time. One of these, for a while, was a very dry young Scot, a classics master at Charterhouse. Most of the week he was alone and he would drop in and propound jokes about English history: he was tirelessly trying them out and refining them. They were the joint work of himself and a gay friend in London who sometimes came down. A pretty chain-smoking girl with a rude tongue, a disturbing wink and an awful cough used also to come down to their parties. It emerged that the schoolmaster and his friend were writing a funny book together and quarrelled so much (the girl told me), that she had once thrown the manuscript on the fire. I don't know if this was true; but once when she was alone there she did accidentally burn some of the furniture when she had fallen asleep over a cigarette. The springs of a chair or two were thrown out on the lawn. She used to bury tins there. The book was 1066 and All that.

When my wife was away acting in a repertory company in the North of England we found a down-and-out sailor in London who came down to look after me. A long time afterwards, years indeed, some of these events became the basis of a story called 'The Sailor': It was at Marlow that the evangelist in The Saint fell into the water.

These stories have been thought well of, but they were

written later in my life; in Marlow they were fermenting in my mind. My task was to finish a long story called 'The Spanish Virgin' for my collection and to go on writing a novel. I had no wish to write a novel and did not know how to set about it, but the publishers insisted. To their surprise my book of short stories succeeded with the critics and readers; instead of selling the expected 600 copies, it sold more than 3,000. It has been out of print since 1930 and so has the novel *Clare Drummer*, which evokes with a novelist's necessary translation of fact into fiction my private Irish experience. It is a nervous attempt to come to terms, but I was trying to write autobiographically without portraying myself. There is a central blur in the book, and the mannerisms are shocking; I am on a see-saw in which I go erratically from awful hyperbole to good observation. The critics noted this and said I was writing off my nerves. *Clare Drummer* sold under a thousand copies and, like the other two books, has long been out of print.

If the reviewers were puzzled by my mixture of feverishness and amateur incompetence, Mr Bassellthorpe – my benefactor – was totally shocked. He had had hopes of my moral character; they were dashed and we were drifting apart. Why were my people so unpleasant? Why were my tastes so morbid and why was I still so pessimistic? I said one could only write as one was. Soon we went off to one of his pleasant lunches. One of my affectations, caught from the older generation, was to carry a walking stick. I carried it under my arm down Piccadilly. The spectacle embarrassed him and he murmured. It was a bamboo stick with a curious head like a polished root and I explained that it was a male bamboo: the bamboos with the crook were female. The shopkeeper had told me. Mr Bassellthorpe was exasperated.

'People have sex on the brain today,' he said angrily. Our lunch was a failure. But he was a man of scrupulous conscience. He wrote me a letter that evening saying that it had come to him that he had spoken of my writing in an un-Christian manner. He apologized, though his opinion remained, and he begged me to try and be a better man. I wished he had not apologized for, like so many people of conscience, he had had his cake and eaten it, with satisfaction.

To be young is painful but exhilarating: to be certain and to pass into uncertainty and on to new certainties, to be conscious of the changes from one hour to the next; to be intolerant of others and blindly interested in oneself. It is so hard to remember youth simply because one loses dramatic interest in oneself. One is harsh; one is all sentiment. It is the time of friendships. I used to think of myself as more exposed than my friends yet clearly I was not. At a moment when I felt wise an elderly and amused doctor said I looked like a bolting pony. A poet, older than myself, said I burned everything up, including myself. I was tame yet I was avid. I was shy and I was aggressive. Goodness knows what any young man is like except egotistical and perhaps fanatical. I was fanatical about writing: the word and the sentence were my religion; everything must be definite. I was rather snobbish about the need to be poor; and, I think, selfish. Not that there was much opportunity for people like myself to be better off. So when I look now at the excesses in my writing, that break out without reason, I see they represent unsatisfied energies, inchoate desires, unresolved dilemmas. Signs of militant weakness. It is pretty certain that the effect of the violent quarrels in my childhood home was to close my heart for a long time. I used to feel, as young people do, older than my years. I had (I thought) seen too much. The trap was that I had not experienced it. I saw people as trapped in their own natures and divided into those who go for power and dominance and those who do anything to keep the peace and make secrecy their defence. There is a theory among psychologists which is less flattering: that an eldest child (and I was that creature) finds himself isolated, leaps at his freedom, becomes even adventurous and self-sufficient – but, untrained by conflict, breaks in a crisis, disperses himself and goes to pieces. I have certainly had to deal with that.

The year of the Wall Street crash I got £75 from my publisher and, under the common delusion that it would be easier to write in France, I went down to Cassis in the south of France to stay in the farmhouse kept by a Frenchman called Roger Nion. I did not know half Bloomsbury had the habit of going there. The peaches were ripe, the sun was hot, the red rocks of the Mediterranean burned against the peacock sea, the cicadas made a din all night in the pines and the dogs of the valley barked at the moon. It was all very gay and lazy. In the cafés the gramophones played, over and over again, pleasant tunes like 'The Sunny Side of the Street'. The street would not be sunny again for many, many years. I was too sun-soaked to write.

Roger Nion was an absurd man. He had been a stage manager. Now he was an elderly dandy who wore a monocle and who went on long bicycle rides on a racing bike. He looked like a dragonfly as he whizzed to the beach. His favourite phrase was 'tout s'arrange'. People thought him a bit of a fraud and a parsimonious French peasant dressed up, but I liked him. His unexpected gift was that he was a powerful and courageous swimmer. It was frightening to see his head bobbing up and down, a couple of miles out in a rough sea. His unmistakably French character came out in a small contraption he had invented for catching flies. It lay on his dining table: this was a small cylinder made sticky with honey, on which the flies that infested the place would alight; the cylinder slowly conveyed them to the glass death chamber attached. Roger used to watch this with satisfaction as he read detective stories. I mention this because it occurs to me that that was what my first three novels were like: amateur machines for conveying my characters into a trap.

When I got back to England I ran into one nervous illness after another. I walked about with a knife sticking into my back by day; when I went to bed my nightmares were about air warfare. I was often sitting with the crowd of Out Patients at hospitals, waiting to be X-rayed. My duodenum twanged. I went into fevers. In Cornwall I got very ill. My habits of work cannot have been helpful. I re-wrote and re-wrote all day and half the night at some periods: the hours and my anxieties must have been hard on my constitution. Samuel Butler has some lines about Radicals having bad digestions. I must have been very Radical. What in fact eventually cured me was success in love, and in my work.

CHAPTER TEN

I MUST go back to the situation at Bromley after my return from Spain. My parents had moved house by this time. I occasionally wrote to my mother but rarely got a reply. The lack of letters and of frequent meetings was, and still is, normal in our family; except for my mother, we all really liked to be 'on our own'.

I went down to Bromley. The shooting-box dream had gone; there had been others, but now I found myself walking up a respectable gravel driveway to a tall, double-fronted Edwardian house, a substantial place, in the best part of the town. The family had gone up in the world. There was a dinner gong in the wide hall, a barometer and Turkey carpets – signs of gentility. In the long drawing-room there was a grand piano which, as I told in my earlier volume, father had secretly bought. The famous pictures called Limpets (by Mabel Lucie Attwell, I believe), of two naked children displaying their rosy bottoms on a rock by the sea, was in place; so was *Wedded*. They were now supported by half a dozen large landscapes of greenery, water and cattle, bringing to the house an appropriate note of the Lake District, for it was called *Rydal Mount*, as were also some 100,000 other houses in England at this time.

Mother was tidily dressed. There was, for the first time, a maid in the house, an elderly religious woman whose eyes gazed with searching eagerness: she was stone deaf – a shrewd move on father's part, because family conversations had the remorseless candour of Yorkshire utterance. The family communicated with this gentle woman by a sort of semaphore and she lip-read. We had never had a housemaid in my time.

I was relieved to see we had so obviously bettered ourselves although the dining-room table, sofas and sideboard had enlarged their old war with each other; in fact I never remember a time when our furniture did not look like evidence of changes in the class war more than anything else. Oak, walnut, cherry, mahogany, flashed their veneers sarcastically at one another.

When I said to one of my brothers that we were going up, he said: 'In smoke!' And, now that my brother, the very successful one, had left home, he added (entirely without malice and as if metaphor alone could describe the situation), 'Rats leave a sinking ship.'

The remark was an example of our family's poetic tendency. There was no sign of sinking. Indeed, the Divine Mind had wisely supplied a chauffeur to drive my father about. Father said: 'I feel I can breathe here.'

But he did ask if I knew the pines and sandy commons near Hindhead. He asked, he said, merely because only the previous week he had been through there on his way to the South Coast on business.

My mother asked if I thought poor Queen Ena was happy with King Alfonso. My mother was worried by my bony appearance. Noticing I had not brought pyjamas for the night, she thought I must be short of money. She looked at me with suspicion: 'Are you still doing the writing?' She always spoke of it as if writing were some unlucky thing – like rain – and that I was out in it without a coat. I was offered a glass of ginger wine.

'That's all you'll get,' she said disloyally. Then switching to near-loyalty: 'Of course, your father always buys the best.'

Father said, in royal manner, 'We always drink it.'

The house, or rather the alterations to it, had cost a lot – and, in fact, the Divine Mind had shown that it was the duty of my remaining brother and sister, who were earning their livings, to live there and contribute to the upkeep. If they rebelled father took this to mean they were trying to destroy him out of blatant ingratitude. There was a fear that Animal Magnetism or the false evidence of the material senses – Mortal Mind, in short – might suggest – and we know the danger of suggestion, don't we? – that they get married and leave home. My father did most sincerely feel that marriage was for him alone. Mine had caused consternation. Still, we were on good terms, so long as we skated past difficult subjects. Hearing that I was reviewing books, he was proud and enthusiastic. It suggested to him that he should buy new books. He did so. Delighted to get out of his factory he was soon in the best London bookshops, buying on a large scale. Seeing a picture of John Stuart Mill at Bumpus's he asked my advice on whether to get the works. He did not read these books, he stacked them up in a wardrobe in his bedroom which was already pretty full of the widely advertised ones. No one was allowed to take them out of the wardrobe. He loved stores and stock.

There was one small cloud. The Divine Mind – here, as usual, at variance with my mother – had brought our grandmother to live in the house: the minister, after some hard years in a rough factory town in Lancashire, had died. Our grandmother had not changed her opinion that my mother, if not still a harlot, had idle dirty London habits, and that our father would have done better 'elsewhere'. My mother occasionally spoke of 'the old b . . .' and mocked her Yorkshire accent. But grandma's tiny inheritance had timidly trebled itself in Courtauld's shares for thirty years. Father had pointed out the folly of letting money run lethargically to fat in this way. He persuaded her to transfer what would eventually be his share for a livelier career in his business. The career was indeed lively and brief; and there was already a faint notion that his brother in Canada might see the attraction of giving his share a canter too. He was a poor working man with a large family who had not made good in Canada and had to look to the future. One couldn't tell, of course, but the Divine Mind might show the way. Father never said this directly: he was opposed on principle to 'voicing one's desires'; the Divine Mind hated you to 'voice'. You prayerfully waited for the Divine Will to 'unfold'. As father said:

'We must not outline what channel will open up.'

Mother, unfortunately, 'voiced' and very frequently.

'Do you believe in this . . .' she said to me. Her face was torn by mistrust. The old story of her pawned engagement ring and other wrongs came out.

'No,' I said.

'You're a wicked boy,' she said. 'Your father does.'

I did not often visit my parents for it was difficult to get an opportunity of talking alone with my mother. If one telephoned, father always answered and one could sometimes hear her voice half whimpering in the background. She had wept when

386

Mr Shaves died; it brought to mind all the deaths in her family.

But each time I went home the situation had become richer. Serious matters in our family were always discussed at meal times. Someone was told to whack the gong in the hall though we were already gathered. We filed in and started; beginning innocently with things like the best kind of stove to have. Presently there were allusions to deeper matters. And they were discussed before my grandmother, as neat, pretty and vain in her eighties as ever. It was safe: like the maid, she too was stone deaf. Conversation was frank, especially if I was there. I will say this for us: we loved to put on a show.

'Will you have a little more, Grandma dear?' my mother would say.

'More?' one of my brothers shouted in her ear.

'Eh, ah fancy a bit of fat, Walter,' my grandmother would say. She loved fat.

'Pass it up quickly, it may be your last chance,' one of my brothers said.

My father tried vainly to silence him.

'After all,' the boy went on, 'she paid for it. And it may be her last.'

These episodes would end with some shy appeasing statement, at great length, from the jollier voice of the Divine Mind. The old lady went to her sitting-room and, on her horse-hair sofa, lay reading a love story in a religious magazine until she fell asleep, under a tapestry picture of Moses smashing up the Commandments at the time of the Golden Calf, a good picture for our family, and one she had woven herself when she was a girl. She had luckily brought a good deal of her furniture with her. We had not enough of our own for the four reception rooms.

Later someone would say: 'You'd better go and see how she is.'

'You never know,' said my young brother.

(I have described some of this in a scene in *Mr Beluncle*, for it oppressed my mind; the novel was very much influenced by Schchedrin's *The Golovlyov Family*.)

The implication was terrible, but so much had money come to obsess us that no one realized it. In her eighties, Grandma might easily pass 'to another plane of consciousness' without warning. She had been heard crying out in the night for William, her dead husband. Or groaning: 'Oh God help me!' Yet she got up brisk and early in the mornings, in her village fashion, and set to work. Once a week she would put on a cloth cap, kirtle her skirt, take up the carpet and linoleum from the floor of her sitting-room and bedroom and, with a pail of water and scrubbing brush, she would be down on her knees scrubbing the boards. She suspected 'London dirt' everywhere. When that work was done, she'd attack my mother for not doing the same to the rest of the large house. Then she'd sit demurely crochetting in her room, making one more doyley to add to her hoard. There were pretty well a thousand in her wardrobe. At other times, she would wrap up one or two of these in paper and slip out to the pillar box at the corner and post it to her son in Manitoba. Once she sent him a strip of linoleum in case he was 'in want'. The postman brought these things back because they were not addressed. When my mother said *she* would send them the old lady suspected a plot, accusing mother of wanting the doyleys and lino for herself, and took to making bigger parcels and throwing them out of the window when she saw the postman come up the drive. He used to bring them back to mother at the back door. The old lady was shrewd enough to see that her little money had vanished.

'Eh,' she would say to my mother, 'this is what you've done to my son.'

'Give it back to her. I'd sooner live in a shed than this,' mother would say. 'I don't want her charity. I like things straight.'

The money, of course, had gone. The story is too painful. But one day, the old lady (now bedridden) said out of her loneliness to my mother:

'You're the only one who loves me. You're the only one.' It was true; my mother looked after her to the end. The burden of dealing with the jealous old lady was hers.

In a year or two, she died. Father always lost his self-control in the large emotional matters of life. He wept. He became helpless. He had no notion of what to do; some bewilderment at the fact that other people existed, independently of himself, made him cling to the idea that events had not happened – perhaps one of his reasons for conversion to Christian Science. He invented excuse after excuse for delaying the funeral, one of the mad reasons being that Miss H would be put out by his absence from the office. Perhaps the reason lay in a sort of Tolstoyan anger at the fact of death; it is certain also that he loved his mother passionately. There the body lay in the house. The result was horror. The dead woman's body burst in the coffin and was borne dripping from the bedroom.

His mother's death had saved father financially. He wept often when he mentioned the little bits of jewellery she had left; and although he laughed, as we all did, at the hoards of crochetting and embroidery she left, he wept as he admired them. He had inherited from her a love of craftmanship and of hoarding things.

Father was on acrimonious terms with his partner. The financial peace did not last long after his mother's death. Desperate second mortgages, and 'borrowings' from my brother began. But a final break with the partner settled it all. I do not know the rights and wrongs of it, but the Divine Mind could do nothing about writs and about lawyers with serious cases. Explaining one of these father said:

'I told him he ought to have been old enough to know it was an ordinary business risk.'

He said this arrogantly and shrewdly, yet immediately a glow would come on his prosperous and optimistic face, as if he had ascended to the Platonic condition of Risk, as if he were Divine Risk in person. He exuded the bliss of insolvency as an ideal to be aimed at; he captivated many. But, unable to share this light, we became, I'm afraid, cautious and were ashamed to feel we might be mean-minded and even guilty. How extraordinary it is that one feels most guilt about the sins one is unable to commit.

The news came one day in the winter that the firm had gone into liquidation. We were all wretched. My brothers had the delicate task of arranging the affair. I was told father made a fine speech at the crucial meeting: he was not a minister's son for nothing, and several of those present were very moved.

And, looking back on it, I see it *was* moving to see a man who had worked so hard and with scrupulous talent, to be his own master, defeated. He was greatly respected in his trade; if he had turned from God to his admiring business friends, he would have succeeded. Inside him was an artist who had not been able to change his style.

In distress I went to see him at his office. I had always been proud of his name plate on his factory and was shocked that 'the business' which had so beglamoured and harassed our lives, was gone. He often said, in his disordered, emotional moments, that, but for his religion, he would 'end it all', and I feared that this might occur, forgetting that it was really one of his energizing self-dramatizing statements. So now I went up the stone stairs that had seemed like prison stairs to me so often, with self-reproach at my inability to rescue him, and with guilt in criticizing him. I felt very close to him. What an emotional state he could put me in! I entered his showroom, once so scented, but now smelling of floorboards, whitewash and empty showcases. He lead me to his office.

'They have to leave you a desk,' he said, claiming his rights. 'Have a cup of tea? The gas is on.'

I have often thought how distressing this meeting must have been for him. I was his eldest son and he identified me with his own father, the Minister and intellectual. My brothers in the business world could and did help him much more than I; but I, like his own father, was an unsettling visitor from outside. He was beginning to wish he had had a life like his own father's. We were at the beginning of that phase so common in the lives of fathers and sons, when the father feels *he* is the son. This is a truth that is missing from a story called 'The Fly in the Ointment' which I eventually wrote about our interview. It was one of those rare stories that require little more than recall from the writer. My father was affectionate and was moved by my calling on him here, for his office and factory were his real home where he had kept so many things private to himself: his gramophone, his photographs, his special coffee cups, the motto containing words of Emerson's. I feared we would both weep; we were saved by a distraction. A large fly flew in from the showroom and father detested flies: emissaries of dirt. He went at it with a copy of the *Draper's Record*. I went at it with an evening paper. We missed. A fury seized us. He got up on his desk to bash it on the ceiling and there, looking down at me, he said sternly:

'You're going bald, my boy.'

It made me feel I was the fly. He was very stern when I helped him down and he said, getting his breath, defiantly:

'We paid a shilling in the pound.'

I asked him what he was going to do. I remember the afternoon sun catching his face as he said:

'I feel' (he always said 'I feel' rather than 'I think'), 'I'd like to take a trip around the world.'

'You want money for that,' I said. I ought not to have said that. He was on to me at once. Scornfully he said:

'Money! That is one thing this has taught me: I don't want money ever again.'

It was I who went home in a suicidal state of mind and not an energetic one either. He looked like being a costly father.

These events in my father's life occurred at a time when my own affairs were in a state of emotional bankruptcy. There had been a sad flaw in my Irish marriage from the start, and wounds can become too appealing and engrossing. My wife and I had both thrown over, long before, the religion that had deceived us. Travel had distracted; we had the sense eventually to be a good deal apart. It is bad when difficult marriages become too interesting. We separated finally and, since we had no children, this was simple.

I had gone to live in a studio in Hampstead. I wondered if I should ever be fully in love. I was excited by the company of women, but the excitement seemed never to go beyond the sexual to a love of the person. Obviously I was one of those who must wait for the *coup de foudre*. Better the certainty of instinct than the muddle of too much thought.

The *coup* came, of course. I knew my present wife scarcely at all before she came to my studio, but at the first passing sight of her I remember my eyes had filled with strange tears. My old, romantic landscaping of girls vanished. I loved instantly the voice and the way she laughed. I *knew* without asking any more. When I spoke to her I scarcely listened to what she said, nor do I think she listened to me. This evening in 1934 – it was appropriately Guy Fawkes Night with the London sky starred by rockets – we skipped away from the door of a political meeting which (we were glad to hear from each other), did not interest either of us. A genius of some kind united us as we got away on a bus in Tottenham Court Road, and the genius has not left us since. We went to Wales where an amorous and eloquent Welsh farmer who came to her mother's house exclaimed that she 'had the bloom on her'. In 1936, when I was divorced, we were married in Hampstead Town Hall and set off to Paris. Everyone, it seemed to me, gazed at her in the cafés, the restaurants and cabarets we went to, and late at night we went laughing up the stairs of our hotel in the Rue Monsieur le Prince, not to the 'cinquième' but something much better. The only bad omen was that there were only refugees from Germany in the Dôme. We went back to a cottage by the sea in Dorset for a few weeks, where I finished a book and played dominoes as the October gales whacked at the roof. From now on I began to live: I became the father of a daughter and a son. Passion had brought out in me the repressed male instinct for responsibility, and I think passion alone among human feelings is the root of this instinct.

I had told my parents of my coming divorce. Father put on his affronted look at first. (He had, I heard, been beside himself with rage when one of his secretaries had got married.) I believe he thought he alone had the right to be divorced. But he got over the offence quickly. He used to drop in at my studio unexpectedly. He felt he would like a studio. The young woman was not there. He pointed out that until the divorce I would have to pay tax as a single man. And another idea had occurred to him.

'Have you made a will?' he asked.

'No,' I said.

'Well,' he reflected a while and then brightened. 'There's no need to. If anything happened to you it would come to me. I'm the next of kin now.'

So he revealed, all innocently, one of the reasons for the fight he had put up against all marriages. He had a longing for his children to belong to him alone, and for himself to rest in the solid sublimity of being next of kin. When we all disappointed him, he moved ambitiously towards becoming next of kin to my Aunt and Uncle in Ipswich, a ticklish campaign that went on for years, but here he was to be out-manoeuvred.

But when he met my future wife her warmth delighted him. The country boy was glad she came from a family of Welsh country people and farmers; he felt vicariously re-united to the land of his boyhood. He mentioned old Yorkshire farmers he remembered; and, not to be chauvinistic, uttered the names of a few Welsh hotels he had stayed at when he was on the road, and named the big Welsh-owned shops in London. He felt at once that here was a young woman in whom he could confide certain discoveries he had lately made, certain truths which would be helpful to us. Within half an hour he was blushing with his latest revelation:

'You see, dear, I have no income. And if you haven't an income, you've got nothing coming in. That's the point.'

And to me, he said, in congratulation: 'I like a girl I can put my arm round.'

True to his emotions he did not come to our wedding in Hampstead Town Hall, nor, since she never moved without him, did my mother; there was no hostility in this though there may have been a sense of propriety.

CHAPTER ELEVEN

In the thirties my life changed completely. I was no longer
the industrious apprentice. Praise – so necessary to writers –
gave me confidence. It surprised me. The act of writing excites
me, but I have little sense of the merits or demerits of my work,
though I have been obliged to recognize its general limitations.
All writers know the gap between aspiration and performance
and it plagues them. But I am curious to know why I have
written this way and not that. If I began to write better it was
for two reasons: in my thirties I found my contemporaries and
fell happily and deeply in love. There is, I am sure, a direct
connection between passionate love and the firing of the
creative power of the mind. I am no believer in the moral of *La
Peau de chagrin* or Shaw's theory of the necessity of abstinence.
The mind of the restrained or sexually discontented man wan-
ders off into shallows. My mind had been abroad too long in a
double sense: not simply in France, Ireland or Spain, but in
a manner that had used only half of myself. Finding my English
contemporaries, I found myself.

I had always dragged behind and, in fact, I was a few years
older than most of the writers who became well-known at this
period. The social conscience of a generation had been aroused.
The cause of our anger lay in our powerlessness in a society
ruled by torpid old men. One could not go to an industrial town
without seeing the terrible sight of unemployed men walking
the streets, ten yards apart from one another and never speaking, wandering from shop window to shop window. I had
known the smell of poverty in Camberwell and Bermondsey.
Our powerlessness had a half-forgotten source in the huge
casualties of the 1914 war. We who had been too young for it
were left with few immediate elders to help us in our contacts
with the old. We simply collided with those elders and got the
worst of it. We began to feel our strength, though unavailingly,
when the Spanish Civil War broke out. I found myself making
speeches at meetings on behalf of the Republican cause. Only

three or four people in England – my friends Gerald Brenan and Franz Borkenau among them – knew anything at all about Spaniards or Spanish history and we saw a new Spain imposed on the reality: this new Spain was not Spain but an export of European ideologies and conflicts across the Pyrenees: Fascism, Communism and European foreign policies. The Civil War on the Republican side was at first a traditional popular rising such as had occurred at the time of the Napoleonic invasion. It sprang from the popular hatred of the disastrous Moroccan war and the resentment in every town and village against conscription. It was a characteristic example of the *furia española*, long expected during the lethargy of the twenties and was doomed to disintegration, especially when the foreigners intervened, for regionalism had for centuries been a force: the unity of the country existed only on paper.

On the Franco side there was the traditional resort to the grim authoritarianism of the Army and the Church. He intended the traditional *coup d'état* but, especially because he came from Morocco, he was felt to be an invader. The reformist ideas of the Spaniards I had known were swept away. Among those murdered I think of Melquiados Alvarez, briefly a Prime Minister. He was an Asturian lawyer with whom I used to sit talking in his garden in Madrid. He was, fatally, a liberal. I think of Lorca reading his poems to a small party of us – murdered too: Unamuno going out of his mind in Salamanca and other friends escaping into exile. The list is long. It was certain, as one set of intervening foreigners after another went through the process of disillusion, that the Spaniards would settle this civil war in their own violent and cruel way; and that for ourselves, this was the first act of the Second World War. In London clubs, usually so good-natured, there were violent quarrels and they were mainly between those under forty and those older.

Spaniards came to our flat. Among them were two who brought a note of farce that ended during the war in a sinister manner. One was a bouncing Spanish journalist who began working in the Spanish Embassy when the Civil War started, under Perez de Ayala, the Ambassador of the Republic. Ayala was an excellent novelist of the intellectual kind, comic, brainy and poetic by turns. He was one of the best talkers in Madrid.

His portraits of members of the government were wickedly entertaining and I loved his novels and his company. He was a man of vocabulary. One of the pleasantest things in the Spanish life of that time for myself was the unaffected willingness of distinguished Spaniards to throw away hour after hour in good talk. No pomposity, no sense of their importance cut them off. They lived in their own fascination with being timelessly human.

I shall call the journalist Paco. He was young, fat and had a stentorian voice. He loved long cigars. He would make loud intimate remarks about his physical state wherever he was. In a club he would bawl across a crowded room, a sentence like:

'My testicles are blown-up like footballs. I cannot sleep with anyone.'

This Sancho Panza hated intellectuals and was always jeering at my views about Spain, but we were on affectionate terms. His constant companion was a rich and fashionable Spanish professor, a dandy and anglophil who had houses in Spain, France and London. He had his yacht and his private aircraft and a notably upper-class English accent. These two friends were born to plague each other and used to drop in on us at late hours and stop half the night. Sometimes a very proper Englishman from the Foreign Office with bowler hat and rolled umbrella would drop in too and reveal an improbable side to his character. He was Rodney Gallop, one of the few English writers who could speak Basque. He could sing Basque songs. Paco would mock the professor's English accent.

'Do you hear that? He says he lives at Sevenoaks. Say Sevenoaks.' Blamelessly the professor said it.

'Do you hear – Sevenucks. Sevenucks.' He chanted it. The professor countered now and then by making fun of Paco's sex life.

'Have you heard about his testicles? Typical Spanish Puritan. All talk about sex, no performance.'

In a few months a change came over Paco. I went to see him at the Embassy. He looked at the door: 'I'm surrounded by spies.'

Naturally: he had become a secret supporter of Franco. We had a violent quarrel about this and we ceased to be friends. I saw him once driving a Rolls Royce down Piccadilly, the picture of happiness, with a long cigar in his mouth. And then, in the Second World War, I found him sitting next to me at dinner where the professor was also a guest, and a young naval officer just back from the Russian convoy. The two Spaniards did their turn. Joyfully they accused each other across the table of being German agents. In the middle of this, Paco was called to the telephone and when he came back, he said to me, in a very changed way:

'I wish we were friends again like we used to be.'

Within a week he was deported to Spain. He was a German contact. Or so the Professor said. The Professor said he had turned him in. I've never seen Paco since; in Madrid I could never trace him after the war. I couldn't help enjoying his follies.

In the thirties those who came from the upper middle class and who had been to Public Schools and the old Universities were easily drawn towards Communism because of the discipline, the training for leadership, the team spirit and élitism at these places. To some Marxism was for a time a scripture and not having met anyone in the working class up till then, they tried guiltily, masochistically and idealistically to get in touch with them, often making absurd declarations of feeling inferior. I was brought up very differently. I had been to school with working-class boys and girls. My parents and relations, my grandfather, the bricklayer, my eccentric great uncle, the cabinet-maker, my mother the shop girl and my father the errand boy and shop assistant in Kentish Town, had belonged originally to this class. Marxism as a dogma could have no appeal to me, but as a way of analysing society and of presenting the interplay of class and history, it stimulated. The fundamentalism and the totalitarian consequences of Marxism were naturally repugnant to one like myself who had been through this mill in a religious form. It would be impossible for me to become a Communist or a Roman Catholic after that; and, in any case, I was constitutionally a non-believer. Rarely have the active politicals had a deep regard for imaginative literature. Writers are notoriously given to ambivalence, and live by giving themselves to the free mingling of fact and imagination.

So although when the Spanish Civil War came I was ardent for the Popular Front, I was much less interested in the 'People' than in the condition of individual people. I was particularly concerned with their lives and speech. In their misleading sentences and in the expressive silences between would lie the design of their lives and their dignity. Sometimes ordinary speech is banal and it is always repetitive, but, if selected with art, it could reveal the inner life, often fantastic, concealed in the speaker. This was the achievement of Henry Green in novels like *Living* and *Back*; and in Hemingway's best stories. Up till now in English literature the 'common' people had been presented as 'characters', usually comic. I had a curious conversation with H. G. Wells about this. I asked him to tell me about Gissing, who had taken his working class and lower middle class people seriously, so that to my mind he was closer to the Russian tradition than ours. Wells began, in his sporty way:

'The trouble with Gissing was that he thought there was a difference between a woman and a lady, but we all know there is no difference at all.'

But when I asked if it were possible to present, say, a lower-middle class man or woman seriously and not as a comic character, he reflected and said 'No.' My opinion was and is that it is, of course, possible; and that the essence is not funniness but militancy. I have rarely been interested in what are called 'characters' i.e. eccentrics; reviewers are mistaken in saying I am. They misread me. I am interested in the revelations of a nature and (rather in Ibsen's fashion) of exposing the illusions or received ideas by which they live or protect their dignity. On the other hand, in the preoccupation with common speech which I suppose I owe to my story-telling mother and to listening closely to Spaniards and others abroad, I did not follow more than I could help the documentary realism that was fashionable in the thirties. The storyteller either digests or contemplates life for his own purposes. The story is a flash that suddenly illumines, then passes.

I write this to explain how I came to write a story called 'Sense of Humour', the first one of mine to make a stir and give me what reputation I have as a writer of short stories. It has appeared in dozens of anthologies and has been broadcast in many languages. The tale had long been in my mind. I had written two or three versions, including one long explanatory one in the third person. None of these seemed right to me. They suffered from the vice of exposition or explanation. I put them aside and eventually saw there was another method; it is pretty obvious, but it had not occurred to me. A now forgotten Welsh writer, Dorothy Edwards, had written a story, in the first person, in which a character unconsciously reveals his obtuseness by assuming an air of reasonableness and virtue; and, in Hemingway, I found the vernacular put to similar use. The words spoken were so arranged as to disclose or evoke silently the situation the people were trying in their awkward way to conceal. The main source of my tale was that commercial traveller I had met in Enniskillen ten years before, who took his girl for rides in his father's hearse. My task was to make him tell his fantastic tale as flatly and meanly as possible, and to see his life through his eyes alone. The tale was written almost entirely in dialogue. I had little recollection of my original but I had known many sàlesmen of his kind, in whose minds calculation plays a large part. I have often been asked to explain the tale; some people found it shocking and cruel, others poetic, others deeply felt, others immoral and irresponsible, others highly comical. The most intelligent interpretations came from French and German critics, thirty-five years after it was written. (I am pretty sure that although I am often described as a traditional English writer, any originality in my writing is due to having something of a foreign mind.) My own suspicion is that the tale is a 'settling' of my personal Irish question; and I am certain that if one is writing well, it is because one is at a point where one is able to define things hitherto undefined in one's own mind or even unknown to one until then.

I am more interested in the question of the 'foreign' strain. Questions of class were very important in the thirties and in giving my uncouth character a voice I was consciously protesting against the dominance of the voice of what is called the high bourgeois sensibility. My narrator was not a 'character' – in the traditional sense– though he was extraordinary. The world he lived in was one of vulgar push and self-interest that was changing the nature of English society. In the next twenty years one would see that England was packed with people like him and his rootless friends. His emergence as a type is commonly misunderstood by literary critics who, owing to the stamp that Dickens and Wells put upon him in their time, have thought of the lower-middle class or petty bourgeois as whimsical 'little men'. But in this century all classes have changed and renewed themselves; they have certainly released themselves from the cosy literary categories of the nineteenth century and carry inside them something of the personal anarchy of unsettled modern life. My own roots are in this class and I know it like the palm of my hand. (The standard view that it is inevitably Fascist is crude and untrue.) In the writing, American influence – particularly of Hemingway – is clear and both from a literary point of view and a social one, this was natural.

I do not write this to claim any great merit for the tale. I am clinically concerned with it as something new in my own life which was brought about by the times and the emancipation my new marriage had given me. I had become real at last. I worked for months on this story, for in writing there is a preliminary process of unwriting, and ideas are apt to be dressed in conventional literary garb in the first instance. (In considering the character of Prince Myshkin in *The Idiot*, Dostoyevsky seriously considered Mr Pickwick as a starting point.) A good story is the result of innumerable rejections. Also, very often, of rejections that are more painful. 'Sense of Humour' was turned down by all likely publications in England and America. I put it away with the feeling that I had made one more bloomer. Then, at last, John Lehmann's *New Writing* appeared and he published it. I got £3 for the story. I cannot say that I woke up to find myself famous but I had modestly arrived. It is a pleasant and also curious experience. I loved being congratulated, especially publicly in restaurants. One admirer, only an acquaintance at the time, and a comically shame-faced womanizer, begged me to introduce him to the girl in the story for whom he had fallen. I had drawn her from several models, but chiefly from a girl I had glanced at in the desk of an Irish hotel. The important thing for me was the story woke me up. It led me on to 'The Sailor', 'The Saint' and 'Many are Disappointed', which became far better known.

When I was writing for the *New Statesman* in these early days, David Garnett was the literary editor and in one of our talks about writing novels he said that when one could not get on with a book, one should create an extra difficulty. That did not help me because difficulty of all kinds surrounds me in writing and writing has always seemed to me the result of being able to throw innumerable temptations from the mind. I have an impatient character; for every page I write there are half a dozen thrown away. The survivors are criss-crossed with deletions. I went through a long period of talking to myself when I went for a walk and again and again I would catch myself saying, with passion, two words: The End. Not necessarily the end of a story or an essay, but the end of the confusion, the end of the statement or sentence. My weakness for images was caused by the poet's summary instinct. I have had to conclude that I am a writer who takes short breaths and in consequence the story or the essay have been the best forms for me and early journalistic training encouraged this.

Because of its natural intensity the short story is a memorable if minor literary genre. There is the fascination of packing a great deal into very little space. The fact that form is decisive concentrates an impulse that is essentially poetic. The masters of the short story have rarely been good novelists: indeed the short story is a protest against the discursive. Tolstoy and Turgenev are exceptions, but Maupassant wrote only one novel of any account: *Une Vie*. Chekhov wrote no novels. D. H. Lawrence seems to me more penetrating as a short story writer than as a novelist. An original contemporary, Jorge Luis Borges, finds the great novels too loose. He is attracted to Poe's wish for the work of art one can see shaping instantly to the eye: the form attracts experiment. It is one for those who like difficulty, who like to write 150 pages in order to squeeze out twenty. At the time of the Spanish war when I had to go to a protest meeting in an industrial town, one of the speakers interested me. I wrote two pages about her and gave up. From year to year I used to look at this aborted piece. No difficulty: no progress. Suddenly, after twenty years I saw my chance. When one is making a speech one is standing with one's body and life exposed to the audience: the sensation is frightening.

Write a story in which a woman making a speech in her public voice is silently telling by the private voice her own life story *while* she declaims something else. To do this was extremely difficult. One learns one's craft and craftsmanship is not much admired nowadays, for the writer is felt to be too much in control; but, in fact, the writer has always, even if secretively, to be in control. And there is the supreme pleasure of putting oneself in by leaving oneself out.

I have written six volumes of short stories and many others that have never appeared in book form. I am surrounded, as writers are, by the wreckage of stories that are half done or badly done. I believe in the habit of writing. In one dead period when I thought I had forgotten how to write, I set myself a well-known exercise which Maupassant, Henry James, Maugham and Chekhov were not too grand to try their hands at. It is the theme of the real, false or missing pearls. I was so desperate that I had to say to myself 'I will write about the first person I see passing the window.' It happened by ill luck (for I thought I knew little about the trade) to be a window cleaner. Whatever, may be thought of this story – I myself do not like the end, which should have been far more open – it revealed to me as I wrote two things of importance in the creative imagination. The first: there is scarcely a glint of invented detail in this tale; it is a mosaic that can be broken down into fragments taken from things seen, heard or experienced from my whole life, though I never cleaned a window or stole a pearl. The second thing – and this is where the impulse to write was *felt* and not willed – is the link with childhood. To write well one must never lose touch with that fertilizing time. And, in this story, some words of my mother's about her father came back to me. He was a working gardener and coachman. It was part of the legend of her childhood that one morning his employer's wife called 'Lock the drawers: the window cleaner is coming.' I did not write about my grandfather but the universal myth relating to theft came brimming into my mind.

The Irish, the Italians, the Russians and the Americans have an instinctive gift for the short story. Alberto Moravia once told me that the Italian successes in this form and their relative failure in the novel is due to the fact that the Italian is so conceited that he dare not look long and steadily at his face in the mirror. I would have thought that the gift is due to the Italian's delight in the impromptu. Frank O'Connor used to say that the form is natural to societies where the element of anarchy is strong and the pressure of regard for society is weak. In English literature we indeed had to wait for the foreign rootlessness and rawness of Kipling before we had a master. Once discovered, this quickly appeared in Saki, in D. H. Lawrence, in the pastorals of A. E. Coppard and T. F. Powys, in Walter de la Mare, Max Beerbohm, H. E. Bates, Elizabeth Taylor, Frank Tuohy, James Stern and Angus Wilson. Late starters, we have done well.

Towards the end of the pre-war time I wrote one more novel. It was called *Dead Man Leading*. The subject was the search for a missing explorer. I had avidly read the lives of Livingstone, the African missionaries, the account of Cheke and Burton. One particularly, the experience of a Frenchman, Caillie, on the Niger – he got to Timbuktoo – especially interested me because of his almost comical masochism. I had detected this characteristic, I thought, in Captain Scot, in Steffansson, whom I had met, and in others who seem to have chosen hardship. The Fawcett story offered a suggestion, though mine had nothing to do with it. I attempted a psychology of exploration. I chose the Amazon for my expedition because I knew the literature of the Amazon well. I constructed a small model of my bit of the river in the garden of a cottage we had rented in Hampshire and, for the rest, consulted a large number of missionary diaries in the British Museum. Missionaries always write down the practical detail. I was stuck at one moment for some items about Manaos which I could not find in books or photographs. One evening when I was returning from London with a rather drunken businessman in the train he told me all about the city. He had just come on leave from a bank there. This novel was more imaginative than my earlier ones; but it came out not long before the war started and that killed it.

More than ten years passed before I wrote another.
At the time of Munich we were living in a flat in a large house overlooking the canal close to London's 'Little Venice'.

Strings of painted barges went by bearing the water gipsies who were still part of London life. I worked in what had been the linen room of this Victorian house and there I helped a young Jewish boxer rewrite his novel about prize-fighting in the East End. In addition to reading for a publisher, I reviewed books, I wrote a story which indicated my angry political mood: it was a satire about a country which was suddenly abandoned by the public statues of its great men who were disgusted by the decadence of its government. The story was too clumsy to be published in any of my collections and I long ago lost the manuscript. I was also working on a short documentary film which was never produced but which introduced me to the extraordinary language of film directors. I was told someone had 'alibied his idealism over on to documentary'. The early documentaries were the first attempt to put a real England, as distinct from the phoney American version, on the screen.

After Munich we saw war was inevitable. Our daughter was a year old; my wife was pregnant again. We wisely went to live in the country. I got out my bicycle, for we did not own a car, and pedalled over Berkshire until I found an empty, isolated, farmhouse in the Lambourn valley, eight miles from Newbury – horse-racing country. Owing to the long decline of English agriculture at the beginning of the century such houses were cheap. I paid £1 a week for a sedate, solid, ivy-covered Georgian house of the spacious farming kind, a place with a large walled garden and apple orchard. The garden ran down to the spring-fed Lambourn river which flooded when the white water buttercups came out. This pleasant place was called Maidencourt – a mis-spelling of Midden-court, I suppose. It lay down a blind lane ending at the railway crossing of the little Lambourn branch line; and then continued as a footpath across the Downs behind us to the Roman Ridgeway above Wantage. From the top there, on a clear day, we could see the spires of Oxford. My wife and I often cycled to Oxford – a good fifty miles there and back – during the war when clothes were scarce, in search of things for our children. I mention this footpath, for it can be easily identified in Thomas Hardy's *Jude the Obscure*, his topography is always minutely exact and is part of his concern with human circumstances. I once saw something close to one of the scenes in this novel enacted in the farmyard behind our house. There were shouts and laughter one afternoon and when I went out to see what was happening I found a girl chasing the farm lads with castrating scissors.

There had always been a farm on our site since Domesday. We had no gas or electricity; our water was pumped down by a windmill on the hill. By hard work in the coal shed, cutting wood, using paraffin stoves, and wearing thick clothes we kept warm. We set about growing huge quantities of vegetables. When Chamberlain finished his short announcement that war had been declared, I solemnly sowed two long rows of turnip seeds. The first winter of the war was fierce. The trees, the blades of grass, the cattle in the fields, were encased in a glaze of ice for nearly three months. One seemed to be walking on breaking glass. Our old-fashioned pump broke down; when my son was born we had no tap water for weeks. We got dozens of buckets from the frozen stream and our pond, and from a house half a mile away. The first water carrying journeys exhausted me, but soon I got uncommonly strong and carried my load as any farm hand does. All telephone wires were, of course, down and one had to walk for miles to get the doctor. I must say I enjoy things going wrong; later on, when the war made every simple act of living difficult, so that I seemed perpetually bicycling to Newbury or Hungerford and back with shopping swinging from the handlebars, I was in excellent health. Domestically, the hardships of the war were felt most heavily by the women, especially by young mothers, like my wife.

We spent the next seven years or so at Maidencourt, the longest time until then I had ever lived in one house. In the war period I kept a diary, as bleakly factual as I could make it, but I am not a natural diarist. I lack the secretive, snail-like temperament, and, I was also so busy writing and reading all day that there was little energy left for making notes. It is all second-rate stuff, but I am surprised by my political outbursts about the state of English society. The war was most of the time a siege for us; we were imprisoned; and I find myself expressing the general view that English society must be revolutionized.

English country life is utterly different from urban life. Because elections were suspended in local government and because I lived in a house of some consideration locally I found myself obliged to become chairman of our Parish Council and had to represent it at the District Council in Hungerford: absurd appointments for an unpractical townee like myself. When the owner of the local Big House, a charming retired colonel, was about to leave the district he invited me to become Chairman of the local Conservative Association. I said I could not do this because I was a Socialist. He replied, 'I don't see that makes any difference.' He sincerely meant it. The war, it is true, did revolutionize life in the countryside eventually. In the Lambourn valley, when I first went there, I found many older labourers who could speak Spanish. When sheep-farming collapsed around 1900 they had been forced to emigrate to the Argentine and Patagonia.

My diary noted these things, but it is mostly a mixture of groans, observations about the weather, the crowd of people who came down to get out of London for a night's sleep, and war incidents. A parachute comes floating down from the sky 'with no man attached'. Spent bullets hit the walls. Bombs fall miles away but in the country sound travels and you think the bomb is in the garden, because every nail in the floorboards gives a jump. I find a comic entry.

Nov. 22nd. A gale all night walloping about *inside* the roof as well as bumping outside the windows and bringing down branches on to the cowshed. Awakened at 5 a.m. by two loud ringing explosions as hard as pick on stone. Lay, heart beating violently, rigid, listening if the children had been woken up. They were not, at least they didn't cry. Then I got out of bed to see what I could out of the window, stubbed my toe. My curses woke up everyone. The baker said 'they' dropped at Kintbury and killed two cows and a horse.

And another entry, too long to quote here, describes one of those short fierce air raids of the last year of the war. I sat at the top of a house in Hampstead recording the fantastic firework display of the London barrage, the sky rippling with magnesium rain, and the carrot-coloured fires. Every object in the house, every cup and saucer, jumped and rattled, and spent shrapnel – or whatever it was – came rattling down against the walls. Sometimes one was excited, sometimes careless in these raids. Sometimes angry or scornful. Once Louis MacNeice and I wandered down the streets in St John's Wood and tried, unsucessfully, to carry away a stone lion from the garden of a destroyed house. The thing was too heavy. But in the raid I was describing, our fears were allayed by John Betjeman, who kept us laughing by assuring a child's teddy bear that he and the bear were all right because they had been to confession, whereas the rest of us, as non-Christians, would certainly be in hell any moment. After a couple of hours the raid was over and then I discovered how terrified I had been: I could not speak clearly because one end of my upper lip had risen up and was stuck to my right nostril. I was not a man who could keep a stiff upper lip. I must have been looking like a rabbit.

There is another note about an evening with George Orwell, who in the melancholy way of one who had been trained for duty when he was young and was inured to suffering, rather liked the war, for he saw it as a fight against the governing class as well as a fight against the Nazis. I went to a flat he had taken at the top of an apartment block; the beauty of the place (to him) was that one could more easily get out on to the roof to put out fire bombs if one lived on the top floor. His health had been ruined by the wound he had got in Spain and he had the strange lonely detachment and fevered half-laughing energy of the sick.

My life was harassed but prosaic. My business on the Parish Council was to stop farmers from letting their cows out, getting the water buttercups cut in the stream when the springs rose, and making plans for the burial of the dead when the Germans invaded us. I joined the Local Defence Volunteers, later the Home Guard, and armed with a tin hat, a Winchester and ten rounds of ammunition, sat up in a thresher's hut at night, waiting for parachutists and listening to the bombers grinding over after 1940. We were thankful to be out of London, for the flats behinds ours in Maida Vale had been blown to bits. The hut on the downs belonged to our sergeant, whose father had been a travelling thresher. He loved the hut because he had had measles in it when he was a boy. It was sacred to him; we were defending not the nation, but the hut and his childhood, and his feeling epitomized what everyone felt about this depressing and unwanted war. The hut had bunks, a stove for making tea; our strong point. One night a drunken roadster tried to get in: four of us marched him away for a mile while he sang Army songs to us and started to show us the scars on his chest. He was our only invader.

In our squad there were the thresher, a shepherd turned gardener; a farmer whose child was dying, a baker's boy who later fought in Burma and an eager simple youth who lived with a blind couple. When we were issued with bayonets he was in ecstasies: he practised bayonet thrusts in the parlour of the cottage while the blind couple sat in the room with him. There was a bit of a row at the hut one night at a time when German aircraft were passing over, because the gardener and I went out on guard and gathered glowworms which he arranged round the brim of his hat so that it was like a phosphorescent halo. Our sergeant said a German plane could easily see them. If the invasion came we were supposed to join up with the Lambourn troop, mainly stable boys; but our lot all agreed they wouldn't do anything to defend Lambourn, a delinquent little place, but would rush home to defend their wives. One summer evening we took turns at trying a very long shot at a hare sat up with its ears pricked in a cornfield. We fired twenty rounds but got nowhere near it. We were as touching a rustic group as any out of Thomas Hardy. I read Gibbon's account of his time in the militia in 1759; his was a drunken regiment. It was difficult for us to get a glass of beer in the country during the war. I grew to have a deep affection for the villagers. The experience stirred me and I wrote a radio play about Gibbon's farcical conflicts with his drunken father in the militia. Like Elizabeth Bowen, Louis MacNeice, Rayner Heppenstall and others, I wrote several radio plays during the war. Before the war the B.B.C. did not care for Left Wing people; and indeed I saw in a producer's list a note about myself. It said: 'Embittered, left wing intellectual.'

Among my wartime obligations was to do fire watching on the roof of the *New Statesman* every now and then. I was

fortunate. There were no air raids on that battered neighbourhood on the nights I was there, but I had arrived one morning
at the beginning of the Blitz to discover it was one of the
only buildings left in Great Turnstile. I climbed through fallen
ceiling rubble and glass in the office to be ordered out by a
policeman who said two unexploded bombs were lying outside. I was trying to deliver my weekly article. The editors had
moved off to the top floor of a printing works, under a glass
roof. I had to walk to the south of the river to it. Under all that
glass one's proof corrections got jumpy when the sirens went
and one's stomach turned over.

The War, as I have said, was an imprisonment. It brought
me into touch with my fellow prisoners in an England I knew
little about: the England of factory workers. I went for weeks
to shipyards; to engineering works, marshalling yards and
railway control centres. I became a documentary reporter. I
spent a short time in an aircraft carrier off the coast of Scotland.
It is fascinating simply to see strange things, though I saw so
many that each experience wiped out the one that preceded it.
I was very conscious of being thinned away to the condition of
voyeur. One particular experience sums up my role. Just after
the Rundstedt offensive, I was sent for a week or two to the
front line Radio Station in Luxembourg when the Germans
were only ten miles away. Since I had been too young for the
1914 war and was too old to serve in this one, I had the common, romantic civilian guilt and it was appeased in the nights
when the Germans sent small rockets into the town and made
the air smell of burned rubber. It was further appeased when I
cadged a lift off a truck-load of American technicians who were
going up to Trier, which had just been captured. I described the
experience in a long article which was published in the *New
Statesman* and often reprinted so I will say little more, beyond
telling the one ludicrous incident.

We seemed to be travelling as we got near to Trier under an
arcade of mild shell-fire and arrived in the town, which was
mostly a mound of stinking damp rubble. The technicians soon
revealed their real purpose. We were really on a semi-looting
expedition: the idea was to dig motor cycles out of a ruined
factory. We were all afraid of snipers – I especially – and of the

Military Police. As we got to the factory, one of their jeeps went by: on the bonnet they had set the town drunk as a mascot. They had put an opera hat on his head: with his simpleton's grin, he added to one's horror of the destruction. When the M.P.s had gone we got into the courtyard of the factory. The weather was wet: the crew were encumbered with sten guns, rifles and other weapons. They had to get rid of their arms while they clambered into the ruins. I was the solution to their difficulty. They asked me to mind their guns. They hung them on me. I stood there in the rain for an hour, a human coat stand, a grotesque and passive human explosive. The expedition failed and we went on to other likely spots. I came away with a couple of bottles of Moselle, a copy of *Le Grand Meaulnes* which I took from a wrecked house – an apposite but characteristically literary choice. Writers always steal books. The only time I was ever singled out as a target in the war was back in Luxembourg: a trigger-happy American fired a couple of rounds at me after curfew. I heard bullets sing past my ears, as in books writers say they do. I took the shots as an uninvited compliment.

There is not much more to say about the war. In one of Elizabeth Bowen's stories a character is made to say of the Blitz – and by extension of the war itself: 'It will have no literature.' In that sense it was like a car smash or pile-up. English writing did not vanish, but for years the experience exhausted us mentally and physically. And then there is nothing as dead as a dead war and, as the pace quickens, the latest war kills the one before it quickly. One is ridiculous to be still alive and the best thing is to keep one's mouth shut. Looking at the war egotistically from a writer's point of view, it was a feverish dispersal and waste of one's life. It is often said that this was a good time, when all private defences gave way, especially the defence of class differences, and that we all came together for once; and one hears regrets that after the war this revolution spent itself and that we went back to our old privacy. We did; though not to the old kind. I am not sure that to be so drowned in the mass was good for the act of writing, for the kind of humanity required of artists is not the same thing as the united public humanness we felt as citizens. A writer soon finds himself wondering how large a helping of human beings his talents can manage, without being swamped by the huge amount of social reality that is forced upon him. The unconscious benefits may be deep; the anarchy of war is a release for a time: the ultimate effects are indirect.

I felt my own case to be uncommonly like my father's when he was taken away from his business by the 1914 war. From that he did not recover. I was luckier: I think I can say, without conceit, that I did recover, but I too was changed. I became a literary critic and in the bizarre circumstances I have just described. I had, of course, been a reviewer, but a more reflective kind of criticism now took up most of the time the war left to me. Although my criticism has been praised, I am not sure that the change was totally for the good. I shall glance at some of the circumstances.

Younger contributors to the *New Statesman* were called into the services and government organizations, so it became my job to write the leading literary article for the paper, almost every week. Since few new books were published, Kingsley Martin and Raymond Mortimer decided that the article must deal with a rereading of the classics. I had to sandwich this task between my war jobs. Maidencourt was a good quiet place for long blinding spells of reading and writing; and though I was often dragged out of it, the long, slow train journeys – it often took five hours to get from Newbury to London, gave more time for reading. The trains were crowded but usually people were too stunnned to talk. So, one week the subject might be Sir Walter Scott, the next Dostoyevsky, after that Benjamin Constant, George Fox, Zola, Gil Blas and so on. When I look now upon the long list of such essays, they seem to fly about or droop like washing on a clothes line. Two thousand words was the limit. In the first year the tone was nervous: my writing is filled in with hesitant or forensic phrases; I was writing against time. I had read widely but I had never 'done' Eng. Lit., French Lit., or Russian Lit. I had no critical doctrine – a shock later on to the platoons of New Critics and later regiments – for critical doctrine is of little interest to the novelist, though it may mean something to the poet. The tendencies of the thirties persuaded me to the historical situation of the

411

writer who was being enjoyed first and *then* examined. We were fond of calling ourselves victims of an age of transition; but it seemed to me that this had been the lot of every writer of any distinction at any time. I was moved by attitudes to social justice; but presently I saw that literature grows out of literature as much as out of a writer's times. A work of art is a deposit left by the conflicts and contradictions a writer has in his own nature. I am not a scholarly man; and I am not interested for very long in the elaborate super-structures of criticism. Some of my critics speak of insights and intuitions; the compliment is often left-handed for these are signs of the amateur's luck; I had no choice in the matter. Anyone who has written a piece of imaginative prose knows how much a writer relies on instinct and intuition. The war had added to my knowledge of human nature. I appear as a disarranged stoic, a humanist with one wall of his room missing – an advantage there, I think, for all writing has one of its sources in the sense of a moral danger to which the writer is sensitive.

So a critic emerged from the hack. I attained a reputation in England and America and found that I was seriously split in two. I had the advantage of being an heir to the long and honourable tradition of serious periodical journalism; and of having, in a minor way, written imaginatively: I am aware of the novelist's methods. I cannot help putting myself in his position as he faces the empty page. I have always thought of myself – and therefore of my subjects – as being 'in life', indeed books have always seemed to be a form of life, and not a distraction from it. I see myself as a practising writer who gives himself to a book as he gives himself to any human experience.

I am very conscious when I am praised of what I owe to two friends who were of great help to me. The first is Raymond Mortimer, a brilliant literary editor who put me on to many writers I knew little about. When I am complimented on having dug up some forgotten author the compliment should go to him. In French and English he has read everything. He is sharp with the careless sentence. My tastes were not always his but his tolerance and friendship were invaluable. My other stand-by was one of the best talkers and letter-writers in England:

Gerald Brenan, who was writing his two great Spanish books at Aldbourne during the war. His village was about twelve miles from ours and we would bicycle over to see each other and have long conversations. He was and is an original, as diverting and yet as serious about life as he is about literature. He lives in a streaming imagination, yet he can be a very stern critic. He is a piquant mixture of the military man, the poet, the scholar and the traveller, and for him life exists to be turned into writing; and when one is with him, one seems to see this happening before one's eyes.

Beyond these two friends was the fatherly figure of Kingsley Martin, the complete and very histrionic Puritan, handsome, masochistic, a restless prophet who contained the fluctuating conscience of the Left and the most impressive if most infuriating editor of an English paper in our generation. He was tactless, affectionate, and (we used to say) was only cheerful when the news was bad. I could never draw the portrait of a man so complex; and there is no need to. He drew his own portrait very honestly and vividly in his own autobiography. He was Meredith's Dr Shrapnel to the life, for under his pacifism was a very violent man and a headlong rationalist.

I am appalled by the amount I have read. This reading has certainly distracted me from original work of my own: for myself – if not for the reader – one or two good stories are worth all the criticism in the world: the best criticism of a story is another story, of a play, another play. In my criticism, perhaps even more than my stories, I am self-portrayed. When I reread those essays written in such numbers over the last thirty years, I am surprised to see how much they are pitted with personal experience, and how much reaction to life itself, either nettled or expansive, has been packed into an epigram or an aside. In penetrating to the conflicts of authors, I have discovered and reflected on my own.

One thing the war did for me was to introduce me to gout. The country doctor glanced at my agonized big toe that looked like a red tulip and said I was suffering from a deficiency of vitamins. Since we finished our small meat ration in the first two days of every week, we lived plainly. Drink appeared only on Mondays and Tuesdays at the pub and I rarely was able to get a glass of wine. The disease recurred and it was not until a devastating attack when the war was over that it was diagnosed. I was on my way to Spain when I was crippled with it. I was told to take aspirins every two hours. I have always been ignorant about medicines for I have always had good health, except in my occasional phychosomatic periods, so I unknowingly over-dosed myself. I got to my hotel room in Barcelona, flopped on the bed and woke up twenty-four hours later with my hat and overcoat still on. Modern drugs have cured me. For a time I blamed my maternal grandmother, the gouty and bibulous old lady from Kentish Town, who had begun her life as a barmaid in Oxford. I supposed I had inherited the weakness from her; but I discovered that the cause lay, among other things, in living off liver and other offal during the war in order to make the meat ration go round. The disease used to attack me when I was about to undertake some long journey or some large piece of work. It drives one to contortions that make people laugh. It is said to stimulate the imagination and intellect and certainly, just before it occurs, one is in a state of startling illumination and euphoria, as happens – according to Dostoyevsky – before an attack of epilepsy.

CHAPTER TWELVE

I MUST go back to 1936 and the crisis in my father's life when his business went into liquidation. One does not expect one's father to fail; he is the hero. When, through weakness, he does so, one is shocked and, for some reason, guilty before the revelations that come out. It was awful to find out that the seeds of this downfall were sown long, long before, and to suspect the taint was in oneself. My austerity when I was young was due to dread of this. In one way the old gentleman was responsible for fathering a set of merciless prigs, and I think only our mother softened us with her strange alternations of disloyalty and decency. She knew her lot would always be a losing gamble and relieved the tedium by fits of vituperation.

What alarmed the rest of us was that this vigorous man was about to be let loose on the world or into a vacuum in which we would have him and his debt-creating genius on our hands. Our mother was ill and in a wretched state. His spry feats and deeply-shaded intrigues had one good effect on us: we were all scrupulous about money; but there was a bad effect. We were not exactly mean, but we had become liable to fits of un-imaginative caution, and mockery. We became wry-minded. We were relieved to have gone up in the world; but the more we knew or guessed about *Rydal Mount*, that solid-looking double-fronted villa in Bromley, the more it looked like a piece of Lake Poetry that had gone wrong. Was the house paid for? How was it paid for? I did not see my parents often and if they came to stay with us in London or Maidencourt my father talked only about food or God. Every two hours he needed nourishment, so between the three large main meals of the day, there had to be a sandwich or a plate of cakes to keep him going in his deck chair in the garden, where he dozed off over his religious pamphlets and woke anxiously listening for the sound of plates and cups. He needed food as he needed credit. As a guest he ate up the day and got very irritable because I worked.

He wanted, he demanded the whole attention of my wife and myself.

He would break into my study and with falsely whimsical voice would say, 'Haven't you done it, old boy?' He always complained that I was a pedestrian fellow; a shower of energizing Biblical remarks used to be thrown at me.

He would close the door and go away sadly. And then pretend to be fascinated when my wife typed what I wrote.

For my brothers and sister, who lived near to him and who saw him often, the matter was different. They were closer to atmospheric changes in his financial life. My brothers were in trades connected with his own. They had known of bank threats and court orders.

It was obvious that his salvation lay in converting his house into flats. But how could more money be raised and where would he live while the conversion was taking place? We trembled. My successful brother had been called to the rescue several times: the rest of us were poor and careful.

Father did *not* tremble. He was exhilarated for – and we were too stupid to realize this – the conversion would mean that he would have *two* dream houses and that the conversion itself would be a superb opportunity for expense. He got himself a temporary job at £4 a week in a Christian Science Reading Room, and left the task to the Divine Mind. I need hardly say that the Divine Mind turned up trumps. Down came the Manna; in came the architect and builders. The next job for the Divine Mind was to find 'alternative accommodation'. (It has struck me since that this modern phrase sums up my father's lifetime ideal. He was fond of quoting the Scripture: 'In my Father's house are many mansions.')

In one of my earliest returns to the house father casually mentioned (as I have related) the pine trees, the heather and the gorse of Hindhead in Surrey. Unknown to us, it had long been his secret intention to live there. The Divine Mind, for once, did nothing. Or, if you prefer, the Divine Mind produced one of its genuine miracles, a miracle so wonderful to the point of farce, so tragic in essence that I was bitter when I heard of it.

My mother, who never spent a penny on herself all her life and hated to go to the door of the house for fear of what legal document would be pushed into her hands, answered the door one day and, clean out of character, went mad and bought a vacuum cleaner from a doorstep salesman. The event is incredible in itself. It amazed, it frightened, it enraged my father when he came home. Having bought the thing she must have suddenly become frightened herself for she hid it behind her dressing table. When father spotted it he was stupefied, he saw he had a rival spender. He was even more put out to hear she was not in debt. She had paid for the machine out of her own pocket.

Where did she get the money? She told some fib about a little present she had had from her well-off sister who often slipped her a pound or two. Father was almost satisfied with this tale, but he was a meddling, ferreting, examining kind of man, and, feeling certain that the cleaner was a swindle of some kind at the expense of an ignorant woman, he got behind the dressing table to look at the machine. In doing so he stubbed his toe. I have mentioned the sensibility of my father's hands: his feet were no less sensitive. They were sentient and thinking feet. He discovered the kind of thing that always annoyed him in a house; some small imperfection which my mother, not having been born in a Yorkshire manse, would carelessly let go. He bent down. Monstrous: the carpet had been incorrectly laid. There was a lump in it. In a minute he had the corner of the carpet up and in his mother's plaintive voice complained of the dust. Under the carpet was a heap of silver coins. Eighty-three pounds, I have been told. My mother's secret savings of a lifetime. She mistrusted banks.

I know this story because my father himself told me it. He was laughing uncomfortably, red in the face, like a boy, abashed, ashamed, almost weeping: not with guilt but with admiration that out of the mouth of such a babe and suckling as our mother, such praise should come. As for herself, she was defeated. It was she who felt guilty, even dishonest. She wept. She confessed. Then after his emotion had died down, father asked the shrewd Yorkshire question: 'Is there any more?'

Mother, gratified by his display of feeling and destroyed by guilt, admitted there was. He had relied so much on the money of the detested Miss H, now jealousy had its victory.

'Yes,' she said.

'Where?'

I am glad I did not witness the scene. My father had the habit of hiding silver articles he had bought secretly among his underclothes. Mother had stuffed another £300 – it is said – in notes between sheets and blankets and in drawers all over the house. I doubt if there was as much. It was with this money that they set out for Hindhead – father's heaven – and found a pleasant little house there.

All conifers, heather, gorse, commons and hills my mother hated and father deeply loved, especially the pine-smelling air. He would stand by the Golden Valley entranced, taking it all into his exhilarated lungs. He loved the name itself: 'Golden Valley'. He said it aloud and he would brace his strong frame as if absorbing some mystical gold. Or because the name sounded like an advertisement, for he liked advertisements too. There was a richness in the air of this high Surrey region, for half hidden in the firs and coppices of birch, were the houses of prosperous businessmen. His local church had many well-off people.

He had moods when he was profoundly amused by himself, particularly in his brash or keen adventures – the salesman who has taken all by surprise or thought of an ingenious way to keep a foot in the door. He blushed when he told of these things – a blush of modest wonder at his genius; or at his disasters when the push landed him in trouble. He dwelled, for example, on a tale of going to see a Mr Y, whom he didn't know, the chairman of a Building Society or a bank; and having been refused an appointment, he decided to turn up at his private house, timing his arrival for about five-thirty when the gentleman would be home. How lovingly he told of the maid who asked him in to wait; how he appraised the furnishings of the library; how inquisitively he began to study some photographs on a desk, after half an hour; how suddenly he saw an alarming face. By accident, he had come to the wrong house. He had come to Mr X's not Mr Y's. There was Mr X's picture – and Mr X had firmly told him some weeks before that if he didn't pay some debt or other, there would be another Court Order. Father got out of the house as quickly as he could, unseen, as Mr X's car passed him at the gate. A narrow squeak.

418

Or again, at Hindhead, this aromatic spot, there was the incident of Lord G's hat. My father's attitude to lords was more north country and American, than the rather snobbish, respectful indifference of the South: if he saw a lord, his way was to go up and shake his hand in a brotherly way. He had gone to a party which seemed to offer opportunities in the prayer industry and there stood Lord G. Whether, from his account of it, my father ever shook Lord G by the hand I cannot say; but it is certain that Lord G was a very tall man with a small head who wore a sporting kind of trilby hat. My father was a short fat man with a large head. As he left the party, my father looked at the hats in the hall and decided by a mixture of accident and design to try on the hat of Lord G. He liked it. He left the party and walked home in it. Mother opened the door to let him in and there he was, modestly triumphant, with this absurd little hat on his head. I say no more. I do not know whether Lord G was in need of prayer at that time, but contact had been made. With extreme shyness, my father said: 'You never know.'

The interlude at Hindhead, beginning as it did with my mother's private miracle, was uncommonly restrained in one way: the villa was small. Here something odd happened to mother, too. She was in poor health; but worse, she was desperate and bored. She was a London girl. She hated Nature. She could not stand conifers; the only acceptable trees for her were the moody, changeable and deciduous. She hated quiet. She knew scarcely anyone in the neighbourhood and indeed my father was terrified that she would make a friend and let her tongue wag. It did wag when it got a chance.

So there was mother stuck among a lot of well-off stockbrokers and commons. A few whimpering telephone calls got through to us; but it became increasingly difficult to speak to her if one rang. Father owned the telephone and rarely were we allowed to speak to her. His egotism was so much more powerful and commanding than hers. She also feared the telephone as she feared the front door. Father commanded us one day to come down at once: she was terribly ill, he said. My wife and I hurried down. She was not ill at all. She was soon rocking with laughter. She was driven to tricks by his enormous righteousness. Obviously they had had one of their weekly

rows and he wanted a breather, for her response to his righteousness was always a wild theatrical scene. She loved 'dragging
up everything'. She got my father out of the room, gripped my
wrist, stared frantically into my eyes and slyly pulled down
some quantities of cloth from a cupboard. It was heavy, expensive material used for upholstering chairs, in gaudy colours
and with a cobbled surface and had what looked like threads
of metal in it. She held up a piece, then another piece and
another. She had been a shop-girl and shop girls have their
fancies when they are bored. While my father was in London mother had made up this cache of valuable material
into a dozen pairs of her obsessional garment: bloomers. She
slipped from the room and came back wearing a fantastic
pair in bright orange; then she pulled them off and tried
on pair after pair. They looked like sofas on her. The stuff was so
heavy that they stood almost upright on the floor, for a second
or two before they collapsed. She screamed with laughter.

'They ought to have had me in the business,' she said. 'I
used to be in the millinery.' She looked at me with her always
questioning look, half serious, half inviting me to join her
fantasy of father recovering his fortunes by manufacturing
upholstered bloomers. She sat down exhausted.

'You've got to do something in this hole or you get driven
out of your natural,' she said and her grey-green eyes filled
with tears.

This happened at the time of Munich. That year the flats were
finished, but had only one tenant. Anyone who could, was getting out of London. Father and mother did the opposite: they
returned to face the Blitz. The town of Bromley was badly
bombed during the war. A lot of the High Street and several
churches went up in flames. Some of the suburban streets
looked like jaws with rotting gaps in them. There were thousands of missing windows and cracked ceilings among the surviving houses. Here, to our consternation, my parents sat out the
whole war. They refused to move. They did come and stay in
the country with us but only in the mid-war lull when the raids
moved to the coast and provinces. They had great courage. Or
was it courage? My first urgent invitation to come down was
answered sharply by my father.

'We can't leave the house.'

And from my mother, whimpering:

'He doesn't want to leave the house with all these things.'
I was angry. One of the traditional explanations of why we
never went for holidays when I was a child was:

'We can't leave the house here on its own, empty.'

Now the house was sacred. It seemed to me that father's
passion for property and things – his capital! – had become as
mad as his mother's and that he was obstinately risking our
mother's life and health, not to mention his own. I went down
several times to persuade them to move. It was always an eerie
experience. One walked up the silent and empty hill in the dusk
to the blacked-out place, where mother clung to me and then
pointed to the long crack on the ceiling with a timid pride:

'Look, Vic, our crack! That was the landmine.'

And father said:

'We've got the water back now.'

During a raid it was my father's habit to go into another
room and pray: he called this spiritual or protective fire-
watching. He refused to have a shelter. Mother, in her irrational
way, would sit in her nightdress on top of the stairs – instead
of sheltering underneath them as one was advised to do.

'I want to get out quick,' she said and saw herself taking a
fast slide down to the door.

One night, when she had sent him out of the room to take
the kitchen rubbish to the dustbin – it was astonishing to hear
her ordering him about; he had never done housework in his
life – she put her familiar grip on my wrist and after leading me
to the windows to peep through the black-out to see if 'he',
i.e. 'that old Hitler' was coming, she took me on a fast, furtive
tour of father's bedroom, opening the drawers and saying in an
excited rage: 'Pants. Shirts. Socks. Collars.' and occasionally
revealing the bits of silver he had hidden there. It was an
hysterical protest against the hoard for which, she slyly conveyed, he was risking their lives. She loathed possessions more
than anything else. She seemed to me like a trapped animal at
that time and she was in a bad nervous state. Yet when he
came back, she was in awe of him.

And a strange thing happened, perhaps briefly typical of

other families in these times. The 'wicked' Miss H who had quarrelled bitterly with my father – the quarrel that led eventually to the break-up of his business – had been bombed out of her house in Dulwich. What passions blew to nothing in that explosion I do not know; but now the elderly Miss H came and sheltered with my parents. The two frightened women got on well and supported each other; my mother spoke well of her. But, lest I should think there had been nothing in the old jealous scenes she had made regularly in our childhood, mother maintained just a shred of the respectability of that passion and said, as she passed the door of the bedroom where Miss H had slept:

'She *always* left the door open at night and called "Goodnight" when *he* passed.'

It was a matter of pride with mother to keep the passions going.

One knows little about the inner lives of one's parents. They were in their late sixties and there was a sort of complicity in their battles. The appalling things they said about each other expressed the fascination of their knowledge of each other and of the undoubted passion that had, at some time, entangled two temperaments so disastrously different. And then, time had brought about an ironical turning of the tables. My father had thought that by becoming a Christian Science Practitioner he had liberated himself and found his true vocation. (Incidentally the Christian Science Church refused to recognize him – I don't know why.) What he hadn't realized was that he had lost his freedom: the 'practice' had to be carried on in his own home. Very few shopping trips in the West End, very few ritual 'hair cuts' at Harrods now. The more she had him in the house, the more adroit she became at preventing him leaving it. He was as housebound as his own father, the Minister, had been.

It was a pity that father never took her to the cinema; with its fantasies her own would soon have become identified. As it was she took up reading. I was astonished to find her reading Dickens and the Brontës. It was about this time that she decided she had cancer – this, of course, was a fantasy that served as a weapon directed at her husband's religion – and she would sit rubbing her skirt at the stomach. The habit began as a sly taunt; but gradually became set and then frantic, so much so that in the next fifteen years she had worn a path away in many of her skirts. She did not have cancer. It was my father who eventually died of it – but that was a long way off. Her nervous illnesses were real enough in one way, but he and we knew how much she could put on, in order to hold him.

'I hold him back, I know I do. I've always held him back,' she would say. But, in fact, he was mystified by his failure to be one of the 'big' practitioners and, since at last he earned only a few guineas once in a while there was nothing to hold him back from. The invalid on the couch controlled him.

Why did he fail in this chosen vocation? So long as they practise in the wealthy parts of big cities, many Christian Scientist practitioners prosper, if prosperity is the test; and in view of the general materialist tendency of the religion it must be. One of his friends, a shrewd fellow from Newcastle who had been 'on the road', succeeded, and father often went to find out the secret. The secret of father's failure was his drastic and egotistic nature. He was more exacting than the holiest. He did not (like his father the Minister) believe in hell-fire and damnation, but he had the same rigid and pleasureless spirit of domineering. The Newcastle fellow was a good man, but he used to beg father to stop dragging the Divine Mind into everything. He urged him to relax. But father was an absolutist, a fanatic. He moved from group to group among the many schismatics which, in others, might have been the sign of an independent spirit; but in him, I'm afraid, it was due to his intolerant compulsion to 'put people in their right place', i.e. to contradict them flatly. His religion was a book religion and he was afloat in a sea of abstract nouns that flowed meaninglessly into one another. He thought everything and everyone outside his religion was waste of time; he often said he wanted God, more and more of God. In the end people felt they were drowning in his unending talk.

'You bore people. You go on too long,' mother would say from the sofa where she lay, longing for respite. The fact is that life had been so totally translated into words for him that it had become meaningless. As a writer, I am uncomfortably aware of the warning in this.

CHAPTER THIRTEEN

THE war was over. Several times I had tried to get on with a novel, but I had to put it aside. We were turned out of Maidencourt because farming had become prosperous and the farmer wanted his house back. We tried London, but London was a sordid and miserable place. For a year or so I was literary editor of the *New Statesman*, but I disliked the job. It gave me little time for writing. Once more we returned to the country on the edge of Savernake Forest. The Americans who had turned down all my stories now published what they had rejected. I wrote a successful novel, on my obsessive subject: *Mr Beluncle*. I travelled again. I wrote *The Spanish Temper*, lectured at Princeton, and went to South America. The diversity of my interests seems to have killed off the novelist, but it was good for a short story writer who needs restlessness. The writer had almost completely absorbed the valet.

But the valet had his difficulties.

My brothers and I had always given money to our parents but now they needed more solid support. Debt forced the sale of *Rydal Mount*. The small profit soon went. Our parents now shared a tiny villa in a depressing street of little houses, with a widow – another stone-deaf woman, an exaltée. When I went to see them she used to greet me with words like:

'Victor, go on giving your good tidings to the world.' She had heard I had been broadcasting.

It was always a gloomy journey to Sundridge Park, for from London Bridge to this place I passed through the bitter scenes of my adolescence. What would my life have been if I had not got that train to Paris so many years before? I remembered my clerkly self with the stiff wing collar, the spot on his chin (I had imagined I had caught anthrax), his nose in a book. I remembered the lowered spirits – after the brief escape into literature in the train – when I walked home to the family quarrel. I saw the golf club father had joined forty years before and where he had never played – one of his day dreams. Now the roles of father and son were reversed. It was I, now, who resembled a stern but worried father going to see an unmanageable son. And I felt sad that my father's ambitions (which had seemed, at one time, so admirable if fear-inspiring) had come to failure. And this led me to think that for all my travels and books, I was a failure, too, trapped in a character I could not escape. Was I, in my own way, as self-deluded as he? Some words of my mother's come back to me:

'All your life you hope, but in the end, you find you have to live without even hope.'

What had she hoped for? Simple security. No more.

The house which my parents shared with the widow was small. Its only distinction was an overgrown hawthorn tree that darkened the sitting-room window. The widow's husband had planted it as a tiny bush, donkey's years before. Father opened the door eagerly and mother would be half-creeping behind him: they had gone to the door a dozen times to see if I were coming. I was taken into the backroom where, what with a desk, a table, armchairs and sofa and a sort of chiffonier belonging to the widow, three people hardly had room to move. Old people cling to their possessions and my parents had imposed theirs on the widow's with comic effect: their carpet covered hers, there were two fenders, two coal buckets, two lots of fire-irons, two sets indeed of most objects. Meals were doubled, for the widow was beginning to fail and could not cook for herself. There was a spare room upstairs stacked from floor to ceiling with the left-overs from *Rydal Mount*. The usual war was going on between my father's religion and my mother's disbelief in it. They were united in a mild battle with the old lady who would take her bath at three in the morning and remain there so long that my parents lay awake fearing she had drowned. Mother enjoyed these eccentricities. The widow had been known to rush out to a passing coalman and cry to him fervently:

'Thank you for all you did for us in the war.'

My father, the exasperated healer, found himself with two invalids on his hands. I must say he showed great patience, especially with the widow who eventually became incapable of looking after herself. Indeed he become a nurse to her. In her exalted way she gave him the Biblical name of David. Father glowed. He was not displeased. He had become a Saint. Mother twitched a bit with her old jealousy and slyness, but laughed it away. She was in her eighties, too. Her resource was her gift for comic observation: father observed nothing except the price of things. It amused her that she who had had to endure a stone-deaf maid and a stone-deaf mother-in-law, should now be living with a stone-deaf widow. She laughed even more because the two quarrelling old odd-job men who came in to sweep the leaves and 'do' the little garden were also stone-deaf and accused each other of stealing, by dumb-show and lip-reading. In place of hope in her life, mother wavered between fear and a sustaining sense of farce. I give a sad account which is shadowed by my own sadness, but I was not a frequent visitor. My brothers and sisters used to visit the old couple very regularly and bring a grandchild or two. This livened them.

Father occupied himself with reading the Bible and writing quotations and thoughts from it on slips of paper which he arranged on his deck or tucked into his wallet. He occasionally had a patient and (if he heard unmistakably from the Divine Mind that his work had been well done) would get into an aggressive state and send out preposterous bills. This led to the inevitable quarrels about money that marked his whole life. He owed some of these patients to one of the Big Men of the religion, but here too an appalling thing happened. The Big Man, famous in London and Boston, strayed from the path; there was a revolt which, characteristically, my father followed. But the revolt turned to a scandal. The awful word 'women' was mentioned; father was horrified. Worse, the Big Man dropped dead.

At this point, father heard of another saint, a woman, of course, who sent out garrulous additions to the revelations of Mrs Eddy from Arizona or California, in the form of expensive News Letters. Here, he told me, was the Truth at last, and his salvation. I was called in to subscribe for them. I gladly did. We dreaded that he was running up huge bills. This turned out not to be so and shows how mean or, at any rate, how calculating I had become. I was alarmed to meet a celebrated bookseller in London who said:

'I met your father the other day. What an interesting man. And what a book buyer!'

The fact was that, rather touchingly, his new dream was to play a part in my kind of life. My success as a writer had an exhilarating influence on him.

Then occurred what I ought to have realized would soon happen. Seeing my name in print so often, he thought he too would turn author; he wanted to be like me. I was called to Sundridge Park and he said he had met a man who was offering him a large sum of money if he would write a popular book on '*true* Christian Science', i.e. not on Eddy-idolatry. Father was agog to do this. He bought a desk, a new typewriter, quantities of paper, but when he sat down to write the book, he couldn't get his thoughts together. Would I help him? The book (he said) was to be 'the crown of his life'. What he meant, he said, was would I ghost it for him? Or, as weeks went by, would I not only write it for him but publish it under my name? The money would be huge. I was very embarrassed at having to turn the idea down. I said he knew I did not believe in his religion.

'I know that,' he said. 'And I know you've written that novel about it, *Mr Beluncle*, with me in it. I glanced at it. I couldn't read it. I don't mind at all. But,' once more his fierce sentence came out, 'let me tell you that without my religion I would have finished myself years ago.'

He was about eighty. But this new Big Man dropped dead too.

In this sad little house, except for the flash of the old rage, his character softened, to our contentment. My wife and I were offered a glass of gin and vermouth – he had always set up as a strict teetotaller – and I was sent to a little room to get the bottles.

'They're on the far side under the bed.'

I came into a room piled with furniture they had not been able to squeeze in with the widow's in the other rooms: there I saw what his last burst of buying had been. It had occurred during the war. He had stored – fearing to starve – hundreds of leaking packets of soup powders, cheeses, biscuits, spaghetti, packets of things now rotting away and enough to keep mice going for years; and, sure enough, under a couple of stacked

427

beds and tables there was a long row of gin, whiskey, vermouth and port bottles he had brought years before – waiting for a rise in the market. I crawled in and got a couple out. He himself took a sip of port and so did my mother. We were very cheerful and gossiped our heads off. I think he read an occasional review I wrote and was very proud when I was praised. He was carried away by the title of one of my books of criticism, *The Living Novel*, which of course he did not read.

'I like that. Living. Life,' he said. 'That's what the world wants. Mrs Eddy says . . .'

The only story of mine I know he read was one published in the *Listener* about two drinking women talking about a flea. It is called 'Things As They Are'. The thought of fleas disgusted him. Fleas were obscene and lower class. If in earlier days, mother suddenly started unhitching her skirts and half-undressing crying with the fever of the hunt, 'Walt, Walt, I've got a flea. I've got a flea,' he would turn green with sick anger. He denounced me for writing a story so vulgar and indecent.

But mother was slowly fading. She crept to the door to greet me no longer, but lay on the sofa scratching her skirt and saying furtively to me:

'It's cancer.'

We forced him to get a doctor who regularly saw her while father argued with him about the errors of medicine. My poor mother did not have cancer; she was suffering from the humiliating ills of old age. Almost toothless, for she either refused or was not allowed to go to a dentist, she could digest nothing. She was worrying, too, about what would become of father if she died.

Early one morning father rang me up, howling – there is no other word – and in tears.

'Your mother has just died. Five minutes ago. I was downstairs making her a cup of tea. I heard a shout. I turned off the kettle and when I got upstairs she was dead.'

I caught the train and was down at the house an hour later. His grief was awful. He moaned and swayed, without control. When his own father, the Minister, died (my brother told me), father had stood in the cemetery and had given out an animal

428

howl of 'Father, I love you,' and had tried to throw himself into the grave. His nature was primitive. My wife followed me down to the house and, on sound instinct, made egg sandwiches for him. Grief does indeed create physical hunger and two or three years later he always spoke of my mother's death and egg sandwiches in one breath.

I had gone at once to see my mother's body. She lay, a tiny figure, so white and frail that she looked no more than a cobweb. I stood there hard and unable to weep. Tears come to me only at the transition from unhappiness to happiness; now I was frozen at the thought of her life. She had been through so much and I had been so much outside it. My father said that a week before she died she suddenly became very young looking, even her hair seemed golden to him, as it had been when he had first seen her in Daniel's shop in Kentish Town.

My mother's laughter is what remains with me; everything turned into a tale in her talk – a tale she would tell, with her despairing work-worn fingers spread over her face, with her laughing eyes peering through the gaps between.

After her death, father stayed with my youngest brother for a long time and was easily managed so long as he could watch Westerns on television. But presently the old restlessness came back. He declared it was morally wrong for old people to live with their children and went back to the widow's house. She too had died in the meantime. She had left him a little money and considering his care and nursing of her, it was deserved. Capital at last.

So once more he set out to prospect the south coast of England for a new house, a place where he could breathe, and where the water was soft and the fish good. We nervously watched his departure to seaside resorts and country hotels. He would return to us to discuss the brochures he had got from house agents. They were always lists of large houses at high prices. These discussions were long. They were in fact not discussions but monologues; he explained that since he lived alone he talked a lot. He did. One monologue, I remember, began at midday; after an hour or so he paused when he was interrupted by grandchildren who looked upon him as a wonder; he continued through two more large meals until one in the morning, in which no one but he said anything. One saw a man fulfilled: he had seen a place in the west country by the sea with four or five bedrooms, three reception rooms, a large garden, near a town noted for its Dover Sole such as he and my mother used to eat after a couple of dozen oysters near Liverpool Street station when they were courting. The cost of this place, was £9,000, add another couple of thousand for alterations.

'But you'll be lonely there on your own. And it's far too big. You ought to live near us or your friends.'

He was about eighty-two. He looked austerely at me.

'I have no friends. They are all dead.'

'And where would you get the money?'

'It will "unfold". *You* could raise it.'

He wanted us to buy him the house. There was a family council. The idea was mad. It was agreed that I would explain to him that none of us could 'raise' such a sum. I wrote to explain this for he never listened. He never forgave me, though by now he had changed his mind and thought the east coast might be more bracing.

'I feel I want to be braced.'

He went to live in lodgings on the east coast and every day went house-hunting. But he got a cold which turned to flu. My youngest brother had an agitated message from his landlady and drove over to fetch him back. They drove the forty miles to my brother's house outside London and arrived in the shopping street in the late afternoon. He asked my brother to slow down so that he could see what the season's 'new lines' were, in the shop windows. The old commercial traveller woke up in him. 'I like this contemporary' was his phrase. 'It's modern.' They drove on to my brother's house and father collapsed as he got out of the car. They got him to a chair and called for a doctor.

'Not the knife. I won't have the knife,' he gasped. He said he was hungry. Then he died. It was not my mother but he who, without pain, died suddenly of cancer.

He had wanted to be buried in Kirbymoorside, his birthplace, but neither he nor any of us knew anyone there. His Yorkshire relations had scattered and gone. A new crematorium, very

430

modern, almost contemporary – his word again – had just opened in the new suburb near my brother's house. My father's body was one of the first to be cremated there. That was a distinction: a new house. He did not believe in the reality of death. He believed that he would 'pass on' to another plane of consciousness and would die and die again until he was the perfect image of the Divine Mind.

The astonishing thing was that he left no debts. He left us all his egotism, as our mother left us her racing tongue. I loved seeing the sad voluptuous pout of his lips as he carved a joint and the modest look on his face when, at my house, he passed his plate up and said, as his own mother had before, 'Just a little more.'

It should have been his epitaph.

Now in my turn I have become an old man though no one would think of telling me I am. And this is not out of consideration, but is due to the frantic cult of youth nowadays. Better doctoring helps. In fact one's age goes up and down, round and about, all one's life. I am seventy, and in my father's phrase, 'I would like a little more.' I shall never be as old as I was between twenty and thirty when, with its deceitful energy, my young body carried a pained, fogged and elderly mind across France, Ireland, Spain and the Tennessee mountains on foot. I am impatient about the time I so dreamily and indecisively wasted then. I am glad that after thirty I got back into touch with my childhood; this gave me my vocation and doing what one wants to do lightens the burdens of life. A writer is more fortunate than most people in being able to carry his work with him. He pays for this happy independence by having to work much harder than the mass of employed people and indeed, today, his profession is not only precarious, but seems to be vanishing. It has been in my nature to work hard but hard work can lead to the idleness of the time-and-motion mind. When the profession dies out it may be possible for the writer to do better the few things he ought to do, instead of the hundred things that are a distraction from it. The cost of literature is far, far higher than the public who get it free in the libraries imagines, and it is getting higher. Once he has proved himself, a writer or any artist needs to be relatively rich, subsidized or in some way kept — think of Goya, Velasquez, El Greco, of Shaw — his leisure does not consist of lying on beaches in the Caribbean, but in a labour delightful because it is fanatical. Scott and Balzac desired wealth recklessly, acquired huge debts and debt is a kind of wealth to those who work furiously within it as these men did. I often wish I had had the guts to get into debt.

But I have done, given my circumstances and my character, what I have been able to do and I have enjoyed it.